The Collected Works of James Clarence Mangan

The Collected Works of

JAMES CLARENCE

MANGAN

Prose: 1832–1839

Edited by

JACQUES CHUTO

PETER VAN DE KAMP

AUGUSTINE MARTIN

ELLEN SHANNON-MANGAN

IRISH ACADEMIC PRESS
DUBLIN · PORTLAND, OR

This book was set in
11 on 12.5 point Ehrhardt for
IRISH ACADEMIC PRESS
44 Northumberland Road, Dublin 4
and in North America for
IRISH ACADEMIC PRESS
c/o ISBS, 5824 NE Hassalo Street, Portland, OR 97213.

© The editors 2002

A catalogue record for this title
is available from the British Library.

ISBN 0-7165-2577-1
Set ISBN 0-1765-2736-7

This book was printed on acid-free paper.

The silhouette of Mangan on the title page
dates from 1822.

ACKNOWLEDGMENT
The publishers wish to acknowledge the financial assistance
of the Arts Council/An Chomhairle Ealaion, Dublin.

Typeset by FiSH Books, London WC1.
Printed in Great Britain by
MPG Books Ltd., Bodmin, Cornwall

Contents

GENERAL INTRODUCTION

The works of James Clarence Mangan (1803–1849) in a full collected edition with a biography of the poet and a comprehensive bibliography are here published for the first time. From the age of 14 until his death at 46, Mangan wrote and published prose and poetry of immense variety of contact and style. His work appeared in most of the contemporary Irish periodicals, from ephemeral almanacs to the antiquarian *Irish Penny Journal*, and from the Unionist *Dublin University Magazine* to the *Nation* of Young Ireland. In all, some thousand poems and dozens of prose pieces—fiction, criticism, essays—comprise his canon. Yet no complete collection of his poetry or his prose has ever before been attempted.

A few editions of Mangan's poetry have been published sporadically over the years, but despite the compilers' enthusiasm and good intentions, each volume has suffered from a cultural or a personal bias. Their editors do not hesitate, for instance, to suppress part of one poem, to combine several versions of another, or to rewrite portions of lines as they think best. The prose has been treated in like manner. All these editions have, in any case, been out-of-print for many years. Only a handful of his poems have become sturdy fixtures in anthologies of Irish writing, and his prose is practically unknown.

Several explanations may account for this neglect. Chief among these is the difficulty of collecting Mangan's writings, published as they were under pseudonyms or anonymously and scattered through many publications, some of them short-lived and obscure. Another, less pedestrian, reason may be that Mangan has been harmed by his image. The traditional representation of him as a pathetic figure dragging out a life of material poverty and moral misery from sordid garret to squalid cellar has been detrimental to his reputation as a poet. People have seized upon this legend—a word which etymologically means *that which has to be read*—and they have neglected the works. In one respect, at least, Mangan is a true *poète maudit* in Paul Verlaine's use of the phrase, that is, a poet whom no one reads.

And yet, the most eminent voices of Irish literature have spoken in his praise. W.B. Yeats declared Mangan "our one poet raised to the first rank by intensity". James Joyce described Mangan as "that creature of lightning, who has been, and is, a stranger among the people he ennobled, but who may yet come by his own as one of the greatest romantic poets among those who use the lyrical mode".

Mangan should now cease to be a stranger. Ellen Shannon-Mangan's biography, the first volume in this series, dispels the sensational myth and legend that have enveloped the poet's life. Jacques Chuto's bibliography of both the poetry and the prose provides a definitive reference to Mangan's work and its sources. Together with those, this complete edition of Mangan's writings, appearing nearly a century and a half after his death, makes it possible for his typically ironic prophecy to be fulfilled:

> Mine inkstand is the Well of Naksheb;—and from each
> Imperishable drop I spread along the page
> Another Veilèd Prophet utters a mystic speech,
> *To be translated only by a future age.**

The Editors

*Italics ours.

INTRODUCTION TO THE PROSE VOLUMES

James Clarence Mangan had profiled himself as a poet years before he ventured into prose. His first poems were published as early as 1818, when he was 15; the first prose appeared in 1832. Yet it is with this publication, of the political satire entitled "The Two Flats; or, Our Quackstitution", that his literary career was truly launched. From then on he published steadily, alternating prose and verse, until the year of his death.

Prose offered the poet a vehicle for his public personæ—Mangan the satirist, the folklorist, the madcap entertainer, and foremost perhaps, the polyglot. In the many *anthologia* articles, the prose commentary, however playful, lent *auctoritas* to the translations, renditions, and fablings. Yet Mangan did not write prose merely to provide a rationale for the poetry. For this the prose is too abundant and varied; its spectrum is broad, ranging from the easily tossed-off—political satire, playful story, light parody, humorous skit—to that which required reflection—the personal essay, biographical sketch, and, yes, fairly respectable criticism.

Mangan's prose has received scant attention. The victim of rapid changes in literary taste, it soon became obsolescent. It paled, inevitably, in the shade of the poetry. Mangan's lasting reputation as a poet—and what is more, a *poète maudit*—may have led critics to regard his foray into prose, with its apparent lack of cohesive thrust, as potboiling. Even the pioneer editor of the prose, D.J. O'Donoghue, questioned Mangan's intentions; in no lesser place than the preface to his edition of *The Prose Writings of James Clarence Mangan*, he wrote, as if insinuating a note of despair in his process of collecting: "To expect a serious work in prose from Mangan would be useless".

What O'Donoghue meant by a "serious work" we will never know. Must it be devoid of levity, or does the *gravitas* of the whole allow for some light touches in the parts? We cannot but conjecture how seriously Mangan took his own prose. He probably regarded an article like "A Dialogue in the Shades", with its accumulation of deliberately excruciating puns and doggerel verse, as a mere clever skit, but "An Extraordinary Adventure in the Shades", for all its emphasis on drink, surely was more to him than a piece of inebriated scribbling—as a genre piece, its haunting expression of delirium deserves a place among such divergent exponents as De Quincey and Flann O'Brien.

Mangan's prose style has been regarded as derivative and strained; he is said to have deliberately imitated the comic and satiric writing that was popular in his day, much emphasis being put in particular on the supposed influence of William Maginn. True, the aphoristic structure of Mangan's "A Sixty-Drop Dose of Laudanum" resembles that of Maginn's "Maxims of Sir Morgan Odoherty", and both writers were fond of hyperbole and extravagance. But then, so were Rabelais, Swift, and Sterne. To say, as does O'Donoghue apropos "A Treatise on a Pair of Tongs": "Excellent fooling, perhaps; but... how unnatural a style for Mangan", is to beg the question of what style *was* "natural" to a myriad-minded shapechanger like Mangan, who, more than any Irish writer before Yeats and Joyce, forged his writerly personality. We know, and admire, the Man(gan) in the Cloak; without it, without that style, *l'homme même* is unidentifiable. Small wonder that Mangan observed, with commendable irony, "I find that almost every thing that is natural in me is wrong also".

Mangan's prose is not comfortable or well-behaved, and often takes the reader by surprise. It is marked by frequent changes of register and sentiment, as in "My Transformation. A Wonderful Tale", which veers repeatedly back and forth from pathos to bathos, before ending on a horse-laugh. Critics have accounted for such shape-shifting by focusing on the purpose of the journals to which Mangan contributed. "My Transformation" was published in the *Weekly Dublin Satirist*, a light-hearted periodical (the same critics explain similar "ups and downs" which occur in "Verses to a Friend, on his playing a particular melody which excited the Author to tears" by the fact that the poem was published in the satirical newspaper, the *Comet*). However, when one finds grotesque elements cropping up also in "The Man in the Cloak", Mangan's adaptation of Balzac's story "Melmoth réconcilié", and even in "Chapters on Ghostcraft", a thoughtful account of German spiritualism, both written for the stolid *Dublin University Magazine*, it seems fair to conclude that such deliberate inconsistency is not a way for Mangan to accommodate his style to editorial policies, but an integral part of his own writing strategies.

There is much more, germane to Mangan's prose, which is apt to confuse the reader. What is to be made, for instance, of the erudition Mangan likes to display—is it genuine or spurious? Or of the information he provides occasionally about his German personæ, Drechsler and Selber—are these glimpses of covert self-revelation? One suspects a soupçon of irony.

Indeed the poet Mangan's attitude to his prose does seem ironic: in an early "Anthologia Germanica", Mangan followed his verse rendering of a prose apologue by Jean Paul with a lengthy examination of its moral. A reviewer who took exception advised "the clever author to indulge his readers with critiques on the distinctive genius of German Poetry, rather than on abstract questions of a cloudy philosophy with which the generality of mankind has no sympathy". Mangan retorted that he desired to appear not as an essayist, but as a translator; he saw little point in engaging "in disquisitions upon the genius or character of every individual from whom it may be our good or ill fortune to translate or travestie a stanza"; in a word, he preferred "the Poetry of poets to the prose of—ourselves". Such seemingly self-deprecatory self-criticism did not prevent Mangan in all his subsequent articles on foreign poetry from setting the translations—or travesties—in frequently copious prose commentary which includes not only considerations of "a cloudy philosophy" but also disquisitions, as often as not unfavourable, on the "Poetry of poets".

O'Donoghue presented Mangan's prose apologetically: "For his prose—well, it is simply the prose of a remarkable poet". No apology is needed. Far from being "*simply* the prose of a remarkable poet", Mangan's prose reflects the essential *complexity* of its author. This the young James Joyce did not fail to see: "Many of his essays," he wrote, "are pretty fooling when read once, but one cannot but discern some fierce energy beneath the banter, which follows up the phrases with no good intent, and there is a likeness between the desperate writer, himself the victim of too dexterous torture, and the contorted writing". One catches here an echo of the line "Tortured torturer of reluctant rhymes" in which Mangan pictured his poetic self in "Twenty Golden Years Ago", while the "fierce energy" which Joyce discerns in Mangan's prose sounds very much like the "intensity" for which Yeats praised his poetry.

Mangan's prose may not reach the fervour of his incomparable verse, but the two modes of writing are so intimately linked that these two volumes are the natural complement to the four poetry volumes: they complete the complex picture of James Clarence Mangan.

NOTE ON THE TEXT

Mangan's prose works are given in chronological order. The text is that of first publication (obvious misprints having been silently corrected), except in the case of the introduction to *The Poets and Poetry of Munster* and of the "Autobiography", which are printed from the manuscripts.

In the articles consisting of verse translations linked together by a critical commentary the remarks dealing specifically with particular poems have been omitted: they are part of the endnotes in the four Poetry volumes.

Mangan's letters fall into two parts: the "Correspondence", which reproduces all the letters extant in manuscript form, and an "Appendix to the Correspondence", which contains other letters as quoted, in full or in part, by more or less reliable biographers and critics.

THE TWO FLATS; OR, OUR QUACKSTITUTION.

AN APOLOGUE.

"Ce gouvernement serait digne des Hottentos, dans lequel il serait permis à un certain nombre d'hommes de dire, 'C'est à ceux qui travaillent à payer: nous ne devons rien, parce que nous sommes oisifs'."—VOLTAIRE.[1]

ONCE upon a time there stood, in a certain part of Kingland, known by the name of Undone town, a large, dull, old building, called by way of pre-eminence, The House. It was a crazy sort of edifice, and was filled with tenants, many of whom were likewise crazy. Their business was to transact,—for weighty considerations,—the affairs of the Neighbourhood: but they generally preferred passing their time either in praising themselves, or in abusing one another. They styled themselves "The Collective Quizdom," and on that account continued for a series of years to be looked up to with a sentiment of almost religious reverence by mohawks, moseys,[2] and spooneys, and, in general, by all those persons who, not understanding the meaning of the phrase, concluded that it was of too sacred a nature to be intelligible. The House consisted of two parts—the Upper Flat, or House of Words—and the Lower Flat, or House of Clamours.

The Upper Flat was subdivided into several departments. The tenants were named Ducks, Mere-quizzes, Err-alls, Wise-counts, and Barrens. There were also a separate class, forming a coterie by themselves, and thence called the Bunch of Bye-shops:—another name for these was the Holygarchy, for their principal occupation was preying. The Ducks were famous at (t)waddling, and were remarkable for a partiality to no quacking but their own. The Mere-quizzes, or, as some called them from their buck-ram stiffness and leaden gravity, the Mar-quizzes, were poor, lifeless creatures; the fairest specimen of the caste was considered to be the Mar-quiz of Longdulldreary.[3] The course of the Err-alls was tracked by their blunders, which the wisdom of the Wisecounts was not competent to remedy. As to the Barrens, their title was singularly significative of their intellectual inanity;—and they constituted the lowest class of any. The motto of all was, "Knowledge is Powder." Their nominal chief was a Puppet in strings (he was called "the Thing"); he was distinguished from themselves by wearing an eccentrically-shaped hat, resembling a bruised kettle with the bottom off; and hence, "the honour of the kettle," "the support of the kettle," "consistently with the dignity of the kettle," &c., were favourite phrases with all.

The stupidity of this batch of beings was only paralleled by their cupidity. They seized everything seizable. (The principal title of the Puppet was "The Great Seizer.") They devoured all substances; even iron; and being particularly fond of axes after tea, they were called "The T-ax-eaters." The Holygarchy alone regularly ate up a tenth part[4] of whatever the Neighbourhood produced. In short, they were all as omnivorous as an army of rats—and, in fact, a gentleman, one day speaking of them, indignantly exclaimed, "they Are-a-stock-o'rats!" an expression, the justness of which was acknowledged by all the by-standers. The Upper Flat had for some time been insufferable. Its only advocates were sinecurists and by-way robbers, with here and there an old woman in a wig—as also *Blockwood's Magazine*[5]—and an odd weekly weakly newspaper, the *John Gull*[6]—and another paper never read more than half through, and called the *'Alf-read*[7]—besides the *Stand-hard*,[8] a nightly straggler and struggler, evidently walking on its last legs.

In most points of view the Lower Flat might be regarded as a less disreputable locality than the Upper. It was eminent for several men of distinguished talent and unimpeached integrity. Every measure of any importance originated here, and the utmost that the Barrens, &c., could do, was to signify their approbation of the measure. Still, still it was a deplorable Flat. The mutual Billingsgate[9] that passed from mouth to mouth, the slovenliness, the apathy, the selfishness, the prejudice and impenetrable ignorance that frequently prevailed, and the corrupt and dirty ways of all kinds encountered in this Flat, rendered it a disagreeable place for minds of a philosophical or patriotical turn. Many individuals were known, by a horrid underground-working system, to have actually burrowed their passage into the House;[10] and Burke-ing traps and Pitt-falls,[11] to ensnare the unsuspecting, were thickly sown at one side of the Flat. This Flat was generally recognized by the names of "The Den of Corruption," "The Sink of Bribery," "The House of Clamours," &c., and as the other Flat was filled with plunderers and robbers, so this was stocked with blunderers and jobbers.

The whole House, in fine, was, as it stood, a public nuisance, and all sensible persons agreed that it was high time to think of remodelling it. Wherever human beings are congregated, we shall see quacks and dawdlers: at all events, Undone town had been, from days immemorial, the grand theatre of Charlatanism. Humorous were the theories—numerous the theorists. The question being the simplest at all, and the obvious expedient being to take down the edifice and construct a new one, such an expedient occurred, of course, to nobody. Patching and piecing, and crutch-propping at most, were talked of, and these merely by the speculators; but even to these every opposition was offered by the peculators,[12] and they regularly carried the day, upon the ground that they (the peculators) had the Eyes of the House, whereas their adversaries (the speculators) had merely the Nose. It was a question, they said, between Eyes and Nose, and the Eyes were numerically to the Nose as two are to one.

The Puppet was himself a Cabinet-maker, but declined interfering individually, stating, as his reason, that he was unwilling to occasion umbrage to the "Ten Teapots"[13] of Europe, by compromising the dignity of his kettle; and suggesting, at the same time, the adoption of the only course that propriety appeared to warrant, viz.: that his Prime-ear should take the Eyes and Nose of "his faithful cormorants" at both sides. In both Flats, however, there were numbers of "old saws," tacks-budgets, and tools of all sorts for hire; many tenants were proficients in boring; there were ex-planers on every bench, and several were in the constant practice of turning. So far so middling.

But,—and here was the rub,—there was, it appears, a mysterious impalpable something, said by sundry persons to exist somewhere: it was called "our Venerable Claptrap Quackstitution in Church and State." The decision of the gravest among the jurisconsults was, that this was an invisible tub-full of the extract of jelly—a decision in the correctness of which the metaphysicians coincided with the jurisconsults, but said that Aristotle had not propounded any rule sufficient to guide them in deciding whether the tub itself were an entity, an abstraction, or a modality, and that in his Ten Predicables[14] he had made no allusion to the tub. To this, however, the jurisconsults replied—1stly, that Aristotle, having never been seen in a wig, was not an infallible authority; and, 2dly, that the tub, being a real tub, could never be regarded as chattel property. The point remained unsettled. Be it as it might, "our Quackstitution" was a bugbear: everything lay at sixes and sevens from a dread of deranging the jelly of "our Quackstitution." Years wheeled on: nothing was achieved. A tenant would talk for seven hours successively on the necessity of a change, and would pronounce the word "Quackstitution" one hundred and ten times, and thereafter another would talk for ten hours and a-half on the contrary side, and pronounce the same word three hundred and forty times; and ten and a-half being more, by three and a-half, than seven, and one hundred and ten being less, by two hundred and thirty, than three hundred and forty, the Eyes would assemble against the Nose, and proclaim that Talker No. 1 had beaten Talker No. 2, by three hours and a-half, and two hundred and thirty Quackstitutions.

But patience will never be an eternal thing, it is really so difficult for human creatures to settle down permanently into stocks and stones.

Wearied, worried, taxed, tormented, robbed, and devoured uninter-
mittingly, the Neighbourhood at last grew uproarious and volcanic.
Assemblies and speeches, vows, placards, thunder and tempest followed in
order. A sensation of uneasiness and alarm gradually pervaded every
department of both Flats. What was to be done? They consulted: the
majority were for dying in ditches, spilling last drops of blood, and doing
other similar matters. One day a special côterie was summoned.

"Our Venerable and Gorge-us Quackstitution is in danger," said the
Mere-quizzes.

"Let us die, then," said the Ducks, "in the breaches of the
Quackstitution."

"It is a love-lie Quackstitution," said the Err-alls.

"It is a bootyful Quackstitution," added the Holygarchy. The entire Flat
sighed.

"It was established by the Quizdom of our ancestors," observed the
Barrens.

"And Ann Tiquity[15] has stamped it with her seal," remarked the
Wisecounts. (Ann Tiquity was an old woman.)

"It has been the Bullwork of Kingland," said one.

"It is the Law and the Profits to us all," said another.

There was a pause. "I think," said Wailingtone[16] to Longdulldreary,
"that our Quackstitution is the perfection of human Wigsdom. Knowledge
is Powder. Vide the wigs of the Holygarchy and my own experience in the
field."

"True," said Longdulldreary to Wailingtone. "What is wanting for the
tranquillity of Kingland is, in point of fact, a Society for the Confusion of
Useful Knowledge.[17] That which is erroneously hight[18] reason, is really
high treason. As regards any Quackstitutional change, I have but one name
for it,—Devilution. There was a devilution in France lately, as I have been
told, (for I never read the papers), and the Devil himself was seen publicly
in Paris, proceeding from street to street to discharge the artillery for the
mob. The mob are dangerous people: they are enemies to all the Drones
and Halters[19] on earth."

"A Devilution," said Wailingtone, "will strike the kettle off the Puppet's
head."

"And annihilate the House of Hangover,[20] depend upon it," said Longdulldreary.

Cumbertheland[21] then addressed himself to the question. "My friends,"
he said, "our Quackstitution is the Quackstitution of Quackstitutions.
Nothing is like it; it is parallel to itself alone; it is the beau-ideal of the
unique; sphinx and phœnix in one; the 'Eureka' that Archimedes missed.
Our enemies themselves must allow it to be good, since, if not good for

something, it must at least be good for nothing. It gives the green acres to the wise-acres. We are the wise-acres;—no man denies it." The speaker then quoted Burgersdicious,[22] Machiavel,[23] Vattel,[24] Puffendorff,[25] and Bombastes Paracelsus,[26] for the purpose of disproving an assertion respecting something that had occurred on the day before, and continued: "Our cause is Holygarchy *versus* Polygarchy, the latter being the mob, the mulctedude,[27] who are many. These powers are now in contest. The power of the Polygarchy has increased, is increasing, and ought to be diminished. If it should continue to increase, the result will disarrange the balance that has in every other age subsisted between both powers. Balances are necessary for balancing things: without a balance it is impracticable to balance anything. (Hear, hear.) I trust that I am perfectly intelligible. The remark was profound, but I trust that I am perfectly intelligible. You will find balances in machinery, in grocers' shops, in watches, account-books, &c. &c. To conclude, I shall merely observe that Hoax, and Trapstick, Hocus Pocus, with Hummery, Mummery, Flummery, Claptrap, Quackstitution, Church and State." This speech was vehemently applauded, and the last sentence declared to contain the pith and essence of all that could be advanced by way of argument for the *One*servative party.

The Neighbourhood called a meeting. "Shall we suffer these Imbeciles to subsist as a political body any longer?" they asked. "What is the Upper Flat but a drag on the Lower?"

The Chairman remarked, that in a proceeding of this nature, temperance and order were indispensably requisite. "Let us," said he, "commence by the commencement. Let the Lower Flat be first purified. This is step the first. After that, the obstructions to other and greater beneficial alterations will be fewer: it will be for our option either to modify or abolish the Upper Flat. My own prepossessions are at present in favour of the abolition. A chariot rolls along gaily enough when there are a dozen blue-bottle flies upon the wheel-spokes;—it is, nevertheless, the belief of men and women, that the same chariot would get on pretty well without the assistance of blue-bottle flies. The flies and we are at issue; it is not very material. But we must, I repeat, proceed with moderation and method. A haze is over the moral horizon, and as yet, we discern objects and principles but dimly: a glimpse only of the attainable perfect is occasionally afforded us. Unity of purpose, sympathy of feeling, concord of opinion,—these are all that is wanting. They are 'the be-all and the end-all.'[28] Struggle for these: isolated exertions are Quixotic in cases of this kind. But possessed of these, precipitancy will be unnecessary. Possessed of these, discovery will succeed to discovery, system to system, until at length, the universal consent of men shall have established a series of ultimate principles, and produced a constitution unsusceptible of any further improvement."

It was accordingly resolved unanimously that the purification of the Lower Flat should commence forthwith, and the meeting having arranged the preliminary measures for the purpose, broke up.

[The conclusion of the apologue will probably be communicated to the COMET hereafter. Meanwhile the writer apologizes for his dullness: he hopes that nothing he has said will be considered as alluding to anything whatever. He has been particularly careful in the selection of his proper names:—dashes would have been suspicious; superficial readers might have easily mistaken Lond-nd-rry for Londonderry; but nobody can suppose Longdulldreary to be Londonderry. He would not have deemed it necessary to append these observations, but for the horrible wickedness of the times, and the increasing number of Radical Reformers; all of whom are assassins to man, and are incessantly destroying the peace of the Aristocracy, by publishing Penny Newspapers and committing other frightful excesses. Vide *the Quart. Rev.*,[29] *Warder*,[30] &c. *passim*.]

ITALIAN LITERATURE.

TO THE EDITOR OF THE DUBLIN PENNY JOURNAL

My Dear Sir,—The Editor of the *Liverpool Mercury* has very handsomely noticed your "Weekly Penny Journal" and has made an extract, including the Aria of which he speaks very warmly.[1] I forgive your remarks, which were made, no doubt, in that spirit which is so peculiar to your country, rash and intemperate. The following Arias are from that great dramatist, whose language you say is that "of affectation," and "more adapted to the opera house" than to what?—"the simplicity of the common feelings of humanity"!! Let the reader judge.

Se a ciascun l'interno affanno	If ev'ry man's internal care
Si leggesse in fronte scritto;	Were written on his brow,
Quanti mai, che invidia fanno,	How many would our pity share,
Ci farebbero pieta!	Who raise our envy now!
Si vedria, che i lor nemici	The fatal secret when reveal'd,
Hanno in seno: e si riduce	Of ev'ry aching breast,
Nel parere a noi felici	Would prove, that only while conceal'd,
Ogni lor felicità.	*Their* lot appear'd the best.

Sembra gentile	How in the depth of winter rude
Nel verno un fiore,	A lovely flower is prized,
Che in sen d' Aprile	Which in the month of April view'd,
Si disprezzò.	Perhaps has been despised.
Fra l'ombre è bella	How fair amid the shades of night
L'istessa stella	Appears the star's pale ray:
Che in faccia al Sole	Before the sun's more dazzling light,
Non si mirò.	It quickly fades away.
L'asilo d'Amore.	

Mr. Editor, as you "would be ashamed to produce a match for the 'Aria' of *my* father-land in the Irish language," it seems that the reason is very apparent. At page 94 you have attempted it indirectly, or without alluding to the challenge, and let the reader pronounce his verdict. True, it is prose,[2] a very good means of escape for the Editor, but your object is easily detected. After all, my dear sir, I respect you as a man of talent, but the following from you is very disreputable, namely, that the "Aria" was "worthy of the land of comfits and confections, of gilt-edged looking-glasses and sugared plums."

Believe me dear sir,

Your's &c.

A CONSTANT READER.

VERY ORIGINAL CORRESPONDENCE.

M Y DEAR PHILANDER[1]—You are a Radical of the reddest hot; so was I, until eleven o'clock this morning. I attribute my miraculous conversion from liberalism to the letter that I enclose: I have read it thrice over; the first perusal was a staggerer—the second floored me—the third and last gave the death blow to all my principles. I am now a Conservative, and shall, for the future, deal in scurrility to a large extent; I have also decided upon hiring myself to that newspaper which pays most; meanwhile, as fair play is a jewel, I request you to give a place to the letter in the next week's COMET. It really bangs Blackwood[2] all to nothing. Your's,

CLARENCE.

IT is ridiculous, my dear Clarence, to mince the matter. I am the worst used animal, the most ruffianishly treated, and abominably handled biped in any twenty towns; the bulk of mankind have conspired to persecute me with a rancour that it infinitely puzzles me to account for; they are leagued and covenanted—sworn and banded to effect, by hook or crook, if not my extermination from society, at least my utter extinguishment as a political star. They would snuff me out the ruffians, with about as much compunction as a philosopher feels when he plants his dexter foot upon the body of a rat! To you, my dear Clarence, whom I respect as a friend, and execrate as a Radical, I will acknowledge that inhumanity of such a sickening nature as this is, has excited my surprise in a much less degree than it has awakened my sorrow. Tom Moore has often told you of Castlereagh's crocodile, who when he had no other business to engage his attention, was accustomed to occupy himself by walking about with his hands in his breeches-pockets, and shedding barrels of tears.[3] There is a remarkable analogy between this crocodile's private circumstances and my own; for I, too, walk about town with my hands in my breeches-pockets, shedding tears for a wager: it is *à qui mieux mieux*[4] between us. I wish, however, to offer one observation: it is not recorded of the crocodile that he ever cursed the Whigs; here, therefore the parallel stops, for night and day my curse is heavy upon the Whigs. You know, my friend, the constitutional placidity of my temperament—how like Epictetus[5] I am, and so forth; but, coming into collision with the wrong-headedness of the age, so frequently as I do, innate integrity and a sense of principle compel me to curse by bell, book, and gaslight,[6] every thing and being in the vicinity of my person. The Gorgon's head[7]—the triple-faced hell-dog[8]—the handwriting on

Belthasar's palace wall[9]—the into-stone-metamorphosing snake-locks of
Medusa[10]—the Cock-lane ghost[11]—the Abaddon-born visions of Quincy
the opium-chewer[12]—the devil that perpetually stood opposite to
Spinello[13]—the caverns of Dom-Daniel[14]—the fire-globe that burned
below the feet of Pascal[15]— were, each and all, miserable little bagatelles by
the side of the phantasmagoria that evermore haunt my brain, and blast my
eyes! "On horror's head, horrors accumulate."[16] The world, this great and
solid globe, is now one immense Whig-Radical, one monstrously colossal
Moderate-Destructive, who goeth about like a roaring lion, seeking whom
he may revolutionize. This, it will be allowed, is a frightful state of things
in civilized society.

When Lord Castlereagh,[17] influenced by pious motives undoubtedly, cut
his own throat, and died without a groan, he set an example which I, to-day,
find myself disposed to imitate, and which, in all probability, a sense of
justice and duty will induce me to imitate at some future period, when
events shall battle against me with a desperation which at present I have no
idea of. In the meanwhile, I feed my fancy with a prospect of better times to
come. Massacre and pillage, as Blackwood's Magazine shows, will, in a few
months, be the order of the day in these kingdoms; and I may yet live to
witness many men who now triumphantly trample me in the mud,
assassinated in open daylight by the daggers of those dupes whom they at
present use as cat's-paws. During these wet and dismal winter evenings, I
have been occasionally cheered by hopes of this description. *Au pis aller*,[18] I
know that persecution is the ordeal of the righteous. The devil will, at the
end of the chapter, take all my enemies into his keeping. It is another,
though a melancholy consolation to me, that I have not a monopoly of
disgrace and suffering. They are the badge of my tribe. How, *inter alia*, it
must harrow up the soul to reflect upon the numerous occasions on which
Conservative candidates, while standing on the hustings, have been covered
from head-crown to foot-sole with a plaister, several inches thick, of rotten
eggs! Only look at Bristol. See how Sir Charles Wetherell,[19] the intrepid
stander-up for the broken-down Constitution of 1688, was necessitated to
skulk out of that town, by holes and by-ways; to crawl, as it were, upon all-
fours, over mire and rubbish, bearing, as he huddled along, a remarkable
resemblance to a draggle-tailed, half-stifled rat, who is occasionally kicked
from the right-hand kennel of the street to the left, and occasionally finds
his energies trodden down by the Mazourka-heeled boot of some swell
Peripatetic. I, like Sir Charles, am a spectacle to the world, to angels, and to
Whigs. My beak is tweaked—my carcass is pummelled—my prerogatives
and privileges, all highly sacred, are matter for horse-laughs—the sanctuary
of my purse is profaned by ruffian fingers—the hooky gripe of the rabble is
at my throat—I am slowly slaughtered by half-inches—in short, I am a

murdered man; and when I shall be fairly expunged from the common-place book of life, the dissecting knife and the dunghill will have the last of me. *Hinc illæ lachrymæ*.[20] But the subject is too painfully interesting to be dwelled upon.

And what, after all, is the head and front of my offending? Why, forsooth, I am a Conservative; a trafficker in boroughs,[21] a public plunderer, an enemy to liberty in general!

First—A boroughmonger? But if a man may carry on business as a cheesemonger, or an ironmonger, without incurring the penalty of being bludgeoned and brickbatted out of human existence, why may he not do so as a boroughmonger? So much money for the cheese, so much for the iron, so much for the borough. It is the simplest question I ever heard of. This furnishes a successful vindication of my doings in reference to borough-trafficking.

Second—Thick-and-thin liars and swearers through deal boards, as, I grieve to say, all the Radicals, without any exceptions are, call me plunderer. Very well, but my reasonings on the question maintain that I am quite the reverse: my reasonings being just, and the reasonings of my opponents ridiculous, the inference is that I am not a plunderer. Hear how I argue:—taxes when they tumble down into the budget, become the exclusive property of the ancient family of the budgeteers; and each member of that highly respectable family plunges, from time to time, his fist into that budget and brings up as much as casually sticks to it. Why should not a Government tax to the utmost practicable extent? In direct ratio with the specific weightiness of a man's purse have ever been his authority and respectability: the richer and fatter a Government grows, the more weight it will acquire; the more influential and vigorous it will become. What goes by the name of plundering the public, is, in point of fact, to a philosophical eye, an incontestible exhibition of intellectual superiority, and moral power;—and there is more talent even in a neat piece of noon-day swindling, than the swindled party is apt to give the swindler credit for. Admitted fully, that, if the booty had been suffered to stop at home in the tills and pockets of the primary proprietors, each individual would be much more agreeably situated than he is, when he sees himself reduced to a state of shoeless and shirtless beggary; but in that case the dignity of the Government would suffer in the estimation of Foreign Powers, and his Majesty's crown might sustain a shove either to one side of his Majesty's head or to the other, so that his Majesty's wig would run the risk of being *dérangé*. The obvious question, therefore, that occurs to a thoughtful man to ask is as follows:—By what precautions shall we best avert these gigantical evils? I see nothing else for it but the levying of tons' weight of taxes, the passing of mouth-gagging bills, the suspension of the Habeas

Corpus act,[22] the general introduction of treadmills, and the establishment of a petty political inquisition in every street, alley, courtway, hole, corner and cranny, throughout England, Ireland, and Scotland.

Third—It remains for me in conclusion, to despatch the charge of illiberalism. Sticklers for liberty and popular bawlers appear not to know that despotic governments are at bottom the freest governments at all. This is proveable with small trouble: he who can act perfectly independent of controul is the freest of men;—a despotical government acts perfectly independent of controul; ergo, a despotical government is the freest of governments. But the truth ought not to be blinked:—liberty is a curse to mankind. Meditative minds will naturally be lost in perplexity to explain how it should be, that the whole human race taken in the aggregate, as a body of agitating boobies, should have been immemorially plunged in sottish ignorance on this question of liberty—such nevertheless is the fact. It is demonstrated by a reference to the state of the social system about a twelve-month before the deluge, and by the opinions of all the antediluvian authorities. Glance at the workings of the liberal principle even in the era we live in; see America, see what a metamorphosis the American people have undergone in fifty years. They were once ardent monarchists; but they rebelled against the King of England and his Aristocracy, and by a special chastisement from Heaven, the spirit of republicanism was permitted to come among them, and to blight all that had been theretofore flourishing in their institutions; so that at the present hour, there is not a member of the American Government that is not an undisguised republican. Such, my friend, is the dawning influence of democracy. The incompatibility of the existence of democratical institutions with domestical happiness is evinced by the fact, that from the infant at the breast to the hoary octogenarian, there is not a human creature in the United States—man, woman, or child, that is not drunk—dead drunk, six times a day. Another splendid argument against democracy is, that it makes mankind an association of butchers; this is exemplified in the campaigns of Washington, whose backwoodsmen mercilessly slaughtered the flower of the British army, at the battle of Bunker's Hill.[23] Democrats, besides, are invariably vulgarians—ruffians—the riff-raff and refuse of society, with neither stars, garters, nor epaulettes—disgustingly ignorant of the mode in which silver forks are handled by the *élite*— savagely ignorant of the *etiquette* at Almack's[24]—Hottentotishly insensible to the advantages derivable from the possession of nobility, by which a man becomes, in a few seconds, magnificently superior in altitude to the grass-hopping populace, and gloriously treads them down on all sides, as so many little clay-clods. If, however, you wish to see this topic and similar topics discussed, unanswerably and at large, I refer you to Blackwood;

tendering you, at the same time, my solemn oath that every syllable in his magazine is entirely true.

Adieu! my dear Clarence. Make what use you please of this letter; I could wish you to publish it in the form of a penny tract, defraying the expenses yourself; but, as it might be chimerical to look for so much generosity at the hands of a political opponent, I shall be satisfied if you procure the insertion of it in the COMET. The circulation of that paper is enormous; and I have no doubt that what I have written, if suffered to appear in its columns, would create a mighty sensation.

Permit me to subscribe myself, your's,

B.A.M.[25]

AN EXTRAORDINARY ADVENTURE IN THE SHADES.

THE DAY of the week was Sunday, of the month the first—the month itself was April, the year 1832. Sunday, first of April, 1832!—*de mortuis nil nisi bonum*,[1] but I really must say that thou wert, in very truth, a beautiful, a bland, and a balmy day. I remember thee particularly well. Ah! which of the days that the departed year gave birth to, do I not remember? The history of each and of all is chronicled in the volume of my brain—written into it as with a pen of iron, in characters of ineffaceable fire! It is pretty generally admitted by the learned, that an attempt to recall the past is labour in vain, else should I, for one, purchase back the by-gone year with diadems and thrones—(supposing that I had the diadems and thrones to barter.) Under present circumstances my only feasible proceeding is to march onward rectilineally, cheek-by-jowl, with the spirit of the age—to abandon the bowers of Fancy, for the broad beaten pathway of Reason—renounce Byron for Bentham,[2] and resign the brilliant and burning imagery of the past, for the frozen realities of the present and the future. Be it so. Whatever may become of me, my lips are sealed—a padlocked article. *Tout est perdu, mes amis;*[3] and when the case stands thus, the unfortunate victim had much better keep his breath to cool his porridge withal, for he may stake his last cigar upon it, that anything more supremely ridiculous than his efforts to soliloquize his friends into a sympathetic feeling, will never come under the cognizance of the public.

The foregoing paragraph is exclusively "personal to myself." I am now going to relate what will be generally interesting.

For the evening of the 1st of April, '32, I had an appointment with an acquaintance whom I had almost begun to look upon as a friend. The place of rendezvous was in College-green, at the Shades Tavern[4]—a classic spot, known to a few select persons about town. At half-past six o'clock I accordingly repaired thither. As yet, my acquaintance, whom I had almost begun to regard as a friend, had not made his appearance. Taking possession of a vacant box, I ordered the waiter to bring a bottle of port and two glasses. He obeyed. Mechanically I began to sip the wine, awaiting, with some anxiety, the arrival of my acquaintance, whom I had almost, &c... But half an hour elapsed, and he came not. Now I grew fidgetty and thoughtful, and began to form a variety of conjectures. At length, for very weariness, I gave this up. Suddenly I heard some one cough slightly. I raised my head, and looked forth at the door. Seated at an opposite table, I beheld a gentleman of tall stature and commanding aspect, striking, indeed, to a degree, in his physiognomy. He was reading a newspaper, and was apparently deeply absorbed in its contents. How was it that I had hitherto neglected to notice this man? I could not forbear wondering. I was unable to account for the circumstance, except by referring to my previous abstraction, the pre-occupied nature of my thoughts, and the agitation which the anticipation of the meeting with my acquaintance, whom I had almost begun, &c., had necessarily tended to produce, in a person of my delicately nervous temperament. Now, however, I was resolved to compensate for my previous absence of mind. I examined the stranger opposite me minutely. I criticised him, without saying a syllable, from hat-crown (he wore his beaver) to shoe-tie (he sported pumps). His cravat, waistcoat, frock, unutterables,[5] all underwent a rigid analysis by my searching eye. I scrutinized all, first collectively and afterwards consecutively; and I owe it to truth and justice to protest, that, upon my honour, the result was decidedly satisfactory. All was perfect, lofty, gentlemanlike. Viewed as a whole, his countenance was, as I have remarked, peculiarly particular. I was, however, determined to institute an examination into it *stückweise*,[6] as they say at Vienna, and I reviewed every feature distinctively and apart. Had I been a *Quarterly Reviewer*,[7] or Professor Wilson himself,[8] I could not have discovered the slenderest groundwork to erect a super-structure of censure on. Had similar perfection ever until that hour been encountered by any? Never and nowhere. I knew not what to imagine; my faculties were bewildered. The thing was too miraculous, it was over-magnificent, extra-odd, super-inexplicable. Who was this man? I had always been a considerable peripatetic, but I could not recollect that in town or country he had ever until now encountered my inspection. Such a figure and such a face I could not, had I but once beheld them, possibly forget; they would have been enrolled among the archives of my memory, as treasures to be drawn lavishly and largely upon, on some future night, when the current of my ideas should run darkly and low, among underwood and over brambly places, and the warehouse of my imagination be ransacked in vain for a fresh assortment of imagery, and the punchless jug should stand solitarily upon the dimly-lighted table, and not a human voice be heard to set that table in a roar. I had never before seen this man: of course, then, it was obvious that I now saw him for the first time. As this reflection, which I conceived to be a strictly logical one, occurred, I filled my glass a fifth time, and sipped as usual. The stranger continued to peruse his newspaper. His attitude was partially recumbent and wholly motionless. It was a reasonable inference from this, that he must be an individual of steady habits and unchangeable principles, whom it might be exceedingly difficult to detach from a favourite pursuit, or draw aside from the path of prudence and duty. Rectitude of conduct is a quality that commands my esteem: if I had before admired the stranger, this consideration annexed to my admiration a feeling of respect. Yes! he was evidently a cautious and fore-thoughtful character—perhaps a little too inflexible in his determinations; but, then, has not inflexibility ever been the invariable concomitant of vast powers? Whether, however, this interrogatory were answered negatively or affirmatively, it was certain that adequate testimony of the positive inflexibility of this man's disposition was as yet wanting; and I should perpetrate an enormous act of injustice in condemning him, unless I had been antecedently placed in possession of every fact and circumstance exercising the remotest influence upon the question. It is essential to the passing of an upright sentence, that crude and precipitate opinions be discarded; and should I, by over-hastily following the dictates of a rash judgment, irrevocably commit myself in the eyes of philosophy, and eternally damn my own character as an impartial observer of the human family at large, would it be reasonable? would it be even politic? Should I not, in fact, deserve to be hooted down wherever I exhibited myself, and driven, like Ahasuerus the wanderer,[9] from post to pillar; seeking refuge now in a cavern, and now in a pot-house, and finding rest nowhere—a houseless wretch—a spectacle to society, and a melancholy memorial to after ages of the ruinous results of that self-conceit which prompts to a headstrong perseverance in opinions of a ridiculous order? What a doom! I shuddered as I silently contemplated the abstract possibility of such a contingency; and then, filling a sixth glass, went on sipping. Still my acquaintance, who was not yet a friend, had not blessed me with the light of his countenance;[10] and my only resource was to watch, with an attentive eye, the proceedings, if any should take place, of the being at the opposite table. I felt my interest in the destiny of the unknown augment moment by moment. Questionlessly, thought I, the Platonical theory is not wholly visionary—not altogether a bam. I must have known this man in some pre-adamite world; and the extraordinary sensations I experience in his presence, are explicable only by reference to an antenatal state of existence. He and I have been ancient companions—fraternized members of the aboriginal *Tugendbund*[11]—the Orestes and Pylades[12] of a purer and loftier sphere. Perhaps I died upon the block for him! Who shall expound me the enigma of the sympathetical feelings reciprocated between master-minds, when upon earth each meets the other for the first time, unless by pointing to the electrical chain which runs dimly back through the long gallery of time, ascending from generation to generation, until it has reached the known beginning of all things, and then stretches out anew, far, far beyond that, wide away into the measureless deep of primary creation—the unknown, unimaginable infinite! There is nothing incredible if we believe life to be a reality; for, to a psychologist, the very consciousness that he exists at all, is a mystery unfathomable in this world. An ass will attempt to illuminate us on the subject, and may produce, with an air of consequential cognoscity, a schedule of what he is pleased to call reasons; but it is all hollow humbug. So stands a leaden-visaged geologist, up to his knees in the centre of a quagmire, and silently and sedulously pokes at the mud with his walking-stick, fancying himself, the while, a second Cuvier;[13] though the half-dozen clowns who officiate as spectators, and whom he takes for assembled Europe, perceive that the poor creature does nothing but turn up sludge eternally. As to the illuminating ass, only suffer him to proceed, and he will undertake to probe infinity with a bodkin, and measure the universe with a yard of pack thread. There are two distinguished plans for the extinction of such an annoyance;—first, to cough him down—second, to empty a pot of porter against his countenance. I have tried both experiments, and can vouch that the most successful results will follow.

The stranger, as I continued to gaze, elevated his hand to his head, and slightly varied the position of his hat. Here was a remarkable event—a landmark in the desert—an epoch in the history of the evening, affording scope for unbounded conjecture. I resolved, however, by no means to allow imagination to obtain the start of judgment upon this occasion. The unknown had altered the position of his hat. What was the inference spontaneously deducible from the occurrence of such a circumstance? Firstly, that anterior to the motion which preceded the change, the unknown had conceived, that his hat did not sit properly on his head: secondly, that he must be gifted with the organ of order in a high degree. Individuals in whom that organ is prominently developed are rarely, if ever, imaginative or poetical: hence it was to be inferred, that the energies of the unknown were exclusively devoted to the advancement of prosaical interests. But here again rose cause to bewilder and embarrass. I could see by a glance, that the unknown was conning a column of poetry, and that his expressive countenance, as he went on, became palely illumined by a quenchless lamp from the sanctuary within; how did this harmonise with my former conclusion? I surmounted the difficulty, however, by reflecting that it is, after all, possible for a man to be, at once illimitably imaginative, and profoundly philosophical, as we find, said I mentally, in the instance of Dr. Bowring.[14] *Bowring?* Ah stupidity! thy name is Clarence. That, until this moment, the truth should never have struck thee! That, only now shouldst thou have been made aware that Bowring himself was before thee! A thrill of joy pervaded my frame, as I reclined my brow upon my hand, and internally exclaimed: yes! it is, indeed, Bowring! It must be he, because it can be no other!

As I had always been ardently desirous of an introduction to that illustrious man, whom I justly regard as one of the leading genii of modern Europe, I shall leave the public to imagine the overpowering nature of my feelings upon discovering that the golden opportunity had at length been vouchsafed, and that I was now free to enter into oral communication with a master-spirit of the age. I paused to deliberate upon the description of address I should put forth, as well as the tone of voice which it would be most appropriate to assume; whether aristocratical or sentimental, free-and-easy or brokenhearted; and also upon the style of expression properest for my adoption, and best calculated to impress the mind of Bowring with a conviction that, whatever my defects might prove to be in detail, I was—take me all in all—a young man of magnificent intellect and dazzling originality, and possessed a comprehensiveness of capacity discoverable in nobody else within the bills of mortality. Whether I should compress my sentiments within two bulky sentences, or subdivide them into fifteen little ones, was likewise a matter of serious importance. So acute an observer of mankind and syntax as Bowring is, will infallibly, said I, detect the slenderest inaccuracy in my phraseology. To betray any philological inability would be a short method of getting myself damned in his eyes; and I should go down to the latest posterity as a bungler and a bumpkin. Mannerism is a grand thing. Let me, therefore, review this question minutely and microscopically, under all the various lights and shades in which it can be presented to the mind, before I pass the Rubicon[15] irremeably.

Mannerism is a grand thing, pursued I, following the current of my reflections. It is the real, heavy bullion, the genuine ore, the ingot itself; every other thing is jelly and soap-suds. You shall tramp the earth in vain for a more pitiable object than a man of genius, with nothing else to back it with. He was born to amalgamate with the mud we walk upon, and will, whenever he appears in public, be trodden over like that. Transfuse into this man a due portion of mannerism: the metamorphosis is marvellous. Erect he stands, and blows his trumpet, the sounds whereof echo unto the uttermost confines of our magnificent world. Senates listen,—empires tremble,—thrones tumble down before him! He possesses the wand of Prospero,[16]—the lamp of Aladdin,[17]—the violin of Paganini,[18]—the assurance of the devil! What has conferred all these advantages upon him? *Mannerism!*—destitute of which we are,—so to speak,—walking humbugs,—destitute of which the long odds are, that the very best individual among us, after a life spent upon the tread-mill system, dies dismally in a sack.

For myself, concluded I, I laugh at Charlatanism in all its branches; but it is, nevertheless, essential that I show off with Bowring. I am nothing, if not striking. It is imperative on me, therefore, to strike.

Six hours of unremitting study a few weeks previously had enabled me to concoct a very superior joke about the *March* of Intellect's[19] becoming a *Dead* March on the *first of April.* This had never appeared. Should I suffer the diamond to sparkle? It was a debatable question whether Doctor B. would not internally condemn me as an unprincipled ruffian for sneering at my own party. I know not, said I:—I am buried in Egyptian darkness on this point; but, *primâ facie,*[20] I should be inclined to suppose Bowring a moral cosmopolite, who could indifferently floor friends and enemies, *con amore.*[21] To humbug the whole world in the gross is certainly a herculean achievement; but the conquest of impossibilities is the glory of genius. Both Bowring and I are living in a miraculous era,—the second quarter of the nineteenth century,—and shall *I* deny to *him* the capability of appreciating one of the loftiest efforts of the human mind? Perish the notion!

I had nearly arrived at a permanent decision, when the progress of my meditations was abruptly arrested by the intervention of a new and startling consideration. Bowring was a universal linguist, a master of dead and living languages to any extent. Admirably well did he know,—none better,—the intrinsic nothingness of the English tongue. Its periods and phrases were, in truth, very small beer to him. Suppose that I were to accost him in the majestical cadences of the Spanish. A passage from Calderon[22] might form a felicitous introduction. Or in the French? I could draw upon Corneille,[23] Malherbe,[24] Voltaire, &c. to any amount. Or in the German? Here again I was at home. To spout Opitz,[25] Canitz,[26] Uz,[27] Wieland,[28]—and oh! above all, Richter—*meines Herzens Richter—(ach! wenn ich ein Herz habe)*[29] was as easy as to mix a fifth tumbler. Of Latin and Greek I made no account; Timbuctooese I was slightly deficient in. As to the Hungarian and Polish, they were not hastily to be sneezed at. The Unknown Tongues merited some attention, on account of the coal-black locks of the Reverend Ned Irving.[30] In short the satisfactory adjustment of this point was to be sedulously looked to. After some further deliberation I at length concluded upon doing nothing hurriedly. First ideas, said I, should be allowed time to cool into shape. A grammatical error would play the devil with me. The great Utilitarian[31] would dub me quack, and the forthcoming number of the *Westminster*[32] would nail me to the wall as a hollow-sculled pretender to encyclopediacal knowledge, a character which I am much more anxious that Oliver Yorke[33] should fasten upon Lardner[34] than Rowland Bowring upon *me.*

As, however, I languidly sipped my ninth glass, a heart-chilling and soul-sinking reminiscence came over me. I remembered to have somewhere read that Bowring was a Cassius-like looking philosopher. Now the stranger before me was rather plump than spare;—certainly more *enbonpoint*[35] than corresponded with the portrait given of the Doctor. Thus was my basket of glass instantaneously shattered to fragments, while I,—like another Alnaschar,[36]—stood weeping over the brittle ruin. This, then, was *not* Bowring! The tide of life ran coldly to my heart; and I felt myself at that moment a Conscious Non-entity!

What was to be done? Hastily to discuss the remainder of my wine, to order a fresh bottle, and to drink six or eight glasses in rapid succession, was the operation of a few minutes. And oh! what a change! Cleverly indeed had I calculated upon a glorious reaction. Words I have none to reveal the quiescence of spirit that succeeded, the interior balminess that steeped every faculty in blessed sweetness. I felt renovated, created anew: I had undergone an apotheosis; I wore the cumbrous habiliments of flesh and blood no longer; the shell, hitherto the circumscriber of my soul, was shivered; I stood out, in front of the universe, a visible and tangible Intellect, and held, with giant grasp, the key that had power to unlock the deep prison which enclosed the secrets of antiquity and futurity!

The solitary thing that excited my surprise and embarrassment was the anomalous appearance which the nose of the stranger had assumed. But a few brief minutes before, and it had exhibited a symmetry the most perfect, and dimensions of an every-day character: now it might have formed a respectable rival to the tower of Lebanon.[37] As I concentrated the hitherto scattered energies of my mind, and brought them soberly to bear upon the examination of this enormous feature, I learned, from an intimate perception, of too incommunicable a nature to admit of development, that the stranger was no other than a revivification of MAUGRABY,[38] the celebrated oriental necromancer, whose dreaded name the romances of my childhood had rendered familiar to me, and who had lately arrived in Dublin for the purpose of consummating some hell-born deed of darkness, of the particulars of which I was, in all probability, destined to remain eternally ignorant. That there is, as some German metaphysicians maintain, an idiosyncracy in some individuals, endowing them with the possession of a *sixth* sense, or faculty, to which nomenclature has as yet affixed no distinct idea, (for our ideas are in fewer instances derivable from things than from names) is a position which I will never suffer any man, woman, or child, to contest. Had I myself ever at any former period been disturbed by the intrusion of doubts upon the subject, here was evidence more than sufficient to dissipate them all. Here was evidence too weighty to be kicked down stairs in a fine *de haut en bas*[39] fashion; for although I had never, until the present evening, come into contact with MAUGRABY, this sixth faculty, this fine, vague, spiritual, unintelligible lightning-like instinct had sufficed to assure me of his presence and proximity. It was even so. Certainty is the sepulchre of scepticism: scepticism is the executioner of certainty. As the believer, when he begins to doubt, ceases to believe, so the doubter, when he begins to believe, ceases to doubt. These may be entitled eternal moral axioms, philosophical aphorisms, infinitely superior to the aphorisms of Sir Morgan O'Doherty[40] touching the relative merits of soap and bear's grease, black puddings, *manches à gigot*,[41] cravats, cold fish, and similar bagatelles;— and I may as well take this opportunity of observing that Sir M. O'D. has by such discussions, inflicted incalculable injury upon the cause of philosophy, which mankind should be perpetually instructed to look up to as the very soul of seriousness, and centre of gravity.

That he whom I surveyed was, identically and *bonâ fide*, MAUGRABY, it would have betrayed symptoms of extravagant lunacy in me to deny; because the capability of producing so remarkable an effect as the preternatural growth of nose which I witnessed, was one which,—as far as my lucubrations enabled me to judge,—had always been exclusively monopolized by MAUGRABY. It was by no manner of means material whether what came under my inspection were a tangible reality or an optical illusion: that was MAUGRABY's business,—not mine; and if he had juggled my senses into a persuasion of the fidelity of that appearance which confounded me, when in point of fact the entire thing, if uncurtained to the world, would turn out to be a lie,—a shabby piece of "*Lock-und-Gaukel-Werk*,"[42]—a naked bamboozlement;—if he had done this, upon his own head be the deep guilt, the odium, the infamy attachable to the transaction. It would be hard if I were compelled to incur any responsibility for the iniquitous vagaries of an East-Indian sorcerer. To the day of my death I would protest against such injustice. The impression transmitted along the cord of the visual nerve to the external chambers of the brain, and thence conveyed, by easy stages, into the inner domicile of the soul, is all, quoth I, that I have to do with. Of such an impression I am the life-long slave. Whether there be other physical objects upon the surface of this globe as well as myself,—whether there be the *materiel* of a globe at all,—whether matter be an entity or an abstraction,—whether it have a *substratum* or not,—and whether there be anything anywhere having any existence of any description, are problems for Berkeleyans;[43] but if there be reasoning essences here below, independent of myself, in circumstances parallel with my own, their opinions will corroborate mine; our feelings will be found to coalesce; our decisions to coincide. In any event, however, no argument arising from the metaphysics of the question can annihilate the identity of MAUGRABY.

Were I to have been hanged for it, in the course of the evening, at the first convenient lamp-post, I could not suppress a sentiment of envy at the superiority over his fellow-creatures which characterised the Indian juggler. Elevate me, said I, to the uppermost step of the ladder,—establish me on the apex of the mountain,—and what, after all, is my preëminence? Low is the highest! contemptibly dwarfish the loftiest altitude! Admit my powers to be multifarious and *unique*; yet am I, by comparison with this intelligence, sunk "deeper than ever plummet sounded."[44] Lord of this earth is MAUGRABY:—his breath exhales pestilence,—his hand lavishes treasures! He possesses invisibility, ubiquity, tact, genius, wealth exhaustless, power undreamed of! Such is MAUGRABY: such is he on whom I gaze. He is worthy to be champion of England, or to write the leading articles for the Thunderer![45]

Gradually the current of my thoughts took another course, and my mind yielded to suggestions and speculations that were anything but tranquillizing and agreeable. I am not prone to be lightly affected: legerdemain and playhouse thunder move me never;—it might be even found a task to brain me with a lady's fan; and hence, the mere size of MAUGRABY's nose, though I admitted it to be a novelty of the season, was insufficient to excite any emotion of terror within me. Viewed in the abstract, it was unquestionably no more than an oddity,—a bugbear to the uninitiated of the suburbs,—a staggering deviation from the appearances that everyday life presents us with;—and if this were the Alpha and Omega of the affair, MAUGRABY was a bottle of smoke. But this was *not* all: it was to be recollected that the nose encreased each moment in latitude and longitude: here was the rub. The magnitude of a man's nose is not, *per se*, an object of public solicitude: the Balance of Power is not interfered with by it, and its effects upon the social system are comparatively slight; but if a progressive increase in that magnitude be discernible, such an increase becomes a subject of intense interest to the community with whom the owner of the nose associates, and will, in course of time, absorb the undivided attention of mankind. (See *Slawkenbergius*,[46] vol. xi, chap. xxxii, p. 658, art. *Nosology*.) It was apparent that in MAUGRABY's case dismal damage would accrue to the proprietor of the Shades. His (MAUGRABY's) nose would speedily become too vast for the area of the apartment; it would soon constitute a barricade; it would offer a formidable obstacle to the ingress of visitors; eventually the entrance to the tavern would be blocked up; all intercourse would thus be impracticable; business would come to a dead stand-still; and an evil whose ramifications no penetration could reach would thus be generated.

But experience alone could testify to the absolute amount of injury that would be inflicted through the agency of this mountainous feature. Extending itself from College Green through Dame-street, Westmoreland-street, and Grafton-street, it would, by regular degrees, occupy every square foot of vacant space in this mighty metropolis. Then would ensue the prostration of commerce, the reign of universal terror, the precipitated departure of the citizens of all ranks into the interior,—and Dublin would, in its melancholy destiny, be assimilated by the historian of a future age, with Persepolis, Palmyra, and Nineveh! As the phantasmagoria of all this ruin arose in shadowy horror upon my anticipations, is it wonderful that I shook, as if affected with palsy, and that my heart sank in my bosom to a depth of several inches? I fell at once into a train of soliloquy.

Too intimately, MAUGRABY, am I acquainted with thine iron character to doubt for an instant thy rocky immovability of purpose. What thou willest, that executest thou. Expostulation and remonstrance, oratory and poetry are to thee so much rigmarole; even my tears will be thy laughing-stock. I have not the ghost of a chance against thee.

MAUGRABY! thou damned incubus! what liberty is this that thou hast dared to take with me? Supposest thou that I will perish, as perishes the culprit at the gallows, bandaged, night-capped, hoodwinked, humbugged? Is thy horn, after all, so soft? I am, it is true, weaponless, unless we consider this glass decanter in my fist a weapon; but all the talons with which nature has endowed me shall be exercised against thee. Still, and at the best, "my final hope is flat despair."[47] I stand alone: like Anacharsis Clootz,[48] I am deserted by the human race:—I am driven into a box, three feet square; there I am cooped up;—a beggarly bottle of wine is allotted to me; *pour toute compagnie,*[49] I am placed in juxtaposition with a hell-hound, and then I am left to perish ignobly.

That I should at this moment have neither poker, pike, pitchfork, nor pickaxe, will be viewed in the light of a metropolitan calamity by the future annalist of Dublin, when he shall have occasion to chronicle the circumstance. The absence of a vat of tallow from this establishment is of the greatest detriment to me, for in such a vat it might be practicable to suffocate this demidæmon. There being no such vat, it becomes obvious he can never be suffocated in it. How then, good heavens! can any man be so senseless, betray so much of the Hottentot, shew himself so far sunk in stupidity, as to expect that I should find one at my elbow? How deplorably he needs the Schoolmaster! How requisite it is that some friend to human perfectibility should advance him one halfpenny each Saturday wherewith to procure a Halfpenny Magazine! He is, this night, the concentrated extract of absurdity: the force of assery can no further go. I protest, with all the solemnity that belongs to my awful position, that if there be a chandler's vat under this roof the fact is the most extraordinary that history records. Its existence is not to be accounted for on any commercial principle. No man can tell how it was conveyed hither, or at whose expense it was established. An impenetrable veil of mystery shrouds the proceeding. The whole thing is dark—it is an enigma, a phenomenon of great importance. I had better leave it where I found it.

My regards were now painfully fascinated by the great magician of the Dom–Daniel.[50] To look in any direction but the one, I felt to be totally impracticable. He had spell–bound me, doubtlessly; his accursed jugglery had been at work while I, with the innocent unsuspiciousness which forms my distinguishing characteristic, had been occupied in draining the decanter. Was ever an inhabitant of any city in Europe so horribly predicamented? It was manifest that he had already singled me out as his first victim. I foreknew the destiny whereunto I was reserved. I saw the black marble dome, the interminable suites of chambers, the wizard scrolls, the shaft and quiver, and in dim but dreadful perspective the bloody cage, in which incarcerated under the figure of a bat I should be doomed to flap my leathern wings dolefully through the sunless day.

Mere human fortitude was inadequate to the longer endurance of such agonising emotions as accompanied the pourtrayal of these horrors upon my intellectual retina. Nature was for once victor over Necromancy. I started up, I shrieked, I shouted, I rushed forward headlong. I remember tumbling down in a state of frenzy, but nothing beyond.

> The morn was up again, the dewy morn,
>   With breath all incense, and with cheek all bloom,
> Laughing the clouds away with playful scorn,
>   And living as if earth contained no tomb.[51]

But I could not enjoy it, for I was in bed, and my temples throbbed violently. I understood that I had been conveyed from the Shades in a carriage. Dr. Stokes[52] was at my bedside: I enquired of him whether he had seen Maugraby hovering in the vicinity of the house. As the only reply to this was a shake of the head, I at once and briefly gave him a narration of my adventure.

Well, said he, I can satisfy you of the individuality of your unknown. He is neither MAUGRABY nor Bowring, but BRASSPEN,[53] of the *Comet* Club. I saw him there last night myself.

Tout est mystère dans ce monde-ci, thought I; *je ne sais trop qu'en croire*.[54]

FLASHES OF LIGHTNING.

"It's good to be merry and wise."
OLD SONG.[1]

"THERE have been some clever letters in the *Age*,"[2] said *Clarence* to *Philander*.[3] *Phil.*: "Yes; but there is one letter, the absence of which obstructs its popularity." *Clar.*: "Illuminate me." *Phil.*: "The letter R; if it had that, it would become the *Rage*."

Clar.: "Talking of letters, those were five *Capital* ones that appeared in the last COMET." *Phil.*: "Which?" *Clar.*: "C, O, M, E, T." *Phil.*: "Well, had I put them in small type, I might have hurt the COMET." *Clar.*: "Illuminate me." *Phil.*: "Perhaps I would have given *it-a-lick*."

"The difference between the Irish Radicals and the Whigs,"[4] said *Phil.* to *Clar.*, "is, after all, merely nominal; but that between the Radicals and the Tories is real." *Clar.*: "It is only half *real*." *Phil.*: "Illuminate." *Clar.*: "The Tories are friends of Peel;[5] the Irish Rads. are friends of *re*-peal."

Clar.: "*Apropos des bottes*:[6] Have you looked through old Mother Mute's Mag.?"[7] *Phil.*: "Yes; every one *saw through* the thing from the first: I just looked at the animal once for all." *Clar.*: "You must have looked twice." *Phil.*: "Illuminate." *Clar.*: "You *re*-viewed it." *Phil.*: "Ah, ha! Have you read the dialogue it opens with?" *Clar.*: "May I *die-a-log* if I have. Yet the Mag. may be of service to literature." *Phil.*: "Bah! You have just such *litter at your* feet in any stable." *Clar.*: "Not that the Mag. will turn out a *stable* concern." *Phil.*: "No; though it takes *hay lofty* tone." *Clar.*: "And may put its unfortunate contributors to the *rack*." *Phil.*: "At all events I fear it can give them little *pour manger*."[8] *Clar.*: "Poh! They may get a *bit* now and then, when they are *sad-led*, just to *stir-up* their *in-tail-lick'd-you-all* powers." *Phil.*: "The poetry of the Mag., however, is rather Miltonic." *Clar.*: "Rather Mill-stone-ic, say I." *Phil.*: "But the story of Bessy Bell and Mary Gray[9] pierced me to the heart." *Clar.*: "That merely proves it to be a *bore*."

Phil.: "*Brasspen*[10] said a bright thing last week to a thirty-first cousin." *Clar.*: "*Qu'est-ce que c'était?*" *Phil.*: "She asked him why Radicalism was abused as a blood-thirsty thing. 'Because,' said he, 'it is *in-Hume-Anne*.'[11] 'Twas good." *Clar.*: "Did she pay him anything for it?" *Phil.*: "Not a ghost!" *Clar.*: "Then he made it *good for nothing*."

A TREATISE ON A PAIR OF TONGS.

> Sure such a pair was never seen,
> So justly formed.
>
> The Duenna.[1]

> Why, man, *it* doth bestride the narrow world
> Like a Colossus.
>
> Julius Caesar.[2]

𝕴 𝖎𝖓𝖙𝖗𝖔𝖉𝖚𝖈𝖊 𝖒𝖞 𝖘𝖚𝖇𝖏𝖊𝖈𝖙 𝖘𝖙𝖞𝖑𝖎𝖘𝖍𝖑𝖞.

THERE is nowhere to be met with in this world, a more interesting spectacle than a pair of tongs. Throughout Japan and the provinces of Tartary,—from boundary to boundary of the Celestial Empire,[3]—among the Moguls, even, not to speak of Van Dieman's land,[4]—in Piccadilly, Philadelphia, Stamboul, Timbuctoo and Bilbao,—I see nothing that I admit to be worthy of standing up by the side of a pair of tongs. It suggests a prolific universe of reflections, each the parent of an additional universe. Contemplate the subject as you will,—handle it as you may, you are certain to discover, day after day, some new quality to blow your trumpet concerning. Small wonder:—it is everlasting as the March of Eternity,—inexhaustible as the depths of Infinity. Only consider, Public, what a pair of tongs really is. Its shape and figure,—the attitudes it unconsciously assumes,—the *materiel* of which it is constructed,—the purposes to which it is destined,—are all topics of the loftiest nature. To discuss any one of these topics apart, should be the work of a succession of generations; to dilate upon the entire conjunctively we know to be a dead impracticability. The bare attempt in any man to do it in 3 vols. post octavo, sickens our stomachs;—it is entirely too revolting,—monstrous beyond measure. Any proposal, emanating from New Burlington Street,[5] and addressed to me, insinuating that I should undertake the business, would prove to us all how slenderly the great European publisher has profited by the intellectual treasures piled behind his counter by Bulwer[6] and D'Israeli.[7] Colburn's lunacy[8] would be at once established as a melancholy fact; and his solitary resource would be to plant himself *solus* on the pinnacle of the Temple of Humbug, and continue there to all eternity, occupying a position too deplorably conspicuous for human imagination, unaided by the Spirit of the *Age*,[9] to be capable of conceiving.

𝔍 proceed now to point out to observers, what a blessed thing it is for mankind that there is nothing like a pair of tongs.

A pair of tongs is an unique object. There is nothing exactly resembling it upon the surphiz[10] of the earth. It is alone: a phoenix: a study for the amateurs of the singular. This is fortunate. If there were any other object from the North Pole to the South, perfectly analogous in form to the tongs, the individuality of the tongs would be at an end: it would, in fact, be merged in the other object. Hence would result a startling question: By what process shall the learned societies of Europe be enabled to distinguish between the identity of the tongs and the identity of the other object? No discovery in physics hitherto accomplished could assist us in framing a satisfactory reply to this question. It is worse than a Chinese puzzle.

𝔍 enter into a mysterious question, to wit, when and by whom the first pair of tongs was built: Nobody can tell me, and thus the thing goes to the devil.

The origin of tongs is involved in obscurity. The period of their introduction into Europe in particular, and among civilized nations in general, has never been clearly ascertained. It is to be deeply regretted that antiquarian research has in few instances been directed to the development of the mystery that hangs over the invention of tongs. This indifference is not merely culpable—it is atrocious:—it inculcates, however, a splendid moral lesson, by pointing out the melancholy consequences of neglect, and by establishing the necessity of diligence and perseverance with regard even to what may be too toploftically termed the *minutiæ* of life. Perhaps a conjecture of my own may be hazarded without presumption. I should imagine that tongs first came into use as soon as they began to be wanted. Any theory which assumes that they existed antecedent to the discovery of fire by Prometheus,[11] in Kilkenny,[12] 5600 years ago, must be baseless;—unless, Public, you and I take it for granted that they might have been applied to widely different purposes,—*par exemple*, to the taking up of little pebbles of lump sugar and dropping them into the mouth of the punch-jug.[13] And considering that the average length and dimensions of tongs altogether unfit them for such an office, the hypothesis must be rejected as the reverie of a drunken dreamer.

𝔍 come down with heavy fist upon the spare-tongs niggard.

Tongs are more frequently handled in the depth of winter, than during the sweltering sultriness of the dog-days;—oftener in requisition where there is fire, than where there happens to be none. The reason of this is obvious: it is because there is a greater occasion for them. Tongs, however, are by no means invariably made use of even in a chamber where the occasion requires their exercise; and this circumstance is generally attributable either to inability or disinclination in the proprietor of the chamber. Possibly he has no tongs:—possibly, though he may have them, he declines using them. Putting case the first as true, he is destitute of the ability to produce a pair; in case the second, he is, though possessed of a pair, evidently unwilling to devote them to the ends to which they were primarily appropriated. Both transactions are of the shabby and beggarly order; but moral jurisprudence will for ever erect a distinction between the pauper and the niggard; and a rational man will be always found ready to give the pauper more halfpence than kicks, and the niggard more kicks than halfpence.

𝕴 𝔴𝔞𝔵 𝔣𝔢𝔞𝔯𝔣𝔲𝔩𝔩𝔶 𝔢𝔯𝔲𝔡𝔦𝔱𝔢, 𝔦𝔫 𝔡𝔢𝔰𝔠𝔞𝔫𝔱𝔦𝔫𝔤 𝔲𝔭𝔬𝔫 𝔱𝔥𝔢 𝔤𝔲𝔦𝔩𝔱𝔶 𝔡𝔬𝔦𝔫𝔤𝔰 𝔬𝔣 𝕮𝔞𝔯𝔱𝔢𝔰𝔦𝔲𝔰[14] 𝔞𝔫𝔡 𝔥𝔦𝔰 𝔠𝔩𝔦𝔮𝔲𝔢: 𝕭𝔢𝔠𝔞𝔲𝔰𝔢 𝔱𝔥𝔢𝔶 𝔥𝔞𝔳𝔢 𝕭𝔲𝔯𝔨𝔢𝔡[15] 𝔱𝔥𝔢 𝔢𝔵𝔦𝔰𝔱𝔢𝔫𝔠𝔢 𝔬𝔣 𝔱𝔬𝔫𝔤𝔰, 𝔱𝔥𝔢𝔯𝔢𝔣𝔬𝔯𝔢 𝕴 𝔪𝔞𝔨𝔢 𝔞𝔫 𝔢𝔵𝔞𝔪𝔭𝔩𝔢 𝔬𝔣 𝔱𝔥𝔢𝔪.

Why should I blink it? The existence of tongs involves the destruction of a certain antiquated metaphysical dogma. Ascertainable by a reference to the writings of Schelling,[16] Gassendi,[17] Reid,[18] Mallebranche,[19] Wolfe,[20] Descartes, Leibnitz,[21] and many more, is the fact, that with the hypothetical exceptions of the Berkeleyans,[22] all philosophers have agreed in the truth of the theory which maintains that there are *in esse vel posse*[23] but two things, *i.e.* body and spirit. This theory is a fallacy. What manner of thing is a pair of tongs? Clearly it is neither body nor yet spirit. It is all head, neck and legs: it possesses therefore no body. It is inert and lifeless; therefore it has no spirit. Hence it is not body—it is not spirit;—and not being body, and not being spirit, the inference follows that it is neither. How frequently have I, during the slowly-rolling winter nights, from midnight till day-dawn, in the solitude of my lamp–illumined apartment, how frequently have I perused the works of those illustrious labourers whom I have named, and of others whom I might have named, if I had chosen to name them, but whom I have not chosen to name, and therefore have not named,—and as I have perused them, how have I been paralysed with astonishment to observe the total omission of any allusion in those works to a pair of tongs! I have ransacked Reid's Powers,[24] Mill's Phenomena,[25] and Brown's Philosophy,[26] in vain. Give me—I have exclaimed, while fathoming, muddler[27] in hand, the depth of my eleventh tumbler,—give me the remotest allusion—the faintest reference to the existence of tongs. I shall be satisfied with the shadowyest semblance of an acknowledgment. In vain, Public. No tongs—no allusion,—nothing whatever. Damning evidence this, of something!—such has been my emphatical exclamation, while fathoming with a muddler the abyss of my fifteenth tumbler. The thing, Philander,[28] was hollow. Any admission of the existence of a pair of tongs would have been death to the systems of philosophy palmed upon us all. Good herrings! how afflicting it is to see men of extensive intellectual resources stooping to such dirty paltriness. The iniquity of suppression is more heinous than the iniquity of misquotation, because the misquoter merely garbles, whereas the suppresser suppresses. He who garbles a fact merely submits it to us in a garbled state, but he who suppresses it entirely, omits it, in fact, altogether.

𝕴 𝔰𝔥𝔢𝔴 𝔴𝔥𝔞𝔱 𝕳𝔬𝔴𝔡𝔶𝔡𝔬𝔴𝔡𝔶 𝔱𝔥𝔬𝔲𝔤𝔥𝔱 𝔬𝔣 𝔞𝔩𝔩 𝔰𝔲𝔠𝔥 𝔰𝔠𝔞𝔪𔭭𝔰 𝔞𝔰 𝔰𝔫𝔲𝔣𝔣 𝔠𝔞𝔫𝔡𝔩𝔢𝔰 𝔴𝔦𝔱𝔥 𝔱𝔬𝔫𝔤𝔰. 𝕱𝔬𝔩𝔩𝔬𝔴𝔰 𝔞 𝔩𝔞𝔪𝔢𝔫𝔱𝔞𝔟𝔩𝔢 𝔥𝔬𝔴𝔩 𝔣𝔬𝔯 𝕳𝔬𝔴𝔡𝔶𝔡𝔬𝔴𝔡𝔶.

A select friend of my own, the late Doctor Howdydowdy, an Englishman of infinite research and surpassing powers of genius, of whose acquaintance, Philander, you would have been vainglorious, never ceased expressing the highest veneration for tongs. To have listened to the indignant eloquence of that man upon the profanation undergone by a pair of tongs, when converted, by hand of vulgarian, into a pair of snuffers! I was accustomed deferentially to hazard a few remarks by way of palliating the enormity. It's all gammon, he would reply, after having heard me out with that lofty patience that characterises elevated minds;—it's all gammon 'at 'ere fudgification of yours!—Darn it!—if a man ha'n'nt got fingers clean enough to trim a glimmer, let him cadge a pair of snuffers and be darned to un!—It is a pity that Howdydowdy should have died as he did, in a ditch. For six months previous to his death he had been subsisting exclusively upon whiskey, a practice that should never be recommended to persons of a delicate constitution. He rests in Bully's Acre.[29]

𝕴 𝔞𝔯𝔤𝔲𝔢 𝔱𝔥𝔢 𝔪𝔢𝔯𝔦𝔱𝔰 𝔬𝔣 𝔱𝔥𝔢 𝔠𝔞𝔰𝔢 𝔞𝔰 𝔟𝔢𝔱𝔴𝔢𝔢𝔫 𝔱𝔬𝔫𝔤𝔰 𝔞𝔫𝔡 𝔭𝔬𝔨𝔢𝔯. 𝕴𝔫 𝔴𝔥𝔞𝔱 𝔴𝔞𝔶 𝔱𝔥𝔢 𝔭𝔬𝔨𝔢𝔯-𝔠𝔥𝔞𝔪𝔭𝔦𝔬𝔫𝔰 𝔞𝔯𝔢 𝔱𝔬 𝔟𝔢 𝔡𝔢𝔞𝔩𝔱 𝔴𝔦𝔱𝔥.

Claims have been authoritatively advanced by plodders and dawdlers in favor of the poker; and the superiority of the poker over the tongs has been warmly contended for by nincompoops and drivellers. The mode of treating these bores and boobies consists in tripping them up and treading them joyously in the gutter. What is a poker?—A bare unit,—a figure of 1,—a Brobdignagian[30] pin,—striking implement, it is true, in the gripe of a savage; but left to itself, abandoned to its own private resources,—seen reclining in its ordinary attitude by the mantel-piece, *nihil*, nothing. What stupid humbuggers there are alive this day! Let no man henceforth syllable poker and tongs in the one sentence.

I dilate celestially upon the effects produced on me by a glimpse of a superb pair of tongs. I prove that nobody has a right to call me a robber.

The preservation of tongs in a state of purity and brilliancy constitutes one of the noblest objects to which human attention can be directed. If a bachelor be so unfortunate as to have neither cook nor housemaid, the concentrated energies of his own mind should be lavished upon the task of burnishing his tongs. When I stalk into a drawing-room, and perceive a magnificent brace of tongs genteelly lounging by the fire-side, I experience a glow of spirit and a flow of thought bordering on the archangelical. Standers-by are instantaneously stricken lifeless with astonishment at the golden tide of poetry which in myriads of sunny streams and glittering rivulets, issues from my lips; poetry as far beyond what you, Public, are accustomed to get from me, as ambrosia is beyond hogwash. With modest effrontery I take a chair; and if my quick eye detect the presence of any thing in the shape of wine or punch on the table, I cheerfully abolish its existence. Impelled as I am, on such occasions, by an irresistible impulse, all apology is superfluous; but to speak the truth, the mingled grace and gravity that accompany my performance of the manœuvre afford superabundant compensation to the company for the disappearance of the drinkables. I may add that I re-establish the spiritless bottle upon the table, instead of putting it into my pocket as a robber would do, or shattering it into shivers upon the hearth-flag as a ruffian would do. Why is this? Because, Public, I, Clarence, am neither a ruffian nor a robber.

Herein I develope the rueful consequences of lazily suffering a tongs to get rusty. My romance conquers me, and I display sentimentalism of a heavenly order.

De l'autre coté,[31] whenever a pair of tongs covered with a cloak of ignominious rust strikes the eye of me, the heart-withering spectre paralyses the majority of my faculties in the twinkling of a bed-post. Darkest pictures arise melancholically and flit in lugubrious guise before my fancy. So pines, ejaculate I, a neglected genius in obscurity,—his prospects shaded,—his powers running to waste,—destitute of a fair field for his talents,—and looking forward to a dreary death and dismal burial in the vicinity of some dunghill! I see Trenck in Magdeburgh,[32] Tasso in Ferrara,[33] Galileo in Florence,[34] and you, Philander, in Kilmainham.[35] (Yet you, Philander, are not rusted, albeit you have quitted one rusty city for another rusticity. You rather remind me just now of a parboiled egg than of a rusty pair of tongs. Why? Because you are under Dunn.[36]) Then flow my tears like rain in winter. The immediate application of *eau-de-Cologne* or *sal volatile* to my temples becomes a matter of pressing necessity; and while this charitable duty is in progress of performance by thee, my own beloved *Eglantine*,[37] I,—totally mastered by the romance interwoven with my nature, unconsciously kiss the fair hand that is thus employed, and bedew it again and again with passionate tears, which gush less from the eyes than from the heart. I am, indeed, a being of incredible susceptibility. I wonder very much that it is not generally known among my acquaintances. But half the world seems to be battishly blind.

(*I shall take up the tongs again, Public, in the next number of the* COMET.)

𝕴 start a poser that would have sorely puzzled Zeno.[38] When 𝕴 have got pretty deeply into it, 𝕴 am unfortunately called off to a bowl of brandy and gruel.

I now approach the analysis of an argument of intense interest. It is taken for granted that a pair of tongs has lost one of its grippers. A question to be mooted then results: whether the remnant be a pair of tongs or not? A presumption in favor of an affirmative conclusion is started from the fact, that although a man (whether a native of the Cannibal Islands, a Chinese, or a Tipperary man) may have lost a toe, he is not the less a man on account of the loss of his toe. But to this it may be objected, that the reasoning is not of universal application; inasmuch as if you,—to purchase a pennyworth of buttermilk for your breakfast,—deduct a penny from twenty pounds, the residue is no longer twenty pounds. Let me conceive the hypothesis that I have a pot of porter on the table before me. I abstract a spoonful of porter from the pot. *Quere*: Is the unabstracted *residuum* of porter left in the quart, a potful of porter or not? It will not be denied by the most determined doubter, that the aggregation of a specific number of spoonfuls of porter is requisite to constitute a total pot of porter. Two spoonfuls will not do. Three are a failure. Four spoonfuls are a decided bam. Five are no go. No man in town will make me a potful out of six. Seven are a beggarly humbug. *Quere*, again, then: Is what remains in the pot a potful of porter or not? If it be still a potful of porter, it must have been more than a potful of porter, antecedent to the abstraction of the spoonful of porter. If it be not a potful of porter, what is it? Is it a potful of froth,—a bubble,—a juggle on touch, taste, and sight? Here we are left to speculate in the dark. Doubt and obscurity surround us on every point of our starless pathway. At every step we make, we sink half a foot deeplier into the bog. We are bewildered, labyrinthed, lost! I am free to admit, however, that, taken in the abstract, scarcely any perceptible analogy subsists between a pot of porter and a pair of tongs. The tongs are of steel or brass; the pot is of pewter. You swallow the porter; no man swallows

tongs. The solitary link of brotherhood between porter and tongs is this,—
that tongs have a head, and that porter has a head. Still I am satisfied with
the general tone of my logic. I perceive that I have shed a wide illumination
upon the subject. I have pick-axically pioneered my way to the original
question, that of the grippers. Is it not, therefore, Public! deplorable,—
must it not be considered dismal,—is it not an awful circumstance that I
should feel at present too dozy and drowsy to push along any farther? My
visage is buried in a basin of brandy and gruel: as soon as I shall have
cleared the basin, off I toddle to bed.

𝔅𝔢𝔦𝔫𝔤 𝔫𝔬𝔴 𝔞𝔤𝔞𝔦𝔫 𝔬𝔫 𝔪𝔶 𝔭𝔦𝔫𝔰, 𝔞𝔫𝔡 𝔣𝔢𝔢𝔩𝔦𝔫𝔤 𝔯𝔢𝔣𝔯𝔢𝔰𝔥𝔢𝔡, 𝔩𝔦𝔨𝔢 𝔞 𝔤𝔦𝔞𝔫𝔱 𝔞𝔣𝔱𝔢𝔯 𝔞
𝔩𝔬𝔫𝔤 𝔡𝔯𝔦𝔫𝔨 𝔬𝔣 𝔴𝔥𝔦𝔰𝔨𝔢𝔶, 𝔍 𝔤𝔬 𝔬𝔫 𝔦𝔫 𝔱𝔥𝔦𝔰 𝔴𝔞𝔶.

The miraculous resemblance between the shape of man and the shape of
tongs cannot fail to make a profound impression upon the most soporiferous
observer. To the moral philosopher it is a source of never-dying interest; the
zoölogist contemplates it in the light of a singular phenomenon; but above all,
it appeals with irresistible power to the sympathies of the philanthropist. It
has oftener than once occurred to me that Robert Owen[39] might, with great
advantage and propriety, commit the superintendence of his parallelograms
to a pair of tongs. The Trades' Union might occasionally, in the absence of
their president, show their independence of all precedents, by moving, "That
until Tom Steele[40] do arrive, the chair be taken by Steel Tongs." Tongs for
ever! Tongs will yet triumph. At some future period, when Reason shall reign
solus,—when illuminism shall really prevail among men,—when Brougham's
Useless Knowledge-books[41] shall be carted, waggon-load after waggon-load,
into the mud of Father Thames,—when the human race shall have become
rational,—when monarchies shall have tumbled, and kings become
nobodies,—and—spiral climax!—when persons like myself, with intellect of
the superhuman sort, shall drop in for an equitable proportion of such snacks
as may be going;—then,—at that time,—in that day,—about that period,
shall Governments and Unions award a tardy tribute of veneration to tongs.
Some better Bowring,[42] yet unswathed, will arise to celebrate the glories of
tongs in all languages!—senators will legislate with tongs in their hands!—
duels will be decided by appeals to tongs!—tongs will, as Warton superfinely
expresses it, "be slowly swung with sweepy sway"[43] from side to side by right
arm of pedestrian,—fair presumption for his dextrality!—and poets will
magnify tongs in all measures and out of all measure,—anapæstic, pyrrhic,
trochaic, dactyle, alexandrine, iambic, and even hexameter,—which that
illustrious member of societies and industrious member of society, Dr.
Southey,[44] has, in his latter days, with miserable want of gumption,
endeavoured to see whether he could have any chance in trying to make a

barbarous attempt at. But I lament to add that in those distant times none of us nineteenth-century men shall be alive,—because we shall all be dead. I speak of the year 7000.

Growing desperate and terrible as I proceed, I attack William Godwin, and threaten to slaughter him.

I guess it is Helvetius,[45] who, in his trumpery book, *De l'Esprit*, observes that a man vegetates like a tree, and that he (Helvetius) would as willingly be a tree as a man. Helvetius has totally omitted to inform us how much he would take to become a pair of tongs. The only mode left to us of accounting for this culpable oversight, is by presuming that Helvetius was as drunk as a piper while he was writing his book. Godwin, in his preface to St. Leon, categorically tells me that "it is better to be a human being than a stock or a stone."[46] Upon my honor, I cannot away with such an implied condemnation of tongs. William Godwin! I contest it with you. Strip, Sir! I will do battle with you on that article. How dare you, W. G., erect yourself into a dogmatist on men, stocks, and stones? Come, Godwin,—come, my man,—whence is your experience? What is the extent of your dabblings in the stocks? Were you ever in the *stock*ing trade,—and if so, how much was your *stock in trade* worth? Have you ever devoured a stockfish? Do you sport a black stock?[47] Come, never shrink from my *attacks*, *man*, as if I were a *tax man*; but answer me: How often do you play at jackstones? How far can you see into a millstone? Did you ever sell even a single stone of potatoes? I am a-*stone*-ished at your *stock* of assurance. You cub, what do you mean? Explain yourself, you varlet! Do you know, you sumph, to whom it is that you stand opposed? Why, you greenhorn of a month's growth, is it possible that you forget that the knotted club of Clarence is already lifted up to prostrate you in your mother-mud, and that you are destined to kiss the bosom of your father-land incontinent? Godwin, I venerate your forty-quill power as an author; and therefore, Godwin, I challenge you to a public disputation in my native city, Dublin, upon this subject; allowing you, as Crichton[48] allowed the University of Paris, the choice of thirty languages, and six and thirty various kinds of verse. There, now;— *c'est là une affaire finie*;[49] so you may take your change out of that, and small blame to you, my gay fellow, for doing so.

Why a man ought not to be tweaked by the nose with a pair of tongs, merely on account of his politics.

Listen to me now, reader. If you have invited a gentleman to dinner, it is a piece of suburban vulgarianism to tweak him by the beak with a pair of tongs, merely because his political opinions are not in harmony with yours. Truth compels me to add, that it betrays devilish impertinence in you; and affords a strong proof that neither your morals nor your manners were properly cultivated when you were a gaffer.[50] Your guest may play the devil; but that is no reason why you should presume to play Saint Dunstan.[51] Your criminality assumes a deeper dye, if you have taken no pains to ascertain whether or not his beak had been soaped before he came into the room; for whenever the beak has not been soaped, and that well, the tweaking is an expressibly painful operation to the tweaked party. In conclusion, I must observe that I have never seen the act done; that I have never heard that any man did it; and that I do not believe any man to be capable of doing it; any man, at least, who reflects that the beak is the leading article of a gentleman's countenance.

P.S. Beak-tweaking is, indeed, very much out of fashion in general. Every one *nose* that it is *beak*ause of the Reform *Bill*.

𝕴 𝖆𝖘𝖐 𝖜𝖍𝖊𝖙𝖍𝖊𝖗 𝖆𝖓𝖞 𝖒𝖆𝖓 𝖘𝖚𝖕𝖕𝖔𝖘𝖊𝖘 𝖙𝖍𝖆𝖙 𝕴 𝖆𝖒 𝖙𝖔 𝖜𝖗𝖎𝖙𝖊 𝖙𝖔 𝖆𝖑𝖑 𝖊𝖙𝖊𝖗𝖓𝖎𝖙𝖞 𝖚𝖕𝖔𝖓 𝖙𝖔𝖓𝖌𝖘, 𝖆𝖓𝖉 𝖓𝖊𝖛𝖊𝖗 𝖌𝖊𝖙 𝖆 𝖉𝖗𝖔𝖕 𝖔𝖋 𝖕𝖚𝖓𝖈𝖍.

I want to put one question. I demand an answer in the face of congregated Europe—of the Comet Club[52]—of the Allied Powers—and of the Black[53]-bearded, Grey-headed,[54] and Blue-devilled[55] Ministry of England. Is there, then, on the *Globe*, under the *Sun*,[56] or in the COMET, a man, with the *pia mater*[57] of an ass's foal, who will tell me that I ought to go on writing upon a pair of tongs to all eternity, without once slipping down to the nearest public-house to moisten my whistler? Why, what a hoggish stupidity such a fellow must have inherited! How muzzy he feels at all times! The world would,—(as Shelley says)—"laugh with a vast and inextinguishable laughter"[58] to see him slowly trailed through some sludgy puddle of interminable longitude, while I, standing alone, aloof from all, would look tearfully on, compassionating the sufferings of the unfortunate man from the depths of my soul,—and swilling (from time to time) as I looked on, protracted draughts from a pitcher of punch, to invigorate my nerves, and preserve me from hysterics. Let me reflect. It is now two, A.M. Taverns are closed. Not a minim of rum under my roof. I am waterless, sugarless, and spir—no, not spiritless! I go forth, Public, in terrible might, amid flashing rain and howling tempest, to storm the city for a beaker, though but of small beer! This is the most eventful morning of my life; and the adventures that I shall meet with before the sun gets up, are to form the subject of a future paper in the COMET.

𝕴 𝖉𝖎𝖛𝖊 𝖎𝖓𝖙𝖔 𝖙𝖍𝖊 𝖔𝖈𝖊𝖆𝖓 𝖔𝖋 𝖜𝖎𝖙 𝖋𝖔𝖗 𝖆 𝖘𝖙𝖗𝖆𝖞 𝖕𝖊𝖆𝖗𝖑, 𝖆𝖓𝖉 𝖋𝖊𝖙𝖈𝖍 𝖚𝖕 𝖆 𝖈𝖆𝖘𝖐𝖊𝖙 𝖔𝖋 𝖌𝖊𝖒𝖘.

We are now to consider what species of scene socialised life would exhibit, in case tongs were a nullity,—that is, if the space they fill presented a blank to the eye of the gazer,—that is, if there were no tongs. Imagine then, Philander,—think, Public, to what extremities we should be reduced! Stars and garters! Public, figure to yourself Francis Blackburne, Esq.,[59] Grey's Attorney-General for Ireland, poking with his fingers among the cinders and semicalcined coals, and dropping them into the fire! Picture to yourself William Conyngham Plunket,[60] Lord High Chancellor of Ireland, descending to such a degradation as this is! *Raking* in his old days! Getting *smutty* in our eyes! Lowering himself to the level of the *Bar*! Disturbing the ashes of the *Grate*! Shaking hands with the most brazen *of fenders*! Showing that he is a *good* warrant at "posting the *coal*,"[61] and a *better* on the *Turf*![62] Instead of hasting away to Coke on Littleton,[63] wasting away his *little ton* of *coke*! In place of poring over Blackstone's Commentaries,[64] fingering coals, which are merely *black stones* (*Common tories*, Phil!) And possibly bringing a *Black burn* on his hands! (No joke, Phil.) The blood, as he stoops, gushes cataract-like to his *cranium*, turning topsy-turvy the mighty kingdom of ideas in brain of Plunket, and sending the king himself adrift, Heaven knows whither, like the Dey of Algiers,[65] or the ex-Rex Charles X.[66] Look at his forehead and suppress your tears! It has come bump into contact with that smutty bar, now a trifle the brighter for the loss of the smut. Did you ever lay eyes on such a dark-browed Chancellor? Only conceive what sums must, in consequence, be disbursed by Plunket, for cleansing lotions, for *Pommade divine*, for ambrosial soap, otto of rose[67] soap, soap of almonds, cocoa-nut oil soap, &c. &c. &c. &c. &c. And yet his is but one instance in many—but *ex uno disce omnes*.[68] Let us therefore, Public, who possess tongs, who enjoy the unlimited use of them, who have received the capability of turning them to account as often as we like,—let us, I say, be careful how we undervalue so distinguished a blessing.

I adduce Jewish testimony on behalf of the antiquity of tongs.

Since I commenced this essay, my excellent friend Moses Cohen,[69] of Dame-street,[70] a philosophical Hebrew (whose cigars I warmly recommend to the "lip-homage" of all devout cloud-blowers) has directed my attention to the following passage in the fifth book of the Jewish Ethics,[71] compiled by Levi:[72]—

Ten things were created on the eve of the Sabbath in the twilight; and these are they: the Mouth of the Sabbath, the Mouth of the Ass (of Balaam), and the Mouth of the Spring; the Rainbow, Manna, the rod of Moses, the Shameer,[73] Characters, Writing, and the Tables. And some say, also the Dæmons, and the grave of our legislator Moses, and the ram of our father Abraham, and also THE PREPARED INSTRUMENT OF A TONGS.

A passage worth the whole of the Talmud! I shall leave it to speak for itself.

𝕻𝖚𝖇𝖑𝖎𝖈 𝖆𝖓𝖉 𝕴 𝖍𝖆𝖛𝖊 𝖆 𝖙𝖚𝖘𝖘𝖑𝖊.

If we dispassionately investigate the nature of our conceptions with regard to the abstract idea of a pair of tongs, we shall discover that it is by no means what the Aristotelians denominate an *ens rationis*,[74] but rather—

PUBLIC (*with outrageous impatience.*) O! curse you and your tongs, and your *ens rationis* to boot! Is there no end to this trumpery? You bore me to death's door! But, bless my soul! Is it possible? He is positively dead asleep! (*approaches and shakes me.*)

I (*yawning and rubbing my orbs.*) You have disturbed me, old woman, in the enjoyment of as hazily-beautiful a doldrum as ever soul of poet revelled in. You have cruelly broken my talisman. For which I feel cruelly disposed to break your neck. My occupation's gone:[75]—asleep, I wrought wonders; awake, my brain-case is a base-built pumpkin.

SHE. But, what, in the name of all that is odd, induced you to select such a subject?

I. Why, old woman,—if I am an original genius,—if nature has gifted me with certain toploftical[76] powers,—

SHE (*interrupting me in an unmannerly manner.*) *Toploftical*! Pah! Do you think that I will tolerate such rebel English?—Like your prohibition, forsooth, against "*syllabling* poker and tongs in one day."

I. What! antiquated dame,—have you, then, never heard of Shakespeare's

> —Airy *tongs* that *syllable* men's names
> In desert wildernesses?[77]

It is clear that you have never been to the Tonga Islands, or eaten (and drunk, too,) your share of a *hog's head* in company with King Tongataboo.[78]

SHE. Well, Sir, *pour couper court*[79]—if you wish me to patronise—I mean *matronise* you, you will desist from a subject only calculated for the meridian of an ironmonger's shop; I lay my injunction on you.

I (*with an air*).—An injunction that the Chancellor shall never dissolve. I yield to the fair—though it is hard. With Schiller I exclaim,—

> Das Jahrhundert
> Ist meinem Ideal nicht reif—Ich lebe
> Ein Bürger derer welche kommen werden.[80]

Adieu! respectable old creature.

SHE. Adieu! my son.

                                                                      CLARENCE

P.S.—Every one remembers Lord Anglesey's modest and quiet *entrée* into Dublin some time back, and Marcus Costello's pair of tongs and pair of black stockings.[81] Costello's conduct on that occasion was looked on, at the time, as a symbolical hint to such of the Marquis's friends as were determined to keep up the *game* "at all *hazards*,"[82] that thus would all *blacklegs*[83] be ultimately caught and suspended. For my part I always, from the bottom of my *sole*, considered it a mark of respect from the noble Marcus to the noble Marquiz for the *heeling measures* set on *foot* by the latter, which I am *shoe-r* it would be *bootless* to enumerate. The Marquis himself says he *under-stands* it in that light, and vows he will take *steps* to put down *White feet*[84] every where. Whiggery, it is said, has got beyond *standing*: if so, Anglesey's first proclamation will make a capital *l-e-g*[85] for it.

THE IRISH LANGUAGE.

TO THE EDITOR OF THE DUBLIN PENNY JOURNAL.

SIR—At page 31, Vol. I. of the Transactions of the Gaelic Society of Dublin, 1808, occur the following words:—"It would be of *great service*, and would facilitate much the reading of the language, if some system were adopted by which the pronunciation of these letters[1] could be rendered more certain." I agree with the remarker, it would be of *great service*.

Count Marcel,[2] a French nobleman, says of the Irish language, that it is "pleine de beautés," and "très expressive;" his remarks have induced me, an Italian, to study your language. But looking into the grammars of O'Byrne and Neilson,[3] they differ so much in their pronunciation that I made up my mind to have a "certain system" from which much advantage would accrue to those who study without a teacher.

In Rev. Paul O'Brien's grammar,[4] p. 6, I find that *a* is (2nd sound) *long* and *slender*, nearly as *i* in f*i*ne, or the German *ei* in w*ei*n, wine; as аѳарс, a horn, pronounced īrk by a Roscommon man, and eerk by a Cork man, having questioned them.

Should some clever Irish scholar who "ama la sua patria,"[5] agree with me in the above remarks, I hope he will undertake, through your valuable publication, a regular system by referring to other languages for example, as C.F. Volney has done in his work entitled "L'Alfabet Européen appliqué aux langues Asiatiques."[6]

I intend, Mr. Editor, (Deo volente) in a few years hence, to travel into Denmark, Sweden, Norway, where I might chance to pick up some valuable Irish manuscripts.

I saw, it is two years since, two interlineal translations of St. John's Gospel, announced in the *Dublin Evening Post*, would your able correspondent O'Donovan, inform me which is the better for acquiring a facility in translation.

Sir, if these few remarks are deemed worthy of insertion I hope for their publication; if they may at all awaken the sons of Erin to cultivate a language which a Mr. Shaw supposes to have been the language of Paradise,[7] I will feel content.

I am, Sir, your humble servant,

A CONSTANT READER.

Clarence-street, Liverpool.

MY TRANSFORMATION.

A WONDERFUL TALE.

Oh! while you live, tell truth, and shame the devil.

SHAKSPEARE.[1]

I SAW Eleanor Campion for the first time in the autumn of 1828. She was then twenty years of age, and a model of all that is witching and winning in woman. She was the most beautiful and fascinating girl I had ever met before, or have ever since known. I had long doubted the genuine existence of an uncontrollable love; and it was a punishment commensurate with the enormity of my scepticism that I should find myself in a few days deeply, incurably smitten. I avowed my passion, and was not rejected. Changed as I am now, in heart and soul, I look backward upon the dazzling brightness of that brief hour with feelings beyond the conception of any save those whose bosoms have burned with a "lava flood"[2] like that in my own. I have wept over the recollection of it with heart-wrung tears. Yet I weep now no more, and the reader will understand why, before he terminates my narrative.

A bond of friendship, apparently stronger than death, had subsisted from childhood between myself and Lionel Delamaine. He was a young man of handsome figure, insinuating address, and extensive accomplishments—certainly my own superior in everything save an unbounded admiration of the beautiful and perfect, and an ardent adventurousness of character. Perhaps it was not altogether in the course of human impulses that I should be desirous of introducing this young man to Eleanor Campion. I well remember that on the very evening of the introduction a presentiment of overshadowing evil hung like a cloud above my spirit. I saw, as on the glass of a magic mirror, the form and character of the change that was about to be wrought upon the spirit of my dream.[3] Those who are familiar with presentiments know that earlier or later they will be realised. So, alas! was it with me. Shape and verification were speedily given to the outlines of my vague imaginings. In one fortnight Lionel proved a villain, and Eleanor a forsworn traitress!—Oh faith! oh honor! oh constancy! are ye, indeed, anything beyond abstractions, hollowly-sounding words to echo ideas begotten in the brain of the visionary?

I tried to summon a sufficient share of philosophy to assist me in sustaining the tremendous shock thus inflicted on me. In vain, in vain. The iron had found its way into my soul;[4] there it rankled and festered: the decree had gone out, and I was thenceforth condemned to be the miserable victim of my own confidingness and the treachery of others. Possibly I might live—might bear about with me the burthen of my agony for long years to come; but my peace was everlastingly blasted, and the common atmosphere of this world, health and life to others, must be for me impregnated with invisible poison. The denunciatory handwriting had been traced along the wall of my destiny;[5] the kingdom of my affections had been taken from me and transferred to a rival. Not, indeed, that I had been weighed in the balance and found wanting. No! Fonder, truer, madder love than mine had never streamed in lightning through the veins of man. I had loved with all the intense fervour attributed only to the heroes of romance, and here was my requital! But so runneth our history in this world of many woes. Perhaps, if my passion had been less fierce and untameable, its course would have shown smooth as the waves do in summer. Such, and so extraordinary is the untoward nature of human fate!

Would not any other in my circumstances have stabbed the faithless fair to her heart, or despatched a bullet through the brain of his perfidious rival? I alone saw how futile such a proceeding must be. Uppermost in my mind floated a sense of loathing inexpressible, but not the wealth of the earth could have tempted me to damage a hair in the head of either Lionel or Eleanor. I wrapped up my heart in the folds of bitterest scorn: this was all, and enough. No thought, no shadow of a thought of vengeance hovered within the sphere of my meditations for the future. I strongly abhorred and deeply despised, and the very intensity of my contempt and abhorrence rendered me impervious to the admission of any sentiment of a more selfish order: in short I was much too proud to be revengeful. Strange idiosyncrasy of mine! Yet not wholly unparalleled, as I have had occasion to witness oftener than once in the course of my experience.

But the ice of pride and scorn will not for ever continue to chain up the warm fountain of love. Again the stream of my tenderness rolled back into its unforgotten channels. Why should it have been thus? I now felt how tyrannous and terrible is the despotism of a hopeless passion. The combination of love with despair probably constitutes the perfect measure of human wretchedness. There are those who may censure my conduct on this occasion as feeble and imbecile. They know not that it was by tedious degrees that I surrendered up my spirit in thrall to the torturing genii who incessantly beset me. Long I battled against my doom, and sullenly I yielded only when an access of temporary delirium ushered in a fever which placed me on the threshold of the grave.

My convalescence was tardy and equivocal; and even when the physicians had pronounced me to be tolerably well re-established, my appearance contradicted their assertion. The steadiest investigation could not enable me to discover that a single particle of flesh existed in my physical system; and, as I dragged myself drearily from room to room in the voiceless cheerlessness of my own house, my dry bones perpetually emitted a creaking and rattling sound, peculiarly painful to the ear of a compassionate listener. My aspect[6] was whitewashy and charnellike. One day, instigated by a faint feeling of curiosity, I measured the longitude of it, and my heart drooped and died within me when I found it to be just thirteen inches. I had also suffered my beard to sprout unchecked for six successive months, so that it now descended to the final buttonhole of my waistcoat. In truth, I was a rueful spectacle. No man, with the slightest allowance of sensibility, could have looked at me many moments without bursting into a flood of tears.

Weeks and months wheeled onwards, but generated no alteration in me, unless for the worse. I had drunk deeply of the waters of bitterness, and my every sense was still saturated with the flavour of the accursed wave. There was a down-dragging weight upon my faculties—I felt myself gradually growing into the clay I stood on, and almost sighed for the advent of the night that should see my head pillowed on the green and quiet mould below me. What was the earth to me? Properly no more than a sepulchral dell, whose very freshest flowers were the rank though flaunting offspring of rottenness and corruption. I tried to look in the miraculous face of the sun; but his glory was shrouded by a pall of sackcloth. The burial of my hopes appeared to have been followed by an eclipse of all that was bright in the universe.

On the other hand I cherished a morbid sympathy with whatever was terrific or funereal in the operations of nature. According to the testimony of the geologists, who have received a revelation on the subject, Ireland will never sustain the visitation of an earthquake: it would, therefore, have been chimerical in me to feed my fancy by the anticipation of such an event. But often, when the whirlwind and tempest awoke, I stood out under the starless firmamental cope, and longed personally to track the career of the lightning, or envelope myself darkly in the curtains of the thunder cloud. The pitless booming of the sea against the naked rocks in winter, possessed a peculiar charm for my ulcerated imagination. To gratify my predilection in this respect, I at length hired a cottage in the vicinity of Monkstown,[7] and during the greater number of the winter nights I spent there, my occupation was to wander from crag to crag, hearkening at whiles to the shriek of the sea fowl or the toiling of the billows, and breathing out my soul on the rack of despairing poetry.

Not until the spring of 1832 did I revisit Dublin. My face, lanker and ghastlier than ever, was, however, completely hidden under a cloak of dark bristly hair, and my beard, which had now grown as far as my knees, completed the metamorphosis. Not a single human soul recognized me! A month afterwards I met Lionel and Eleanor, arm in arm, crossing Carlisle Bridge.[8] They stared at me, but betrayed no symptom of recognition, and I felt, for the moment, proud and thankful that they knew me no more. The sum of my aspirations was, to be blotted away from the memory of all, but most from that of those who had associated with me in the beautiful meteor period of my now extinguished youth.

Meanwhile the gloom and horror of my condition augmented hour by hour. Having long lost all appetite, I ate but on one day in the week. My resource was to smoke perpetually on the other six. I pursued this system for some time, but finding my withered up frame undergoing a still further reduction in consequence of the exhaustion of my salivary glands, I adopted the expedient of supplying the deficiency by drinking two gallons of water daily. Many persons may regard my habits as evidences of a deranged intellect; I shall not controvert their conclusions. Questionlessly my dreams were peopled with the most horrible, and hideous, and misbegotten *spectra* that ever rioted in the desolated chambers of a madman's brain. Frequently have I started from my bed in the hollow of the night to grapple with the phantasmagoria that flitted before me, clothed in unnameable terrors—and merely stumbled over, perhaps, some small utensil in the neighbourhood of the bed. Sleep-walking was also an occasional practise with me, and it was a favourite recreation of mine during my unconscious paroxysms, to jump from the roof of my house into the centre of the street below.

The house I dwelt in was in a remote and isolated quarter of the city. Solitary, silent, and prison-like, it was nevertheless a dwelling I would not have forsaken for the most brilliant pleasure dome under the Italian heaven. To the rere of the house extended a long and narrow court yard, partly overgrown with grass and melancholy-looking wild flowers, but flagged at the extremity, and bounded by a colossal wall. Down the entire length of this wall, which was connected with a ruined old building, descended a metal rain spout; and I derived a diseased gratification in listening in wet weather, to the cold, bleak, heavy plash, plash, plash of the rain, as it fell from this spout on the flag beneath. I have sat nine hours consecutively at my back parlour window, with a cigar between my lips and a pitcher of pump water at my side, to hearken to this dismally monotonous echo. To such a state may that intellect of man, which familiarly travels beyond the stars, and undertakes to fathom the infinite, be reduced by the blight of one, only, lonely, but glorious hope!

Few and rare were the visitors who speckled my solitude. I had voluntarily broken the magnetic bonds which unite man with man in socialised being. Whenever I happened to be addressed, either at home or abroad, I generally answered by the briefest monosyllables in our language; sometimes, indeed, merely by a groan, and occasionally by a peculiar howl, half human, half canine, such as may be supposed to proceed from the throat of an individual under the spell of lycanthropy.[9] How all this was taken troubled me little. This human world had died to me; the lights and shadows of life's picture had long since been blended into one chaos of dense and indistinguishable blackness; the pilgrimage of my blank years pointed across a desart where flower or green thing was forbidden to live; and it mattered not how soon some shifting column of the sands descended and swept me into its bosom. Thereafter darkness would swathe my memory for ever; not one poor sigh would be expended for me; no hands would care to gather mine unremembered ashes into the sanctuary of an urn. Why then should I affect an emotion that I could not feel? Or what cared I if those who thus attempted to break down with their feeble fingers the adamantine barrier that severed me from a communion with mankind, perceiving the futility of their enterprise, retired from my presence in disgust and despair?

Was it at all within the circle of human probabilities that this dreary state of things should be destined to pass away one day abruptly and totally, and be succeeded by a millennium of hilarity and glee indescribable? I must hurry to the crisis, for the readers of the SATIRIST will doubtlessly be anxious to learn the details of this marvellous transformation.

On Thursday evening, August the 15th, 1833, as I was seated in my back parlour, reading Burton's Anatomie of Melancholie[10] before a few dying embers, I was startled by the sudden entry of an old acquaintance who advanced, and, shaking me by the hand, hastily apologised for his refusal to take a denial from my servant, and added that he had news for me of the most cheering character.

There was something in his accents that thrilled through me unaccountably. Possibly the fire that originally burns on the altar of an ardent heart can never all perish. Man, as Godwin observes, is more of a human being than of a stick or stone.[11] Even the enchanted prince in the Arabian tale, metamorphosed as he was, was marble only from the waist downwards.[12] I looked up in the face of my acquaintance, I gathered courage for a phrase or two. What mean you? I asked: Do you not know that unseen hands have dug my grave, and that I am even now tottering into it?

You are the devil of a long while tottering into it, he answered, but my business is to establish you stoutly on your pins again. Look here! he continued, taking what appeared to me to be a newspaper from his pocket. Look at this! and he held it at arm's length before me. I gazed, as if fascinated, and saw at the head the words "THE DUBLIN SATIRIST."

Some mysterious power appeared to be at work within me. I already began to experience the beneficial efficacy of my friend's intrusion. A wild emotion, hitherto undeveloped, caused the blood to dance through my arteries, as I exclaimed "That paper—that paper, then, is"——

"The panacea for all descriptions of blue devils[13] and fifteen-inch visages," answered my visitor. "Come, my anchorite," he added briskly, "let me hear you read a paragraph or two."

He placed the paper in my hand.

I began, but had not accomplished three lines before my risible faculties were summoned into immediate requisition. I chuckled with ineffable delight.

"I guessed how it would be, my trump," said my companion. "Go on. Haw! haw! haw!"

I proceeded, but tears of laughter gushed from my eyelids, and my attenuated frame was shaken by a convulsive ecstasy. I flung myself upon a sofa and bellowed like a bull, until the house reverberated again. The servant, astonished at the hubbub, made his appearance before us with uplifted hands and gapping goggles, but was forthwith pushed into the hall and tumbled down the kitchen stairs by my friend, who then returned into the parlour to laugh over the circumstance.

It was midnight when we separated, after an evening of the most uproarious merriment that imagination can picture. His last words, however, were solemnly enunciated: "Remember the instrument of your cure—remember THE SATIRIST, and be grateful!"

Next day I sent to Thompson's in Henry-street[14] for a case of his best mowers. I was a renovated being. Surely, never within the remembrance of man has such another apotheosis occurred. I am now the victim of one everlasting, never-dying fit of laughter. Morn, noon, night—times and seasons,—places and persons, are all one to me.—I laugh, as Shelley says the caverns of the dædal earth laugh, "with a vast and inextinguishable laughter,"[15] at all periods and before all people. As Jean Baptiste Anacharsis Clootz[16] was orator of the human race, so I am laugher of civilised society. I occupy the laughable office of grinner-general to the public at large. Democritus[17] laughed all the day long, but while he slept his countenance was characterised by a stupid seriousness of expression, whereas awake or dreaming I am perpetually practising the guffaw. Lord Chesterfield observes, "There are some persons who have a habit of always laughing when they speak, so that their faces are perpetually on the grin."[18] This is precisely my case. I am grinning night and day like a mountebank through a horse-collar. I now begin, for the first time in my life, thoroughly to understand that the grand business of my existence is grinning. The only disastrous effect of my present mode of life is that it has partially damaged my beauty, for my teeth, from exposure to the atmosphere, have shifted from a pearl white to an ebony tint; and a brace of wrinkles, as deep as the bed of the Nile, have unfortunately established a permanent residence at the sides of my mouth.

I have now communicated to the public an undecorated statement of facts. I say to them, in conclusion, "look on that picture, and on this."[19] Such was I: such am I. They may draw the inference. It cannot be too frequently impressed on the sufferer that for sixpence a week he may purchase an immunity from all his woes. If he want further information let him come to me, and I will wager a hogshead of O'Connell's porter that three weeks shall not elapse before he pens a magnificent ode in praise of the wonder-working powers of THE SATIRIST. He will find me any evening in the six, at Cohen's cloud-compelling[20] Divan in Dame-street,[21] where the most superb cigars in Europe may be had for a beggarly trifle of cash.

A DIALOGUE IN THE SHADES;

BUT NOT A "DIALOGUE OF THE DEAD".

Talkers—MYSELF AND A FRIEND.

"It's good to be merry and wise."—OLD SONG.[1]

I.—   COME, shall we have the other flask?

HE.— Permit me to decline.

I.—   Decline? Do you mean hic, hæc, *hock*?[2]

HE.— No, but merely to observe, that although

> "Tipplers drink many times before their dinner,
> The sober never taste of rum but once."[3]

I should get the name of a toper.

I.—   Pooh!

> ——"What's in a name? The *nose*
> By any other name would smell as sweet."[4]

Do you intend swelling the number of Jackson's dinner-party on Monday?

HE.—No: my opinion is, that a dinner-

> "Party is the madness of many for the gain of a few."[5]

I.—   And mine is, that it is the madness of a few for the gain of many. By the bye, I met Jackson to-day, as he was stepping out of Green's, the fishmonger's. A fellow was staggering across from Castle-market to Coppinger's-row.[6] "Now," said Jackson, "wouldn't it have been wiser for that unfortunate fool to have left his trifle of change with our friend Green here, than to have melted it down in a half-pint?" "Brutus would have thought otherwise," said I: "don't you remember his spirited reply to Cassius, who wanted him to buy fish, instead of whiskey, for a hog[7] which he happened to pick up on the Rock-road?"[8]—

> "*Buy herrings!* I had rather coin my blood
> For *drams*."[9]

HE.— The bibber[10] was too strong in Brutus. We find him haranguing a batch of ragamuffins with the words—

"Friends, *rum'uns*, countryfolks, and lubbers."[11]

O'Hoolaghan, however, a poet of the Firbolgs,[12] accuses him of shying the genuine potteen,[13] and says of him—

"Trom-ól se munloch ó mhaidin go n-oídche."[14]

That is—

"He muddles with hog-wash from daylight till dark."

I.— Many a great man has had his failing. Look, for instance, at Agamemnon, as apostrophized by Achilles—

"Thou swiller of gin, with the heart of a hare, and the front of a dog!
Thou never to battle to sweet Tipperary didst joyously jog."[15]

But, as to Brutus, his habit of muddling exflunctified[16] his appetite. Pomponious Atticus[17] records that a penny roll served him for two days; and that one day, dining with Cæsar, he merely demolished one potato; upon which Cæsar, tendering him a second on the point of his fork, said—

"Eat two, Bruty."[18]

HE.— Not a bad story, but rather low.
I.— Excuse me, it's a *hi*-story. You yawn desperately.
HE.— Yes: I was travelling all night; and yet—pity me!—I must cross[19] two long letters this evening.
I.— One to the lively Lucy, and one to the placid Isabel.

"Oh, mirth and innocence! oh, milk and water!
I love you both, and both shall have my praise."[20]

HE.— (*rather confused.*)—Well, and what may your commentary be?
I.— Why, that you are like Goldsmith's "Village Schoolmaster"—

"'Tis certain you can write, and *sigh for two*."[21]

HE.— Beshrew me, but I guess I shall match that.— (*He sweeps the decanter off the table, which descends with a hideous crash from the centre of gaiety towards the centre of gravity.*)—There! that wreck is

> "Even as a broken bottle, while the glass
>   In every fragment multiplies, and makes
> A thousand images of one that was,
>   The same, and still the more, the more it breaks."[22]

I.— Be it so: I can tell you, however, that although

> "You may break, you may shatter the glass if you will,
> The scent of the liquor will stick to it still."[23]

But, I think you have said you were travelling all night?

HE.— Yes; and the chaise-wheels stuck here and there in some horrible holes on the Ballygruddery road,[24] so that I was cruelly fagged, and almost capsized.

I.— Aye: Pope speaks of those holes on the Ballygruddery road; but his opinion is, that they all form a subterranean junction somewhere. He says that—

> "All are but part of one stupendous *hole*."[25]

HE.— I was about to tell you that, as I went slowly up hill yesterday, I overtook a man leading a bear with one hand, and carrying a basket of eels in the other. It was sweltering hot, and the flies were making rather free with the poor fellow's nose; but as his hands were full, he could only, like Lord Burleigh,[26] occasionally shake his head in indication of his disapproval of their want of breeding. Undoubtedly, thought I then, this man judges it to be better

> ———— "To *bear* those *eels* he has,
> Than *fly* to others that he *nose* not of."[27]

Him followed a gaffer,[28] who, by the aid of a stick, was driving a cow to the nearest market town, and the next line immediately occurred to me:

> "Thus conscience doth make *cowherds* of us all."[29]

I.— And yet I venture to say that he hadn't been used to *con science*.

HE.— There you err: he was trying experiments in *a-cow-sticks* at the time. But, *apropos de rein du tout*,[30] is it true that old Crabtree[31] is "gone to the tomb of all the gabbleheads?"

I.— Fact: and just before his death he pathetically uttered two lines of rhyme, which it would be difficult to find a parallel for within the whole compass of English poetry. Here they are:

> "When men behold old mould rolled cold around my mound of ground, all crowned with grass, alas!
> Mankind, though blind, will find my mind was kind, refined, resigned, but shrined, like gas, in glass."[32]

HE.— Psha! mere jingle and clink. But if you wish to see something really distressing in the elegiac way, here (*takes a document from his pocket-book, and presents it to me*) is half an hour's relaxation of mine to dim your goggles withal.

(*I immediately open the paper, and read, with faltering tone, tearful eyes, and breaking heart, the following Elegiac:—*)

LAMENTATION FOR THE DEATH OF JOE KING, LATE ANGLER AND FISHER.

> Poor old Joe King, the fisherman, has paid
>   That weightiest of debts, called Nature's debt,
> The only debt he paid, I'm much afraid,
>   For all was fish that popped into *his* net.
>
> He, like a critic, was well used to *carp*,
>   Albeit he had not read a single book;
> And if his *lines* were, *in the end*, too sharp,
>   He sometimes won his victims—*with the hook!*
>
> And though he never *spared the rod* (his wishes
>   Being opposed to that indulgent plan),
> 'Tis plain they did not think the *man officious*,
>   Because they never cried, *O! fish us, man!*
>
> They say there's treasure in "the deep, deep sea,"[33]
>   Yet he who *pries* may chance to meet a *blank*;[34]
> However, as to angling Joey, he
>   Got now and then a *check upon the bank*.

Woods, wilds, and forest trees, were things his soul
  Was evidently never made to reach;
The only *ash* he knew of was *ash*-oal;
  He climbed no *beech*, but stood upon the *beach*.

Yet he was used to *pine*, and felt *ash*-amed
  Whene'er without *ash*-oal he came *ash*-ore;
Then *wood* his wife (whom *Ivy*-rafter[35] named,)
  Deal him a *box*, which made him *sick-o'-more!*

And while she thus *fir*-ociously assailed
  Her lord and master, 'twas a horrid sight!
Yew would have thought *Oak*-on-*elm*-ight[36] have failed
  To ex-*tree*-cate him from his rueful plight.

Yet, Joey now and then took heart of grace;
  And when potteen had made his utterance thicker,
He'd swear upon his *soal*[37] he'd leave the *plaice*,
  Unless she went and pawned *her rings* for liquor.

In architecture he was no great shakes;
  But those who tell us he knew nought at all
About the building science, make mistakes,
  Because he sometimes used to *make a hawl!*

'Tis strange!—but *Joe King* was not fond of *joking*,
  Which proves a man may *sell* what *fish* he can,
Without in reason forcing or provoking
  People to brand him as a *selfish* man.

Yet, though his turn of mind was rather sad,
  And though he rarely ventured on a jest,
Still, when he stood beneath a *bridge*, he had
  An arch way then about him, I protest.

And oft, while drawing in his nets, he'd make
  What some philologers would call an odd use
Of words, for he'd exclaim—"Come now, I'll take
  A comfortable view of my *net produce*."

And when Jack Reilly died, with scythe in hand,
  Mowing the mead, Joe, sighing o'er and o'er,

Observed—"I'm sorry, and you understand
   My reason is—poor Jack is now *no mower!*"

But, Joe's no more himself! For, t'other day,
   After a dinner of *hashed* veal and *peas*,
He perished in a storm; so let us say—
   Pease to his *hashes* in the rolling seas!

HE.— Well, what's your opinion?
I.—   It is half a dozen centuries before the "Lament of Tasso"[38]—it beats
      the "Elegy in a Country Churchyard"[39] and Schiller's "Wail of
      Ceres"[40] all to sticks.—Nothing can be more melancholical, except
      the "Death and Burial of Cock Robin."[41] In short, my dear fellow, I
      shall now, as Robert Owen[42] says, "develope to you a secret, which,
      until now, has been hidden from mankind," and, improving on
      Owen, I may add, also from womankind.
HE.— I comprehend: you have squared the circle.
I.—   I intend to do so, as soon as I shall have a little leisure. But, mark
      me now! this elegy is the guarantee of Ireland's future glory.
HE.— I don't instantaneously flare up.
I.—   You are a little too smoky! Don't you see that on Saturday, the 21st
      of June, 1834, the elegy is enshrined in the museum of the SATIRIST;
      that seventy thousand beautiful eyes become so many flowing
      fountains of tears; that cambric rises exorbitantly; that linen drapers
      look up delightedly; and that by a sympathetic action commerce in
      general revives, sun-bright faces are everywhere visible, auction-
      rooms are shut up, the Mendicity Asylum[43] is pitched into the Liffey,

              "To sink or swim, as heaven pleases,"[44]

      and Ireland, to make use of a quotation adopted only on *one*
      occasion by Mr. O'Connell, and therefore interesting, from its
      novelty, stands forth again—

                    "Great, glorious, and free,
          First flower of the earth, and first gem of the sea!"[45]

HE.— On voit bien, mon ami que vous devenez ce qu'on appelle ici
      hoxmontary. Allons. (*Rises.*)
I.—   (*Also rising*)—Il vous sied bien, vraiment, de m'accuser d'etre
      hoxmontaire, vous qui êtes maintenant aveugle comme un hibou. Si
      j'avais envie de le faire, je pourrais vous *exflunctifier teetotacieusement*.
      Mais allons.[46]   (*Eximus.*)

LOVE, MYSTERY, AND MURDER.
A TALE.
(Foundered on Facts.)

CURTIS—Let's ha' thy tale, good Grumio.
GRUMIO.—Lend thine ear.
CUR.—Here.
GRU.—There!—(*gives him a box on the ear.*)
CUR.—This is to feel a tale, not hear a tale.
GRU.—And, therefore, 'tis called a sensible tale. This cuff was given thee to knock at thine ear and bespeak thy listening. Now I begin.[1]

Taming of the Shrew. Act IV. Sc.I.

CHAP. I.
An Ugly Portrait.

IT IS a bad thing, on the whole, to be a tyrant and a throat-cutter, at least in these times; and why? Because every body reads the DUBLIN SATIRIST. Don't you see the logic of this? Then go to: you have been groping all your lifetime, and to the day of your demise you will be a muzzy-headed man. I particularly, nay, pathetically request that you will at once, and for ever, abandon your foolish resolution to read this story; so, off with your goggles, for I regret to state that they will never afford you the slightest aid in seeing your way through a mile-stone.

Such a man, however,—that is a tyrant and throat-cutter—was the Conde Ugolino di Bulbruzzi.[2] His castle stood on the top of an inaccessible rock;[3] and it was surrounded by four towers, called the North Tower, South Tower, East Tower, and West Tower. Of these the East Tower was the least tower, but the West Tower was the best tower. It was calculated, according to Cocker,[4] that the Conde was worth six hundred thousand scudi annually; but it was a heart-rending fact, that this enormous income sprang from assassination and pillage—these being the modes by which Italian noblemen generally make out a subsistence, as I clearly find in Mrs. Radcliffe's romances.[5] This Conde that I am writing about was an abominable assassin. He had murdered several hundreds of persons,—suppose we say coolly, in round numbers, 700; and the carcases of these unfortunate people were left to rot in dungeons, an hundred yards below the level of the sea, while their unappeased spirits stalked about the tapestried chambers and winding galleries of the castle in swarms.

Mrs. Radcliffe, however, has told me that all these people were murdered—not by the Conde in person, but by his proxy—a "monk." The name of the monk was Hugo Gundalpho.[6] He wore a cowl over his face, and generally carried a dagger in one hand and a lamp in the other. He never either ate or drank; so that in fact it was a sort of miracle how he subsisted. All the recreation he allowed himself was the occasional use of a tobacco-pipe, the smoke of which drove away the ghosts. Not that he was a man to stagger before a ghost; quite the contrary, for he always pushed them out of his way. The truth is, he had studied metaphysics very deeply, and was therefore profoundly ignorant of the nature both of men and ghosts.

CHAP. II.

A Pretty Picture. A Family Groupe.

The Conde had killed his wife with a poker, but a beautiful daughter still remained to him. She was a paragon of loveliness, and shone in that lugubrious old castello like a sweet floweret in the wilderness, an ivory pillar in the desert, a pearl in the abyss of ocean, or a shilling in a bagfull of halfpence. Many of the neighbouring Condes, Marcheses, Barones, &c., had been suitors for the happiness and honour of her hand; but her sire, by his bearish repulsiveness of manner, by tumbling some of them down the stairs and stabbing others when they became over troublesome, had freed his dwelling of those intruders; so that, for many months before the period our story opens at, the only inmates of the castle and towers were the following, viz:—the Conde himself, his daughter Amelrosa, the Monk with the cup[7] and dagger, and the domestics; for I reckon the ghosts as nobodies.

CHAP. III.

How to bother a buffalo, when you have not time to load your gun.—Falling in love by accident.

It was a bright, bloomy, bland, blessed, and beautiful summer's day. The earth and the skies, having no very serious business on hands, were laughing in one another's face. Upon this day, Amelrosa was peripatetically recreating herself by a romantic walk on the borders of a coal-black forest near the castle. She had been walking about half an hour, when the day grew astonishingly hot, and the sun began to blaze in an appalling manner. Amelrosa, who had no parasol, and was quite unattended, calculating, after some time, that the heat was too enormously awful to be endured, was preparing to return, when, at that moment, from an adjoining thicket there came rushing, with lips of foam and eyes of flame, an infuriated buffalo, and with great expedition, considering his bulk, advancing towards the spot where Amelrosa stood. Overcome by terror, the young lady was about to faint, and would have fallen a prey to the rage of the quadruped, had not a young man, in a hunting dress, stepped up, (of course precisely at the critical moment,) and levelled the buffalo to the earth by a blow from the butt-end of his fowling-piece. The buffalo magnanimously expired without a groan. Then the youth, hastening to the support of Amelrosa, whom he discovered nearly exhausted with terror, exhorted her to be of good courage.

"Fairest lady," said he, "abandon apprehension. The career of the monster was terrible, but brief. One blow from the butt-end of my fowling-piece sufficed.— The buffalo is no more."

"Generous youth!" said Amelrosa, "I owe thee my life." She then blushed, as she added, taking out her purse, "I have not much to offer thee in return, cash being rather scarce in this quarter; but this purse contains fifteen pence; and here," continued she, extricating a rose from her tresses, "here is something that I give thee to wear for my sake."

"Next to my heart!" said the youth, pathetically; and, having first put the purse into his pocket, he stuck the rose in a button-hole of his hunting-frock.

"Farewell, generous youth!" said she.

"Hadst thou not better accept the assistance of my proffered arm, noble lady?" asked the youth. "I will accompany thee to thy castle portals. These wilds are perilous; perhaps another buff——"

"It may not be," interrupted Amelrosa. "Knowest thou the name and quality of her whom thou hast rescued from death?"

"Nay," replied the young man, "I know not."

"The Conde di Bulbruzzi is my father."

"Ha!" cried the youth, striking his forehead violently against an oak tree.

"And know, brave young man, that I am—his daughter."

"Marvellous!" exclaimed the youth. "Thy father, lady, is my implacable enemy. Nevertheless, I will accompany thee to the gate."

"Never, gallant youth!" said the lady. "Adieu, we may meet again."

"Hear me!" said the stranger.—"Wouldst thou, then—wouldst thou, perhaps—wouldst thou—I say, wouldst thou——"

"Proceed."

"Meet me on the battlements of the North Tower, at midnight, when the owl is hooting? I know that all ordinary access is excluded, but love is bold; I will swim across the flood, and mount the rock."

"Yes, thou lovest me!" said Amelrosa, "thine eyes betray the truth. Doubtlessly thou art of high descent?"

"My father was," answered the youth; "for he lost his life by falling from the top of his castle into the ditch below."

"It is melancholy that thy father should have died in a ditch," said Amelrosa, mournfully. "But adieu, noble stranger,—at midnight we meet once more."

"At midnight, then," said the youth.

He kissed her glove, and they separated.

CHAP. IV.
A sheep's head—and pluck,[8] (i.e. *resolution.*)

About the same hour, on the same day, the Monk was seen gloomily perambulating the kitchen of the castle, with something under his cloak, which was evidently too big to be either a lamp or a dagger. At last he stopped, and addressed the chief cook. "What does the Conde dine on to-day?" he asked.

"On potatoes and fish," said the cook.

"Hearken," said the Monk; and approaching the cook, he drew from the folds of his cloak a sizeable sheep's head. "The Conde is dyspeptic; fish disagrees with him; boil this sheep's head, therefore, and let it be served up to him this day. Do this, or beware of my stiletto."

"Your commands shall be obeyed, Padre," answered the cook. The Monk then left the kitchen, and the cook stepped out into a back yard, with the sheep's head in his hands, and tossed it into the sewer, where it was immediately captured by a troop of hungry rats.

CHAP. V.
Murder will out.

Midnight was waning into morning. The Conde traversed, with irregular strides, the eastern corridor of the South Tower. As he heavily brooded over his own dark imaginings, like a murky tempest over a troubled ocean, a step approached. Presently the Monk appeared; his cowl was drawn over his face; he bore a lamp in one hand, and in the other a stiletto.

"Whither repairest thou?" asked the Conde.

"To the northern corridor of this tower," the Monk answered, in a sepulchral tone. "But, Conde, I have tidings of ominous import for thine ear."

"Say on."

The Monk paused. "Hast thou supped?" he demanded.

"I have taken a bowl of gruel," said the Conde.—"Wherefore askest thou?"

"It mattereth not," said the Monk, abstractedly.—"Yet once again,

Conde; of what materials was thy dinner banquet to-day constituted?"

"The materials were herrings and potatoes. Thou knowest that I am no Apicius.[9] But wherefore askest thou?"

"There was a sheep's head," observed the Monk, gloomily.

"Ha! villain! traitor! assassin!" cried the Conde. "I see the drift of thy cross-questioning. I know well that that sheep's head was impregnated with an accursed poison. Hence! lest I be tempted to trample thy withered carcase into impalpable powder!"

"I must first get my pipe," said the Monk, coolly; and taking up the pipe, which had been lying on a table, he glided out of the passage like a spectre.

CHAP. VI.
Ten appointments and one disappointment.

It may be easily supposed, that the meeting of the lovers was characterised by the deepest tenderness, the finest sensibility, the most enrapturing ecstacy, and the most eternal protestations. An hour and a half glided away, at the end of which time Amelrosa began to grow sleepy, and an appointment was made for the following night. As I mean to make this an egregiously short history, I shall merely mention, that the lovers met on the next night, and the next, and the next, and the next, and the next. They also met on the next night, and on the next, and on the next after that, and likewise on the next. Thus, they met on ten successive nights. But, after the tenth night, the Lord Lieutenant of the Castle[10] issued a proclamation, and they met no more! As the French say, I go to explain the mystery.

CHAP. VII.
People must occasionally descend in this world.

The Monk had gone out on the battlements of the tower one night, to indulge himself in a solitary walk in the fresh air; for he had been considerably annoyed by meeting, on that evening, with a greater number of ghosts than he really thought the castle could hold.—He had been walking for about ten minutes, when, hearing two people conversing at some distance, he drew near, and, hiding himself behind a projection of the wall, overheard a great deal of poetry, which only wanted the ornament of rhyme to make it superior to that of Ariosto.[11] On the next day the Monk recited a few passages of this poetry to the Conde, by way of getting his opinion on them; and the Conde swore that he would force his daughter to confine herself within the limits of plain prose for the future. Being a determined man, and a hardened villain to boot, he put his threat into execution; and, in half an hour afterwards, the wretched Amelrosa found herself incarcerated in a horrible dungeon, a hundred and twenty feet below the level of the sea. This dungeon had been hewed out of the solid rock by an experienced architect, and was principally inhabited by toads and lizards, who subsisted upon the vapours that rose up from the ground, the slime of the walls, and such other articles of food as they could collect.

Here this persecuted maiden spent fifteen days and nights, being supplied, during that period, with bread and water for her diet, by command of her inexorable father. On the sixteenth day, while groping about the dungeon, she felt a chasm in the wall. Animated by hope, she exerted all her strength, diminished, as it had been, by the bread and water regimen, and pulled out a stone, and, after that, a variety of other stones. She was now able to insinuate her slender person through this Hole in the Wall,[12] and walked cautiously onwards, until she came to a flight of stone steps, which led her, after an ascent of an hour and a quarter, into an immense natural vault, or cavern. To her great delight, she now heard the booming sound of the sea; and in a few minutes more she once again banquetted her eyes on the great picture of ocean and sky. Oh, Liberty!— but I shall postpone my grand apostrophe to thee until that black day, long anticipated and at last to lower, when, with a pair of bellows in my hands, I shall discover myself seated before the wreck of a fire, in a neat but narrow apartment of the Stone Jug.[13]

CHAP. VIII.
An aquatic excursion.—A truly original flare-up, with comments thereon, by a pair of illustrious obscures.

Amelrosa waited in the cavern until the approach of nightfall, and then came out. Fortunately there was upon the strand a boat, of inconsiderable dimensions, constructed to hold one person, being three feet long by two feet broad; and she found no difficulty in launching this into the waves. The moment afterwards she stepped in herself with the grace of a Naiad; and a fresh breeze springing up from the land, the boat drifted out rapidly. She had neither oar nor sail to accelerate its progress; but the propelling force of the wind was quite sufficient to urge it onward. It drifted all that night, all the next day, and all the next. There was in the boat a small quantity of mouldy biscuit and a decanter of pump water, which had been left there by the navigator who had been last in it; and these were of material service to her during the two days. But on the third day, when she had no more biscuit to eat, and no more pump-water to drink, it was no wonder that she found herself growing faint and peckish. On the fourth day a flying fish tumbled into the boat, which, of course, the circumstances of her condition compelled her to masticate cold and raw. On the fifth day she chewed her slipper, and found it remarkably tough. On the sixth day she luckily caught an eel by the tail, which had been making a voyage of discovery from an adjoining river, and had thus met the fate of all enterprizing travellers. On the seventh day she captured a booby, and ate it with the feathers on, washing them down with salt-water. On the eighth day a tempest arose, and capsized her little boat; so that she saw herself necessitated to perform the remainder of her voyage sitting on the keel. On the ninth day, however, the storm increased to such a pitch, that the hapless girl, quite unaccustomed to the sea, was scarcely able to maintain her position, and grew sea-sick beyond description. At length, on the tenth day, and when the boat was nearing land, the combined influences of thirst, hunger, weakness, despair, and the violence of the storm, bereft her of all consciousness, and she would have been drowned, if just then a billow, the magnitude of a church, had not at once swamped the boat, and swept the unfortunate girl at least half a furlong over the waters and through the breakers, until at length it dashed her on the beach.

A great concourse of spectators had assembled on the shore, in ecstacies at her picturesque method of navigation. But now the storm arose to a tremendous degree of fury. Thunder pealed without intermission. The sea was one mass of foam. At last a blinding flash of lightning streamed from the heavens, and in a moment after, the waves, far as the eye could reach, were in one blaze! A general cry was now heard—"The sea is on fire!—the sea is on fire!" There was a chemist present, who had taken lodgings near the sea, for the purpose of prosecuting a series of experiments, the object of which was to enable him to extract milk from oyster-shells: there was also a geologist standing by, who had been poking the whole day in a little mud-hole, two inches deep, with a walking-stick, with a view to discover how many thousands of years older than the creation that part of the globe was. The chemist observed, that the phenomenon before them was indubitable evidence of the inflammable character of muriatic phlogiston,[14] and that he had long suspected the combustibility of the sea. The geologist, hearing this, replied that the chemist was mistaken, and that the conflagration was simply the result of a volcanic eruption in the bowels of the ocean, as he could prove by a number of documents in his pocket, marked A. B. C. D., &c. &c. The chemist shook his head; upon which the geologist laughed; upon which the chemist frowned; upon which the geologist sneered. The chemist then said, that it must be self-evident that the geologist's theory was erroneous; for that he (the geologist) was a beggarly ragamuffin, who lived on a two-pair floor,[15] and wore the shabbiest castor[16] in ten thousand. The reply of the geologist to this was, that on the contrary, it was manifest that the chemist was as ignorant of the nature of the phenomenon as a hog is of heraldry, because he (the geologist) was able to kick him (the chemist) through the streets like a foot-ball, and mash his bones instanter. The entire of the discussion was reported on the spot by an eminent note-taker; and printed copies were afterwards despatched to the various literary and sciencestuffical institutions of the island.

But, to return to Amelrosa.

CHAP. IX.

An inconstant youth.—The misfortune of being over-sensitive.

The island upon which Amelrosa had been cast was called Weathercock Island. It was a very fine island, and thickly peopled with men and women. The women spent their time in endeavouring to outwit the men, and the men in endeavouring to outwit one another.

When Amelrosa recovered her senses she found herself in bed. A fisherman had brought her into his hut, and his wife had extended every species of succour to the unknown forlorn. In another week she was able to walk up and down, and in a week afterwards was preparing, after a speech expressive of her lifelong gratitude to her preserver, to depart; but the fisherman stopped her. "You had better abandon your intention," said he, "at least for a few hours longer, when the procession shall have passed by. Otherwise you may meet it, and be trampled to death by the crowd."

"Procession! What procession?" asked Amelrosa.

"What! have you not heard the news? Do you not know that the Prince of Weathercock Island is to be married to the Princess of Pearlpowder to-morrow?"

"I have heard nothing of it," said Amelrosa; "who is this Prince? Pray describe him to me."

The fisherman described him to the best of his capacity and recollection. As Amelrosa listened, her heart grew sick. O, Perfidy! thought she, thy name is man.[17] From the description, it was evident that the Prince and her unknown lover were one and the same individual. She related her disastrous tale to the fisherman. "And this," she concluded, weepingly, "this is the ingrate for whom I sacrificed my virgin heart—this is the wretch for whose sake I suffered myself to be flung into a dungeon—for whom I embarked in a boat three feet by two, chewed my slipper, and caught a live eel by the tail, besides capturing a booby—though that, indeed, a girl can do at any time. O woe! woe!" And as she thus spoke she fainted away.

There was not a smelling-bottle in the entire hut.

CHAP. X.
Oh, such a sight!

The procession was a grand one, and went off tolerably well, not more than about seventy persons being trodden under foot by the horses, and not more than a hundred and twenty killed in party rows. The music was enchanting, only a little too noisy; and there was a miscellaneous variety of red, blue, and yellow rags, streaming from the ends of long poles, and called banners: these had a very fine effect. Followed in the wake of the procession about fifteen thousand people; a small proportion of these was composed of idlers, loiterers, and pocket-pickers; there were also a few philosophers, who came to study human nature and stare at the show. The procession moved on in regular order until it came opposite the King's palace, when it stopped.

CHAP. XI.
An heroic, or heroinic purpose.—Love's labour lost.

Nothing that the fisherman and his wife could urge was sufficient to dissuade Amelrosa from setting out for the city and seeking an interview with the Prince. She would positively go; and accordingly the good couple gave their blessing and a small sum of money, and then bade her an affecting farewell; and the little housedog, who could scarcely be restrained from following her, howled after her in a melancholy manner as she crossed the threshold.

The metropolis was not more than a mile from the fisherman's cottage, and Amelrosa soon reached the King's palace, which was in the suburbs. The crowd had dispersed, and only a few guards, for dignity's sake, were promenading before the gates. Amelrosa inquired whether she could see the Prince, and was ushered into a spacious hall, where, in a few moments, a gorgeously-apparelled young man came to demand her name and business. "Tell the Prince," she replied, "that Amelrosa di Bulbruzzi demands an audience—public or private, she cares not which;" and her eyes, as she spoke, flashed lightning. "She is certainly a woman," said the young man, as he ascended the stairs to convey the message. He speedily returned, and told Amelrosa that the Prince was then occupied in affairs of state, and in an important consultation with the Princess of Pearlpowder as to the size of her bracelets; but that he would give her a public audience in the evening, and that she was welcome to the festival. Amelrosa, upon hearing this, left the hall and the palace with a proud look and a lofty bearing, and as soon as she had reached a solitary part of the street, burst into a flood of tears.

CHAP. XII.
The pranks of a Prince.—A mad world, my masters![18]

She continued wandering about the suburbs and weeping for the remainder of the day. At night the city was brilliantly illuminated in honor of the Prince's approaching marriage. Amelrosa again repaired to the palace; she was arrayed in a dress of simple white, and wore a pair of green slippers, fancifully turned up at the toes: altogether she looked dazzlingly lovely. A buzz of admiration was heard among the courtiers as she passed from room to room, her name every where preceding her, and when the great doors of the saloon were flung open for her admission, her appearance created an universal sensation, and about three hundred eye-glasses were instantly levelled at her. The Prince, who was seated on a throne fourteen feet high, and sipping punch, rose up for a moment, bowed coldly, and again sat down; upon which the entire assembly immediately took the hint, and Amelrosa was suffered to remain standing near the door.

An unpleasant pause ensued. At last the Prince having drained his beaker, again arose and descended from his throne by means of a stepladder. "Ladies and gentlemen," said he, addressing the guests, "I feel awkwardly situated. I am naturally of a bashful disposition. I do not know how to disclose what, nevertheless, I feel compelled to say. I have taken two beakers of punch, and the result is—that I am willing to take a third. Unite, therefore, your stentorian lungs with mine, and shout aloud, "Hurrah! for the powers of punch!—hurrah! for the powers of punch!"

And the guests arose, and all simultaneously shouted, "Hurrah! for the powers of punch!"

Amelrosa advanced and endeavoured to gain a hearing, but in vain. The Prince protested that upon his honor he could not give any one an audience until he had concealed his eighth beaker. In the meantime he drew from beneath a sofa a three-legged stool and tossed it into a corner, that the unhappy damsel might, if she pleased, accommodate herself with a seat. The Prince tossed off six beakers with miraculous grace and rapidity, worthy of the son of a king. Then, taking from his breast a small horn of silver, he blew a thrilling blast, and a dead silence ensued.

"Let each guest take his plate in his hand," said the Prince. The order was obeyed; and the Prince bounded lightly on the table, and commenced dancing a hornpipe, during the progress of which he was loudly applauded. When the hornpipe was finished he blew another blast. Silence followed as before.

"It has been ascertained," said the Prince, "that the most serious study to which the energies of man can be dedicated, is—balancing a turkeycock's feather." One of the gentlemen in waiting then presented a turkey-cock's feather to the Prince upon a golden salver; and the Prince, for at least fifteen minutes, continued balancing the feather upon his nose in such a superior manner as to elicit universal approbation.

A third time the horn was blown. "Now," said the Prince, "every man is at liberty to cut his own throat." The guests heard this in silence, and seemed to be perfectly satisfied with the fact of the liberty, without resorting to any practical method of testing the truth of the assertion. "Then," cried the Prince, "let every man cut his neighbour's throat: let those who wear plain cravats cut the throats of those who wear fancy cravats."

This was agreed to be a rational proposition. Every man laid down his plate and took up his knife. The ladies in the meantime fanned themselves, anticipating hot work. In that critical moment, however, the great door of the saloon opened, and the Princess of Pearlpowder entered, attended by her maids in waiting.—Of course all hostilities were immediately abandoned. The Princess bowed graciously to the assembly, who, after returning the salute, leaned back in their chairs and began to pick their teeth; and the Prince conducted his Princess up the steps of the stepladder, and established her on the throne.

CHAP. XIII.
An old friend, who will soon have a new face.

In the meantime the neglected Amelrosa, who had too much of the spirit of a woman to sit upon a three-legged stool when a throne was prepared for her rival, remained standing alone and unnoticed in a distant part of the room. She felt as if her heart were breaking, and when the Princess of Pearlpowder came in, tears involuntarily flowed from her starry eyes. The better to elude all observation she retired behind a pillar; but what was her horror on discovering already planted there a tall figure in a cloak and cowl with a stiletto in his hand! The shriek she uttered as she bounded forward was terrific, and drew the eyes of all upon her.

"The Monk! the Monk!" she exclaimed; "he is here—he is here!—oh save—save—for mercy's sake—" Her emotion deprived her of further utterance.

"Who talks of Monks?" asked a small philosopher who was present. "We have no Monks in this country. This is the land of philosophy, of universal benevolence and humanity. We have pillaged all the monasteries and expelled all the Monks."

CHAP. THE LAST.

Is he a beef-eater now?—Oh murder! murder! murder! murder!—A wise man takes everything quietly.

Now came the *denouement, eclaircissement, finale, Aufklarung*, winding up, or whatever else it may be termed. The supposed Monk rushed from his hiding-place, and flinging off his cloak and cowl, stood revealed as a symmetrical young man of about five-and-twenty, habited in a very handsome garb. "Lady," said he to Amelrosa, "I am thy friend—fear not. But thou, wretch!" turning towards the Prince,—"Tremble! thou hast basely betrayed this, thy first love!"

"I deny the charge," said the Prince coolly. "She was not my first, nor my twenty-first. She was my twenty-second. The Princess of Pearlpowder was my twenty-third."

"What!" cried the Princess of Pearlpowder, "am I affronted to my face? Never will I survive the indignity!" With these words, frightful to state, she drew a pair of scissors from her pocket, and stabbed herself to the heart.

Weeping, wailing, and uproar followed. The *ci-devant* Monk challenged the Prince to single combat on the spot. The Prince took up the three-legged stool and hurled it at his adversary, two of whose front teeth were smashed by the blow, and who became so deeply exasperated with the treachery of the Prince, that, flinging aside his stiletto, he snatched a large carving knife from the table, and severed his head from his body at one stroke. The bloody head rolled about the dinner-table, and at length settled itself into a soup dish.

This was a melancholy state of things, but the worst was not yet over. "Now, lady," said the *ci-devant* Monk, "hear me! I have wrought thee heretofore much wrong, for which I avow my penitence. Suffer me now, O fairest, to ask thee one question. Is thy heart disengaged? And wilt thou bestow it on the most devoted of thy slaves?" As he spoke he bent one knee to the floor, and took her lilywhite hand in his own.

"Never!" answered Amelrosa, with dignified solemnity. "Though I was not the first love of the Prince of the Weathercock Island, he was mine; and it is in vain for me to think of another. Woman loves but one, and but once!"

"Then," said the other, "this be thy fate!" and he buried the knife in her bosom up to the maker's name—"and this be mine own fate!"—and he plunged the same knife up to the extremity of the handle in his own heart.

There were four bloody corpses now lying about the apartment; and as there was every appearance that the tragedy had terminated, the assembled guests, male and female, rose to take their departure. A great many jokes were enunciated on the occasion as the party descended the different staircases; for the inhabitants of Weathercock Island are a mercurial people.

In about an hour afterwards, the old King, the Prince's grandfather, who had been out shooting snipe, returned, and was acquainted with what had occurred in his absence. "Come," said he, to a privy councillor, "come, we will see with our own eyes." An attendant led the way and opened the doors of the saloon. The ghastly and bloody spectacle burst upon him in all its horrors; for no one had dared to remove the bodies until the King's pleasure should be known. The King gazed on the scene in silence for about a minute; and then shaking his head—not with a right and left, but with an upward and downward motion, for another minute, he turned to his companion and said, "*Shuck!*"

"True," said the privy councillor; "and it strikes me that I would hardly at this moment consider your crown equivalent in value with the sum of five shillings."

"At all events," remarked the King, "the evening is waning, and it is time for me to exchange the crown for a night cap."

"All fair and square," said the privy councillor, "provided you are not obliged to put on the *bonnet rouge*."[19]

ANTHOLOGIA GERMANICA.—NO. I.
THE LYRICAL AND SMALLER POEMS OF SCHILLER.

W HEN Father Bouhours,[1] more than a century ago, propounded that solemn and entertaining question of his, *Un Allemand peut-il avoir de l'esprit?*[2] and satisfactorily established the impossibility of such a monstrosity by a pithy *Point du tout*,[3] he confidently felt that he had bolted the door for ever against the pretensions of *L'Allemagne* to eminence in the Belles Lettres.[4] His categorical negative was thenceforth to constitute an unscaleable wall of separation between the German mind and the Spirit of the Age: it was supererogatory, so contended his partisans (and they were a legion) to construct any other or stouter; people are not obliged to build up a tower of argument to the altitude of Pelion piled upon Ossa,[5] where a single drop of ink is an overwhelming extinguisher: the Germans are a barbarian race, and must therefore continue so: *le maître l'a dit; cela suffit*,[6] and so thought the *maître* too. Taking the contrasted positions of both countries in those days—the palmy state of France, and the dark and downtrodden condition of Germany, into consideration, we shall perhaps pause before we adjudge the absurdity of Bouhours to be worthy of everlasting reprobation. At all events, his conquest over his own note of interrogation continued for a tedious length of years quite indisputable. The coldblooded sarcasm of Voltaire, when, remarking the blunders of some Prussians who had been sent to Ferney to assist him in a rehearsal, he exclaimed, *"Il ne faut pas s'en étonner; je demande des hommes et l'on me donne des Allemands!"*[7] affords painful evidence of the sort of estimation in which, even but sixty years back, the Germans were held by the most enlightened people in the world. But as time rolls, man progresses and nations grow out of their nonage. Fortune is herself too full of freakishness and frolic to tolerate the notion of suffering either peoples or systems to stand perpetually stock-still in the one old attitude. Neither is it because A has been unfortunately precipitated into a ditch, while B, C, D, and the rest of the alphabet speed merrily and rattlingly onward to their journey's end on the roof of the Diligence, that he, the Overthrown, is necessarily condemned to diet upon lizards and make his bed amid the mud for the residue of his days. So Germany at last awoke from her long slumber, and shewed the small psychologists who had pronounced it a death lethargy, that they had been "darkening counsel by words without knowledge".[8] And then, (very singular to publish,) it came to pass that the French themselves were the foremost to hail the prodigy with pleasure. The countrymen of the philosopher who wanted men instead of Germans, and of the honest dogmatist who fixed a pumpkin upon the shoulders of every creature who enunciated the *ch* after a fashion differing from his own, were the first translators of the *Leidenschaften des jungen Werthers*,[9] and by them was that (then) extraordinary work rendered celebrated throughout Europe. Ever since also, to their credit be the chronicle, they have exhibited zeal indefatigable in bringing more prominently forward into the daylight of the South the best and boldest of the German writers. So that if Bouhours were now to shake off the dust of the cemetery, and revisit the glimpses of the Parisian moon,[10] the Revolution of 1788,[11] and eke that of 1830, much as he might be startled to hear of them, would dwindle into comparative insignificance in his eyes before the great moral revolution which has taken place in France in favour of German intellect.

The Annals of Locomotion, if such Annals there be, cannot, it is true, furnish an instance of a tardier march than the march of Germany towards the goal of distinction. To Martin Opitz,[12] a Silesian, and a versifier of some talent, who flourished in the first and second quarters of the seventeenth century, and whose rhymes even in this our day read prettily and smoothly, attaches the renown of having founded the first modern School of Poetry in his native land. But the followers of Opitz, and the followers of his followers, although remarkably numerous, were not remarkably respectable; and nearly one hundred years elapsed before Germany displayed any decisive indications of a capability to create a name for herself. It was not until the early part of the eighteenth century that alterations for the better became generally perceptible. Appearances, then, for the first time assumed an aspect rich in promise. Men of poetical tastes began to be sensible that to guarantee an enduring reputation something worthier must be substituted for the stilted pedantry or mumbled mysticism which their predecessors had established as the standards of perfection. Among the names of this epoch which merit commemoration may be mentioned Gellert and Hagedorn,[13] as also Rabener,[14] Haller[15] and Weiss,[16] none of whom will utterly sink into oblivion, so long as purity of thought and harmony of diction shall continue to find advocates in Germany.

Yet were none of these, none of all who were then most popular, even with Klopstock[17] at their head, sufficiently gifted to be able to communicate a permanently noble tone to the literature of their fatherland. There needed the avatar of some untrammelled and untrammellable spirit who, by a manifestation of energies thitherto undreamed of, should coerce the suffrages of all, and strike with force electrical through and through the very core of the universal mind. In a fortunate hour, as the Orientals phrase it, Goethe commenced his career of triumph. Him followed Schiller. Both names are hackneyed, but one cannot help that. The land of the Teuton has cradled no other two greater than those two.

As to the author of Wilhelm Meister, whose "praise is hymned by loftier harps than ours",[18] we pass him by with a benison. Tranquilly may he slumber in that pavilion, to Immortality dedicate, which, while yet a denizen of the earth, he himself laboured night and day in the sweat of his brow to construct. Our present object is to bespeak attention to a few vagrant reliques, originally belonging to Schiller's cabinet, and which found their way into our hands by a series of accidents. We have (for no base purposes) disguised them to the best of our poor ability; but we should, after all, be loath to hear that they had forfeited their identity. They are short poems of a lyrical and miscellaneous description, and, we should hope, marketable merchandise yet. If otherwise we shall experience a certain regret, but no compunction.

"It is the bright day that brings forth the adder".[19] Yet it has been the rare lot of Schiller almost wholly to escape censure. Few writers have acquired a lifelong and posthumous popularity equal to his. Attempts, however, mean as they were abortive, *have* been made to disparage his excellence. His title to originality has been canvassed. It has been questioned whether if *Götz von Berlichingen* had never appeared the world would ever have had *Die Räuber.*[20] But causelessly. Schiller unquestionably embodied in himself all the elements of a mighty nature, qualified to stand alone, and assume an independent bearing among myriads. He is one who in any age would have achieved for himself a dowry of immortal notoriety. He has accomplished for the Drama what Goethe with all his powers could never compass—he has conferred upon it stability, definiteness, consistency, everything. His prose productions, too, are characterized by an originality essentially distinct from that which beams through the pages of his illustrious contemporary. In that sovereign control exercised by Goethe over the creations of his thought Schiller is deficient; in Goethe's grace he is deficient; he lacks the playful vein, the versatility, the Protean, Voltairean faculty of metamorphosis and self-multiplication possessed by Goethe, but his great individuality is, by reason of this very deficiency, only the more conspicuously developed. Above all, he is as a poet fairly the compeer of the other. With tens of thousands he is more popular still. The judgment of the multitude, it is true, is a perilous criterion. But, viewed with reference to his positive merits only, Schiller is confessedly a poet of transcendant power. Little doubt can exist that if he had bequeathed his Lyrics to the world uncompanioned by any second legacy his name would have been greenly garlanded, his genius labelled as magnificent and he himself classed among the first masters of song. Is the truth exaggerated by this panegyric? Those who with understandings to appreciate and hearts to feel have studied them in the language they were penned in are fitliest qualified to answer the question.

It is these Lyrics that we propose, as we have said, to introduce to the reader. Their great hallowing charm is the captivating, rather than faithful resemblance they bear with the realities they profess to be images of. Schiller has judiciously forborne from carrying into them any portion of that stormy vehemence, and blasting invective, for which his tragedies are sometimes remarkable. This is precisely as it should be. Schiller was aware that if the might of Tragedy lies in the fervour of its appeal to our passions, Poetry has won its distinguishing triumph when it succeeds in interesting our affections. His poetry, therefore, will be found to be of a majestical and mild order, occasionally philosophical, but more generally pathetic, and at all times attempering ardour with meekness, like the enthusiasm of a woman. Take, for instance, his *Mädchens Klage*, in which he darkly depicts the desolateness of a susceptible heart, outliver of all its early loves and sensibilities, yet still unwilling to cast away even the ashes of its extinguished fires.

* * * * * * * * *

The composition of riddles has fallen very much into desuetude in these latter days. Small is the wonder, it may be replied, when the race of little children is no more—extinct like the mammoth and dodo. True, my good Madam, or Sir, and Life itself has superseded every other riddle: an additional misfortune is, that this puzzles more than it amuses. But the crabbedness of some rhythmical riddles was always a colossal obstacle in the way of their popularity. Where solutions are apparently achievable with facility, it is a pleasure to enterprise them. Otherwise, what is Bacon himself, with his Novum Organum open before him to refer to, but a voyager at random, putting out to sea in the dark, chartless and pilotless? One glance, however, at the *Parabeln und Räthsel*[21] sufficeth to shew that though our friend Schiller excelled as a decorator of Truth, he was ill skilled in the art and mystery of disguising her: his drapery is in fact the sheerest gauzework; beautiful to the eye, and arranged *comme il faut*,[22] but intolerably transparent, and withal *too* easily stripped off. *Voyez un peu.*[23]

* * * * * * * * *

Schiller has left upon record a striking apostrophe, penned at three and twenty, to the grave of Rousseau,[24] and of this a translation lies beside us; but there is a little bird who whispers us that we must heroically reduce it to a heap of tinder—so, there! we have done so. He—but no—it is evident from our promptness to obey her that *this* little bird is a *she*—she tells us that if we should suffer it to go forth, Schiller himself would have the very blackest crow in five score to pluck with us hereafter; and her we verily believe. When Schiller wrote this apostrophe he knew neither himself nor the author of Emilius.[25] Succeeding years afforded him practical proof that the necessary tendency of such writings as those of Rousseau must ever be to disorganize the structure of Society, and drive the ploughshare of destruction over the fairest harvests of the heart. That "Grand Panoramic View of the French Revolution"[26] which was unrolled before the eyes of Europe, and had more spectators than admirers, spoiled his fancy for Spectacle in general; and he, the Poet of Enthusiasm all his life, nevertheless lived to discover that the hiding-places wherein the personifications of his early abstractions had taken refuge were not traceable upon any known geographical *mappe-monde*. These experiences were not lost upon him; and, in truth, it might be difficult to name a poet whose works abound more in testimonies of deep reverence for the ancient and canonized forms of life than Schiller's. Our limits warn us to be as slightly diffuse as possible, but the lines to the *Mädchen von Orleans* are so characteristical of the changed spirit in which Time and Truth at length taught him to survey many things, that we cannot forbear allotting them a place here. In these lines Schiller stands face to face with Voltaire; and bitterer than the draught that Francis Arouet has been called from the Vaults of the Pantheon to swallow, need no epicure in wormwood wine desire his potation to be.[27]

* * * * * * * * *

It may here be remarked, in conjunction with what has already been stated, that, owing to an uncommon, though not isolated idiosyncrasy, Schiller was never able to perceive the beauty of that species of wit which has become so famous under the title of *persiflage*. He understood the Philosophy of Sneering as indifferently as Champollion[28] understood the Hieroglyphics. He did not teach, with Rabelais, that Jackpuddingism[29] constitutes the genuine business of Life, or think, with Byron, that the Universe is merely a wider showbox. His mind, like that of Dante, and Wordsworth, and Milton, and every great poet whose genius is an *integer*, was wholly unpoisoned by any sympathy with the Ludicrous. *Für eine Comödie hatte er einst einen Stoff gefunden*, (says one of his biographers) *fühlte sich aber zu fremd für diese Gattung.*[30] No doubt. Like Manichæus,[31] he recognised but two Realities, the Good and the Evil, and he loved the one and he loathed the other too intensely to make a mere laughing-stock of either. Mephistopheles, it is true, was born in his day, and travelled (by night) from France into Deutschland with purpose to circulate the Devil's Elixir—a yet more infernal decoction, by the bye, than Hoffman's[32]— among the unsophisticated pipe-smokers of the North. But if Goethe had not caught him and up-shut him in a cage, (casting at the same time a somewhat showy and tawdry robe over his nakedness, so as to render him an attractive object of popular curiosity) Schiller, believe it, was the very hero upon Earth to have planted his great heel, shod with pitiless iron, upon the head of the Denier,[33] and emphatically squabashed him for an eternity of twelvemonths.

Even the lighter weapon of playful satire exhibits (and one is glad that it exhibits) an awkward appearance in his grasp. It is a cat o' three tails, flourished up and downward by a stalwart knight, who can never doff his armour or dismount from his charger. The most forlorn part of the joke is that this little instrument of annoyance is exercised against shadows.

* * * * * * * * *

In the next selection I shall endeavour to convey to the reader some idea of two of Schiller's longer poems—The Lay of the Bell, and The Message to the Iron Foundry, the former of which is without a parallel in the anthology of any country. In the meantime I shall take the opportunity afforded me by the conclusion of the present notice to cite the testimony of Goethe to the worth, talents and sufferings of his friend, (for of the last he also had his share.) Schiller needed not the eulogy of Goethe; but Goethe's voluntary tribute of homage at the shrine of one certainly his inferior in general intellectual power, is truly honorable to himself.

[Here follows a translation of "Epilog zu Schiller's Glocke"]

ANTHOLOGIA GERMANICA.— NO. II.
SCHILLER'S LAY OF THE BELL AND MESSAGE TO THE IRON FOUNDRY.

WE have asserted that no parallel to the *Lied von der Glocke* can be found in the Anthology of any nation. The assertion may have been a hazardous one. Yet there is no necessity, as far as we can see, for timorously qualifying it; and we shall point out why.

In the first place, Every production, the birth of an original mind, is and must be characteristical of its parent only. It must be evident that no poet, no matter how gigantic his powers of conception, how comprehensive his habits of speculation, can possibly belie or compromise his intellectual identity. It is, in truth, a gross assumption, that which supposes the existence of such an attribute of Genius as Universality. They who are accustomed to negligently fashion their conclusions rather more in accordance with the unsustained and unexplained opinions of others than with the evidence furnished by those facts which the analysis of the mind in all ages supplies us with, may think differently. But no argument can establish an essentially erroneous position. What is called Universality will be found to be a mere specific form of Individuality. Though the Ocean girdles the great globe its waters have limits. The sun takes "a comprehensive survey"[1] of a certain number of planets; but there are other suns, surveyors of other planets, on a perhaps yet more comprehensive scale than his. The intimate acquaintance possessed by a gardener with the properties of the plants, fruits, and flowers of his own garden, is by no means a guarantee that he is qualified to undertake the cultivation of another garden, whose plants, fruits and flowers bear not the remotest resemblance to those of his own. The gardener's knowledge is to universal knowledge as three acres and a perch are to the territory of the world. Does anybody suppose that if Shakspeare had been tasked to the composition of a metaphysical romance, he would or could, constituted as his genius was, have bequeathed us a work at all capable of rivalling St. Leon?[2] The expectation were about as reasonable as that of a man who should fancy that an oak ought to produce pomegranates as well as acorns. Schiller himself, it will be conceded by such as are familiar with the character of his writings, could scarcely have screwed his courage so far up to the sticking-place[3] as to have grappled with a theological epic; but if he had done so, and come off conqueror withal, the chances are still infinity to one that between *his* Messiah and the Messiah of Klopstock there would be as little affinity by relationship as between Monmouth and Macedon.[4] They who are either sceptical or curious may examine his tragedies, and see how far they are like to those of any other dramatist, alive or dead. If we had no second argument to appeal to, therefore, here is one that would of itself suffice to convince us that the *Lied von der Glocke* must be an isolated production.

But we have another argument. It is an isolated production, because it is a purely *local* production. That is, it could only have been produced by a German. This conclusion will be at once acceded to when the nature of the poem is understood. The intrinsic action developed by the poem is almost a nullity. A bell is founded, and that is all. The description of sermon that an Englishman might be expected to preach from so meagre a text, would, it is to be feared, be somewhat wiredrawn and weak—an unfavorable sample, on the whole, of pulpit oratory in the second quarter of the nineteenth century. There is a feast when the founding is over: among the beakers and platters the Englishman might, to be sure, be in some degree at home: he might draw up a catalogue of the eatables and drinkables, and chronicle the few brilliant things of which the motherwit of the assembled company instigated the utterance. But beyond this his tablets would exhibit a ghastly blankness. Not that the failure, after all, could be so justly ascribed to the incapacity of the man himself as to the deficiencies of his education and his unfortunate lack of experience. He had never seen a bell founded any where. Obviously he should have travelled and taken up a residence during the winter months at Stutgard or Weimar. There he would have been better taught. In the German towns the founding of a bell is, be it recollected, an event that excites considerable interest. The founder publicly notifies his intention several days beforehand: he advertises it in the newspapers, specifies time and place, and invites the people to come and witness the process. A little festival is, as I have mentioned, also solemnized on the occasion, and a name is formally bestowed on the bell, by which name it is ever afterwards recognised. But as none of all those ceremonials are known or heard of out of Germany, it follows that we have here an additional reason why the poem in question should be one of a peculiar character. Accordingly, we find that even in Germany it is regarded as such. Lessing and Wieland[5] lived and died unvisited by the conception. The forty volumes of Goethe may be explored in vain for such another. It is a solitary sparkle struck from the glowing spirit of SCHILLER alone.

So much by way of preface or prologue. It is now time to allow the poet to come forward and declaim for himself as best he may. The reader will observe that the cardinal beauty of the poem consists in its episodes, and in the skill and address with which these are introduced. Thus the junction of the metals suggests one episode, the possibility of fusion another, the danger of explosion a third. Neither should the mechanism of the versification be overlooked or contemned. Though the metre incessantly varies as the subject ranges the variations are always in accordance with the finest principles of harmony. Let any one, for example, examine the episodical passage of THE WEDDING-BELL, and he can hardly forbear from admiring the curious felicity with which it is imagined and constructed. Schiller's correctness of taste in his adaptation of the versification he employed to the matter he treated of has never been surpassed.

* * * * * * * * *

Schiller, according to the opinions of the most competent German critics, did not eminently excel in the Ballad: at least he is generally regarded as being surpassed by Bürger and Uhland in all that constitutes the poetry of that species of composition. But, though this judgement may not be altogether erroneous, it is beyond question that, simply taken as narrative-pieces, Schiller's Ballads are invested with a grace, a pathos, and occasionally a majesty rarely equalled in the most finished efforts of other writers. As specimens of the pathetic, *Hero and Leander*[6] and the *Cranes of Ibycus*,[7] but more particularly *The Hostage*,[8] (*Die Bürgschaft*,) a tale founded on the popular anecdote of Damon and Pythias,[9] may challenge a comparison with any productions of a similar class in any land. *The Diver*,[10] also, which versifies a historical incident in the reign of King Robert of Sicily, is a powerfully graphic story, and in *The Combat with the Dragon*[11] we recognize one of the most beautiful of modern allegories.

None of these Ballads, however, can be said to be of a purely imaginative class. Schiller, indeed, in most instances, preferred a slight basis of authenticated fact to rear his airiest superstructures on. Whether from an absence of sympathy with the unmitigated elements of the Ideal, or from a nervous dread of coming into hostile collision with that rather understood than expressed popular sentiment which overhastily supposes that wherever the Ideal is found unassociated with the Actual, it is necessarily excluded from the territory of the Possible, or else from what phrenologists would call a deficiency in constructiveness—a deficiency which, even where every other intellectual faculty is in full vigor, brings with it a consciousness of irremediable incapacity—he shrank from drawing as largely and liberally on the resources of his own mind as an acquaintance with his works would lead us to believe he might have been justified in doing; for even *Der Geisterseher*,[12] (The Spectre-haunted,) the very best of all his prose fictions, is made up of some half dozen fragments which are united without any apparent connection, and conduct the reader to the close of the book without allowing him to arrive at any conclusion. Thus also for the materials of the following tale Schiller is indebted to some ancient legend. His commentators are not agreed as to what particular author he may have found them in. Böttiger[13] states that the story is of Alsatian origin, and that Schiller met with it while at Manheim. For ourself, we remember that while as yet we were very young and little, we read it with intense interest in a translation of a work by the learned Spanish Jesuit, Rodriguez[14] (the same Rodriguez alluded to in Dryden's preface to *The Hind and Panther*, as well as in the poem itself). The Ballad founded by Schiller on the story may be said to be the most extensively popular of the author's minor poems, for it has been dramatised under various titles, not merely throughout Germany, but by most of the continental theatres generally, and in all instances with the happiest success. Whether in an English garb the Ballad itself be equally capable of pleasing the lovers of English poetry will be better determined by others than by us.

[Here follows "The Message to the Iron-Foundry"]

ANTHOLOGIA GERMANICA.—NO. III.
MISCELLANEOUS POEMS AND METRICAL TALES.

W AS KLOPSTOCK imbued with the true spirit of Poetry? To enable us to become satisfied on this point it would be requisite that we should possess an unclouded conception of what it is that properly constitutes Poetry. Unfortunately there is little probability that we shall ever acquire such a conception. That Poetry is, in some sort, an object of perception to the understanding, as a species of composition distinct from and superior to Prose, is admitted by all. But that there are certain characteristics by which the recognition of it is rendered an easy matter to the uninitiated, we are compelled by the voice of universal testimony very strongly to doubt.

Voltaire observes that *Quand des hommes éclairés disputent long-tems sur une chose il y a grande apparence que cette chose n'est pas claire;*[1] and if we find that inquiries into the nature of Poetry have effected little besides bringing into collision a greater variety of discordant opinions than could be elicited by the analysis of any other subject within the range of literary discussion—if we find that, like the spirit it emanates from, Poetry would appear to make itself comprehended rather through its operation than in its essence, we may infer that it is idle to appeal for an explanation of the mystery that envelopes it to any tribunal but that of individual experience. Perhaps, therefore, the utmost that can be unhesitatingly advanced is, that whenever, either in creating or criticising a poem, belief and feeling are at issue with abstract deduction, the judgment will incur less hazard in suffering itself to be biassed rather by the former than by the latter, and that poetical genius will make its most successful appeals to the sympathies of mankind, when, taking counsel of none, it confides in its own impulses, and assumes license to follow those alone fearlessly and at large.

Whether KLOPSTOCK acted thus or acted otherwise, the age has not yet decided, and may not immediately decide; but we apprehend that if the decision were pronounced tomorrow, it would not be found to furnish such a justification of his pretensions to poetical eminence as his reputation at home and abroad might at first appear to warrant.

It is beside our purpose to enquire whether KLOPSTOCK be or be not entitled to the merit of having constructed an Epic. We will grant that he is, though we are far from being satisfied that we could not adduce arguments that should establish the contrary. Aristotle tells us that in framing an Epic we must in no iota deviate from the principle upon which the Iliad is modelled. Castelvetro,[2] however—no insignificant authority in his era—asserts that if the details of the Trojan war be matter for the historian, the Iliad cannot be regarded as an Epic, for that the essence of the Epic is pure Fable, unadulterated with the slightest admixture of fact. Again, Tasso[3]—on what grounds we forget—insists that the Epopee[4] is at once destroyed by the introduction of the gods; so that, according to this great poet, the ancients had not a single Epic at all to boast of! The settlement of such a controversy is not a very important desideratum. It is sufficient for us to perceive that the Messiah of KLOPSTOCK is a poem not particularly distinguished for either power or brilliancy. We need only read it to become convinced that the author—though his exertions contributed to the breaking asunder of those contemptible strawbands, the twist-and-plait-work of GOTTSCHED and Co.,[5] which for years had fettered the rebellious intellect of his country—had not energy enough, was not gifted with audacity enough, to prosecute a higher triumph, and assert for himself such an originality as could alone qualify him to rank among the Masters of the Lyre.

But though we cannot, because of his Messiah, allow him to enter the same temple with Milton, Camöens,[6] Dante, Goethe, and Byron—all explorers of realms new and strange in the world of Song, which have since recognised them as sovereigns—we should, on the other hand, be loth to condemn him to the common dust and obscurity wherein today lie sepulchred the Scudérys,[7] the Perraults,[8] the Mambruns,[9] the Chapelains,[10] and the thousand and one additional pupils of the gyve-and-fetter school all over the globe. We cannot do so, without injustice, so long as his Odes remain to challenge our admiration, in however qualified a measure we may feel disposed to bestow it.

They are not, it is true—these Odes themselves are not, in every respect, what we could wish them to be. But they develop much power of thought and much power for the communication of thought. Their harmony is rarely at fault, and their diction is frequently felicitous. With all their defects of repetition and redundancy, they are compositions to be proud of; and we would venture to predict that whatever, after the lapse of ages, shall remain unimpaired and undimmed of the celebrity of KLOPSTOCK, will be found to have been based upon the excellence of his Odes alone.

Two of those odes we shall now select for translation....

[Here follow "To Ebert" and "To Giseke"]

These odes are in perfect harmony with the sombre character that marks a great portion of German literature. But in justice towards

KLOPSTOCK it should be stated that his temperament was commonly averse from gloom. He was not one of those painters who have a passion for darkening, and who uniformly pourtray the universe in a sad-coloured vesture. We would even say that the tendency of his poetry is to beget confidence rather than despondency. He is a solemn writer, but, except in a few instances, he rarely indulges in disheartening views of life. Not that if he had done so his glory would have suffered depreciation in the estimation of his countrymen. Perhaps if he had dug the graves he is so fond of alluding to deep enough to hold both soul and body many of them might have liked him all the better. A true German poet revels in the corruption of the sepulchre with the perseverance of a Ghoule. Open his books, and the word *Grab*[11] meets your eye at each verse, and this not merely in elegy, but in every form of miscellaneous composition. To illustrate our observation, we take a volume of KALCHBERG[12] at random, and transcribe one of his apostrophes.

[Here follows "To my Grave"]

Even the song-writers of Germany are at seasons apparently more desirous of being crowned with yew than laurel. If they pen a madrigal they will probably tell their sweetest—as the poet we have just quoted does elsewhere—that her locks are growing grey while she hesitates to choose a lover. If the theme be bacchanalian, the odds are that, with KOTZEBUE,[13] they quaff their wine *den Ruhenden unter dem Grase* (to the slumberers under the sod). Let the reader, for curiosity's sake, just turn to the fourth volume of this Magazine, p. 673, and he will be struck with the singularly *gay* tone of the song he will see there (a translation from HÖLTY[14]). We now give a second song from the same writer; but this, it will be perceived is of a happier description than the other.

[Here follows "Song Exciting to Gladness"]

Germany, like France, has always abounded in didactic poets. Shelley, in the preface to his "Prometheus Unbound", acquaints us that if there be any description of poetry that excites his abhorrence it is the didactic. His own poems are in correct accordance with his principle, for they teach nothing to anyone. Yet Shelley, as an enthusiastic lover of German poetry, could scarcely have failed to perceive that the noblest portion of that poetry is the philosophical. We do not mean to say that the exertions of those who labour to array the treacherous and brittle maxims of a system of false metaphysics in the dyes of poetry are to be applauded; but we revere and admire such sentiments as the following:—

[Here follows "The Two Sorts of Human Greatness"]

If the didactic poets of Germany are on a few occasions betrayed by their themes into insipidity or stiffness, many of the prose moralists fall into the contrary error, and disfigure their essays or etchings by exuberance of embroidery and decoration. We should, last of any, be disposed to utter a disrespectful syllable against RICHTER, but that he has now and then squandered the wealth of his mind on fantastical fripperies none will doubt.[15] In ·the tale we are about to versify there are some puerilities, which we think were better absent, and we shall therefore pass them over. Perhaps we should apologise for violating our original intention of extracting from none but poets, if the violation here were not rather apparent than real. RICHTER's language, though to the eye it is prose, to the heart speaks with more than the fervour of poetry.

[Here follows "The New-Year's Night of a Miserable Man"]

A caviller may possibly take an objection against the conception here developed. With apparent plausibility he may urge that the nature of the incidents renders the moral null. He may thus argue. Septuagenarians do not so deplore the loss of their youth. It is undoubtedly the province of dreams to revolutionize the feelings, to awaken buried regrets, and generate unwonted channels for the current of our tears. But this fact is one of those recognized results from the constitution of our being, which our noontide hours regard rather with commiseration than with sympathy. Let us suppose that an individual were subjected for a short period to the operation of a necromantic spell, and in that short period were compelled to endure unutterable agonies of remorse for his past offences. Is there any necessary link of alliance between such a contingency and the perpetual prolongation of the excitable state of mind which wrought him so much temporary torment? Would he, because of the anguish he had undergone, feel the more disposed to anathematize his own delinquencies? Would he not, contrariwise, charge that anguish upon the monstrous nature of the illusion he had been held in thrall to, and gather more abundant encouragement to persevere in error, directly he should discover that Nature and Necromancy were at issue on one of the least intangible points in Ethics, the connection of Crime and Punishment? We shall answer this argument. It is true, that the Youth and the Old Man are separated, each from the other, by irremoveable barriers; true, that there is no common bond of sympathy between them. But this abstract truth cannot argue aught against RICHTER, because he advances no assumption capable of being interpreted as attributing to the Old Man in actual life any such sensations and reflections as the dream of anticipated age awakens in the Young Man of the Poem. Assuming as fact the hypothetical case already stated, we should say that much would depend on the idiosyncrasy of the spellbound individual. The probability is, that if he were at all capable of drawing rational inferences—if he were at all susceptible of any influences independent of mere physical influences, he would conclude that the remorse he had suffered was not severer than his transgressions demanded; and that if the balance between criminality and justice were rigidly struck, the legislation of the known, and that of the unknown world, would mete out the same chastisement to his soul. He would so conclude, we think, not merely from the mysterious nature of the human spirit, and its boundless capacity for suffering, but from a comparison of the circumstance in question with his own interior experiences on many occasions. We admit that the moral of the story *is* likely to be powerless. We never knew a moral that was otherwise. The resources of the devil are not so exhausted but that he can bring a sufficient array of artillery to bear upon the rank and file of a few vowels and consonants, however compactly the column may be set. But RICHTER is, nevertheless, to be praised, because, though in this world a good man is required to do little more than weep for the evils that overspread it, (for when he would warn, a rushing whirlwind comes and drowns his voice,) not all men are good, and it is less in accordance with the indurated natures of many to weep than to scoff.

* * * * * * * * *

ANTHOLOGIA GERMANICA—NO. IV.

WE have not forgotten our German. Months, it is true, have elapsed since we last presented our readers with any of those gems from the rich mines of German poesy wherewith we were wont to deck our pages. Yet our studies have not been discarded, although they have been laid aside. They have been laid aside, not because there was any intermission in the depths of that worship which, in our soul, we pay to the grand, albeit sometimes gloomy spirit that presides over the song and legends of the land of Goethe—but because other, and far less pleasing occupations intervened to disturb the stillness of our devotion, and we have not had a peaceful hour to weave an offering that might be worthy to lay upon the shrine. But now, once more, we return again to our old employment—once more we bring down the volumes from the German shelf of our library, and turn over the leaves, that we may cull the choicest extracts, and translate them into the language that, after all, is the language of our love. For though there be those who would cry shame upon us for the confession, we do confess that to our ear no language sounds as pleasing as that of England; and we would not exchange our own mother tongue, with all its harshness, and with all its imperfections, (harshness, it is true, that has never grated upon our ear, and imperfections that we never have detected,) for all the languages that either modern ages or antiquity can boast. No, not for the rich and sonorous melody of the Greeks—not for the terse and racy conciseness of the Latins, nor for the almost boundless vocabulary of the German, nor yet for the soft and melting flow of the Italian. And why should we? Is it not the language of our homes? Is it not that in which we remember the voices of our parents, and of the friends of our youth? Is it not that in which we first heard the words of tender endearment, in which we first listened to the teachings of religion? Is it not thus twined, as it were, in hallowed association with all our recollections of this world, and all our hopes of the next? and where is the linguist, we care not how ardent his devotion to other tongues, who will not return, with all the fervour of first love, to his own? Ay, and as the thoughts of first love will arise unbidden, we know not why, at a moment when we did not wish for them—is not the language of England that in which we spoke the words of young and ardent, and generous, affection to one who—but no matter, we must not become sentimental, and surely to our readers we will need far less excuse than we have already made, for loving the English above all other languages.

And yet we love the language of Germany, and we admire her poetry, and therefore it is that we would pay to that poetry the highest compliment we can, that of translating it into the language that we honour most; wishing at the same time that our strains were worthier to do justice to its merits. Come, then, reader, we will have another Anthology. Come; the meadow is rich with flowers of a thousand tints—we mean the meadow of fancy and of imagination, in which we would have you to wander with us for a little while. All the summer you may have been wandering in the meadows, and on the mountains of our loved isle—you may have pulled the primrose on the bank, and the heath upon the hill—and wooed the coolness of the summer breeze, as it wafted the perfumery of the wild flowers along the moor or the lake, and while thus you could wander, we called you to no other Anthology—but Autumn's keen blast has swept the flowers from their stems—the scythe of the mower has passed over the sward of the meadow, and the wild flowers you used to admire are now lying stored up snugly in the farmer's hayrick, and the breeze comes sharply along the lake or moor, untempered by a single breath of rural sweetness, and there are no blossoms now upon the valley or the hill. Come, then, now, with us, and we will lead you where the Autumn's breath can never wither the bloom of the garden. Come, and we will guide you to a plain where the flowers are changeless in their hue, and perennial in their bloom, and we will laugh to scorn the rude nipping frosts that will soon be coming over the earth. We will have another of our German Anthologies; we trust it will not be the last, and so, gentle reader, dropping our metaphors, we will soberly and quietly introduce you to

THE POEMS OF MATTHISON AND SALIS.[1]

If we were asked what it is that constitutes the leading characteristic of German Poetry, we should be disposed to answer—Too adventurous an attempt to assimilate the creations of the ideal with the forms of the actual world. Throughout that poetry we can trace a remarkable effort to render vivid and tangible and permanent those phantasmagoria of the mind which by the statutes of our nature are condemned to exhibit an aspect of perpetual vagueness and fluctuation. And as this is the prominent characteristic, so it is the darkest blemish of German Poetry. Let no absurd admirer of the style that approximates to the unintelligible tell us that we censure as an imperfection what we should, if we properly entered into the spirit of the writer, applaud as an excellence. Advocates for the highest possible degree of perspicuity in poetry we are and shall always continue to be, because we are persuaded that it is the want of that perspicuity which, more than any other want, has contributed to the growth of the popular indifference at present so prevalent with regard to poetry, and has made the eldest-born of Heaven, even in the eyes of her own worshippers, an object rather of wonder than of love. Remote from us be the narrowness of soul that would underestimate or contest the capabilities of genius. Imagination may in many great poets have its own wondrous forms, and seem to produce its own strange creations, without any restraint, save that of which the ancient critic speaks—

$$\text{"}\varepsilon\iota\sigma\ \nu o\mu o\sigma\ \tau o\ \delta o\xi\alpha\nu\ \pi o\iota\eta\tau\eta\text{."}^2$$

But even this latitude, wide as it is, is not infinite. The "$\tau o\ \delta o\xi\alpha\nu$" was always a barrier, however distant it might appear, if all was left to the poet's discretion—the existence of discretion was presumed, and we hold it to be all but an axiom that if, while Imagination operated, it had not, after all, limited its operations to a sphere whose boundaries were prescribed and sentinelled with jealous vigilance by Reason and Precedent, we should at this day possess but a scanty show indeed of poetical monuments to boast of. We would venture to say, that we should scarcely be able to produce one that would be accounted worthy of more than the momentary gaze of admiration we bestow upon the shifting colours of the air-bubble or the kaleidoscope.

Men of a strongly-marked poetical temperament are not, we concede it, likely to be over logical in the management of an argument, or scrupulously consecutive in the development of their ideas. If their ingenuity be such as to acquire for them a character for originality of thinking, it is well; we are pleased; and all reasonable expectation has sufficient to be satisfied with. We shall never quarrel with them if they disclaim all pretensions to be reverenced as masters in the art of mystifying, or even, to go no further, of precise and subtle reasoning. But it is the peculiar and grave calamity of great genius that so soon as, overcoming all intermediate obstacles, it has obtained a height from whence it might smile contempt upon the contingencies that menace its downfall, it not infrequently—urged by an impulse, the enigma of which is only to be solved upon some unopened leaf of its own perplexed philosophy—foregoes that enviable eminence, precipitates itself headlong downward, and is lost thenceforth and for ever in an abyss "deeper than plummet ever sounded."[3] It would appear that there lies somewhere in the geography of the human soul a *terra incognita*, which hardy speculators have been in all ages ambitious to penetrate. The possible existence of this Land of Shadow we are not prepared to deny; but the hazards of a voyage to explore it, to establish its boundaries and analyse its mysteries, come to us, we confess, unrecommended by any rational prospect of a counterbalancing remuneration. Not so, however, have thought the German metaphysicians and poets. They—ardent and withal inapprehensive souls!—have now and then tempted the dangers of the

Great Deep that heaved between them and the bourne of their longings. But better had they been less rash, for they who went, went and returned no more. Either they suffered shipwreck against the rocks on the coast, or else, if they landed, they perished amid the insuperable wildernesses around them. And the legacy they have bequeathed to mankind is, alas! nothing worthier than a memory which, while it excites to commiseration, has failed to produce the desirable effect of warning subsequent adventurers from similar enterprizes.

For the predominance of the evil we have alluded to various causes may be assigned. Perhaps the structure of the German language may originally have had and may still have much to answer for in the production of it. The indefinite facilities afforded by that language for the expression—or at the least for half-comprehensive attempts at expression—of emotions which we of a less favoured land than Germany have experienced from generation to generation, without well knowing how to communicate the biography of them to others, are, it may be, to be chidden for that multitudinous array of mystical sentences which we find darkening the pages of such men as Schelling,[4] Novalis,[5] Tiedge,[6] and Richter. But whatever the cause of the evil may be, it is unquestionable that the evil itself exists, and that too large a proportion of German poetry is, not merely obscure, but in the positive sense of the phrase, unintelligible. Wearing the outward mask and semblance of that which it professes to be, it stands exposed, when stripped of those, as a revelation of incongruities and absurdities—a picture, the grouping of which presents us with but a mass of blots and shadows, an anomaly with which the heart cannot sympathise—which the understanding is powerless to grapple with. It is, after all, beautiful, but conventionally beautiful, not intrinsically. It is like the grotesque architecture of a dream, which seems enchanting only because the reasoning faculties have predetermined not to abide by the canons of true taste in their judgment of it. There is a certain deranged arrangement in it which we long to call chaotic. It is the perfection of magnificent inanity.

This taint, however, it is but justice to state, has not ulcerated the whole body of German poetry. The volume before us is in a great degree exempt from it. Here we have evidence that the streams of Castaly[7] may flow as purely through German channels as through any other. The productions of Salis and Matthisson—honoured be their names!—breathe, we are happy to say, all that unsophisticated freshness, all that simplicity of language and integrity of sentiment, which we conceive to be the richest ornaments the poet can decorate his page with. They are also distinguished for an elevated tone of moral principle—in this age no slight praise.

* * * * * * * * *

The feelings of Matthisson as a poet appear to have been rarely excited beyond that equable, though by no means everyday level, which best qualifies a man to appreciate at their fair worth all the blessings around him, without leaving him in any great degree liable to be injured by the shocks he may encounter through existence. To the hurricane and turmoil both of the physical world and the human passions he is a happy stranger. He is the amanuensis of Nature in her mildest moods, and he chooses poetry as the medium of her thousand-voiced communications to mankind. He is rejoiced when he listens to the carol of the lark, and glad because he sees that the primroses are blowing; "his heart leaps up when he beholds a rainbow in the sky;"[8] and, if he can also weep as he hears the mould fall upon the coffin of a brother, his tears, though sincere, are neither bitter nor exhaustless, for he is a believer in the promised Resurrection.[9] He does not, like too many, detect the flavour of poison in every draught that the wells of humanity supply him with: he is evidently unwilling to suspect that anything unholy or polluted can emanate from such a source. True, his effusions are occasionally tinged with melancholy; but it is not the melancholy of despair or even of common human grief that shades the page: it is the overflowing of a heart whose yearnings for the Beautiful "nought under Heaven's wide hollowness"[10] can satisfy, and whose longings after the unobtainable sympathy of the Fair, the Excellent, and the Noble, of all centuries and countries, though German enough, perhaps, in their character to excite a smile in *us*, are as deep a spring of pain to him as the severest trials of Life can be to the worldly-minded. Hence, though the Elegy is a favourite form of composition with Matthisson, he does not sorrow for the dead "as one who hath no hope;"[11] for his sentiments are, in their darkest phases, rather sad than gloomy; while the Laments that he pours forth to the living, though unsurpassed for pathos, exhibit not half the despondency and bitterness of which such subjects might be supposed susceptible.

* * * * * * * * *

For the present our labour of love is over; and now, ten words with respect to ourselves. It has been alleged against us that our Anthologia are somewhat deficient in the information which essays purporting to treat of German literature should contain.[12] In these papers, however, we desire to appear not as essayists, but translators. As translators we are very much at a loss to discover what species of information it is that our censurers or counsellors require of us. Do they wish us to furnish histories of the lives and adventures of every poet we chance to take down from the shelf, embellished, for default of honester materials, with "anecdotes from authentic sources," and so forth? We hope not. All these may be met with in the *Biographia Literaria*, or the Annual Obituary; and we have no ambition for encroaching on the office of the conductors of either one or the other. Or do they, perhaps, expect that we are to engage in disquisitions upon the genius and character of every individual from whom it may be our good or ill fortune to translate or travestie a stanza? Our brief and unceremonious reply is, that such disquisitions are read but by a few, are scarcely half understood by those few, and are never cared for or recurred to by the many or the few. They will continue to be written, we admit, so long as ideas are at all marketable commodities, if only to prove that the writer is capable of writing what the world are incapable of appreciating; but if they ever produce any definite impression, it is, and will be, that the author has been depicted—not as Truth would have depicted him—not as he would or should have depicted himself—but as the prevailing humour and peculiar views of his commentator inclined. We believe that the heart and the intellect of a poet are ever more easily susceptible of analysis by a simple reference to his works than by the aid of the most elaborate explanatory criticism that ever passed through the press. There is a time-honored adage about the supererogation of hanging out a bush where the wine is tolerable; and we object upon principle to flourishes of trumpets, either before Tom Thumb[13] or "His Majesty Sardanapalus, the king, and son of Anacyndaraxes."[14] Apples of gold, though people do occasionally set them in net-work of silver, can afford to shine very well by their own lustre. If the poetry be worthy, its worth will constitute its best recommendation. If it be otherwise, the most eloquent pleading in language is "leather and prunella."[15] These are our undecorated sentiments. We are vain enough to imagine that, if they were also the sentiments of others, neither the cause of poetry nor that of common sense would be a loser.

Thus much in temperate explanation of our preference of the Poetry of poets to the prose of—ourselves. If this be not satisfactory, we shall readvert to the subject in suitable season.

ANTHOLOGIA GERMANICA.—NO. V.
FAUST, AND THE MINOR POEMS OF GOETHE.

F AUST may, in one respect, be looked upon as the *chef d'œuvre* of Goethe. It is the most remarkable by far of all his productions. *Werther*[1] is painful, is harrowing, if read for the first time; every particular line of it pierces to the heart like a javelin tipped with poison. *Wilhelm Meister*[2] reveals to us the searching philosopher, the lucid and comprehensive reasoner, the dialectician to whom all principles, all sciences, all systems are familiar, and in whose hands the duskiest hieroglyphical characters in the Encyclopædia of Nature assume at once an illuminated appearance: this is the noblest work of Goethe. The *Dichtung und Wahrheit*[3] may, perhaps, be pronounced the most interesting; as well on account of the multitude of its facts as on account of the light which, by means of it, Goethe, unconsciously to himself, lets in upon some of the thitherto dark and inexplorable recesses of his own intellectual constitution. But there is no classing *Faust* with or beside these. Its individuality forces it to occupy a position apart from all of them. It is a book *sui generis*. It is, and to latest ages must remain, the most imperishable of all the monuments of the marvellous genius of its marvellous author.

Yet not because of its intrinsic importance; certainly not because we should pronounce it a work which the spirit of Utility, or even of Utilitarianism, would care to patronise. For any high moral purpose it may be deposited on the shelf as valueless. It inculcates nothing either consolatory or ennobling. It possesses no tendency to elevate him who reads and studies it above his fate or his fellows. There is no lesson conveyed by a single page of it, the perusal of which tempts a man to exclaim, This is indeed a legacy!—this is worthy of being treasured up in the memory for ever! It communicates no restorative, no freshening impetus to the soul of him who, having set out in quest of Truth, droops by the way-side when storms begin to muster, and clouds first overcast the prospect. It is a specimen of mere but of magnificent Power. This is the attribute which we have always regarded as constituting the distinguishing excellence of Goethe as a writer. But there are in *Faust* more of the elements that go to the composition of this attribute than in all the other great works of Goethe together. We regret that we cannot, within the narrow limits allotted to us for these our introductory remarks, enter into such a discussion as would establish the correctness of our assertion beyond the possibility of controversy. At present we can only refer to the book itself, and request a comparison of that book with the other books we have mentioned. But this may suffice, for we are persuaded that no soundly-judging person can examine and criticise all in a spirit of impartiality without giving his unqualified assent to the justness of the opinion we have advanced.

As a poem *Faust* cannot fail to strike even the most lethargic reader. It will strike, however, less by any innate beauty than by the consummate skill and exquisite ingenuity of artifice displayed in its construction. The poetry, simply as poetry, is by no means worthy of ranking with that of some of our own first-rate dramatists. We look in vain for any passages capable of competing with the thrilling monologues in *Manfred*[4]—whether we speak with reference to poetical beauty or poetical effect. Let us not, however, mistake. In the generality of cases we might insist upon being allowed the benefit of such assertions as these, because in the generality of cases nothing but a false timidity can compel the German muse to veil her face beside the English. But, as we have mentioned Byron's drama, we will observe, in justice to Goethe, that one source, perhaps the only source, of the poetical superiority of *Manfred* to *Faust*, is unquestionably to be sought for in the native nobility and intrinsic altitude of the character of Manfred as contrasted with that of Faustus. That Goethe, if he had undertaken the portrait of such a character as that of Manfred, would have failed to exhibit all the splendour and emphasis and energy of Byron we have no evidence for asserting. His own hero is made of materials different in many respects from those of which Byron's is constituted. Goethe, too, it cannot be denied, has gone extreme lengths for him. He has hedged him round with quite as much divinity[5] as was compatible with a decent solicitude for the maintenance of the *vraisemblable*. But even Goethe could not give him genuine dignity. We care but little for the man Faustus; little for him in poetry, less in the world. Divest him, indeed, of the robe which Goethe has embroidered for him, and you leave him slight title to more notice than falls to the lot of any other inheritor of the penalty of Adam. You discern nothing but a human being, somewhat unhappier, it is true, than his fellows, but scarcely differing from them in any particular of a more prominent nature than his unhappiness. How many of the more cultivated order of minds should we not presume that there are, whose progress through this mysterious existence is characterised by the same suffering, the same scepticism, the same vague ambition, the same vicissitudes of enthusiasm and lassitude that make miserable the days and nights of Faustus! Are there in reality such in the world? Assuredly. We do not, it is true, meet with them. Why do we *not* meet with them? *Because they are in the world.* Being *in* the world they appear as *of* the world; the thick veil of worldly error and worldly illusion interposes betwixt us and them, and the

naturally strong outlines of their individuality grow dim and undefined to the eye. Besides, the heavy moral atmosphere their souls breathe without intermission presses upon themselves. Even they, confused in their perceptions and disorganized in their faculties, are not always conscious that they suffer more than others. *No one among them is capable of seeing himself in the same point of view in which he regards the Faustus of the drama.* "The world is too much with them"[6]—though it is still more with those who would scrutinize and understand them. Hence the utility and lofty moral excellence of the poet. He disperses, by his wizard art, the mists which envelope the shapes of Actual Life, and marshals those shapes before us, apparelled, perhaps, in a more gorgeous vesture than the philosopher might require to see them arrayed in, but preserving, withal, their indestructible identity, and all those distinctive peculiarities of aspect and proportion which render it impossible that any one of them shall be confounded with any other of them. Goethe has done so much for Faustus, and if he has failed in awakening our deeper sympathies in behalf of the child of his creation, not to any defect in his art is the failure attributable, but to the essentially common-place character of the being the record of whose struggles against the constitution of Nature and the universe he has rendered imperishable.

In thus impliedly asserting, however, that Goethe *has* failed to interest us, we exclude from view, it will be noticed, the hypothesis that the drama is susceptible of an allegorical interpretation not obvious to most perusers. We do so, because in Poetry, as in Prose, we are sticklers for an adherence to the apparent and superficial signification of all that comes before us in the guise of Language. It is too much the fashion of the age to look for mysteries where they do not exist, and to magnify them where they do exist. If this be controvertible it is at all events too much the fashion of the worshippers of Goethe. With these persons the philosophy of *Faust* comprehends the whole circle of theoretical knowledge, and the mysticism that lurks under the philosophy is something too sacred to be discussed by the uninitiated at all. "As Mephistopheles," observes an analytical and original thinker of our day, "represents the spirit of Denial, so Faust may represent that of Inquiry and Endeavour: the two are by necessity in conflict; the light and the darkness of man's life and mind."[7] But what proof, capable of satisfying a rational inquirer, that Goethe designed him for such is adducible from the poem itself? Certainly none. On the contrary, concede the assumption, and we are revolted by a worse conception than any the brain of Mephistopheles himself could have engendered; for at the very outset of the enterprise he is supposed to meditate, "the Spirit of Inquiry and Endeavour" is compelled to select the Accursed of God and Man as an indispensable auxiliary in the prosecution of his plans, and in the end becomes his irredeemable dupe and victim. We need only glance at the fearful position in which the necessity of adopting such a course, to meet such a requital, would establish Mankind with reference to the Power that willed them into existence, to reject the idea with instant abhorrence. At the same time, as we are not of the number of those who would reduce the labours of Goethe to the level of those of an every-day story-weaver, who estimates the extent of his merits by the involutions of his weft and the gaudiness of its texture—we will allow it to be likely that Faustus may have been intended for an impersonation of some certain attribute or principle. Perhaps—and if we err in our conjecture we are contented that our error shall be ascribed to an inability to fathom the fountains of any philosophy save that which appeals for the soundness of its tenets to the experiences, the hopes, the aspirations and sympathies of universal Mankind—perhaps Goethe was desirous of typifying in the destiny of his hero the evils that necessarily spring from the possession of an ill-organized mind, when Discontent and perverted Knowledge combine to maintain it in perpetual thraldom. Faustus, we know, is a man who drinks, in a somewhat deeper proportion than many, of the common chalice of wretchedness whereof we are all partakers. But he is scarcely singular in his sufferings; if at all singular he is singular only in the rebelliousness and desperation generated in his heart by the obstinacy with which he continually broods over those sufferings. His rebelliousness it is that renders him unapproachable by expostulation, and forms a source of bitterness for ever welling up in his bosom. We would liken his case to that of an intractable culprit, condemned, with a multitude of others, to, let us say, a year's imprisonment for a violation of the laws. This man stands aloof from all the others. His companions are perhaps more easily reconcileable to the rigour of their sentence: each of them sees what the constitution of Society exacts in such cases; he sees that he is not in a worse predicament than those around him; he feels that, although he is in prison, he is still the master of his mind and volition, and that his thoughts are chartered to range the universe, and above all he is aware that when the period of his incarceration shall have terminated he may join the mass of his fellow-men, a wiser and a better member of the community than before. With such a being, even though he repine, you can reason. But with the other you cannot reason. He wraps himself in the mantle of his pride and sullenness, and when he speaks you perceive from the fierceness of his invectives and from his denunciation of the barbarity exercised against him that he has not a thought to spare except upon the injustice of his degradation and punishment. Now "look upon this picture—and on this;"[8]—one is the ordinary man, the other the Faustus, of Society. Let it not be urged against us that the consciousness of misery furnishes in itself a *prima facie* case against all argument. We have no wish to deny this truth. We are aware that "the heart knoweth its own bitterness,"[9] and that, being no Zeno,[10] as the mind is, it cannot so successfully play the self-impostor as to become persuaded that substance is shadow, and reality illusion. No: we commiserate Faustus. It were impossible for us to do less. But equally impossible is it for us to blend with our commiseration a single particle of respect. There is about Faustus too much of unmitigated selfishness, too reckless a disregard of the Future, too little of that sublime resignation to Destiny which glorifies the sufferer, too little of a catholic feeling for the afflictions of his species, there is too much and too little of these about Faustus to accord with our notions of the constituents of a truly estimable character. In short, upon the supposition that Faustus is a living emblem of "the Spirit of Inquiry and Endeavour," or any spirit of a corresponding order, the history of his calamities and struggles is a satire on the constitution of Society and his destruction another on Divine Providence. We say *destruction*, because it is manifestly the object of Goethe to produce an impression that he is destroyed. Some, we know, contend that, after all, he is not. But he *appears* to be, and, in this instance, at least, we are bound to confide in appearances. His abandonment of this "visible diurnal sphere,"[11] takes place under circumstances too unequivocal to license us in the hope that he will henceforth be the denizen of a brighter one. We can find nothing in the poem to justify us in the belief that Goethe intended to leave us in the supposition that he was ultimately saved, and we cannot attach much weight to the speculations of those who choose to invent a termination of their own for the drama. In the work of Goethe we believe that Faustus is destroyed; and his destruction is, we repeat it, a libel on Divine Providence if the theory of the writer we have adverted to and the theories of all those commentators, English, French and German, who have criticised the character of Faustus in a similar spirit with that writer, be not utterly hollow and untenable.

It is not, therefore, as a work which recommends itself to Mankind by its utility that *Faust* is to be judged. We are far from wishing ourselves to be understood as intimating that it does not contain abundant materials for such reflection as must naturally spring out of the subject it deals with. But as this species of reflection is never productive of any beneficial end, as at best it terminates in leaving us where it found us, and in the majority of instances tends to bewilder and weary, we are justified in making no account of it. *Faust*, as we have already said, is a specimen of pure Power. It is the boldest and most vivid manifestation of Power that, as a poem, the whole world, perhaps, is capable of exhibiting. Of such celebrity as is acquirable from an imposing display of all that is comprehended under this term—fervor of sentiment—force of delineation—fidelity of character—

grace and occasionally gorgeousness of diction—the voice of literary Europe has given Goethe the full benefit; and greater celebrity than this Goethe himself, we believe, never aimed at for his work, and certainly never could have rationally anticipated.

There are now several so-called translations of this poem in English, and there is one translation which we do not class with those—conceiving, as we do, that it is precisely such a work as Goethe himself, if he had written in English, would have bequeathed us. It is unnecessary to add that we speak of the translation by Dr. Anster;[12] and it were little, indeed, for us to say that Dr. Anster has given to the world a translation of *Faust* far and away the most finished and faithful of all the translations—it were little for us to state that no eulogium can do justice to its various and transcendant merits—but it will, we trust, be considered (at least by all who have read the German work) as the best praise that can be bestowed on it—that it is—and no emphasis can exaggerate the force that properly attaches to the words—*a translation of Faust*—a veritable and glowing image of its original. Of the other translators we have little to say. The merit of having accomplished the closest *literal* version certainly belongs to Mr. Blackie;[13] but this gentleman, though he manifests considerable power over language, appears to be deficient in rhythmical judgment; and, on the whole, his endeavour to "recast," as he says he wished to do, the original drama is scarcely a happy one. The Faustus of Lord Francis Egerton[14] *is* the Faustus of Lord Francis Egerton. We say nothing of its multiplied sins of omission and commission; for whatever the imperfections of the volume may be, they are more than counterbalanced by its excellences; but it is not Goethe—it is not a translation. Of the version by Mr. Syme[15] we shall merely observe that it is obviously inferior in general power to every one of the others; nor do we entertain a high opinion of that which the Honorable Mr. Talbot[16] has given to the world. It is but fair to state, however, that in all there occur from time to time passages of striking poetical beauty, the merit of which, as far as a felicitous mode of rendering sentiments from another language can confer merit, the severest criticism will not withhold from the translators.

Dr. Anster's version of the "Prologue in Heaven" has been deservedly applauded above that of any other translator; and, if we recollect well, the "Hymn of the Three Archangels," as rendered by him, has already been transferred to our pages. We take the liberty of again calling attention to this chaste and eloquent piece of—we had almost said—composition, by the side of which we place the translation of Mr. Blackie. Underneath we give Lord F. Egerton's version, and a fourth, which has not yet appeared.

ANSTER	BLACKIE
The three Archangels come forward.	*The three Archangels come forward.*

RAPHAEL.	RAPHAEL.

The sun, as in the ancient days,
  'Mong sister stars in rival song,
His destined path observes, obeys,
  And still in thunder rolls along:
New strength and full beatitude
  The angels gather from his sight,
Mysterious all—yet all is good,
  All fair as at the birth of light!

The Sun doth chime his ancient music.
  To brethren-spheres' contending song,
And, on his fore-appointed journey,
  With thunder-pace he rolls along.
Strength drink the angels from his glances,
  Though no one comprehend him may;
God's works of grandeur unconceived,
  As bright as on creation's day.

GABRIEL.	GABRIEL.

Swift, unimaginably swift,
  Soft spins the earth, and glories bright
Of mid-day Eden change and shift
  To shades of deep and spectral night.
The vexed sea foams—waves leap and moan,
  And chide the rocks with insult hoarse,
And wave and rock are hurried on,
  And suns and stars in endless course.

And swift, and swift, beyond conceiving,
  Spins Earth its self-revolving flight;
Alternates Paradisian brightness,
  With gloom of deep and fearful night,
Wide foams the sea in mighty currents,
  Beneath the rocks, with murmurs hoarse:
And rock and sea are onward hurried
  In one eternal circling course.

MICHAEL.	MICHAEL.

And winds with winds mad war maintain,
  From sea to land, from land to sea;
And heave round earth, a living chain
  Of interwoven agency.
Guides of the bursting thunder-peal,
  Fast lightnings flash with deadly ray,
While, Lord, with Thee thy servants feel
  Calm effluence of abiding day.

And storms loud rage with storms contending,
  From sea to land, from land to sea,
And weave around the globe unwearied
  A chain of deepest energy,
The lightning's desolation flameth
  Before the pealing thunder's way,
But still, O Lord, thine angels worship
  The soft revolving of thy day.

ALL.	THE THREE TOGETHER.

New strength and full beatitude
  The angels gather from thy sight;
Mysterious all, yet all is good,
  All fair as at the birth of light.

Strength drink the angels from thy glances,
  Though no one comprehend thee may;
Thy works of grandeur unconceived
  Are bright as on creation's day.

EGERTON

Song of the three Archangels.

RAPHAEL.

The sun his ancient hymn of wonder,
  Is pouring out to kindred spheres,
And still pursues, with march of thunder,
  His preappointed course of years.
Thy visage gives thy angels power,
  Though none its dazzling rays withstand,
And bright, as in their natal hour,
  Creation's dazzling realms expand.

GABRIEL.

And still the earth's enduring motion
  Revolves with uncomputed speed,
And o'er the chequered earth and ocean
  Darkness and light by turns succeed.
The billowy waste of seas is boiling
  From deep primeval rocks below,
Yet on their destined march are toiling
  The rocks that stand, the waves that flow.

MICHAEL.

The whirlwind and the storm are raging
  From sea to land, from land to main;
And adverse elements engaging,
  The trembling universe enchain.
The lightnings of the dread destroyer
  Precedes his thunders through the air,
Yet, at the nod of their employer,
  The servants of his wrath forbear.

CHORUS.

Thy visage gives thy angels power,
  Though none its dazzling rays withstand,
And bright, as in their natal hour,
  Creation's dazzling realms expand.

OURSELF

The three Archangels come forth.

RAPHAEL.

To frater-worlds the sun is pealing
  His choral roundelay of yore,
As, in his marked-out orbit wheeling,
  He tracks his thunderous course once more.
His glorious face, all else consuming,
  But lends the angels prouder might,
And lo! the eternal bowers are blooming
  As first they bloomed in Eden's light.

GABRIEL.

And circling, circling swift as lightning,
  Man's globe revolves in shifting show;
Now Heaven's own beams the scene are
  brightening,
  Now Night falls black on all below.
Around the rocks, with maddest motion,
  The toiling billows foam and curl;
Now rise the rocks, now rolls the ocean,
  In ever-sleepless wheel and whirl.

MICHAEL.

And tempest-voices shout their anger
  Round strand and main, from sea to shore.
And, answering Earth's appealing clangor,
  The roused-up Deep's recesses roar.
But though before the bolt career the
  Loosed lightnings in destroying might,
Thy ministers, O Lord! revere the
  Mild beauty of thy Day and Night.

THE THREE IN UNISON.

Thy glorious face, all else consuming,
  But lends the angels prouder power;
And lo! the eternal bowers are blooming
  As erst in Eden's primal hour.

On the superior merits of Dr. Anster's version we need not comment.

Mr. Blackie's resembles the original most—except in harmony. Lord F. Egerton's retains the double rhymes of the German and reads well, as far as euphony is concerned, but there is less character in it than in any of the others. "Though none its *dazzling* rays withstand," and "Creation's *dazzling* realms expand," are lines indicative of haste and heedlessness. "Yet on their destined *march* are toiling the rocks that *stand*" appears less German than Irish, and "at the nod of their employer" is forced and feeble. The first half of each stanza, however, especially of the third, is, we are bound to say, remarkably good.

* * * * * * * * *

But Goethe, though he rambled at times into the fields of the Marvellous, never looked for his happiest harvest in them. He felt himself on strange ground, for he loved the domains of Nature and Reality; and the statues which these twain had set up in the gallery of Time, were the gods before whom, from first to last, his idolatry—if we may so speak without irreverence—exhausted the greater portion of its fervour. Goethe appears to have been skilled in the languages of the East. But his acquaintance with these was not made available in administering to the popular appetite for those monstrous fictions with which the stores of Oriental literature abound. He has transferred to his own pages perhaps just as much of the minds of other men as was worthy of being made immortal. Everywhere he gives us the *tableaux vivans* of Man and Man's world—if not exactly as they are, at all events exactly as his eye took their dimensions. Some odd pages, indeed, smell so much more suspiciously of the Weimar, than of the Wonderful Lamp, that we read them twice over, before our doubts are altogether dissipitated. But all are alike genuine.

* * * * * * * * *

One objection that might be made to the poetry of Goethe, is, that though the morality of it, taken *cum grano salis*, answers, or might answer well enough, he seldom chooses to put it forward so prominently as to place it altogether within our reach. Like Pascal, he seems to think it requisite *presque toujours de tenir une pensée en arrière*.[17] He forbears, when he fancies he has painted his bird, to write under the painting—*This is a hawk*, but trusts to the discernment of all the ornithological to distinguish between it and a hernshaw. We suspect that the apprehension of being stigmatized as trite and formal may have been a greater bugbear for Goethe than he chose to acknowledge; and yet he knew, as well as any, that trite and formal writers vaunt a majority of readers, and are always on the safe side as far as intelligibility and straightforwardness originate a ground either for obtaining praise or securing sympathy. There is something, therefore, to fret for in his fastidiousness, or his fear, or whatever else we like to call it. This world, the generality of us at length find out, though "the best of all possible worlds,"[18] is not the wisest. *Les hommes*, remarks Voltaire, *réfléchissent peu; ils lisent avec négligence; ils jugent avec précipitation; et ils reçoivent les opinions comme on reçoit la monnoie, parce qu'elle est courante.*[19] In dealing with mankind, the most self-sufficient of us all should ever bear in mind the apophthegm of Bacon, that "every thing must be received in proportion to the measure of the recipient."[20] The moralist who proceeds upon the principle that instruction is a tangible article, a purchase-and-saleable commodity, that may be doled out at the rate of so many farthings per ounce, is absurd enough, but not more so than the mystic who writes Æsthetics for the unæsthetical, and who, if poetical, is dreamy, and if philosophical, is drowsy. It may be, however, that Goethe, as we have often thought, wrote less with a view to the wants of the age he lived in, than in the anticipation of an era when much that is now abstruse and clouded, as well in ethics as in metaphysics, shall become the subject of familiar inspection and analysis.

* * * * * * * * *

An imperfect acquaintance with the mannerism of Goethe might mislead into a belief that in many of his lesser lyrical productions he has left himself liable to be charged with slovenliness of composition, and now and then with a propensity to dilate upon very contemptible topics. But they who have studied him thoroughly run little risk of falling into such an error of judgment. Goethe sometimes treats philosophically questions which no exercise of intellectual art can render philosophical; but he is at any time far from degrading either himself or his subject: he may be obscure, perhaps impenetrable, but he is never clumsy, never weak, never wanting to his own conceptions; and though his principles are not always definitely developed, it is possible that they are susceptible of a definite development. As we have already observed, Goethe probably wrote more for an undeveloped Future than for his own era. He probably anticipated a period when words shall cease to be the lifeless and colorless instruments of Action which in many instances they now are; and when the images which Thought shall sculpture and send forth in silence, though they may "come like shadows," will not "so depart,"[21] but will stand each in its appropriate niche in the mart of the Universe, and promise a permanence defying decay or oblivion. Throughout his works we frequently stumble upon skeletons of thoughts whose gigantic and foreign aspect startles us, but which, we have no doubt, hands competent to the task will hereafter fill up with the flesh-and-blood essentials of vitality. It forms indeed, the great glory of this wonderful man, that his obscurity rarely strikes us as being other than veiled luminousness, and that we often learn more from it than from the meridian intelligibility of others; as in the blurred background of an antique and faded picture, the eye is apt to detect forms and resemblances which it seeks in vain where the colors burn brilliantly on the canvass. Even where his reasoning does not convince, *it always looks as though it ought to convince*; because, although you half suspect that his premises are arbitrary or fallacious, every successive link in the chain of his dazzling argument shines out in the day-beams of Truth with all the tangibility and lustre of the solid gold. Where he is in the right, he is in the right with such a palpable and peculiar obviousness that you seem to have already acquired a sort of guarantee against the possibility of being led into error by him elsewhere. Where his theory is illusive, you incline rather to distrust yourself than him—rather to question the sufficiency of your own judgment than the tenableness of any position he may have advanced. His unsurpassed equability, his perfect appreciation both of his own skill and the strength or weakness of his adversary, and the perspicacity with which his eye takes in at a glance all objects within its gaze, bear him victoriously onward, and he manages to achieve a conquest where a thousand contingencies would appear to menace him with defeat. If, after all, there be any thing essentially insignificant or ephemeral in his writings, it will, of course, sink to its proper level, and be forgotten, as it ought to be. Goethe himself would have been among the first to repudiate whatever was unworthy of being associated with his name—he would have counselled others to repudiate it.

> Laszt fahren hin das allzu Flüchtige;
>   Ihr sucht bei ihm vergebens Rath;
> In das Vergangnen lebt das Tüchtige;
>   Verewigt sich in schöner That.
>
> Und so gewinnt sich das Lebendige
>   Durch Folg' aus Folge neue Kraft;
> Denn die Gesinnung die Beständige
>   Sie macht allein den Menschen dauerhaft.
>
> So lost sich jene grosze Frage
>   Nach unserm zweiten Vaterland
> Denn das Beständige der ird'schem Tage
>   Verbürgt uns ewigen Bestand.[22]

ANTHOLOGIA GERMANICA.— NO. VI.
THE GERMAN FABULISTS.

GONE away from all of us for ever is the fine spirit of docility and simplicity that characterised our forefathers. Gone is the spirit that distinguished those days when, to enable a child to read, it was considered requisite to initiate him in the alphabet beforehand; and when a man who wished to discuss at large any particular subject, endeavoured, in the first place, to acquire some slender information with respect to it. It went,

"Nor cast one longing, lingering look behind,"[1]

when modern France, like the ancient Sphynx, arose to propound to the world that embarrassing riddle, Why Liberty should be the worst species of slavery, and Knowledge the densest ignorance; and, like the same Sphynx, destroyed all who were at a loss how to solve it. The memory of it—we mean of the spirit, not the riddle—may, indeed, still be cherished by some of us, and a faint conception of it may be formed by others; but the spirit itself has departed—has for ever forsaken the temple. Would that any exertion of ours could avail to conjure it back! That any sacrifice in our power to make were efficacious for the purpose! Had we Aladdin's lamp[2]— Gyges' ring[3]—the wishing-cap of Fortunatus[4]—Paganini's violin[5]—the lyre of Orpheus[6]—the collar of Moran[7]—the sword of Harlequin[8]— Prospero's wand[9]—St. Leon's *elixir vitæ*[10]—the finger of Midas[11]—the wings of Icarus[12]—the talisman of Camaralzaman[13]—the flying horse of Prince Firouz Schah,[14] there is no one of all the thirteen we should shrink from bartering for that which we have lost. But the contingency may not be: we but succumb to bootless regrets—

The Beautiful is vanished, and returns not![15]

and policy, philosophy and philanthropy alike dictate to us a reverence for the existing age, and a due regard to its moral and literary wants and interests.

Are we asked, however, why we assert that this spirit no longer tabernacles among us? Alas! is not its absence but too manifest? Have not the records of those years wherein Lafontaine and Gay[16] amused and amazed mankind, become so dulled with dust, that even the latest Patent Amber Spectacles are insufficient to aid us in deciphering the page? Are not those writers superseded by Beranger[17] and Byron? Is not, in a word, FABLE a dead letter? Fiction, it is true, still survives to delight or confound us; and its field (always arable ground) continues, we admit, to be sedulously cultivated by the extensive circle of our acquaintance. But, largely as our acquaintance may deal in Fiction—and some of them are no inexpert masters and mistresses of their business—we are still compelled to deplore the disappearance of our venerable friend, Fable. Aesop,[18] Casti,[19] La Mothe,[20] Phædrus,[21] Hagedorn,[22] Lafontaine, Yriarte,[23] Gay, Weiss,[24] Karamsin,[25] and nine hundred, four score and ten others, making a total of one thousand—these, all these—a mighty host—have perished as silently, but as utterly, as that of Sennacherib.[26] And if we be justified in adding, with Schiller,

> Alles Schöne,
> Alles Hohe nahmen sie mit fort;
> Alle Farben, alle Lebenstöne,
> Und uns blieb nur das entseelte Wort,[27]

is not our conclusion a correct one, that Simplicity and the true Spirit of Humility have ceased to dwell upon the earth?

We thus, as it were, confound Fable with the Spirit of Simplicity. Be it so. And henceforth we are satisfied that both phrases shall be deemed convertible. Fable, then, is lost to us. It exists but as a tradition. *Fuit Ilium.*[28] We need not go on to repeat, without end, our sorrow for this. It ought to suffice that we have made solemn profession of it once. Let us be believed.

And we do really feel in our heart of hearts that we ought to be believed. There was in the Departed much that was estimable beyond emeralds—

> Much that we love, and more that we admire,
> And *nought* that we abhor—[29]

much that gave it a great advantage over every other *genre* of poetry. It was considerably shorter than the Epic, and therefore considerably better. It was didactic in its nature. It embodied a reasonable share of small incident. According to Voltaire, *c'est précisement par des détails que la poësie nous charme;*[30] and in Fable we had details in abundance. Then it was acceptable to all classes and castes. Swift's Laputan architect[31] projected a peculiar mode of building a house: the workmen were to commence with the roof and labour downwards to the foundation. In like manner the nobler kinds of poetry must address themselves in the first place to minds of an elevated order, and must sink deeply into these before they can be made to accord with the conceptions of meaner understandings, or cease to be "caviare to the million."[32] But with Fable the case was contrariwise. This interested at once the natural feelings of the mere human heart; it spoke before all to the mass of mankind; its appeal was to *le bon sens qui court les rues*;[33] and the remark of Quintilian, that Fable produced its chief effect upon brutish and ignorant persons,[34] was, in our opinion, founded on correct observation, and is, if properly understood, powerful testimony in its favour. Not that it went a–begging for any man's testimony. Like the late William Cobbett,[35] though in a separate sense, it was its own best panegyrist. But, upon all accounts, its memory merits to be hallowed among us. And as nothing abandons us without leaving a substitute—as Love but yields to Indifference—as when the fire dies we retain at least the ashes—as the decease of the conqueror is the signal for the erection of a statue of bronze in his place—as when the golden lyre ceases to vibrate the "quicksilver small-talk"[36] that had been checked in its course, again flows—as Aesop's old lady, when the cask was exhausted, still felt revived by the effluvium that issued from it[37]—as daylight, when it goes, commends us to the "majesty of darkness"[38]—as beauty is succeeded by rouge and wrinkles— so for the reality of Fable itself—the being—and whether this be a modality, a quiddity, or an entity, we leave Leibnitz[39] to settle—we have got all the consolatory and luxuriant reminiscences associated with it; and long, long may they continue to shed a melancholy charm over our private studies and solitary reveries!

But it is time for us to begin the business of our Anthology. Our present object is to submit to the English reader some specimens of the German mode of fable-making.

Germany, a century ago, like every other country in the earlier epochs of its literature, was famous for the number of its fabulists. If no one of these attained to any great eminence in his *métier*, they all, nevertheless, received the homage of the age, and purchased an applause now sought for in vain by men of much superior talent, and the value of which, moreover, was then enhanced by the consciousness that it was the result of genuine kindliness of feeling for services rendered to the heart and the understanding. None of them were poets; they never betrayed any divine intoxication of soul; they shewed neither nerve nor verve; they wanted power, pathos, passion; they had no terrific force of delineation; they did not know how to be eloquent, and yet they pleased those for whom they wrote—we will even add that they please *us*. If we were to account for the satisfaction they give us by saying that they are *natural*, we should, perhaps, compress into one phrase all that can be advanced in explanation of the secret of their influence. They are natural—natural in their humour, natural in their tastes, natural in their language, in their incident, in their characters, in every thing. The sly dash of satire, too, with which they spice, now and then, the insipidity of ordinary narrative, is another recommendation of them in our eyes. We should have liked them without it; but we like them all the better with it. We are honest in making this declaration—let us not be regarded as the less humane or kind-hearted.

Our first sample is from Gellert.

The Traveller.

Of old, ere History began
   Her chronicles, we understand
   There somewhere lay a certain land
Wherein was nowhere found a man
Who did not stutter when he talked
And did not hobble when he walked;
And he who stuttered most in talking,
And he who hobbled most in walking,
Was held, by Custom's ancient law,
   Pro tem.[40] the leader of the fashion.
A traveller, wandering thither, saw
   With great surprize and some compassion
This odd and *outré*[41] state of things,
Surpassing all imaginings.
Quoth he, 'Twere charity to set
   This crazy folk a good example:
   My opportunities are ample,
And doubtless I'll reform them yet.
So, forth he went, and up and down
Began to promenade through town
At ease: the people followed after
   In rushing groups, and as they eyed
Him, all burst into roars of laughter.
   "O, G—G—Gemini!" they cried;
"Re—m—m—mark his g—g—gait!
He w—w—w—w—walks quite straight!"
Our foreigner, beholding this his
   Peripatetical experiment
   Received with such unseemly merriment
As groans and laughter, sneers and hisses,
Conceived it was his bounden duty
   To try and talk them into seeing
The moral and æsthetic beauty

Of walking like a human being.
"My friends," he said, "you all are wrong
And I am right: *you* limp along,
I move correctly. Don't you see
That every man among you hobbles?
Henceforth take pattern, then, by me."
　　Alack! the laughter but redoubles.
"Hear him!" they cried; "h—hear him utter
His words!—he c—c—cannot stutter!
Yet he pre—t—t—tends to teach
　　Us how to u—u—use our legs,
　　And b—b—b—b—b—b—begs
We will a—d—d—dopt *his* speech!"

Covered with mockery and disgrace,
Our friend was fain to hide his face
And leave the land. I see, alas!
　　He mentally remarked, that when
　　We seek to serve our fellow-men
　　We must not vaunt our own humanity
　　Or skill, or else we wound their vanity.
Self is the idol of the mass.

We like this fable. Yet Gellert, we suspect, was not aware how inartificial the construction of it really is. The details want congruity. People may be blind to their own faults; but they are never found united in sentiment upon the propriety of condemning as faults the accomplishments and excellencies of others. Passing this over, how is it made manifest that the traveller could have conferred any real benefit on the absurd people in the fable? Here is a country all whose inhabitants limp in their gait and stammer in their speech. A stranger comes among them who neither limps nor stammers. He tries to bring them over to his own mode of talking and walking, and he fails. Perhaps he ought to have failed. We assert that his first care should have been to ascertain whether the people themselves were not fully satisfied with their own proficiency in the arts of peripateticalism and oratory. There is an old proverb, that no one but the wearer knows where the shoe pinches. We may add, as an appendix to this proverb, that when the shoe pinches, the pinched will be apt to take it off of his own accord, and without the suggestion of a prompter. The traveller, we fancy, might have set himself very much at his ease when he saw that the people whom he pitied did not pity themselves. But he, forsooth, was a reformer. So will Brougham[42] and *clique* try to force their Useful (?)

Knowledge-books upon the attention of a people who care not a hazel-nut for their books, and are much happier without them. The intellectual portion of the community being the reflecting portion, it is odd that one of their commonest errors should be that of presuming that all the men, women and children in the world are possessed, or ought to be possessed, of the same tastes and capacities as those which have been bestowed on themselves. We like the fable, however, and, as we do like it, we give a second.

[Here follows "The Green Ass", of which these are the concluding lines:]

> However silly anything may be,
> If new, 'tis sure to catch immediately.
> In vain philosophers declaim;
> The world has always been the same.
> Experience of his folly is the mirror
> Wherein each man must wait to see his error:
> Nor need our lecturers idly fancy
>   That all depends on a didactic tone:
> This is no part of Nature's necromancy—
>   She works improvements but by Time alone.

Art, however, works improvements chiefly by the printing-press; and wherever this can be employed in the removal of unhappiness, or the abolition of such errors of opinion or conduct as affect our welfare, we give it a decided preference to the doing of nothing at all. Moreover, we really like to be busy and bustling. Godwin observes, in his "Thoughts on Man," that if it should enter into his head to kill an individual with whom he might be quietly conversing in his (Godwin's) own house, one of his motives would be a desire of bestirring himself, "a wish to be alive and active."[43] The killing of an acquaintance as a resource against the possible contingency of a yawn is a *recherché* idea; but in sober truth we abominate all inaction as heartily as Godwin.

> To act, to suffer, may be nobly great;
> But Nature's hardest lesson is—to wait.[44]

Instead of standing by the river-side until the waters had passed by, we would rather occupy ourselves, if we had nothing better to do, in ladling them, like St. Augustine's dream-child,[45] into pitchers. There is only one situation in which we should be contented to trust to the progress of Time for the amelioration of our condition. That situation is the one in which

Beckford, author of Vathek, has placed King Solomon in the Hall of Eblis.[46]
We do admit, that under circumstances like those by which that king was
constrained,

> levius fit patientia
> Quidquid corrigere est nefas.[47]

But this is an extreme, not to say extra-mundane case—and so *revenons à
nos moutons.*[48]

[Here follows "The Cuckoo", of which these are the concluding lines:]

> "I wonder the dunderheads aren't ashamed!
> Well, then, I protest, as they give me no praise
> I'll trumpet myself to the end of my days."
> So saying, away to the forest he flew,
> And ever since then has been crying *Cuckoo!*

Self-preservation, say moralists, is the first law of Nature. Self-
aggrandizement, proclaims all experience, is the second. Did Professor
Gellert, then, mean to insinuate that where an individual conceives himself
defrauded of his equitable proportion of eulogy, he is reduced to the rigid
necessity of becoming his own Chief Trumpeter? If he did, the only
observation we shall make is, that we do not consider him more than half
as reprehensible as we should do if our morality were doubly as austere as
it really is. Not, however, that we are by any means his apologist in this
instance. But we cannot overlook the many admirable lessons of wisdom
inculcated by his fables generally. We should be loth to exhibit the isolated
brick we have taken from the monument of his genius and industry as a
sample of what the monument is. Besides, Gellert does not stand
altogether single in this oblique mode of recommending a man to take as
much care of his own interests as he thinks proper. Aesop, indeed, was
always immaculate. La Mothe we allow to be irreproachable. But, to say
nothing of Guichard[49] and Dorat,[50] Lafontaine does not upon all occasions
come out of the crucible seven times purified.[51] For the transgressions of
Pilpay,[52] too, we are at times compelled to mourn; and whenever we see him
stagger upon the level ground of his own philosophy we mourn the more
because he is our friend. There is a sad fable of his on record, which, as it
is short, we shall communicate. A certain rabbit had the misfortune to get
into debt to a large extent. He owed to an ox, the proprietor of a meadow,
the charges of a twelvemonth's board; he also owed more or less to all his
neighbours. Whenever he stirred abroad he was sure to be worried and

badgered by a tribe of creditors, who tracked his whereabouts like the shadow of destiny. "Pay me for the grass," cried one; "Pay me for the bran!" said another; "Pay me! Pay me! Pay me!" was the incessant demand. Of course the rabbit was greatly perplexed; he could not tell what to resolve on. At last, one day, as he was walking in a field, he saw a dead gazelle on the ground. Ah! said he to himself, this is just the thing. He flayed the gazelle and drew the skin over himself, adjusting it about his body and head as well as he could. By and by some of his creditors came up. "Ah! my poor gazelle," said every one, "my poor creature, how small and thin thou art grown! What has happened to thee?" "Alas!" said the other, weeping, "it has all come of the rabbit. I interrupted him in some sorceries; he cursed me on the spot, and I withered away immediately. My friends, may Heaven defend you from vexing the rabbit!" "Do you hear what he says?" said one to another. "The rabbit cursed him, and he has withered. For the love of Heaven, let us not do anything to vex the rabbit, lest he curse us also!"

The moral of this fable we take to be that a clever man has it always in his power to outwit his creditors.

* * * * * * * * *

ANTHOLOGIA GERMANICA.—NO. VII.
KERNER'S LYRICAL POEMS.

W E grow every day fonder and fonder of the German Muse. True, we did, in a former paper, reprobate that practice of "darkening counsel by words without knowledge",[1] in which some Transalpine poets and philosophers have surpassed not only *the* Man of Uz[2] in the ancient days, but every man of us in the modern. "We have," as Burke flatteringly announces of his anti-Gallican contemporaries, "real hearts of flesh and blood beating in our bosoms,"[3] and cannot afford a cordial welcome to those flitting and gibbering phantoms of sentiment that visit us in a garb, compared with which the Coat of Darkness in the Nursery-story[4] seems a garment for the Angel Gabriel. But our dislike for the style Germanesque has never interfered with our admiration of the style German. *Vive le sublime* was always—who dares deny it?—our ineraseable *devise*. And at worst we are not bound to despise all that we cannot understand. Neither must the delinquents we reprehended be condemned *en masse*. The stepping-stone that stands midway between the Sublime and the Misty should not be placed upon a level with that which separates the Sublime and the Ridiculous.[5] The last infallibly prostrates a stalker, no matter how good an understanding he may have been on with his stilts the moment before; the first only elevates him to the clouds. The Misty is, in fact, as it strikes us, but a loftier species of the Sublime. Where one begins, and the other ends, it may be difficult to state; but each will be uniformly found to have some affinity with the other. Nothing is perhaps wholly and hopelessly unintelligible, if our indolence or incapacity do not make it so. The key to every enigma, we should recollect, is only hidden, not lost. The treasures of the Great Deep are now garnered up in caverns, to the end that when at last laid bare for inspection, their magnificence may the more irresistibly dazzle all eyes. The retirement of "Glorious Apollo"[6] behind a curtain of cloud superinduces a temporary eclipse; but the heavens are not the less blue beneath. In other words, Poetry, about which so much has been said, at such great length, to such little purpose, is at all times— Poetry; and where its "serious sayings darken to the mystical,"[7] we shall not quarrel with those who refer a portion of the obscurity to the limitedness of the reader's faculties. As Poetry we hail it, welcome it, and pay it homage; and though we may regret to hear it speak a language unfamiliar to our ear, we must ever recognize with delight the thrilling tone whose magic Poetry from the beginning of ages has monopolized.

The truth is—for in the end we are all driven to the truth—that though the German poets are in too many instances chargeable with strange obscurities of expression, there is another and a worse fault which, since we have begun to study them more intimately, we trace even more generally throughout their writings. This fault, for want of a fitter name, we shall call *prosiness.* But a definition of German prosiness, as it is found in poetry, is, be it noted, one of those things that a single dash of the pen is apt to accomplish more hurriedly than happily. How to convey an adequate notion of it we do not know. Stupidity is one thing, and senility is another; while dreaminess lays claim to an individuality distinct from that of either of the twain. Now the peculiarity of the German poet, and that which renders him very insufferable is, not so much that he manages to effect an amalgamation of all the three, as that he dishes up the gallimaufry[8] with a ludicrous air of solemnity, and lays it down before you after the fashion of a suburban ale-draper,[9] whose "Pay on delivery" is a notification that he considers you are getting to the full as good as you brought. One is reminded of the Barmecide in the Arabian tale,[10] who presided over a sumptuous banquet of empty platters; or, more appropriately, of Chamaheewah, King of the Tonga Islands, while strutting up and down before his court in the old, red, lead-buttoned coat of a common English soldier. Our own literature—thanks even to our dulness!—has nothing like to this. Dr. Johnson we believe it was who ridiculed the idea of throwing the words:

Come, lay your knife and fork across your plate,[11]

into the form of an iambic line. But even the sickliest English nambypambyism is remarkable for a *keeping*, a coherence, a congruity of parts, which, though insufficient to rescue it from contempt, prevents it from shocking as a monstrosity. The German, on the other hand, is just as remarkable for the absence of this coherence. Both are bad; but although if we were required to patronise one or the other we should so far deviate from the venerable custom of "choosing the lesser of two evils," as to select neither, we confess we should readily damn the second to a deeper gulf of oblivion than we should the first. *A bas la bagatelle, mais au diable la sottise.*[12]

Let us not be misunderstood. We cannot object to the employment of prose-language in poetry, where it is in character, or may be essential to the integrity of the poem. All that we insist upon is, that we have a right to repudiate it where the poet, in the plenitude of his emptyheadedness, tries to pass it off upon us as the most felicitous of all modes for the development of poetical conceptions. And is not the imposture now rather too common in

Germany? Is it or is it not true, true to the letter, that more than a moiety of all the productions of all the German poets are beneath criticism—that they are a stigma upon the national taste—that they bear about the same resemblance to poetry which a collection of visages chiselled out of a timber-log by some bungling booby, less accustomed to the chisel than to the pick-axe, might bear to the "human face divine"[13] of Greece or Asia? With great confidence we assert that it is; and we challenge contradiction from any literary authority in existence. We allude not now to those outrageous violations of the Aristotelian canon—the standing reproach of German literature—which everybody has heard of and nobody palliates. These are diagnostics peculiar to diseased intellect, and nothing besides; and a reflecting mind will no more find fault with them than with the ravings of lunacy. They are attempts to illustrate whatever is most senseless in theory, or least tangible in principle, and, of course, to be uniform, *must* be absurd. We speak merely of the comparative dryness and insipidity of German poetry generally. And how dry, how insipid this is, let those tell who having studied it *au fond*, are best qualified to pass judgment on it. Common-places that the ear grows intolerant of in conversation,—driftless paradoxes—clumsy descriptions—lack-a-daisiacal lamentations—rhodomontade—puerility—nonsense—these are the stock in trade of the German poet; and if any one wonder that his business should ever be a flourishing one, let it be borne in mind that he, the same poet, is the exception to the rule that "a prophet hath no honor in his own country,"[14]—and this not, of course, because of his own deserts, but because of his *lieber Deutschland's*[15] immemorial proneness to patronize all sorts of common-places, driftless paradoxes, lack-a-daisiacal lamentations, rhodomontade, puerility and nonsense. Were it otherwise, where were the six-compound-epithetted Tiedge,[16] with his baffling nouns, about as tangible as shadows; or Hölty, who, whenever we indulge in a rural stroll with him, grows enthusiastic upon horseponds and haystacks? How had it fared with Klopstock, whose feeble phraseology is only the more pitiable for its feebleness, because for a space it dupes ear and eye with a semblance of force? Or with Bürger the celebrated, whose platitude, save in two or three of his ballads and lyrical pieces, is alas! unendurable? Or what had become of those twin-giants, Werner and Schubart; seeing that neither of them knows what to do with his club, unless he sit down upon the highway and split pebbles with it? Or of Tieck, who, rich and imaginative beyond all praise as his prose is, was the first writer whose poems ever helped us to a perfect conception of the meaning of the word *twaddle*? Or of Novalis[17]—but no—erroneous as the views of Novalis were with regard to the nature of poetry, we cannot doubt that if he had lived, his comprehensive understanding would have corrected them. Time will yet gather the ashes of Novalis in an urn apart: in the meantime let not common hands presume to weigh them.

Schiller, in one of his ballads, introduces a man who takes a human head out of a wallet, or some such receptacle, and another who guts a fish and finds a ring in its entrails. Where poetry is based upon historical incident, it may be said, the minuteness of detail becomes a thing of course. True; but why create the necessity that makes it a thing of course? When a Solon[18] puts on a fool's cap he must shake the bells: but men of sense will wonder why he put on the cap at all.

Heine, lacking matter for a stanza, goes out to inspect the sea and sky, and then and there, bursting into a Della Cruscan[19] extacy, he declares that the waves are like *green horses* with silver manes; and that the "eternal sun," in the "eternal blue" above his head is "the Rose of Heaven, the fierily-blooming." *Ex pede Herculem*[20]—we need not multiply examples. But this is the average tone of German poetry when it treats of suns, and seas, and soforth.

In a ditty by the Baron de la Motte Fouqué a saunterer, with his chin upon the top of a wall, accosts a clump of trees in a garden, and begs to be informed whether they can prepare a commodious place beneath their shade for him to repose in, forasmuch as he is "a life-weary man". The reply of the trees is, that they have good reason to bewail old times, because they no longer enjoy in the garden the same health and spirits that fell to their lot when they were blithe and young in the forest. Never suppose, good reader, that here a snake lurks in the grass; the pen of la Motte Fouqué is innocent of satire. The colloquy appears modelled upon that described in the *Merry Wives of Windsor*: "I went up to her and called *Mum*; she cried *Budget*."[21] But the Baron, no doubt, before he put it in type, was at the trouble of ascertaining how far trees are in the habit of shifting their positions to suit the convenience of loungers, and also to what extent a man tired of life may be refreshed by sitting under a sycamore.

Ludwig Uhland is the most distinguished poet now alive in Germany. We have opened a volume, as broad as it is long, of his works, at a little poem entitled *Einkehr*, viz: *Turning-in*, or Stopping as a guest at a tavern. Of the same the following is a correct literal translation:

> With a tavern-keeper, wonderfully mild,
>   Staid I lately as guest:
> His sign was a Golden Apple
>   On a long bough.
>
> It was the good Apple-tree
>   At which I took up my quarters;
> With sweet food and fresh froth

Did he nourish me well.
There came into his greenhouse
   Many lightwinged guests;
They tripped it freely, and banquetted,
   And sang to the best of their ability.

I found a sweet repose-giving bed
   On delicate, green mats:
The tavern-keeper covered me himself
   With his cool shadow.

I asked him what the reckoning was;
   And he shook his head:
Blessings on him always
   From hat-crown to shoe-sole!

"Do you know, you ignorant woman," asks Mons. Jourdain of his wife in Molière's *Bourgeois Gentilhomme*, "do you know what it is that I am talking at this moment, what it is that I have been talking ever since I opened my mouth?" "Yes, certainly; downright balderdash," answers the lady. "Not at all, you stupid being," exclaims her husband: "it is *prose*: I have been talking *prose* the whole day to you. Every thing we say must be either poetry or prose: whatever is not prose is poetry and whatever is not poetry is prose."[22] Nothing can be clearer. Uhland might get by heart the valuable aphorism of Mons. Jourdain with vast advantage to his future labours. But what is the gist of the five stanzas we have quoted? Or were they perhaps produced at the early age of six? There is no prefatory announcement saying so. What is the gist of them? If any body be but good enough to tell us we shall feel thankful, and pour "blessings on him always from hat-crown to shoe-sole".

Tieck puzzles us yet more. Look, for example, at his little piece, *Der Wanderer*.

In the rush of winds on a stilly night (!)
   Goes forth a wanderer.
He sighs, and weeps, and treads *so* gingerly!
   And calls to the stars—
My bosom heaves; my heart is heavy;
   In silent loneliness,
The Whence and the Whither unknown to me,
   I pass on through joy and sorrow.
Ye little golden stars,
Ye remain for ever distant from me,
         Distant, distant,

And ah! I confided in you *so* gladly!
Thereupon something tinkles round about him;
 And the night grows brighter;
Already he feels his heart not *so* heavy.
 He thinks he has lately awakened.
O Man! thou art far from and near to us,
 But alone thou art not.
Wert thou to confide in us thine eye would see
 Often our stilly light.
We, little golden stars,
Are not for ever distant from thee.
   Gladly, gladly
Do the stars think of thee.

But enough of this maudlin drivel.

Altogether the prosiness of German poetry may be regarded as the unsightliest blotch upon the surface of that poetry. Tell not this in Leipsic—publish it not in the streets of Stutgard[23]—but believe it nevertheless. If the Germans, for the credit of their literature, be anxious to get rid of such an eye-sore, they must by all means discourage the further disfigurations of the blotchers. They must give countenance to none but men of lucid, and stern, and straightforward intellect, who are capable not only of thinking, but of thinking *severely*, and who possess, moreover, the power of making such a display of their thoughts before the world as neither they nor the world need be ashamed of. When such men alone are popular through Germany, Germany will, properly speaking, be a poetical nation. Until then she may solace herself with the consciousness that the dreamers and dawdlers she patronises have already acquired an illustrious reputation at home, and will acquire the same reputation abroad, as long as nobody knows anything more about them than their names.

But how happens it that the taste of the German public should not have long since decided upon the applicability of this or that subject, of these materials or those, to the purposes of poetry? The question is naturally asked, and easily answered. The German public have never cared to pronounce any decision upon the matter. In the earlier stages of their advancement in literature they were notoriously incompetent to pronounce any. Throughout the entire of the seventeenth century, those classes who were at all distinguished from the crowd by intellect or education, were marshalled under opposing literary leaders, no one of whom ever understood what it was that he was doing, excepting whenever he tilted against and overthrew an adversary. For a great portion of the eighteenth the contest among the combatants was a struggle to determine whether the English or the French were to be considered as the models for Germans; just as if the shadow of a necessity existed that men in possession of a copious and vigorous language should hire foreign prompters to show them in what way the obvious principles of common sense and poetical beauty were to be developed through the medium of it. And today, though the progress of mental cultivation has achieved much, and though reviews and reviewers abound in the land, the people of Germany are too indolent to interest themselves in a question, the settlement of which, judging from the past, may, to be sure, appear to all but the enthusiastic utterly hopeless. They take what is given them, and take it satisfied and gratified, for they can get nothing better, and, were they even to get something better, they would not at once perceive the advantage. The system, it must be allowed, though it has no tendency to extend the celebrity of the poet, is agreeable and accommodating enough, so far as his immediate interests are concerned. Not he, but his translator is to be commiserated. Most to be commiserated of all is his English translator, who, having the severest judges in Europe for his critics, is often reduced to the necessity of either making himself ridiculous by his desperate fidelity, or criminal by his departures from it, however marvellously these may improve the original—as in five instances out of six they do, and by a process of no more magical skill than is involved in the substitution of brilliant and elevated sentiments for plain and stupid ones.

The indolence we have spoken of as characterising the German public must of course react upon the German poet. It must in a great measure paralyse in himself all incentives to extraordinary exertion. If his purchasers are contented with the Mediocre, with the Paltry even, why should he tire his spirits and exhaust his energies in endeavouring to inoculate them with a reverence for the Transcendant? Motives to the perpetration of such folly as this are hardly ever sufficiently numerous under the circumstances. The German poet may not be always behindhand in a desire to lead universal opinion captive. But applause is so very easily attainable a jewel in his country that he never dreams of paying a higher price for it than his neighbours pay. He would rather be simply praised to the skies for dipping his pen a dozen times a day in the inkstand, than lauded to the tenth heaven[24] for dipping it a hundred times a day. His ambition and love of ease enter into a mutual compromise of principle, and the public are the dupes of the compact. Such a *pococurante*[25] spirit as his may seem to be enviable. It is despicable. In contrasting the condition of the German poet with that of the English we must acknowledge that the genuine and sterling advantage abides with the English. The German poet is hugged and fondled out of his proper independence. He is beslavered with the slime of popular adulation, until he becomes a spectacle for the pity of the rational. The English poet is left to himself. He is cast upon his own resources. He is compelled to make head against all obstacles; and his power to annihilate those obstacles is made, and fitly made, the test of his genius. The consequence is that he either attains eminence and celebrity, or is thrown down, trampled on and forgotten, as Nature intended. It is all (among us) just as it ought to be. There is no error more decided than that of supposing that a mind of a great and original tone requires what is called encouragement or patronage. On the contrary, such a mind should voluntarily erect an impassable barrier between its own operations and any support that others might be inclined to tender it. All support of the kind, like that which the ivy affords to the oak, would, in fact, have a latent tendency to impair its vigorousness. Popular favour too frequently bereaves its idol of that freedom of thought without which it is impossible for any man to calculate upon the ability of accomplishing an enduring benefit for his fellow-men. It is like the Magnetic Mountain in the Persian Tale,[26] which mariners hailed at a distance with delight, but which, as they approached more and more within the sphere of its influence, drew out from their ship all its nails and clench-bolts, and thus left it to drift or founder. And if the pinnace of the German poet, after living its hour in the sunshine, goes down and is seen no more, where lies the wonder? We know where the blame lies.

It may be inferred from what we have said that we are dissatisfied with ourselves for having undertaken these Anthologia. But we have always considered any deprecation of censure for our own attempts to be quite out of the question. The entire weight of the blame rests upon the authors from whom we versify. We cannot, like the experimentalist in Gulliver,[27] undertake to extract a greater number of sunbeams from a cucumber than it is in the habit of yielding. Beyond the mere ability to classify, the discernment necessary for selecting and rejecting, there is neither labour nor knowledge that we will submit to be tasked for. Still we uniformly do the best we can both for ourselves and our originals. The maker of the volume now before us, for instance, may hold no very exalted rank among the poets of his native land. He is an imitator of the *very* imitable Uhland,—a pupil also of the Matthissonian[28] school—a lover, that is, of Nature, sparrows and trochaics. But it is our business to cast a veil over his blemishes, and bring forward nothing but his excellences, or what we presume to be such.

* * * * * * * * *

"Kerner", says Bernays,[29] "is a lyric poet in the true sense of the word. A feeling of the gentlest and most amiable kind predominates in all his poems, while he skims but lightly over the external objects of his muse, whether in joy or sorrow." Very good; but we prefer elevated and healthy feelings to "gentle" and "amiable" ones. In the greater number of these poems Kerner does little else than weep, listen to birds and brooks, hide himself in hedges, and apostrophise the zodiac. His *Dichtungen* may be said to be made up of an aggregate collection of *Thränen, Vögel, Blumen, Bäche,* and *Sterne,* with here and there a *Grab*[30] to bury himself in; for he dies off six or eight times, and of course retreats into a sarcophagus on each occasion, until he thinks it time to come out again and exhibit himself as large as life to his acquaintance. Kerner is a great favorite with the good people of Suabia; but he ought to recollect that poetry has no more necessary connexion with graves, birds, and tear-dropping, than it has with pillow-cases or potato-ridges. Its business is to enshrine great sentiments and superb delineations in the eternal crystal of a peculiar form of expression. The form may subsist where the sentiments and delineations are wanting, but its value will be upon a par with that of the casket when the jewel is absent. There are a few such caskets up and down through this book.

* * * * * * * * * *

Most people besides Kerner make pretensions to the faculty of dreaming; but we have never yet had the happiness to meet with any one who knew how to dream properly. For ourselves we lament to state that the Rip-Van-Winklish[31] soundness of our slumbers for eleven hours out of the twenty-four effectually prevents us from dreaming at all. We are not excitable even by opium, though we have repeatedly devoured stupendous quantities of that drug—and we now begin to despair of ever becoming a vision-seer. Once, and once only in the course of our life did Somnus[32] mount guard so negligently on the citadel of our imagination as to allow Morpheus[33] to enter it; but oh! that was a glorious moment, when we beheld Stamboul arise before our mind's eye in all its multifarious gorgeousness, glittering with mosques, kiosks, minarets, temples, turrets, and the rest of them! We surveyed them with extacy. We knew that we were dreaming, and that we might perpetrate any devilment with impunity. "Here, to all appearance, we are," we exclaimed; "the streets are redolent with life around us; the firm earth is resonant under our boot—the sun hath a saffron, but clear brightness in Heaven—and yet all this is the merest sham—for we are at this moment at home in our own bedchamber, a thousand miles from hence. What is to withhold us, if we please, from annihilating this proud city by the breath of our nostrils? First, however, let us signalize ourselves in some less startling way." Our attention was by-

and-by attracted by a colossal pillar, inscribed with sentences from the Dutch poets. How absurd! thought we; this must not be,—and exerting our volition, the pillar disappeared. A moment afterwards, however, we recollected the peculiar prerogatives of a dreamer's imagination; and we smiled. A man then came by, bestriding a rhinoceros. This time we were not to be hoaxed; and we merely demanded of the rhinoceros whether he was going to hunt. "Following the horn, at least," answered the rhinoceros; and we laughed so intemperately at this piece of wit that death appeared for a time almost inevitable. In the midst of our convulsions a Spahi[34] approached us, and asked us, in English, if we were not the scoundrel who had picked his portmanteau an hour before of a diamond tobacco-box. "Go—haw! haw! haw!—to the devil," we replied, half suffocated. In an instant he cocked and levelled his carbine. "Do your worst, non-entity!" said we; "we are—ho! ho! ho!—sound asleep." But though his piece continued levelled he seemed irresolute whether to pull the trigger or not; and we, profiting by his apparent indecision, marched away unimpeded, and strode into a cloth-bazaar. Forthwith from an interior apartment advanced to meet us, with a curiously convolved chibouque[35] in hand, an old Mussulman, who, after a salaam, enquired our business. In the meantime we had cast our eyes upon a juggler's garb, and were determined that it should leave the bazaar in our company. We moreover decided upon paying the owner nothing, and withering him to powder by a look, if he murmured. "But, perhaps," we observed aloud, "it may be as well to preclude the practicability of murmurs;" and as we spoke we seized the twisted chibouque and pitched it to a distance of some twenty yards. We were then proceeding to put our pulverising project into effect; when to our unbounded amazement the fellow rushed upon us, and grappled with us, seizing us by the coat-collar, while he shouted for help most lustily. This was too good. We burst into a horselaugh. Our captor, however, still maintained his gripe, and at length, shifting

From gay to grave, from lively to severe,[36]

we grew stern. "How dare you," we exclaimed—"*you*, the creature of our imagination—the production of a temporary attack of night-mare, brought on by an extra quantum of cheese and claret—the child of our stomach—the begotten of our phantasy—how dare *you*, a pseudo-being, who have never had existence, *you* a make-believe, a bull-beggar, an unreality, a humbug, a nobody—how dare you assume the privileges of vitality and substantiality? Grovel in the dust at our feet this moment, handful of rubbish!—Down!". And extricating ourselves by a violent effort, we lifted our clenched dexterhand, and were about, probably, to inflict a ruinous wound upon the bedpost, when Mussulman, bazaar, city and all melted away into thin air, leaving nothing behind but the remembrance of a dream, which Dr. Macnish,[37] in his next edition of the "Philosophy of Sleep" is welcome to transfer to his pages for a trifling gratuity.

* * * * * * * * *

There are three stanzas in this volume, one addressed to Kepler,[38] one to Schubart, and one to Frischlin.[39] We shall...give the third in the Kernerian tongue,—as an apt illustration of what we have called the style Germanesque.

Frischlin.

Ihn schlossen sie in starre Felsen ein,
   Ihn, dem zu eng der Erde weite Lande.
Doch er, voll Kraft, zerbrach den Felsenstein,
   Und liesz sich abwärts am unsichern Bande.
Da fanden sie im bleichen Mondenschein
   Zerschmettert ihn, *zerrissen die Gewande.*
Weh! Muttererde, dasz mit linden Armen
Du ihn nicht auffingst, schützend, voll Erbarmen.[40]

We knew, some years ago, a worthy citizen, who, whenever he got upon his legs to speak in his club-room, always, by some unaccountable fatality, broke down after the fifth sentence—generally in the midst of a Demosthenic exordium, which made the failure appear the queerer—and remained for the rest of the night lost in a dense fog of tobacco-smoke. Somewhat akin to his case is often that of the German poet. He begins in a tone of thunder, as if he would bring Heaven and Earth into collision; but while you are waiting to see what will come of it, he calls for his pipe, and you thenceforth lose him in the fog. You have scarcely time to admire his efforts at scaling the firmament, before you are startled to behold him drop "plumb down"[41] into a quagmire, like a bullet through an exhausted receiver. To see him when he is setting out you would fancy that he will tolerate no impediment to the prosecution of his enterprize. The fiercest and deepest rivers cannot appal him; his triumphant skiff makes no account of their waters. Mountains shew but as phantom-barriers; and were they otherwise he has wings to overfly them. But when forest, and ravine, and wilderness, and jungle have been traversed, it is his misfortune that he is too apt—like Rabelais' giant,[42] who, after devouring thirty windmills, was choked by a pound of butter—to close his career by slipping into a ditch, where he lies helpless, "himself bruised and his clothes in tatters." Schiller and some other men of first-rate genius excepted, every German poet is more or less unequal, is more or less incompetent to sustain the same rôle from the opening act of the drama to the closing. The fire that he commences with kindling at your very core burns down for want of fuel; and then you feel doubly chilled, and are fain to rake the dead ashes for a few sparks to warm your fingers at. He labours to agony to upheave a mountain; and anon you discover him stretched at its base, exhausted by his exertions, and tracing upon the sand a lament over their futility. His imagination (where he has any) runs, like a heavenly herald, before his conceptions, developing, as it passes along, whatever was hidden before, and illumining all places that thitherto lay shrouded in shadow; but here and there you discover afterwards that a line of lamps has gone out, or was more probably never lighted up at all; and these interspersed gaps of blackness must necessarily derange, and do derange, the beauty of the entire *coup d'œil*.[43]

> Nimm einen Ton aus einer Harmonie,
> Nimm eine Farbe aus dem Regenbogen
> Und Alles was dir bleibt ist Nichts, so lang
> Das schöne All der Töne fehlt und Farben.[44]

SCHILLER'S DRAMA OF WALLENSTEIN'S CAMP.

COLERIDGE, who translated, in his own unapproachable manner, Schiller's tragedies of *The Piccolomini*, and *The Death of Wallenstein*, chose to leave untranslated the Prelude of *Wallenstein's Camp*, by which those tragedies are introduced. The prelude is in rhyme, and in eight, nine, ten, or eleven syllable metre; and Coleridge's apology was that there were not rhymes enough in the English language to match the German, and that the metre would be rejected by the taste of the English public. Presumptuous as we may be deemed for dissenting from Coleridge on any subject, we think his first plea inadmissible. The fallacy of the notion that the rhyming capabilities of the German tongue surpass those of the English we exposed in a former paper;[1] and our experience, since we penned that paper, has not modified our original impression. We still believe that the English rhymes are more abundant and various than any other rhymes. We have never yet met with a Spanish, French, Italian, Dutch, or German line, which we found it impracticable to render by a corresponding English line. If translators have declared certain tasks impracticable, the declaration may be a proof of their unwillingness to undertake those tasks, but cannot be a proof of any thing besides. They find it convenient to talk of impracticability whenever it is not practicable for them to conquer their own indolence. It was less troublesome to the waggoner in the fable,[2] when the wheels of his cart got imbedded in a miry rut, to sit down by the way-side, and invoke Hercules, than to apply his own shoulder to the vehicle. The truth lies at the bottom of the well of the translator's incapacity in the shape of want of spirit. His case is the reverse of that of the man, who, when asked whether he could play on the fiddle, answered that he did not know, as he had never tried: the translator has tried, and succeeded, and yet will tell you that he is afraid to attempt a common street-melody. If "fools rush in where angels fear to tread,"[3] surely men of great powers occasionally sin in the contrary extreme, and, though only "a little lower than the angels,"[4] are a thousand times more timid even than they. It is not the way that is wanting; it is the will. The statue is in the marble, said Praxiteles[5] to his pupil; the point is to hew it out. The equivalents lie ready for all translators; the business is to look for them in the right places. We remember an arithmetical puzzle of our childhood: Given an eight gallon cask of brandy, and two empty vessels, one made to hold five gallons, the other to hold three: so to divide the brandy, as that four gallons shall remain in the cask, and four in the five gallon vessel. This *vexata quæstio* posed us for a length of time, because we kept continually pouring the liquor into wrong vessels. The generality of translators are just such pourers of liquor into wrong vessels. The right vessels, however, are always at hand, though they are not to be discovered without consideration. Enough of this here. Perhaps the objection that the verses of the prelude are too lax for the taste of the English public is entitled to somewhat more attention. Yet we question the validity of even this objection. A large class of readers relish poetry all the better for its freedom from the buckram trammels of the regular metre, "where, one link broken, the whole chain's destroyed."[6] The largest class of all care little about metres. In the *Vicar of Wakefield* the Vicar observes to his travelling companion, that modern dramatists appeared anxious to imitate Shakspeare rather than Nature. "To say the truth," said the other, "I don't know that they are anxious to imitate anything at all."[7] Coleridge may imagine that the English people prefer the metre of Pope's Homer[8] to that of Chapman's;[9] but for us, we believe that they entertain no marked metrical predilections in favour of any poem whatever. We think that in metres, as in the staple of metres, they like "everything by turns, and nothing long".[10]—The question is not, What metre the poem is written in: the metre is but, as it were, the *tournure*[11] of the garb in which the poem is attired: the question is, Whether the poem be worth reading. We shall here, to the best of our limited ability, give the reader an opportunity of deciding that question to his own satisfaction.

The great name of Schiller consecrates all his works. But let the piece be judged by its proper merits, not by the celebrity of its author. "The magic of a name"[12] is very often upon a level with every other species of juggle. There is quite enough in *Wallenstein's Camp*, we hope, to secure it attention for its own sake; and in this hope it is that we present a translation of it to our readers. They will now be able to estimate the precise extent to which the severe genius of Schiller was capable of deviating from its otherwise uniformly lofty path. Beyond the point to which it has in this instance verged in search of the familiar and humorous, we may reasonably conclude that it could not wander—and *Wallenstein's Lager* may, so far, be looked upon by Schiller's admirers scarcely less in the light of a curiosity than in that of a poem.

[Here follows "Wallenstein's Camp"]

ANTHOLOGIA GERMANICA.—NO. X.
TIECK AND THE OTHER SONG-SINGERS OF GERMANY.

LUDWIG Tieck, man-milliner to the Muses, poet, metaphysician, dramatist, novelist, moralist, wanderer, weeper and wooer, a gentleman of extensive and varied endowments, is, notwithstanding, in one respect, a sad quack. Such rubbish, such trumpery, such a farrago of self–condemned senilities, so many mouthy nothings, altogether so much snoring stupidity, so much drowsiness, dreariness, drizzle, froth and fog as we have got in this his last importation from Cloudland, surely no one of woman born before ourself was ever doomed to deal with. We now, for the first time in our life, stumble on the discovery that there may be less creditable methods of recruiting one's finances than even those which are recorded with reprobation in the columns of the Newgate Calendar.[1]

Our opinion of the literary merits of Tieck generally is, as Robert Owen[2] would say, "a secret which has hitherto remained hidden from mankind." Be it then, on the 1st of March, 1837, made notorious to all whom it may concern, and also to all whom it may gladden, that for our German friend we cherish the highest imaginable veneration. As a critic we hold him perfect, as a *raconteur* pluperfect, as a philologist preterpluperfect. That is, he shines, we conceive, in syntax, in story-building, and in the art of twaddling on the belles-lettres. We confess we are proud, proud as a peacock, of being able to bear testimony in his favor thus far. Nothing could give us greater pleasure than the privilege of smoking the pipe of peace with him on all occasions whensoever; unless he would allow us to advance one step further and join him in grinning away his hypochondriacism, of which last article, or rather substantive, his inglorious constitution appears to have laid in a stock by no means as easily transferable as stock in general is.

But *Omnia vincit veritatis amor*,[3] as Ferdinand Mendez Pinto observes in his Quarto;[4] and candor compels us to repeat that our esteemed friend is, as a poet, an egregious quack. For two hours we have been tugging at these two volumes for two consecutive stanzas that might convey to our mind some shadow of a notion of what it was that the writer fancied himself about, and we are now commencing hour the third in a vain search after the same phantom. We scan the page and blink like an owl over it, our countenance preserving the while that steady expression of stupifiedness which the plodding through Cimmerian[5] poetry is so apt to communicate to the august lineaments of the human face divine.[6] Certes, either he is mysterious beyond the capacity of the children of men,[7] or we are Impenetrability personified.

All that we can gather, is that he is delectably miserable. He maintains almost from first to last one monotonous wail, as mournful and nearly as unvarying as the night-lament of the Whip-Poor-Will[8] in the forests of South America. He simpers and whimpers; and yet, one cannot tell whether he would fain be thought glad or sad. He plays the poetical coquette between Fortune and Misfortune, and might adopt for his *devise* the plaint of Uberto, in Pergolesi's Opera, *La Serva Padrona*:[9]

> O un certo che nel core,
> Che dir per me non sò
> Se è odio o s'è amore;
> Io sto fra il si e il nò,
> Fra il voglio e fra il non voglio,
> E sempre più m'imbroglio.[10]

Trifles and things of nothing also exercise prodigious power over him. It is easy to see that, if tempted to "make his quietus," it will be with nothing savager than "a bare bodkin,"[11] and that a yard of packthread will be quite sufficient to aid his efforts at exhibiting a case of suspended animation in his own person. Hotspur complains of being "pestered by a popinjay,"[12] but Tieck's patience, like that of Tristram Shandy's uncle,[13] is put to the test by a blue-bottle fly. He is knocked down by a bulrush every half-minute in the day, and reverently kisses the face of his fatherland fourteen hundred and forty times in twelve hours. A dead leaf throws him into convulsions, and at the twittering of a swallow the heart of the poor man batters his ribs with such galvanic violence of percussion that at three yards' distance you suspect the existence of hypertrophy, and are half-disposed to summon a surgeon. Like Gulliver in the hands of the Lilliputians,[14] he is the victim of a million of tiny tormentors, who slay him piecemeal, the ten-thousandth part of an inch at a time. The minuter his calamity, too, the more he suffers. He may exclaim, with the lover in Dryden's play, "My wound is great, because it is so small!"[15] The colossal evils of life he passes over *sous silence*,[16] as unworthy the notice of a sentimentalist. Like the bronze figure of Atlas, he can stand immovable with a World of Woes upon his shoulders; but a single disaster, particularly if it be very slight, is too tremendous for his equanimity. The last feather, it is said, breaks the horse's back; but Tieck's back is broken by one feather. He is ready to oppose, as our friend Fergusson[17] would say, an "ironbound front," to the overwhelming allurements of an entire parterre, while a simple *bouquet* brings on an attack of *delirium tremens*. He can lounge through a flower-garden half-a-mile long, his hands in his pockets, a Peripatetic in appearance and a Stoic at heart; but "dies of one rose in aromatic pain."[18]

Under such circumstances one should suppose that he was much to pity. The case is the contrary. His sufferings are the sole source of his pleasures. Reversing the saying of the frogs in the fable,[19] what seems death to you is sport to him. Every emotion that tenants his heart must pay a rack-rent,[20] or the income of his happiness is so far deficient. Like Sindbad in the Valley of Diamonds,[21] the lower the gulf he descends into, the wealthier he becomes. If he be found in tears, it is a proof that he is lost in extacy. He not only agrees with the author of Hudibras,[22] that "Pain is the foil of pleasure and delight, and sets them off to a more noble height,"[23] but goes further, and, like Zeno,[24] makes pain and pleasure identical. To help him to an annoyance or two, therefore, is to confer a favour on him that awakens his most lugubrious gratitude. He is like Brother Jack in the *Tale of a Tub*,[25] whose felicity consisted in planting himself at the corners of streets, and beseeching the passengers, for the love of Heaven, to give him a hearty drubbing. Or he reminds us of Zobeide's porter in the *Arabian Nights*, who, as each successive load was laid upon his aching shoulders, burst forth with the exclamation: "O fortunate day! O, day of good luck!"[26] But why waste our ink in these vain illustrations? There is no saying what he resembles, or what he is or what he does, except that he doubts and groans, and allows his latitudinarianism in the one volume to carry on the war so soporifically against his valetudinarianism in the other, that not Mercury himself, if he took either in hand, could avoid catching the lethargic infection, and dropping dead asleep over the page.

The apex of Tieck's cranium must, we should think, display a mountainous development of the organ of Self-esteem. It is quite manifest that whatever he chooses to pen becomes in his own conceit inerasable and inestimable. A piece of bizarre barbarianism that Rabelais would have blotted out on a first reading is reckoned as the production of Ludwig Tieck, worthy of being enshrined in gold and amber. With submission, nevertheless, to our esteemed, he here reckons without his host; that is, without his host of readers, and also without us, his knouter, who are a host in ourself. The world, we would beg to assure him, gains nothing but dead losses by such acquisitions to the staple stock of literature. Where a man's genius, indeed, is very *prononcé*, where "his soul is like a star and dwells apart,"[27] people have an excuse for attaching importance to his extravagances. But Tieck, if a star at all—and he is rather a starling than a star—is but one of a family constellation, whose number may hereafter, when Time shall have brushed away the dust from our moral telescopes, appear as augmented as their glory will appear diminished. If we hold up all we have got from him between our eyes and the light, we shall be rather at a loss to discover in what it is that he has transcended his neighbours. The grotesque make of an article, he ought to recollect, is but a so-so set-off against its inutility. Common sense judges of all things by their intrinsic worth. A pedlar scarcely guarantees the admiration of a sensible purchaser by shewing him a pair of bamboo sandals from the shores of the Bhurrampooter,[28] or a necklace of cherry-stones strung together by a child born without arms or legs. We want not that which is unique and singular, but that which is of paramount and permanent interest. The Roman Emperor who rewarded with a bushel of millet-seed the man whose highest ambition it was to cast a grain of that seed through the eye of a needle, set an example of contempt for mountebankism which we are at length beginning to copy. We do not now-a-days, like our ancestors, barter an estate for a Dutch tulip.[29] Not exactly, Ludwig! Your thoughts, Ludwig, are not one gooseberry the more valuable to the public on the score that they are your thoughts exclusively. "I cannot be expected," says Goldsmith's Chinese,[30] "to pick a pebble off the street, and call it a relic, because the king has walked over it in a procession." If the Useful should take precedence of the Ornamental, how far into the rear should it not hustle the Fantastic? Poets generally reflect less to the purpose than other men, or they would have long ago found out that the world is weary of their impertinences, and that nothing satisfies in the long run but what was of sterling respectability from the beginning. A publican can think of nothing better for luring the thirsty crowd into his pot-house than a Hog in Armour, and a poet must clap some parallel monstrosity over the door of his own *sanctum sanctorum*,[31] or he fears that he will not be left in a situation to quarrel with his company. But Nature, after all, does not often back the appeals of the Bedlamite.[32] "The common growth of Mother Earth—her humblest tears, her humblest mirth,"[33] suffice for the generality. Few people catch mermaids in these times and still fewer are caught by them. A phœnix is a nine days' wonder—a sight to be stared at and talked of during a season; but our affections are given to the goose, and she is honored from Michaelmas to Michaelmas.[34] Let Tieck but bring us geese into the market and we shall be satisfied. We will not even object to go to the length of puffing off all his geese as swans. The sole stipulation we make with him is, that he shall close the gates of his Phœnix-Park.[35]

Tieck is our particular friend. We have called him a quack. Our freedom of speech is a proof of our friendship. For the world we have little but hypocritic smiles and silver lies. Tieck deserves better, and we have favored him with a gentle trouncing. He must not droop, therefore, but contrariwise rejoice. He must pluck up heart. There is pith and stamina within him. We depend on him for yet giving us something rather less remarkable for platitude than his *Bluebeard*[36] is. The Titian of *The Pictures*, the Prometheus of *The Old Man of the Mountain*[37]—above all, the concoctor of *The Love-charm*[38] can never be destitute of the means of retrieving his poetical reputation. But the task is one that will exact the sacrifice of his entire cistern of tears. If he undertake it, it must be with nerves of iron and a brow of brass. It was not, he should remember, by enacting Jackpudding[39] under the mask of a Howling Dervish,[40] that Milton or Goethe grew to be an intellectual Colossus. Annual self-exhibitions at Leipsic Fair may be all very well for nondescripts and nobodies—the awkward squad of the literary army—the tag-rag-and-bobtail of the bookmaking multitude, who are glad to pocket sixpence by hook or crook, and will bawl and bray the whole day long for half a dollar, but Tieck ought to be above those degrading shifts and antics. His mode of procedure is obvious and simple. He aspires to the title of a poet. Very good: let him give us conceptions we may make something out of; and sentiments that our flesh and blood hearts will respond with a thrill to. He need neither overleap the pale of the world, nor yet grovel in the low and swampy places of the world. Enough of work, we warrant him, will he find to do in the right spot. He can build himself a magnificent mansion, with "ample room and verge enough"[41] in it to entertain the whole circle of his acquaintance, "yea, the great globe itself,"[42] if his architecture be not of the clumsiest. Embrace, O, Tieck, the Beautiful and True! Abandon the Factitious and the False! The bowers of Poetry, bestrewn with roses, and overarched with evershining laurel, shall no man visit but with Nature's passport! You cannot assimilate Kant and Shakspeare. Metaphysics and Poetry are by no manner of means nitrogen and oxygen. They dwell best asunder. Each should be kept at a distance from the other, as brandy should be kept at a distance from water. The *tertium quid*[43] produced by the attempted amalgamation of both is a nauseous humbug. If any doubt of the truth of our assertion overcast your mind, peruse your own poems and doubt no longer.

* * * * * * * * *

A poet need not, indeed should not, be a preacher; but we have a right to demand that the tendency of his writings shall in all cases be favorable to the encouragement of human hopes and energies, and in no case favorable to the depression of them. Man is a sane and ratiocinating being, or he is not. If he be, here is so much poetry made subservient to the interests of untruth and absurdity. If he be not, still nobody has an apology for trying to make his condition worse than it is. Those who live like Mirabeau[44] may, to be sure, like Mirabeau, find it necessary to call for music to stun them in their last moments—and, by the bye, Tieck and Mirabeau seem to have hit on the same idea—but the generality of people stand in no need of a flourish of trumpets to herald their entrance into eternity. We firmly believe that no tranquil-minded man ever yet took it into his head to regard Life as a mystery,[45] or Death as a terror. If poets would now and then reflect before they write, what an *amas*[46] of rhodomontade would be fortunately lost to the world!

* * * * * * * * *

Turn we now to our other volume, the "Popular Songs of the Germans." M. Klattowski has here strung together a brilliant array of poetical pearls. His selections are in general judicious and excellent. The few exceptions we would not particularise; there are motes, as well as beams, in the brightest of eyes, and spots on the "bright eye of the universe,"[47] himself; and so, considering these things well, we hold our peace. In all respects beside a handsomer affair than this we shall not look on soon. No meaningless bombast, no clumsy gibing, no distorted humor, no stupid extravagance, no, or next to no, mawkish mockery of sentiment affronts us here. The book, to tell truth, shame the devil, and, we fear, somewhat annoy M. Klattowski's feeling of nationality, is just such an agreeable and sparkling book as we should have expected a German Song-book not at all to be. The notes, also, are a great acquisition, and for those we give M. Klattowski unqualified praise. They extend to fifty pages and embody much useful information. They are quite as instructive as the lyrics are entertaining. Indeed the *utile* and the *dulce*[48] were never more gracefully blended than they are in this little work. Altogether, we pronounce it, in perfect good faith, a production highly creditable to the taste and talents of M. Klattowski.

* * * * * * * * *

M. Klattowski lays particular stress on the merits of a certain tiny ode of Klopstock, of which we confess we can make nothing. It runs thus:—

Die Fruehen Graeber.

Willkommen, o silberner Mond,
Schöner, stiller Gefährt der Nacht!
   Du entfliehst? Eile nicht, bleib, Gedankenfreund,
   Sehet, er bleibt; das Gewölk wallte nur hin.

Des Maies Erwachen ist nur
Schöner noch wie die Sommernacht,
   Wenn ihm Thau, hell wie Licht, aus der Locke träuft,
    Und zu dem Hügel herauf röthlich er kommt.

Ihr Edleren, ach, es bewächst
Eure Maale schon ernstes Moos!
   O wie war glücklich ich, als ich noch mit euch
    Sahe sich röthen den Tag, schimmern die Nacht!

LITERAL TRANSLATION.

Early Graves.

I welcome thee, silvery moon!
Mute and beautiful Guide of Night!
   Dost thou flee? Flee not yet! Bide, O, Friend of Thought!
    Lo! she abides: 'tis the clouds only that pass.

The waking of May is alone
Sweeter still than the Summer night,
   When the dew, bright as day, droppeth from her locks,
    And to the mountain aloft blushing she comes.

Ye Nobler, alas! on your tombs
Grows already the mourning moss:
   O, how blest once was *I*, while I still with *you*
    Saw the day redden at dawn, and the night gleam!

"Whilst contemplating," says M. Klattowski, "on a fine summer-night the starry heavens, the poet is filled with sadness at the recollection of his early departed friends, and he expresses his deep-felt emotion in these verses." What! friend Klattowski, call you that sample of drowsy drivel emotion? Twaddle, man, boarding-school twaddle. Read it again, read it in our version—the phrases the same, the metre the same as those of the star-surveyor, and acknowledge that any thing more thoroughly impregnated with the concentrated quintessential extract of wishy-washyism has yet to pass through a printing-office. Pretty phraseology, too, we have in "*Wie war glücklich ich*," and "Des Maies Erwachen *ist nur schöner noch wie!*" But Klopstock made it a point to sacrifice sense to sound, and both to metre. He possessed the finest metrical ear ever granted to mortal. Gifted with this, and a *penchant* for tear-shedding and plethoric adjectives, he made incredible way among his countrymen for a season. But his reputation is now fast waning, and in a few years more, the great light which so dazzled the Saxon owlets of the last age will die off like the burnt-down wick of a farthing candle. He was, in fact, little beyond a mere mechanician, and if he had been called Stopclock, instead of Klopstock, the name would have tolerably well typified the man.

* * * * * * * * *

"It is the speaker's last argument that weighs with me,"[49] said Byron. It is to the last word of a song that our ears tingle. There is a vibration from the last word that we miss in every other word; mirthful, if the song be mirthful; melancholy, if the song be melancholy. We always look down at the end of a ballad, and if the last word be pretty, we fall at once in love with the entire, as the Prince in the fairy-tale fell in love with Cinderella directly he cast eyes on her slipper. The last word

> Comes o'er our ear like the sweet South,

(not Dr. South, the preacher,[50])

> Breathing upon a bank of violets,

(a leaf-bank, if not a branch-bank,) and

> Stealing, and giving odour,[51]

(like a pickpocket abstracting a scented handkerchief.)
It so happens that the last word of each of our last two ballads ["The Fisherman" and "The King of Thule"] is *more*. Talismanic word! which puzzled Horne Tooke,[52] and which the world so well understands, the sound of which in England is Life, and in France is Death.[53] It calls upon us for other songs. Long let it so continue to call. Let the echo of that call visit the cells of our brain oft in the deep midnight for months to come. We will yet hear and answer. But now, and for a season, our lips are sealed. Unless we alter our mind. A contingency which may occur. Nobody knows. At present, however, our resolution is firm.

> The torch shall be extinguished, which hath lit
> Our midnight lamp—and what is writ is writ.
> Would it were worthier![54]

We close this Anthology by a poem from Kerner.

"Reading and writing," says honest Dogberry, "comes by nature."[55] There is a good deal of truth in the remark; more by half than Shakspeare imagined. A poet takes to ink as a duckling takes to water: "he lisps in numbers, for the numbers come."[56] It is all instinct. The individual is passive in the matter. He is like a voyager at sea, without power to leave the vessel he is in, or arrest its progress. He follows the Will-o'-the-Wisp of Rhyme, "a weary chase, a wasted hour,"[57] because he must follow it, and for no other reason. So rushes the iron towards the loadstone, the moth towards the flame, the earth towards the sun.

At the same time it is to be noted, that as to "reading and writing," the poet uniformly reads and writes just as much and as well as, and no more and no better than Nature ordains. This is the age of wonders; but still every body cannot excel everybody, even in poetry. It is a result of the natural, no less than of the canon law, that there shall be many Priors and few Popes.[58] The eloquence of one man will shake thrones, where that of twenty other men cannot interfere with the equilibrium of a three-legged stool.

With these irrefragable truths we have been familiar from childhood. It would, therefore, be quite impossible that we should ever censure anybody for his or her intellectual deficiencies. We have never presumed to censure our particular friend Kerner. We have expressed some pity for him generally, because, in despite of etiquette and education, we now and then express what we feel, but we have never threatened him with the tomahawk.

He is unfortunate, poor fellow. Nature has, as yet, only half taught him to read and write. His *Reading-made-Difficult*[59] is still in his venerable hands, and when we ask for a specimen of his calligraphy we are invited to contemplate a blurred copy-book, full of pothooks and hangers. What then?—His brains were not of his own constructing. The worst that can be said of him is, that he has made indifferent poetry because he was unable to make different. We are not irrational enough to condemn, or even to contemn him. On the contrary, we have doled out, to the fraction of a penny-weight, the precise avoirdupois quantum of panegyric that his deserts called for. Surely, therefore, he ought to be contented.

But if, as we suspect, he remain still as dissatisfied as ever, we would just request his attention to the following translation, and ask him whether he be not, after all, our debtor to a very serious extent.

[Here follows "My Adieu to the Muse"]

LITERÆ ORIENTALES.
PERSIAN AND TURKISH POETRY.—
FIRST ARTICLE.

I.

" *CE n'est pas la route ordinaire de l'esprit humain de voyager vers le nord,*"[1] observed Count Segur,[2] when Napoleon's troops caught cold and died off in Russia. Looking at the disastrous result of the Russian expedition, no intelligent person will dissent from the Count. In reality, the great art of securing a triumph in reasoning is to make your conclusions wait upon your facts. A conjuror who jumps down his own throat sets no heads shaking except the very woodenest; all the philosophers proceed immediately to prove the possibility of the Impossible. It is well to be ingenuous, but better to be ingenious. Of all begetters of theories, commend us to events: a mere hypothesis wants bulk, muscle, marrow; it is an impalpability, an *ens rationis*,[3] a ghost that one may evoke, and again lay in the Red or Black Sea of his inkstand at his leisure or pleasure; but a principle grounded on a fact is Pelion based upon Ossa,[4] is a fixture in the great Warehouse of Argument, a Cheops' Pyramid[5] stereotyped. The safest of all inferences deducible from the occurrence of a circumstance is the antecedent necessity of that occurrence. If a million Frenchmen march into Russia, conquer the country, and come home again laden with trophies and triumphs, this is natural; cold, according to Beaupré,[6] renders men capable of extraordinary exertion. If the same million are killed by the Cossacks, this also is natural; frost destroys French enthusiasm as infallibly as Irish potatoes. To shew, when any thing is, that it should be as a consequence of course, is the business of the theorist. So in *Candide*, when the academician is asked why the Eldoradian sheep was red, and why it had died on leaving Eldorado, he is considered as giving a praiseworthy and prizeworthy explication in demonstrating by $a+b-c=z$ that the animal must have been of that color, and could not have lived in Europe.[7]

The Count's opinion, however, chances to be right in the abstract; and we should have said so at once. Warm and bright climes are preferable to chilly and cloudy. Poussin thought it essential to the effective development of his Arcadia to represent the sunset as illumining the looks of his shepherds.[8] We even bury our dead with their faces towards the Orient. The Greater and Lesser Lights of Dante's Paradiso[9] were never borrowed from Northern skies. "The savage loves his native shore;"[10] so at least saith the ballad; but nationality is not always rationality, and taste is confessedly questionable where its canons cannot be made answerable. Some difference may be presumed to exist between Italy and Iceland. No soil not classic is consecrated ground; we may believe the contrary when we are satisfied to refer the question to the arbitration of the Houzouana[11] or the Troglodyte, for a tedious and excellent account of whom, consult, inquisitive reader, the pages of that respectable traveller, La Vaillant.[12]

The mind, to be sure, properly to speak, is without a home on the earth. Ancestral glories, genealogical charts, and the like imprescriptible indescriptibles are favorite subjects with the composite being Man, who also goes now and then the length of dying in idea for his fatherland—but for Mind—it is restless, rebellious—a vagrant whose barren tracts are by no means confined to the space between Dan and Beersheba.[13] It lives rather out of the world. As the stranger said at the sermon, when asked why he did not weep with the rest of the congregation, it "belongs to another parish." It is apt, when in quest of its origin, to remount quite as far as the Welshman who across the middle of his pedigree wrote, *About this time the earth was created*. It is a Cain that may build cities, but can abide in none of them. It repudiates every country on the map; it must do so; it should; it would not be Mind if it did otherwise. But, all this notwithstanding, matters as they regard the general truth advocated by Segur and ourself remain where they were. No private principle worth preserving is interfered with by reason of the dominance of a certain great catholic feeling in the human spirit. Abstract in its nature, such a feeling is ever compatible with the coexistence of particular and temporary preferences and prejudices. We do confess that the Mind, with all its indifferentism, looks rather Eastward than Northward; do acknowledge, are proud to acknowledge, that, whatever the human sympathies it has, they are with the East, or with its conceptions of the East. That shadowy species of affinity which the Mind in its complacent moods delights to assume as subsisting between the Orient and its own images of Genii-land possesses rich and irresistible charms for human contemplation. Imagination feels averse to surrender the paramount jewel in the diadem of its prerogatives—a faith, to wit, in the practicability of at some time or another realizing the Unreal. If the East is already accessible, so may be at last—the reverse who dares prophesy?—"the unreached Paradise of our despair;"[14] and so long as the Wonderful Lamp,[15] the dazzler of our boyhood, can be dreamed of as still lying *perdu* in some corner of the Land of Wonders, so long must we continue captives to the hope that a lovelier light than any now diffused over the dusky pathway of our existence will yet be borne to us across the blue Mediterranean. Alas! wanting that which we have not, cannot have, never shall have, we mould that which we really have into an ill-defined counterfeit of that which we want; and then, casting a veil over it, we contemplate the creature of our own fancy with much the same sort of emotion that may be supposed to have dilated the breast of Mareses, the artist of Sais, when he first surveyed the outlines of the gigantic statue himself had curtained from human view.[16] Yet it is on the whole fortunate that Speculation can fall back upon such resources. Slender and shifting though they seem, they serve as barriers against Insanity. From amid the lumber of the actual world prize is made of a safety-valve which carries off from the surface of our reveries the redundant smoke and vapour that, suffered to continue pent up within us, would suffocate every healthier volition and energy of the spirit.

When we speak of Mind, readers must understand us to mean Mind *par excellence* Mind. Visions of lovers and poets, and lonely *rêveurs*, who have read no metaphysics, and are therefore best qualified to become original metaphysicians, subtlest of the subtle, flit before us as the word assumes shape under our quill. Of mathematicians one perhaps in a thousand comes, but even that one hardly lingers. Few ploughmen dazzle us, and no *millionaires*. But the absence of these last is of small import, nor are we now quarrelling for the assertion of any principle. Power and Beauty best vindicate themselves. Multiform and omnipresent in their manifestations have they ever been; and he who passes ninety-nine altars without worshipping must perforce kneel before the hundredth. There is a reverence independent and apart which neither poet nor man of the world can well refuse to the East. The universal consent of nations assigns to Asia a character it assigns to no other portion of the globe. The title of Rome herself to any celebrity beyond that derivable from her military triumphs must be shared with Asia, the "mother of science, and the house of gods."[17] Asia was the cradle of the human race, was man's primeval world. We look to it from childhood as "the land of the sun;" our young ideas of glory, antiquity and enchantment are associated with it. The coldest of cosmopolites must feel that it is the Great Caravanserai at which he is oftenest disposed to put up in the resting pauses of his pilgrimage. To trace with effect the revolutions of centuries to their source he must turn to Asia. If he would know how empires were founded, how society was formed, how civilization originated, Asia must be his book of reference. If he be desirous of an acquaintance with the history of the establishment of governments and legislatures, with the history of the earliest discoveries, with the history of the first wars and the first conquests, he must seek them in Asia. Picture to yourselves, you who think but travel not,—behold, you who travel and think not, those monumental miracles of ancient conception, those stupendous relics of the Past, which seem to have been bequeathed to the Present as much in defiance of the comparative labours of all succeeding generations as in a sublime despair of rivalling Deity. Look upon these as they are; reflect on what these were; and wonder, if you can, that the traveller of old, treading the earth of the East for the first time, should have fancied himself half-restored to Eden, and that even the sword of the seraph over the Prohibited Walls[18] should have appeared to gleam from afar less in menace than in invitation.Where flourished gardens then, it is true, we stray in wildernesses now; where palaces rose we find roofless walls and broken columns. But the justness of the trite remark, that Greatness though in decay is Greatness still, is nowhere more fully exemplified than in the East. Amid the ruins of Palmyra, and Balbec, and Babylon, and above all of Persepolis,[19] the wanderer becomes deeplier convinced than ever of its truth. Tabor[20] is to-day the holiest of mounts. The name of Galilee remains eternal. In the shrouded and tabular inscriptions of Egypt we meet still those mysterious hieroglyphs, of whose less unfamiliar counterparts, "the *Mythi* of the breast,"[21] we are suffered to gain glimpses when the lightning of Inspiration and Genius plays over their surface. Our conclusion, then, is not an idle one. Poet, artist, archæologist, philosopher, philanthropist, warrior, mystic, religionist—all may meet in Asia, as on ground common to all. Each will be acquitted of all supererogatory enthusiasm, even if, as he looks around him and exclaims, "This is my own, my native land!"[22] every responsive chord in his heart vibrates to the utterance of the sentiment.

II.

The literature of such a country, as well modern as ancient, must be supposed to comprehend a variety of knowledge in the highest degree interesting to investigators. It is not wonderful, therefore, that attempts should have been from time to time made in Europe to obtain for it the publicity it deserves. But although from the fifteenth century to the present period there has been no deficiency in the number of minds willing to devote their energies to the task, it is only within the last two-score years that any progress in it worth noticing has been made. It is matter for regret that the old Orientalists entered upon their labours without any distinct notion of the nature of them. They were alike ignorant of their own, of Asiatic, of human nature; they saw not the multitudinous difficulties opposed to the successful prosecution of their undertaking, and they wanted the comprehensiveness of judgment which could alone have enabled them to grapple with those difficulties when encountered. They were men who had been taught to think, rather than men who had learned to think; and, stopping short in their researches where Custom and Indolence dictated, it probably never occurred to them that any further advance, even if practicable, could be regarded as necessary. They had acquired, perhaps, a knowledge of history, but they had not acquired any knowledge of the principles upon which the great events and great characters of history should be judged; and an attempt to blend the conflicting and discordant elements of the Past and Present, of the Remote and Proximate into one harmonious total was as far beyond their ability as the idea of it was beyond their capacity. They regarded the Asiatics as a subordinate and degraded caste of mortals, without troubling themselves to anatomise with too much curiousness the reasonings they had arrived at their conclusions by. Europe stood with her face to the light; Asia lay buried in shadow; the contrast was undeniable and was made the most of. It would indeed appear a habit inseparable from the constitution of many minds to estimate all things, all peoples even, at the worth which they assume in the eye while they are immediately under survey. "Goethe," observes Carlyle, "reckoned Schiller happy that he died young, *that we might figure him to ourselves as a youth for ever;*"[23] and with the memory of Goethe himself few, possibly, will ever associate any image but that of the octogenarian. The old Roman, as he looked with contempt on the barbarian Teuton and Briton, could scarcely have imagined a period when Germany and England would contest the victory of intellectual pre-eminence with the majestic Mistress of the World. Voltaire, forgetful of the palmy days of Jerusalem, doubts that the Deity could have selected a nation of cast-clothes-men as the repository of his favors,[24] and Hume condemns the whole colored population of the earth to imbecility perpetual. The old Orientalists were unfortunately so organized as to be incapable of viewing the existing condition of Asia *as it stood in relation to the system of the world from its beginning.* They could not have anticipated the excellent remark of Wieland,[25] that "to understand human affairs and human beings aright, we must scrutinize them, not in detail, or as they appear in single places or epochs, or as they stand in connection with this odd thing or that, or as they lose or gain by being involved in the clouded atmosphere of opinions and passions, but as they refer to the Whole, in its origin, progress and termination, and in all its forms, movements, ramifications, and consequences." Their error was involuntary. But the result was that they communicated few or no impressions of Asia that were not imperfect and unsatisfactory. They tested the genius, habits, and prejudices of one continent by the genius, habits and prejudices of another; and because the two continents differed—because the moral character of Europe was reckoned austerer than that of Asia—because Asia was not Europe, the literature of Asia was pronounced unworthy of a comparison with the literature of Europe. The inference was mysterious, but not more than two-thirds a *non-sequitur* after all, and drawn with all imposing gravity besides; and so, many believed, and few questioned, and none contradicted. Writers and readers were alike misled—the writers by their own convictions—the readers by the plausibility of the writers.

But enough and too much of these men. Time has trodden them down, them, their works, their memory; their light, like the lamp in the tomb of Cicero's daughter,[26] could burn only in an atmosphere of darkness;—directly the *Appian Way*[27] of the human mind was upbroken by the first pickaxes and crowbars of the French Revolutionists, it died, day-extinguished, storm-destroyed. They have passed away, and bolder enquirers occupy their places. Fairer views, prospects worthy of the name at length begin to open upon the admirers of Orientalism. "The night is far spent, the day is at hand."[28] The dawning of a new era is heralded by many a rising star and gilded cloud.

We begin to perceive how much we have hitherto been in the dark, and how much we are still. Even such a perception is no insignificant advantage. Knowledge is not Power, but Knowledge readily suggests a mode for the acquisition of Power. We have gained an accurate insight into the extent of our deficiencies. To this naturally succeeds the decisiveness of action which will soonest enable us to supply those deficiencies. Supplied they must be, or else any important, any available progress towards the attainment of our object, the publication, that is, of the worthier portions of Eastern Literature, ceases to be matter of reasonable hope. Of course, therefore, we should be zealous and indefatigable in our endeavours to supply them.

"Contarini Fleming," says the Younger D'Israeli, "wrote upon the wall, *Time*."[29]

Our inscription would have been, *Hope and Exertion.*

III.

Our chief desideratum is undoubtedly a Literary History of the Oriental Nations, but more particularly of Persia and the Arabias.

The question then is, Whether the compilation of such a work be practicable. We hesitate not in pronouncing it to be quite practicable. Considerable industry, calm patience, unremitting perseverance, a little discriminating power, a talent for collocating, selecting, arranging and distributing, these are essential to the accomplishment of the task; but, apart from these, nothing. An exception, on second thoughts, may be made in favour of the *con amore* feeling which usually accompanies literary drudgery of all kinds. This included, we need no other requisites. It were disingenuous, however, to omit acknowledging that the laborer, whoever he be, will have much up-hill work to achieve. There are difficulties in his way, and their name is Legion, for they are many.[30] He may be young; all the better; his youth is no objection; he will grow old enough over his desk, for years must elapse, a quarter of a century perhaps, perhaps more, before he will have reduced his chaos to order. The merit of his undertaking will, perhaps, be better appreciated when we have embodied in a rapid *esquisse* a statement of the peculiar nature and character of the obstacles that will contribute to retard him.

The primary difficulty to be confronted is confessedly in the materials from which the required information is to be derived. All are of course MSS. Of these comparatively few have reached Europe; and those few are productions of different eras, penned in differing dialects, and abounding in provincialisms, local allusions, idioms, word-abbreviations and the duskest ambiguities of expression. A leaf-by-leaf examination of one of them never fails to dishearten a tyro. But as we suppose our drudge to be no tyro—as we suppose him an indifferent proficient in the Eastern tongues, and as the time, toil and thought he might expend in perfecting his proficiency, would not be ultimately thrown away, we refrain from directing attention more pointedly to this difficulty. We draw upon our fancy, and imagine it mastered in the first month of a brain-bracing Winter.

A more dubious result would possibly succeed the attempt to collect, collate, compare and classify the variorum copies of the same MSS. scattered abroad as they are, and parcelled out among the libraries and public institutions of Europe. If we presume that our historian elect visits the East in person, the objection drawn from this second difficulty, it is true, in a great measure vanishes. But upon such a presumption he is, on the other hand, likely to be affrighted from his propriety[31] altogether, by new considerations, and those of a very embarrassing description. What they are we hasten to explain.

In the East, be it noted, there are two sorts of Annals—Public Annals and Private Annals.

The Public Annals are chiefly those of the Arabian Chroniclers, Ebn Aher, Abulfeda, Makrizi, Abulmahassan and others. They are made up of records of the political events of each successive year, interspersed with brief notices, in the manner of our newspaper obituaries, of the remarkable men who have died within the year. Beyond their exactitude these annals have no recommendation. In style and matter they are contemptible. They are dull, drowsy and monotonous, or rather have no tone whatever. We cannot call them literary. They could be of no service to the literary historian.

The Private Annals are pure biographies. They are narratives of the sayings and doings, dreamings and schemings, lives, fortunes and misfortunes of such men of all grades and calibres, lettered and unlettered, officials and expectants, as had in their day any pretensions to wear pantoufles[32] an inch higher in the heels than the mere rabble wore them. Throughout most towns of the East, but principally in Mecca, Medina, Bagdad, Damascus, Ispahan and Bassorah, these Annals abound and superabound in piles of volumes, "ten thousand times ten thousand and thousands of thousands."[33] From the age of the Hejira to the present times, Renown has enacted the part of an auctioneer in the East; and every Mussulman has had assigned to him an immortal lot who has been able to bid up to the price of it. It is a great mistake to fancy that the Orientals know nothing about any body except Haroun Alraschid and Sinbad the Sailor. They shew you the written lives—half of which were first taken and then undertaken—of "small poets and great prosers,"[34] period-rounders, law-expounders, harem-founders, and theologians whose *hue* and *cry*[35] were White and Omar, or Green and Ali.[36] You have the lives of Muftis, Cadis, Hakems, Agas, and Effendis, and, in the same volume with these perhaps, the lives of the fathers, mothers, brothers, wives and children, aunts, uncles, and cousins by dozens of the same Muftis, Cadis, Hakems, Agas, and Effendis. Even the grammar-school-masters, and the quack-physicians, and the country-jugglers, and the town-criers, and the court-buffoons, and the fig-and-date hawkers, and a host of the like illustrious obscures have been made welcome to hide their undiminished heads for an eternity in the sepulchres of the Great Biographical Cemetery.

Now the literary history of a country, though it may be said to properly consist of two parts, the history of its literature *per se*, and the history of the lives of its literary men, rests its chief claim to importance on the history of its literature *per se*. If we take both parts in conjunction as a circle we shall find that the first part embraces about three hundred degrees, and the second part the remaining sixty. Of these two parts, therefore, the first part is of a magnitude and moment far transcending the second. Its business is to acquaint us with the state of literature generally and particularly, its origin, its growth, its influence on society and the arts, its various revolutions and the causes that may have operated to accelerate or retard its progress. It is obvious that although in this history, this first part, mention may incidentally occur of literary writers, they should appear, wherever they are introduced, only as accessories; the types are not licensed to "prate of their whereabouts;"[37] they are not the staple of the work; they "come like shadows, so depart";[38] their successes or disasters are affairs with which we have no immediate concern. It is in the second part of the literary history, that is, in the literary biographies that we look for these; and even there we expect to find that the biographer has allotted to the portrait of each writer a wider or narrower space in the literary gallery as the writer himself was more or less distinguished in his rôle. Such biographies are unquestionably of some collateral utility to the literary historian. But they do not in the most latitudinarian sense of the term constitute literary histories. They are histories of the lives and labors of men whose lives and labors have been subservient to the advancement of literature, and they are nothing more. They can scarcely of themselves answer all the purposes of the literary historian.

Unfortunately, however, it happens that throughout the East few or no sources of information besides these are discoverable. The single basis whereon to rear the superstructure of a literary history of the East may be said to be the literary biographies.

Here, then, is a formidable difficulty, and, attaching to it all the importance that really invests it, we should at once admit that the compilation of a *perfect* literary history of the East cannot be hoped for. But the truth is, that we never dreamed of such a chimera as a *perfect* history. We are satisfied to have the best history that can be given us, "with all its imperfections on its head"[39] and the compiler's. The difficulty we have just dwelled upon does not we think interpose an insurmountable wall of separation between our wishes and their final accomplishment. Viewed, however, even with reference to stipulations as moderate as ours, we still acknowledge it to be, as we have said, formidable in its way; and it were wise to weigh and ponder it fully before hand.

We now come to and we shall conclude with an embarrassment, which though of a minor order, comprehends in itself such a number of annoyances that the historian, even if he had none other to make head against, might feel tempted to abandon his pen in despair when considering it.

In the East there are but a few proper names of individuals. Abdallah, Ali, Hassan, Mohammed, Hussein, for example, are common to thousands. To remedy the inconvenience that might be supposed to result from this tendency to homonymousness the Orientals annex to the family-name of the chronicled person, 1, a *conya*, or surname, taken from the name of his eldest son, as *Abu*-Mohammed, *Abu'l*-Hassan (father of Mohammed, father of Hassan). 2, the name of his father and often the name of his grandfather. 3, a name taken from his place of residence. 4, a name taken from his birth-place. 5, an honorary title, chiefly appended to the names of cadis, sheikhs and imams, monks and doctors, as *Bohal-eddin*, Splendor of Religion, *Djelal-eddin*, Glory of Religion, *Tadj-eddin*, Crown of Religion; and in the order of this nomenclature the last name is put first. Thus to designate aright the famous physician Abd-alladif we must call him Mouwaffik-eddin Abu-Mohammed Abdalladif Ben Yusuf Mousouli Bagdadi, *viz*: The Protector of Religion, father of Mohammed, Abdalladif, son of Joseph, living at Mossoul, born at Bagdad. Yet this is by no means an exaggerated specimen; several other surnames of the same kind are frequently added. The perpetual recurrence of such a multiplicity of names and titles must tend in many ways to confuse a literary historian; and the more naturally when he finds the same individual chronicled in one page under his honorary title only, as *Djelal-eddin*, in another under his family-name, as *Abderaman*, in a third under his father's name, as *Ebn-Arabshah*, some where else under the name of his son, as *Abu'l-Abbas*, and perhaps again, and where one would least look for it, under the name of his native province, as *Scheherestani*. D'Herbelot[40] has recorded no fewer than fourteen Persian writers, all of whom pass under the common cognomen of Karamani, from their province, Karaman. Here is perspicuity! But this is not all. The transcribers of the MSS. have frequently confounded the titles *Abu* and *Ebn*, or else, for abbreviation-sake, have omitted them altogether, and written down as Abd-alla or Abd-eraman him who was in fact the father or the son of Abd-alla or Abd-eraman. Then there are a great many authors whom public celebrity has been accustomed to distinguish so exclusively by one only of their adjunctive titles that even the native biographers find it impossible to trace either their family names or their other surnames. Lastly, many hundreds of books bear the same name, and the names of most books are conceived after such a many-worded and no-meaninged fashion that even de Sacy,[41] Schlegel,[42] Casiri[43]and Von Hammer,[44] to mention but a few investigators out of many, have been foiled in the attempt to establish their signification.

For the dryness of these details we should deem it our duty to apologize, if we did not feel convinced that those who have accompanied us thus far will agree with us that notwithstanding their dryness they are not destitute of a certain degree of interest. We have been desirous to specify the nature of the preliminary step towards rendering available, that is, transferable into our own land's language, all that may be really valuable in the literature of the East. There is nothing like knowing where we are, what we are doing, how we are circumstanced and whether and when the exertions we are engaged in are likely to be successful. Exceedingly satisfactory would it be to us if we could encourage the hope that in, say, thirty years hence, supposing the many-colored thread that binds our nights to be spun out through that period, we should witness in the publication of such a history as we have adverted to a proof that our suggestion had been acted on. The work need not be more voluminous than the *Bibliothèque Orientale*,[45] which, by the way, has long called for a companion, perhaps we should say a substitute, considering that D'Herbelot, after all, was able to do little more than catalogue some thousands of names, and that since the completion of his catalogue a century and a half have passed over. We have mentioned the sort of compilation that we regard as indispensable and we have enumerated the principal obstacles that will embarrass the compiler. We have said and we again say that those obstacles appear surmountable by time, zeal, and steadiness. We have merely to add that when surmounted, we, or those who shall come after us, will be at length enabled to deal out to the Oriental Muse that full measure of justice which the limitedness of our views at present with respect to the true merits of the poetry of the East must prevent us for a season longer from according her.

In the meantime we, whose motto was always *Aide-toi, le ciel t'aidera,*[46] must do the best for ourselves that circumstances will permit. Our business just now is with Persian and Turkish Poetry merely, the merits of which we shall endeavour to discuss as concisely as possible.

IV.

It is rather remarkable that nobody should know with any certainty to which country of Asia the oldest poetry belongs. Augustus Schlegel[47] is disposed to advocate "the great priority" of the Sanscrit, though he allows the powerful rival title of the Arabic. Sir William Jones[48] patronizes equally the Indian, Arabic, and Tartarian; Langlès[49] the Manchew-Tartarian alone. Abel-Remusat[50] appears to support his own arguments in favour of the Chinese with considerable effect, while Von Hammer exalts the Ancient Persian, albeit he, too, somewhat like Schlegel, pronounces the Arabic "a venerable dialect, whose poetry is allied to the Hebrew, and owes its origin to an immemorial epoch." It would be foreign from our purpose to enter into any discussion upon these conflicting theories. If, however, we were to hazard a conjecture, it would be in favour of Von Hammer. The works of that accomplished scholar we have attentively perused and studied; and, after as impartial a comparison between his arguments and those of his opponents as we were capable of, our conviction is that although many extravagant assertions have been advanced with reference to the peculiar antiquity of the Old Persian,[51] there is evidence enough to satisfy a rational mind that it is a language and can boast a poetry coeval with the earliest dawn of civilization among mankind. Our decision with respect to the Arabic would be less positive. That the Arabic, as a language, is entitled to every deference, we at once concede, but its poetry is far from striking us as being of a very elevated order. Elsewhere, indeed, Von Hammer himself confesses that "*die höchste Poesie des Arabers ist das Werk des arabischen Propheten, der Koran,*"[52] the sublimity of which in his opinion transcends that of the *Moallakat*[53] itself, but which in our opinion, and we really think in the opinion of any unprejudiced proficient in Arabic and judge of poetry, is about as paltry and bombastic a budget of rhapsodies as exists on a shelf. Mohammed in truth hated poetry and poets.[54] He is candid enough to admit his own total want of "the vision and the faculty divine."[55] *We have not taught Mohammed the art of Poetry*, says the Koran, *nor is it expedient for him to be a poet.* And again, *I swear to ye by that which ye see, and that which ye see not, that this is the discourse of an honourable apostle, and not of a poet.*[56] The concluding verses of the twenty-sixth chapter of the *Koran* contain a very drawling and stupid tirade against poets in general, for which we refer to the book itself. The following also are a few of the elegant sayings current among the Arabians as having been uttered by its author. *Poetry is the devil's horn-book.*[57] *Better for thee to fill thy stomach with garbage from a dunghill, than with poetry.*[58] *Cast mud in the face of the poet.*[59] There was no necessity for Von Hammer to rest his appeal in behalf of the merits of Arabian poetry on the *Koran*; (in fact the romance of *Antar*, also an Arabian production and of comparatively modern origin, is alone worth a dozen *Korans*.) But when of his own accord he chooses to do so, and declares that he has nothing nobler to back his argument with, he may be assured that if even the disciples of his own school appear to swallow open-mouthed every proposition he lays down for them on the subject, it will be *cum grano salis.*

That which is certain at all events is, that the poetry of Persia ranks much higher in critical and popular esteem at the present day than the poetry of Arabia, or, indeed, the poetry of any of the many other lands of the Orient. Its pre-eminence over that of Arabia is disputed in Europe with little plausibility and less reason. The rich raciness, the terrible strength, and undenied beauty of some kinds of the Bedouin poetry have earned for the poetry of Arabia a celebrity to which it is not in strict right entitled. The poets of Yemen, or Arabia Felix, have little to recommend them; and in fact, the productions of the Arabian poets generally, as they were, for the most part, penned at the courts of the khalifs, exhibit just such a nervelessness and absence of character as might have been expected from men "thus trammelled and condemned to Flattery's trebles."[60] If now and then, at intervals a century apart, some gifted Bedouin started up and electrified his countrymen with strange melody the very singularity of the phenomenon operated to prevent it from being referred to as an evidence of national genius: the poet, it is true, was apotheosised, was elevated to the sphere of a demigod, but a barrier so much the more impassable was therefore supposed to sunder him from the multitudes below, "the common growth of Mother Earth."[61] When Volney visited the East, he did not forget the Arabs of the Desert, and his testimony as to them is, that, *"Toute leur littérature consiste à réciter des contes et des histoires dans le genre des Mille et une Nuits."*[62] The Arabs, however, it is to our purpose to remark, are well aware that even this work is of Persian origin; and the supremacy which Persian poetry assumes over every other is but feebly contested by them. That supremacy is ceded with still less reluctance by other nations. It is acknowledged that no poet has as yet made his appearance in Arabia, China, Tartary, India, or the Ottoman Empire, who has succeeded in transferring the laurel from the brows of SHEMSEDDIN MOHAMMED HAFIZ[63] to his own.

With regard to Turkish poetry, its excellences and defects, whatever they are, belong to a modern epoch; it is an imitation, an echo of Persian poetry. *Die persische Poesie*, writes Von Hammer, *ist die Sonne, welcher die Sonnenblume osmanischer Dichtkunst zugewendet, Farbe und Wachsthum danket.*[64] Drechsler[65] has confirmed our conviction of his utter incompetency to assume the criticaster by his contemptuous condemnation of this poetry in the gross. Goethe rather sneers at it—the poetry, that is:— he seems to forget that a nation which may be said to have itself sprung up on the borders of the Caspian but six hundred years ago cannot be expected to exhibit a literature characterised by a very marked degree of individuality. Rückert and some other busy bodies have been at a world of unnecessary trouble to depreciate the Ottoman poetry, as owing what little notoriety it has acquired to an extraneous source. "The poetry of Turkey," says the Leipsic *Handbuch einer allgemeinen Geschichte der Dichtkunst*, "possesses no intrinsic force, beauty or merit *of its own*; all its harmony and vigour are borrowed from the Persian and Arabic. There may be one exception in the compositions of BAKI, who died in the year 1600, and who acquired a very extensive reputation as a lyrist of peculiar powers."[66] This, though meant to be severe, is half panegyrical. Nobody ever dreamed of claiming originality for the poetry in question; nor need we care whether it be original or not. If it really possess beauty, harmony, and vigour, it is of no consequence whatever to us or any body, whether they are borrowed or inherent. It would certainly be a novelty in the prize-ring if the claims of the pugilistic victor to the championship of an hour were rejected on the ground that his father was as hard-fisted a punisher as he. It is to be lamented, meanwhile, that these shadowy attacks by nobodies upon an imaginary citadel, have not been productive of some substantial advantage, by at least awakening curiosity. More than once it has been proposed to give all parties fair play by shewing through the medium of a Turkish Literary History how far either party may be under a mistake; and some left-handed attempts have been made at getting up such a history, but of course, without success. One Introductory Part of the *Literaturgeschichte des Osmanen* has, it is true, been given to the world by Eichhorn; but the second and more important portion, that which moots the question of the poetry and oratory of the Turkish nation, though it has been twenty years printed, seems to be much less nearer publication now than when the author first took it in hand. The publisher, who, it seems, like Philosopher Square,[67] does everything according to a certain system, originally decided on bringing out the *Turkish History* in the same volume with an embryo *Hungarian* and *Polish* History; and for twenty years no German has been found willing to undertake the latter. The fact that in Germany it has been proved an easier matter to procure a compiler of Turkish songs and speeches than a compiler of Polish and Hungarian does not astonish us.[68] The Poles and Huns, we believe, never sing or speak upon any occasion; and he who should undertake to furnish a list of their poets and prosers would find himself pretty much in the situation of the gentleman who proposed to write a Treatise on the Rats of Iceland, and was obliged to begin and end his work thus:—*There are no rats in Iceland.* But we cannot help regretting that Eichhorn should persist in adhering to a foolish resolution formed a score of years back, when his adherence to it is so prejudicial to the interests of the cause that he wishes to forward. May his heirs, executors, administrators, or assigns turn out more enlightened than he, and agree among themselves that even the literary world can manage to subsist and grow robustuous "without either rhyme or reason" from Poland or Hungary!

We are wandering, we fear, beyond the strict boundary-lines of our applotted territory. Let us pause. We pause, therefore. A sea of argument stretches out before us and the waves thereof curl about our feet. But we forbear to plunge in. Reflection recurs, and we receive a *check* on the *bank*. We advance no further. And yet we stop not—to apologise. Least said, quoth the proverb, is soonest mended. At all events, it is soonest ended.

V.

To resume, then.

But no; we shall not resume. For even now we can perceive that many fair—no, not fair, but red—lips are beginning to open in qualified commendation of us. And qualified commendation, be it noted, in lieu of growing "fine by degrees, and beautifully less,"[69] too often encreases until it terminates in unqualified condemnation.

A basket of flowers lies before us. Will your ladyship do us the high honor of accepting a bouquet from our hands? Many thanks—oh, that finger!—surely it was a Peri's! Madam, the selection has been made with some taste,—this moss-rose strikes us as exceedingly beautiful. Pray, young lady, take a passion-flower—do. O! you've got one already, have you? Sir, we can supply you with some heart's ease. You shake your head—ah! well,—which means ill. Sir, sir, don't crush the poor flowers, they have done you no harm—see, now, you have torn all the leaves to pieces! Come, honest man, keep off. Ho, there! you with the forty fingers, what are you running away with? Do not, do not, ladies and gentlemen, do not, for charity's sake, crowd upon us so! What! more, twenty more, fifty, five hundred, ten thousand, millions, trillions, octillions! We shall be stifled, smothered, trampled into powder! Mercy! Mercy!

We are "alone once more."[70] The crowds are gone; are gone in chase of butterflies. But the flower-basket is here still. And the flowers are fresh and blooming and innocent as ever. They look, many of them, for all their youthfulness, like ancient acquaintances. Wherefore a misgiving masters us, on the sudden, that not all are exotics. The deuce a matter, nathless, good folks. We shall await with decorous gravity the decision of the horticulturists. They know a vast deal about the matter indeed. Meanwhile, here are the flowers, laughing in our faces, as though to rebuke our solemnity. Come, cull and choose, you who will, for you are welcome.

Dropping metaphor, for the management of which our Aristotelian intellect ill qualifies us, we conceive it to be time to introduce to the notice of our readers a few first-rate samples of Persian and Ottoman Poetry. More than a few the length to which our preliminary remarks have extended precludes us from offering in this article; but we shall at least make a beginning; and here, now, at the outset, we request it to be understood, that we shall avail ourselves of all such sources of information as may be open to us,—premising only this, that we shall hold ourselves responsible for all that we may here or hereafter assert, and that our translations shall be our own and our own only.

* * * * * * * * *

In general . . . we have no objection to the imagery of Eastern Poetry. And in any instance but one objection. It is here and there obscure, without being original. The poet is too fond of ellipsis; he occasionally leaves so much to be comprehended, such reasonings to be supplied, that one grows sceptical of the existence of a meaning at all under his phraseology. Saadi relates that a sage met with an old man who was bewailing the death of his son. "Why weepest thou?" demanded the sage. "When a pearl, yesterday, fell from my hand into the sea, no man said to me, That should have floated on the surface." And he pauses for no reply. If the syllogism be not obvious here it will seem odd that one man should be expected to cease weeping because another has dropped a pearl into the sea. But while we cannot help considering this tendency to obscureness a fault we must confess on the other hand that the condensation of expression it induces is sometimes in skilful hands very impressive and striking.

* * * * * * * * *

"In the East," says Sir William Ouseley[70] (*v.* his *Asiatic Researches*) "it is the belief of the commoner sort that pearls are formed in the shells of fish from drops of rain which they absorb." No. 293 of the Spectator furnishes a story illustrative of this belief.[72] In one of Lopé de Vega's Pastorals there is a shepherdess who weeps by some sea-shore or other; and, says the poet very old-schoolishly,—

> El mar, como invidioso,
> A tierra por las lagrimas sali,
> Y alegre de cogerlas,
> *Las guarda en conchas y convierte en perlas.*[73]

The tears of Oriental skies, however, it would appear from the testimony of another poet, have generally but a remote prospect of falling at last into the hands of the jeweller. Oysters are often in love, and, we suppose, drink deeply to stupify their feelings; and hence a scarcity of Pearl Necklaces, and thence French Revolutions[74] and a variety—we beg pardon, a number—of *odd* volumes on the same.

* * * * * * * * *

It is our policy, roamers as we are through the Enchanted Caverns of Oriental Poetry, to commence our scheme of operations, like the pupil of the Dervish Noureddin[75] in the tale, by picking up from the ground a few stray jewels of slight weight and no very brilliant water, before we proceed to ransack the coffers and carry off the ponderous golden vases that lie piled about us. So opens an Indian juggler his exhibition by tossing two or three small brass balls into the air, yet by and by brings down more stars than pave the visible heaven to play in dazzling dance around his head. It is in harmony with order to preface great achievements by little; thus the Russian Gastronomer, Alexis Ruganoff,[76] when about to devour a hog, a sheep, and an ovenful of loaves, regularly introduced his three courses by one horn of brandy. We need not therefore, we hope, offer any former apology for confining ourselves in this leading, but we trust, not leaden, article of ours, to those terse and laconic pieces of poetry whose brevity, when it fails to display the soul of wit, will at least make dullness more endurable.

* * * * * * * * *

"My adversary," says Scaliger,[77] in one of his controversial folios, "*ought to blush when he sees the lengthiness and tediousness of my work, which he hath in some sort necessitated me to write, that so I might put him down.*" Now, we are anti-Scaligerian, take us generally, and by the mustachios of Mohammed himself we swear that with the brevity and beauty of this article the public must be enchanted to a degree rather, to say the truth, too painful to be dwelt on; and with respect to which, therefore, propriety dictates to us the preservation of a dignified, we will not add, a stern, silence. They, the said public, shall not feel otherwise, on penalty of being fiercely cut, every anti-human soul of them, wherever we encounter them, at home and abroad, in street and square, north, south, east, west, at church, mart, levee, and theatre. Let them, and they may abide by the consequence. We know how to "shame the fools."[78] Our native city shall be in our eyes as a City of the Dead, and WE, agreeably to the Fichtean[79] philosophy, the only existent individual in town. We shall pace the *trottoirs*, perceiving nobody, astounded at our own solitariness, and musing, with Baconian profundity, over that instability of human affairs which in the space of thirty days has removed from the metropolis a population so celebrated for its singular dissensions, to substitute in its stead a type of plural unity—to wit, Ourself. Like Alexander Selkirk, we shall be "out of humanity's reach, and must finish our journey (to the suburbs) alone."[80] WE in short, shall be everything and the public nothing, after the manner of the Second and Third Estates of the Abbé Sieyés.[81] Till, upon some bland morning in October, weary of wandering hither and thither in this astounded, musing, and misty-eyed state, we shall at once halt, and proceed, with a majesty of manner worthy of the world's wonder, to appropriate to our own use all such cash and portable valuables as may have been thoughtfully left in our way throughout the wilderness around us; chanting, the while, sundry snatches of songs and songs of snatches by the Arab Robbers of the Desert.

In the meantime we think that after all we have sung we are entitled to a call; and so we call for a series of rounds of applause, to be repeated and renewed until our further pleasure be signified, for our concluding ditty.

[Here follows "The Time of the Roses"]

Among the "elegant extracts" in this volume is a tale by TIECK, scanty in incident,—the characters merely stalking to and fro in long cloaks and short boots,—but rich in sentiment and "thoughts that lie luckily too deep for tears."[1] We suppose it may have been given us by way of compensation for the fatigue of reading thirty poetical pieces from the pen of the same writer, filled with sighings and sobbings for tom-tits and robins. We have never, by the way, been able to understand why there should be such a contrast between Tieck's poetry and his prose. In other German writers the characteristics that pervade the novel distinguish the poem also. Goethe[2] for example is uniform through his fifty volumes. *Faust* and *Werther*[3] are fractions of a common integer. We may regard them as we regard an opal: the hues are many, the stone is one. So with Wieland[4] and Schiller and their copied copyists. So, in fact, with all literary Germany except the author of the *Phantasus*.[5] Tieck, like Brockden Brown's Carwin,[6] is a biloquist; he is duplex, double-systemed, two-souled. Like Hoffmann's Medardus,[7] he is linked with a *Doppelgänger*,[8] but the comparison is not to his advantage; for the second-self of Ludwig Tieck might be mistaken for the man in the moon, or his own *Scheuchvogel*.[9] His poetry is the shadow, as his prose is the light of his intellect. It baffles alike description and analysis. There is something on the surface of it that mocks our penetration; so that when we try to look at it stedfastly we feel as if our eyes were filmed over with scales. It appears to us at once bright and dark, like polished ebony. It is akin to the "dazzling gloom" that Shelley speaks of in his version of the May-day Night-scene.[10] It is a painted sky of night-clouds where the moon of the poet's imagination is content to abide for ever in her first quarter. One phase only of his genius is revealed by it, and that is the *chiaro oscuro*.[11] It is a versified magic lantern, not unlike the one which Kerner, who, though a great man, is no conjuror, has lately transferred to his publisher for the puzzlement of reviewers and the wonder of antiquated gentlewomen.[12] We should care little for all this if there were not a certain attraction in Tieck's poetry coercing us to read in defiance of our judgment. In Maturin's *Montorio* there is a character, (his name we forget) a timid man, who when the assassin's knife is at his throat, and he shakes and quakes from head to foot, and his hair stands erect with horror, feels a strong inclination to break into a horse-laugh. We, as we pore over Tieck, are circumstanced somewhat similarly with this shaking quaker, whose name we now recollect to be Filippo.[13] Every stanza is a basilisk which we at once abhor and are fascinated by. One half of our sensations are at war with the other half. We are dragged different ways at the same moment, like Ravaillac[14] by the wild horses. We make energetic efforts, of course, to emancipate ourselves by plucking out the heart of the mystery that lies at the bottom of our thraldom. But the poet laughs us to scorn. His genius is a stumbling-block in our path. It is a rock of strength to himself—a rock of offence to us. It is like a scroll from Herculaneum; the longer we scrutinise it the more embarassing it seems. It grows more and more convolved and intricate each moment; it is an abyss without bottom, a snare, a pitfall, a maze, a labyrinth, the chance of extrication from which appears as remote as that of deliverance from the Living Charnel appeared to Sindbad the Sailor.[15] As Schiller says of the universe, "We call aloud to know what it means, and are answered by the echo of our own words, as if one had shouted down a chasm."[16] It poses, tantalizes, frets, exasperates us. We cannot, charge as desperately as we will, make way through the phalanx of those intellectual cohorts; we exert ourselves in vain to penetrate the triple blinds of sentiment on the wrong side of which the mind of the poet is in full activity, stripped naked like a Roman athlete at his exercises, and exulting in the security and secrecy of its might. As thought after thought comes forth and fronts us we greet it "with open heart and tongue affectionate and true,"[17] but our straightforwardness and warmth of feeling are requited on the instant by some look of intense frigidity, some *noli me tangere*[18] influence, as if, after all, the stranger and we were existences of antagonist orders. Afar off, the cheat appears a magnificence—"the distance lends enchantment to the view"[19]—but when we come to lay hold on our prize the mirage has vanished, and our hands are filled with sand and our hearts with sadness. It glitters, but wants transparence; we cannot see into the core of it; it is brilliant and opaque, like a spread-out sheet of silver. It reminds us of a melo-dramatic spectacle during which we are blinded by the lights, and stunned by the music, and suffocated by the heat, without catching more than a few words, here and there, of the piece. And yet we read and read, still hoping against hope for better things and more intelligible! We are perpetually the victims of the same delusion. Experience profits us nothing. Like Sisyphus,[20] we bowl the stone for ever up the hill, and for ever grasp it on its descent with renewed infatuation. The poet conquers and reconquers us, until the last fragment of our independence is torn into shreds; yet, like the British Army, we cannot believe ourselves beaten. We are taken captive with scarcely a struggle while our confidence is at the proudest pitch, as the reeling drunkard is laid prostrate he knows not how, at the moment when he fancies himself a match singlehanded for a thousand hosts. In vain we arm ourselves like a Goliah;[21] our panoply is useless; if Tieck "throw but a stone the giant dies."[22] He writes *veni, vidi, vici,*[23] on the back of each of his poetical despatches. If now and again he hoists the white flag from the top of a page,[24] it is not a sign that he surrenders, but that *we* are vouchsafed an armistice till he shall think proper to resume hostilities. A fillet is bound over our eyes while we are glorifying ourselves on our perspicacity. The will of the wizard overawes ours. We are dragged on whithersoever he pleases, as Van Wodenblock[25] in the story was by his magic leg. We are "fooled to the top of our bent,"[26] and never perceive, except by glimpses, and "through a glass, darkly,"[27] that the juggler has been mocking us all the time. As a man in a dream, entering a well-known house to gaze on "old familiar faces,"[28] finds himself all at once in a foreign habitation, an enchanted pile; and astonished, alarmed, and confounded, but unreflecting, roams from chamber to chamber, encountering sphynxes, hippogriffs, talking birds and walking statues, and yet still pursues his wanderings, hoping to the last to meet those he is in quest of, so we, while wondrous fancies flit before us, and undefined shapes multiply around us, and all the phantasmagoria of a morbid intellect crowd about us, explore page after page of the mystic volumes that present us with them, and still expect to discover in the end the secret soul of all—hidden, perhaps, in some unsuspected nook, like the soul of the licentiate Pedro Garcias, in the preface to Gil Blas,[29] or diffused over the entire surface of the writer's imaginings, like star-light over a deep flood—a subtle gas, with whose peculiar properties our faculties could become intimate only after we had been breathing it so long as to forget our ordinary atmosphere, as the eyes of a man who passes from a bright room into a dark one must learn to accommodate themselves to the change before the haze that rests on surrounding objects can be dispelled.

The conclusion we would come to with respect to Tieck's poetry, is as follows. It is an emanation from, not an exertion of, intellect. It is neither action nor passion; it merely indicates the *perception* of these. It exhibits many blemishes and many beauties, but it will always be a favourite with imaginative young people from eighteen to eight and twenty. To all others it must be caviare. Its worst fault is its sickly egotism. This is the "green and yellow"[30] silk twist upon which all Tieck's poetical pearls are strung. He seems incapable of "subduing himself to the quality of his conception;"[31] he has not the heart to break down the walls of the sanctuary, within which, "fold over fold, inextricable coil,"[32] his *amour-propre* twines around the pillars of his thought: take what form he will, he is haunted by his individuality to the last, as the princes in the Arabian Nights, though metamorphosed into birds and apes, are condemned to retain their consciousness. The style is beautiful, except where the author attempts the legend. The matter is made up of weepings, about nobody knows what—and wanderings about, nobody knows where—flash-in-the-pan *éclats* of sentimentalism—hop-skip-and-jump sketches of narrative; for anything like a regular "story, Lord bless you, he has none to tell, Sir"[33]—dusky allusions to past events, unintelligible to every body else, perhaps to himself, and baby babble about flowers, in which he sees a resemblance to mankind, for the very dreamy reason that the head of man is inclined to thought, and the head of the flower to the light, and that when man begins to nod, the flower droops.[34] Having said so much, we shall be excused for not at present offering any translations from Tieck. We pass on to the next writer in the volume before us, JUSTINUS KERNER.

This gentleman is considered by some as belonging to the same school with Tieck. There is, however, a noticeable difference between the two parties. Tieck is a very metaphysician in his poetry, delighting to anatomise what he feels, and descanting *à la Socrate* on topics which few but himself understand or care about: Kerner never troubles us with the analysis of any of his emotions; he merely tells us that he is glad or grieved, *und damit Lied am Ende.*[35] Again, Tieck rarely appears unequal or incongruous; Kerner is so much a contrast to him here, that he sometimes begins a poem where he should end it, and then, to mend the matter, stops short in the middle, fancying he has finished. The only points of resemblance we can see between them, are their egotism, and their common German propensity to weep for dead sparrows and rave about the breakings-up of iceponds. Tieck, though he sonnetizes half the poets of his fatherland, never alludes any where to the existence of such an individual as the Suabian physician—a proof that he has little community of feeling with him—while Kerner lavishes the entire of his little stock of panegyric on Uhland.

* * * * * * * * *

We must take the liberty of pushing aside our respected friend, La Motte Fouqué, with his show-box of tourneys and banquettings, to make space for SCHUBART.

Poor Schubart! Who can ponder the story of his life without admitting him to be as indisputably entitled to the *sobriquet* of the Unlucky as Gregory Hipkins[36] himself, or even Miss Edgeworth's Murad?[37] Schubart was born in 1739—was sent to school—was a dunce—and was flogged—went to study divinity at Jena—managed to get into debt with every body there—came home wrecked in his health—turned musician, then tutor, then player, then hack-scribbler—worked himself into innumerable scrapes in each capacity—married a wife and immediately afterwards quarrelled with and separated from her—obtained the post of leader of an orchestra at Ludwigsburg, and lost it again through his untameable impetuosity—revenged himself by writing a satire on the Ludwigsburgers and their orchestras generally—had his house (accidentally) burned about his ears and at the same time found the town itself too hot to hold him— was banished by the authorities to Stutgard—was driven thence to Heidelberg, and thence to Manheim, where through the interest of Count Nesselrode he was appointed to an honourable situation in the Musical Academy—caricatured "with the best intentions," every member of the Academy—was cashiered in consequence—travelled to Munich— embroiled himself with divers respectable families there—raised a tremendous hubbub in every house he set foot in—was obliged to decamp post-haste—went to Augsburg, and there established a newspaper in which he lampooned the whole world and the Augsburg magistrates—was of course shewn to the gates of the town by the said magistrates—capered off to Ulm, the entire population of which he raised in arms against him—and fell, at last, into the clutches of the Duke of Wirtemberg, who locked him up in the fortress of Arnsberg, where for *ten years*, compassionate reader, he remained loaded with irons, and received a scanty supply of bread and water daily for sustenance! Like Trenck,[38] however, he was endowed with indomitable fortitude, and learned to dance in his chains;—the same emptiness of stomach, moreover, to which Novalis[39] traces the origin of his own extraordinary activity of brain appears to have aided the development of Schubart's genius, for he produced all his readable poems in his dungeon. On his enlargement he opened a theatre in Stutgard and was about to commence, besides, a variety of literary undertakings, when, in 1791, he was attacked by an illness which terminated in his death.

* * * * * * * * *

LITERÆ ORIENTALES.
TURKISH POETRY.—SECOND ARTICLE.

A PORTION of the long-expected work of the Baron von Hammer-Purgstall[1] on the Poetry of Turkey has at length been published. It has not given general satisfaction. In many respects it may be regarded as a valuable acquisition to the library of the Orientalist, and particularly on account of the interesting information it communicates on the past and present state of literature in the Ottoman Empire. But altogether the book, we fear, is dull; it smells oppressively of the lamp. It contains, indeed, several hundreds of selections from the Turkish Poets; but, alas! of these hundreds there are not a dozen pieces intelligible, not half a dozen readable, and not three,—the quarter of a dozen—what we could pronounce admirable.

Considering what manner of man M. von Hammer is, this, we think, is hard. Every body who knows M. von Hammer knows that he is one man in a million. He has achieved an enduring reputation as an universal linguist and philologist. He is perhaps the first Orientalist of his era. His general knowledge it would be difficult to match by that of any other living individual. In his character of poet, of poetical translator especially, we consider him the antipodes of contemptible. He is somewhat gaudy and unequal in his prose writings, but his talents for research and discrimination, his capabilities as a compiler, are too well known to require our eulogy. For upwards of thirty years, moreover, he has distinguished himself as the almost sole advocate of the excellence of Turkish Poetry. It was incumbent on him when the time arrived for establishing the fact of that excellence on a more permanent basis than mere general assertion, to adduce evidence that his encomiums had not been lavished without reason or before he had satisfied himself of their justness by laborious and critical investigation. He might have recollected that the rock upon which Sir William Jones[2] had split was the practical antithesis of following up a series of panegyrics on the peculiar beauty of Persian poetry by a few starveling verses from HAFEZ and others, rather more prosaic than ordinary prose. The character of M. von Hammer never can be at stake; but though a man may gain a reputation by a great deal of talent, he requires, to sustain it, a trifling share of tact. If the Baron could not have added another brick to the pyramid of his fame he should at least have left it standing as it was and have been contented to repose within it. His course has been somewhat injudicious, and is certainly calculated to afford a triumph to the anti-

Ottoman party, already pretty rampant, among the literary *sapernientes*[3] of the Continent.

The work is called a *History*[4] of Ottoman Poetry, but the share of narrative it comprises is not copious. It is for the most part made up of selections from the writings of persons by courtesy called poets, which selections appear in the form of rhyme or of blank verse, as suited the convenience of the translator. As a sample of those selections we give the following ghazels, transcribed from the first pages we may happen to open the book at.

We have opened it at p. 150.[5]

GHAZEL.

AUS LAMII'S DIWAN.

Durch Wunder ward des Busens Feld zum Gülistan
O Herzensräuber, seh mit einem Blick mich an!
Ist's Wunder, wenn sich meine Thräne spiegelt roth,
Da heut der Freud gekleidet in Syringenroth,
Im Leichentuch fall' ich wie Wasser dir zu Füszen,
Wenn du Cypresse mich mit einem Wink willst grüszen,
Nur einen Augenblick hör meine Klagen an,
Wenn ich wie Nachtigall erseufz' im Gülistan.
O schleppe mich, wie Schatten, durch des Staubs Gewimmel,
Denn wenn ich gleich nur Staub, so bist du doch der Himmel,
Das Ach! der Nachtigall beeng' nicht deine Brust,
O Knospenlippichter! eng ist der Erde Lust,
Es will dich tödten Lamii, der, den du liebst,
Was ist's, wenn einen Augenblick du Aufschub gibst.

GHAZEL.

FROM LAMII'S DIVAN.[6]

The field of the bosom became a rose-garden with wonder.
O, robber of the heart! look on me with a glance!
Is it (a) wonder if my tear is mirrored red,
When the friend (is) to-day clad in red sprinkling.
I fall as water in a graveshroud at thy feet,
If thou, cypress, wilt greet me with a nod,
Hear my lamentations only a moment,
When I sigh in the rose-garden like (a) nightingale.
O, trail me like (a) shadow through the cloud of dust,

For, though I (am) only dust, thou art heaven,

The Ah! the nightingale (should) not straiten thy breast,
O, bud-lipped! limited is the earth's pleasure.
Lamii will kill thee, he whom thou lovest,
What (matter) is it, if thou givest respite a moment.

Again we open it at p. 145.[7]

GHAZEL.

AUS LAMII'S DIWAN.

Dein Schönheitsgarten ist vom Bartflaum
    grün geworden
Es wächst der Liebe Raserey; ist's Lenz geworden?
O Schöner, deines Flaumes Zeilen sind am Rande
Zur Glossenschrift von dem Koran der Schönheit
    worden,
Wiewohl sultanische Moschee sich einfach ziemt

Ist sie zuletzt mit Bildern ausgemahlet worden.

GHAZEL.

FROM LAMII'S DIVAN.

Thy garden of beauty is grown green from the down
    of the beard.
The madness of love encreases; is Spring come?
O, Beautiful! the lines of thy down are become
A glossary on the margin of the Koran of Beauty.
Although it beseems the Sultan's mosque to be
    simple
It is in the end decorated with paintings.

Der Trennung Feuer sengt die Liebenden wie Mücken,	The fire of separation singes the lovers like gadflies,
Dann wascht sie Huld; es ist der jüngste Tag geworden,	Grace then washes them; it is the Judgment-day.
Dein Schönheits Jusuf wird für Moschus aus gewogen,	Thy beauty's Joseph is weighed out for musk,
Zum Käufer ist Suleicha des Flaums geworden,	Zuleika of the Down is become a merchant.
Um deiner Wangen Flur im Frühling zu begrünen,	To make the meadow of thy cheeks verdant in Spring
Ist Flaums Basilikon Violenstreu geworden,	The basilick of (the) down is become a violet-parterre.
Das Haar zog LAMII, der Schönheit vor den Flor,	The hair drew LAMII before the meadow of beauty,
Deszhalb sind Herzen hier zu Klagenden geworden.	Therefore the hearts here are become bewailers.

How far inferior in pith and originality these lines are to the lunatic burst of Nat. Lee,[8] beginning, "O, that my lungs could bleat like buttered peas!" We make just one other extract at random.[9]

GHAZEL.

Es ist das Aug' in Herzensgluth getauchet mir,	My eye is dipped in the heat of the heart,
Von diesem Feuerquelle Alles raucht an mir,	From this fount of fire everything smokes nigh me.
Wenn ohne dich ich in des Herzensgluthen brenne,	If I burn without thee in the heats of the heart
Erscheine ich als Leichnam, den man peinigt mir.	I seem as (a) corpse, which people torment (in) me.
O schenke! schenke ein dem, der nicht Liebe hauchet,	O, pour, pour out to him who breathes not love,
Von Liebe bin ich trunken, Wein gebricht nicht mir,	I am drunk from love, I want not wine.
Ich schliesze zu das Auge, um dein Bild zu sehen,	I close the eye, to see thine image.
Geschlosz'nes Aug' ist nicht in Schlaf getauchet mir,	My closed eye is not dipped in sleep.
MUHIBBI seufzt im Schmerz der Nacht aus Seelenadern	MUHIBBI sighs from (the) veins of (the) soul in the pain of the night.
Begeisterung, nicht Hauch der Laute, haucht aus mir.	Inspiration, not breath of sound, breathes out of me.

In what corner of M. von Hammer's brain was his good taste slumbering while his fingers were busy in filling his volumes with such trash as this?

But enough of so ungracious a theme. We must see whether it be not practicable to exhibit the Ottoman Muse in apparel somewhat more attractive than that which decorates her here.

For us, we make no boast on behalf of Oriental poetry. We are not so wrongheaded as to assert the superiority of the Asiatic to the European languages. We assert no superiority on any side, and no inferiority. The languages of all civilized nations, philosophically considered,—that is, considered with reference to the only principles applicable to the consideration of languages,—are unquestionably upon a common level as far as regards the vocabularies of genuine thought and feeling. No one of these languages can be richer than another, because no one of them comprehends an ampler stock of ideas than another. Phantomy and fantastic *nuances* of apprehension there may certainly exist in some of them of which others are destitute; but these are nullities; we can no more class them with the healthy and tangible births of intellect than we could include in a census of the earth's population the myriads of spirits who may be dancing on the point of every needle. For all legitimate purposes of conception and expression we believe that the English language, the German language, and the Turkish language are upon a perfect equality one with another. We believe that that which is good poetry in any one of these languages may be made to appear equally as good poetry in any other of them, if the translator be possessed of skill enough to make it appear so, and that translators may be possessed of such skill there can be no doubt.

The simple question then for discussion and decision would appear to be, Whether Turkish Poetry, or any portion of it, be good or not. We will give a brief statement of the result of our own investigations on the subject.

Suffering the more voluminous poems to remain untouched for the present, let us confine ourselves to a review of those immediately within our reach, and more available for the purposes we propose to forward.

The ghazels,[10] elegies, odes and songs collected by KINALIZADE, AASHIK, REEAZI, KAFZADE and the other Oriental compilers and commentators of latter times, amount, by the best computation that we can make, to about ten thousand. The relative merit of these productions is of course apparent at a glance, and the critic experiences no difficulty in disposing of them off-hand. Our classification of them takes this order:
There are:
Of the inane and characterless, three thousand.
Of the religio-mystic, three thousand.
Of the mad metaphoric, two thousand.
Of the bombastic, one thousand.

These would furnish a total of nine thousand. One thousand, however, would still remain unclassified, and these one thousand would perhaps redeem the worthlessness of the other nine thousand. In reality the fact bears us out in our conjecture. There are in or about such a number of tolerable, of good, and even of first-rate poems in the MSS. of the compilers we have named—poems which would have been worthy of translation into German, as we trust they will be deemed worthy, even by our humble hand, of translation into English.[11]

From this proportion, then, of the entire, we propose to give our versions; and if we fail to interest, as now and then perhaps we may, the fault is our own, and we are willing to bear the odium of it.

* * * * * * * * *

To convey an idea of the spirit and character of the religious poetry of the Ottoman writers we select a passage from the *Nedshatul-Gharik*, or Salvation for the Perishing, by one of the HUDAYIS. The work is in alternate prose and verse, a mode of composition by no means rare among the Orientals.

Passage

FROM HUDAYI II. NATIVE OF ANATOLIA. OB. 1628.
LIES BURIED NEAR CONSTANTINOPLE.

The Prophet spake to MURAD, saying: Into how many classes, thinkest thou, will the wicked be divided on the Judgment Day? Murad answered: GOD and his Prophet can tell. Then, said the Prophet, hearken thou: at the Last Day there will be ten divisions of the wicked; for some will be apes and others swine, and some will be hanged with their feet upwards and their heads to the earth, and others will be blind, and others deaf, and there will be some gnashing their teeth and vomiting fiery pitch, and some will have their hands and feet cut off, and some will be buried up to the mouth in mire, and the carrion bodies of others will exhale a horrible stench. GOD and his Prophet, said Murad, can tell who these are: who are they? The Prophet answered, saying: Hearken thou: the apes are the flatterers; the swine are the sensual; those hanged with their heads downward are the unmerciful; the blind and deaf are the unbelievers and the hard-hearted; the vomiters of fiery pitch are the liars; the maimed are the envious neighbours who ruin others, those buried in the mire are they who live in too much luxury, and the carrion-bodied are they who abandon themselves unrestrained to libertinism. Afterwards the Prophet spake to ABOU HOREIRA: O! ABOU HOREIRA, Thy best safeguard is prayer, and thy best prayer is the confession of faith, THERE IS NO GOD BUT GOD. Every good work will be weighed on the Last Day except this confession of faith, THERE IS NO GOD BUT GOD; for O! ABOU HOREIRA! if this were put in one scale and the nine heavens and the seven oceans in the other, the heavens and the oceans would all be outweighed by the confession, THERE IS NO GOD BUT GOD. O, Man, saith HUDAYI, that walkest in darkness and art proud of blindness, dream not that thou canst cling to the weak reeds that grow up from the marshes of this world.[12]

* * * * * * * * *

KAFZADE has preserved a good repartee by this YAKINI. He had one day taken his place at an entertainment above a certain Molla MOOSTAFA ZABRIS, celebrated for being able to repeat all the chapters of the Koran off book, and the Molla grew wroth. "O, Effendi," he exclaimed, "is it you who give my father's son this dirt to eat? Have you no regard to decency and the fitness of things? By your beard! say, does it become you to take precedence of me? Of two books, one the Koran, and the other a book of profane science, which do men lay uppermost?" "They lay the Koran uppermost," answered the poet, coolly, "but as to the *wrapper* of the Koran,[13] they thrust that into any corner."

* * * * * * * * *

There is a very curious old Turkish poem, called the *Mulhimet*, or the Revelation, a sort of calendar in verse, originally written by SALAHEDDIN about the beginning of the fifteenth century, but which continued to receive emendations and additions from various writers up to the middle of the seventeenth. From this authority we learn[14] that people should begin to build on Saturday, to plant kitchen-gardens on Sunday, and to travel on Monday, and should slay animals on Tuesday, take physic on Wednesday, commence perilous undertakings on Thursday, and make love on Friday. We would suggest, however, that the duty of Friday might be very appropriately merged in that of Thursday, as making love is rather a perilous undertaking in its way. Wednesday is the unlucky day of the week, for on that day no fewer than seven persons have, from time to time, found their way out of this world—namely, King Pharaoh[15]—Nimrod, the Mighty Hunter[16]—Lot[17]—the rebel trio, Core, Dathan, and Abiron[18]—and lastly the giant Og,[19] who at the time of the Deluge stood only up to his knees in water.

* * * * * * * * *

And now to conclude.

The *Iskander Nameh*[20] is a Mystic Epic Poem of the thirteenth century, by the Ottoman poet AHMEDI. Both as a poem and a philosophical composition it is held even at the present day in great veneration by most Mohammedans, but more especially those of Turkey. The subject, as the title imports, is the Life of Alexander the Great,[21] but the work embraces multiplied and complicated disquisitions on almost every branch of literature and science. It may, in fact, be regarded as an Oriental Encyclopædia of metaphysics, history, geography, natural philosophy, civil polity, and religious doctrine. It is divided into thirteen cantos, containing altogether more than sixteen thousand lines, and is ornamented with seventy-five gorgeous illustrations.

An introduction to the poem discusses, in a series of protracted dialogues, the respective rival claims of the ancient Persian emblems of Love, Purity, and Beauty—the Taper, the Butterfly, Wine and the Censer, on the regard and affection of the descendants of Adam. The poem itself opens with a recondite and abstruse treatise on the unity, attributes, occupations, and names of the Godhead—an eulogy of the poet on himself, and a long list of his own names,[22] amplified by minute explanations first of the ostensible and then of the real signification of those names—a solemn hymn in praise of the Prophet—a selection from the Prophet's traditional sayings—a discourse upon the nature of Truth—a panegyric on Wisdom— an apostrophe to the properties of the human spirit—and an examination into the doctrine of the Metempsychosis.[23] The action of the poem at length develops itself by a review of the state of hostilities between Philip of Macedon[24] and Darius of Persia.[25] The poet pours forth a lament for the world while suffering under the scourge of war. He praises the physical wonders of the globe, again treats the unity of God, considers the emptiness of past renown, and offers some speculations with regard to his own celebrity in after ages. Alexander is born and educated. The poet lauds the advantages of learning. Philip dies, and the poet laments the transitoriness of life. Alexander summons before his throne the Wise Men of Greece,[26] of whom, instead of seven, there are but four—namely *Aristo* (Aristotle), *Iflatun* (Plato), *Sokhrat* (Socrates), and *Bokhrat* (Hippocrates[27]). Alexander enquires what the original substance of the globe was. Aristotle answers Fire—Plato, Water—Socrates, Earth—and Hippocrates, Air;—but Khisra, the Guardian of the Fountain of Life,[28] suddenly appearing among them, declares that God created the world out of nothing; and the four philosophers confess themselves vanquished. The poet examines those proofs of the unity of God that may be adduced by Reason. He gives four chapters of Wise Sayings by the four Wise Men, and announces Aristotle to be the type of Reason, Plato of Imagination, Socrates of Memory, and Hippocrates of Practical Philosophy; and the canto closes by a brief recurrence to the state of affairs between Alexander and Darius.

Canto II. begins with a philosophical enquiry into the nature of Sleep and Dreaming, of which the poet recognises two species, the real and the illusive. Darius despatches a messenger to Alexander to demand tribute, which is refused: the messenger then, to typify the numerousness of the Persian armies, silently pours out a sack of millet-seed on the ground before Alexander, and Alexander orders in a cock who picks up the whole of the millet-seed. Of this the poet supplies the metaphysical elucidation: Darius is human cupidity, and Alexander the soul; the millet-seed are the many faults of our nature, which the cock, who is Religion,[29] overcomes and destroys. Alexander and Darius prepare for war; but Darius, betrayed by his generals, is assassinated. The poet deplores the blindness and wickedness of a portion of mankind, and, as a remedy for the evils that afflict the world, recommends a general abstinence from crime, and an adherence to the precepts of Wisdom and Reason.

Canto III. opens with a statement of the dimensions of the planets. The earth is not square, but round; it is six thousand eight hundred farsangs[30] in circumference, and two thousand one hundred and sixty-four farsangs in diameter: the firmament above the earth is thirty-three thousand farsangs in thickness: the firmament above Mercury is four thousand and fourteen farsangs in thickness, &c. The poet expatiates on the works of creation, and condemns those learned men who employ their talents for atheistical purposes. He discusses the nature of the soul and the nature of the body. The soul is an abstraction, a pure consciousness, without solidity or extension, diffused everywhere in a *cognizant* capacity, but not actually existing in any one spot:[31] the body is a structure composed of nine jewels, two hundred and forty-eight pillars, seven hundred and twenty hinges, three hundred and sixty fountains, and twelve gates, and is guarded by eight sentinels. The nine jewels are the flesh, blood, saliva, nails, muscles, skin, fat, hair, and teeth; the two hundred and forty-eight pillars are the bones; the seven hundred and twenty hinges are the nerves; the three hundred and sixty fountains are the veins; the twelve gates are the two lips, two ears, two eyes, &c.[32] and the eight sentinels are digestion and respiration, self-respect, creativeness and cautiousness, the propensity to oppose, the love of fame and the love of life. An ambassador is sent from Keid, the Indian king, to Alexander, and Alexander presents him with a pot of lard; the ambassador punctures the lard with needles, and Alexander melts down the needles in a furnace, upon which the ambassador transmutes the molten mass into a pocket-mirror. A metaphysical explanation of this by the poet follows: the pot of lard is the soul, filled with covetousness; the needles are pungent words of wisdom which penetrate it, and which, being melted down in the furnace of order, become a manual of philosophy, and finally take the form of a mirror of self-knowledge. Follows another treatise on the unity of God; and the canto ends by a detailed account of the creation of the world.

In Canto IV. Alexander goes to India, and hunts lions among the mountains. This is an allegory: Alexander is Reason, and the lions are the Passions. The poet sings a hymn to the Creator. Alexander wages war with Porus and his elephants: Porus is the soul, subjugated by Passion; the elephants are the evil powers of the soul, and Alexander is Reason.

In Canto V. the war with Porus is continued, and Alexander combats and kills a dragon.

Canto VI. commences with a description of the devil. The poet divides philosophy into theoretical and practical. He dissertates upon bravery, self-diffidence and integrity; and exhorts the world to be virtuous. A prayer to God follows, and Alexander goes to China.

Alexander, in Canto VII. sets out for Zanguebar and reaches the Mountain of Snakes; from thence he proceeds to the Island of Quackquack, so called because the fruits on the trees of the island are birds which, by an instinctive intelligence, cry out *Quack, quack*, whenever a traveller visits the place;[33] and from thence he sails to the Island of Atvarib, the inhabitants of which have dogs' heads. The poet minutely describes the crab and the musk-deer, and furnishes a reason for the phosphorence of organised bodies, and especially of dead fish. He gives an account of men who have fishes' heads, and fish who have human heads, and describes a singular animal which swims by day, and flies by night. Alexander goes to Java; he builds the city of Serendib, and then sails to the Island of Sulamit; proceeds from thence to the Valley of Diamonds, and then sails up the Indian Archipelago, until he reaches a great Mountain of Wonders, in the centre of which is a crystal palace, protected by forty-eight talismans. Finally, he goes again to China, and arriving at Shadkiam, the capital,[34] which contains a dense population of magicians, genii, and philosophers, he enters into a discussion with the latter on the essential properties of bodies, which is prolonged to the close of the canto.

Canto VIII. describes a rock into which a Peri has been banished for three thousand years. The poet displays his knowledge of mineralogy and metallurgy, and then returns to Alexander, who engages in controversy with a Mandarin on the power of the Creator. Those evidences of a First Cause furnished by Creation are considered by the poet. Alexander goes to Cashmere and constructs the Dyke of Gog and Magog. The poet describes the Nile, the wonders of Egypt, the building of Alexandria, and the Pharos of that city, which he regards as a symbol of Reason. This canto ends with prayer.

Canto IX. treats exclusively of the heavenly bodies, their nature, their number, and the influence they exercise over the affairs of mankind.[35]

Canto X. is devoted to an account of the preparations made by Alexander for going to war with Kaidafa, Queen of the Amazons.

In Canto XI. the poet recommends the study of navigation, botany, metaphysics, mathematics, astrology, and natural history generally.

Alexander applies himself to acquire information with regard to the moral and physical condition of mankind, past and present, and engages in a discussion with Aristotle on the probable occupations of great warriors and great statesmen in a future existence.

Canto XII. begins with giving a list, in chronological order, of the Shahs of Ancient Persia, which is continued down to the epoch of Mohammed. A list of the Arabian Khaliffs follows, to the age in which the poet flourished. This canto alone is, in point of length, nearly equal to half the poem. The author pronounces a glowing panegyric on himself at the end, and vows vengeance against the whole race of womankind, on account, principally, of their hair and their duplicity, neither of which can be painted as black as it is.[36]

The last Canto opens with a fable of a cock and a bull, a fox and a parroquet, the drift of which is not obvious.[37] Alexander goes to Jerusalem, and from thence returns again to Egypt. His good-fortune has now reached its acmé. He goes again to India, leaves India for Djinnestan (Genii-land), and Djinnestan for the *Land of Darkness*; his armies are scattered through wildernesses, and perish; and finally he himself lies down to die, under the shade of a tent, with a golden cupola above him.[38] The last illustration represents Alexander's mother weeping over the sarcophagus of her son; and the poet concludes his work by a lament for his hero and fifteen other laments for fifteen philosophers, *viz.* Hippocrates, Plato, Matrimus, Rufus, Bertas, Philo,[39] Socrates, Bias,[40] Pythagoras,[41] Bidagoras, Aristippus,[42] Solon,[43] Zeno,[44] Heraclitus,[45] and Aristotle.[46] In a sort of postscript he congratulates himself on his achievement thus:

> Glory be to GOD that this sublime and
>   Glittering string of pearls at last is finished!
> That these noble pebbles, each a diamond,
>   Greet the eye in lustre undiminished!
> Certes, of the master-hands of China,
>   None can paint a picture of such splendor:
> Persia cannot boast of so divine a
>   Work, so philosophic, yet so tender.
> Beauty sparkles here in all its phases;
>   Tulips, hyacinths, and flaming roses,
> Weighty words, plump couplets, jewelled phrases,
>   Be the treasures this rich book discloses,
> And each stanza, as thou seest it written,
>   Was compared beneath my own inspection
> With the original of same, as fit in
>   Cases where a work demands perfection.

Our next article will probably terminate our review of Ottoman Poetry. It will depend upon circumstances whether we shall afterwards enter upon Persian and Arabic. At present we have no great inclination to either. To acknowledge the truth, at the close of our paper, *we dislike Eastern poetry.*[47] Its great pervading character is mysticism—and mysticism and stupidity are synonymous terms in our vocabulary. No luxuriance of imagination can atone for the absence of perspicuity. A poet above all men should endeavour to make words the images of things. He should not disdain to graduate in the school of the logician. The shadow on the wall can as easily strike a blow as the poet can produce an impression without lucidness both of conception and language. It is the error of poets that they consider themselves bound to be at all hazards original. They are ignorant that the value of originality is to be tested by the character of the originality, and that the Dull is something totally different from even a remote modification of the Entertaining. They may be assured that every thought worth expressing has already been expressed forty thousand times over. Ideas resemble all other things; there is but a certain usable number of them in the world; and though that number may be vast, it is not infinite. The very phrase, "march of mind,"[48] indicates the existence of a goal, or it follows that we are all in the monstrous condition of travelling without a prospect of terminating our journey. The stock in trade of the mind—an embargo being first laid on all commodities, the sale of which were a fraud on the purchaser—(and really a poet should have as much conscience as a pedler) is soon catalogued. "The thing that hath been is that which shall be,"[49] only into another shape transmuted. To repudiate all that is antiquated, merely because it is antiquated, as the Hindoos drive the aged of their kindred into the Hoogly,[50] is fashionable, but wrong. Poets do not stand the higher in the estimation of the rational for writing insufferable nonsense about embalmed reminiscences, and sunny tresses, and spirit-voices. Instead of creating nondescript forms out of no materials they should rather endeavour to mould the existing materials into new and more beautiful forms. In doing this they would be rendering service to the world and to themselves. Mysticism would disappear from literature, and poetry for the first time stand a reasonable chance of becoming in reality what hitherto it has been only in name—popular for its intrinsic excellence.

ANTHOLOGIA GERMANICA.—NO. XII.
THE LESS TRANSLATABLE POEMS OF SCHILLER.

THE greater number of Schiller's Ballads remain undone into English; but nobody who has read them can be at a loss to discover the reason that they have been thus neglected. They are dull; and dulness of composition induces repugnance to translation; for that which people do not get through *con amore* they seldom get through with *éclat* to themselves or satisfaction to others. Half the impracticability of shaping a sow's ear into a silk purse is owing to the disgust of the artist upon taking the bristly material in hand; his antipathy paralyses his operations, and he bungles the job. A translator, in grappling with his original, should be possessed by a feeling akin to that which animates the matador in his contests with the bull; but if there be positively nothing in that original which can awaken such a feeling, it is clear that it must continue to slumber. The energy can be elicited only by the occasion. In other words, none but good poems are susceptible of being well translated. For it is in this department of literature as it is in love; the maintenance of fidelity towards the beautiful is always easier than it is towards the ordinary.

Let us not be accused of injustice towards Schiller. We merely echo the opinion of the best German critics. It is admitted that, great as the other powers of Schiller were, he wanted those which constitute the perfect ballad-singer. His genius, essentially dramatic and didactic, never accommodated itself gracefully to those restrictions which a judicious adherence to the established forms of narrative must, in a greater or lesser degree, impose on a writer. Where he had to deal with but a few incidents, and those few were of a striking nature, he could depict them vividly enough, especially in prose; but his monologues and dialogues are acknowledged, after all, to be the best parts of him. Speech-making was, in truth, his forte; while, as a story-teller, he sank below zero or Mother Bunch.[1] Next to his *Song of the Bell* (which is all spoken by the bell-founder,) his *Lament of Ceres* is his finest rhymed poem; but it is pure declamation throughout. On the other hand, his *Cranes of Ibycus* is a piece of lifelessness that would be at present ejected from the Balaam-box[2] of a half-penny miscellany; but it is narrative throughout. And the difference observable between these twain is a sample of the difference that subsists between all his poems of the declamatory class and all his poems of the narrative class.

Candour, however, demands from us the admission that among the latter there are two which, though displaying many imperfections, exercise considerably less of a soporific influence over us than nine-tenths of the rest. One of these is a ballad foundered [*sic*] on the story of Damon and Pythias and is warbled in this manner:

[Here follows "The Hostage"]

The conduct of Pythias[3] in this ballad is of course intended to enlist the sympathies of the reader; and his energy and intrepidity are certainly incontestable. But energy and intrepidity, as it happens, are in themselves such excellent qualities that in witnessing the exhibition of them we sometimes forget to enquire whether the circumstances demanding that exhibition might not have been controlled in the beginning, and the resources of the exhibitor thus husbanded against a season when they should be really wanted. That we do so forget is to be attributed to us as a fault. When a man chuses to set his own house on fire the grand and striking *coups de théâtre* that he may show off in rescuing his wife and children from the flames, while they elicit shouts of applause from us, should not hinder us from recollecting that his heroism is barely the *amende honorable*[4] he makes to his duty when the consequences of his folly have become apparent. The slaying of dragons we account praiseworthy; but when somebody tells us that the slayer is in the habit of making the dragons he slays we qualify our encomiums. Pythias was himself the creator of the necessity for all the hubble-bubble, toil and trouble[5] that he put himself to. Being condemned to death for his want of cautiousness, he begs a respite of three days, and this being accorded, off he scampers, at the rate of twenty knots an hour, on a wild goose chase nobody knows whither. Now it is clear to us that this proceeding was uncalled for. He interfered with the regular course of justice. Punishment may not in every case follow hard upon conviction; but a high-minded criminal must always be extremely unwilling to solicit any postponement of the penalty that his crimes have provoked. Pythias should have scorned to beg a favour from the Tyrant. He should have looked the dagger at him that was taken from his waistcoat pocket, and gone to death without parley or ostentation. Above all, he should not have jeopardied the life of his dearest friend for the satisfaction of cranching a pie-crust and tossing off a glass of wine at a wedding. Not a soul upon the face of the earth wished or wanted him to make a parade of his incomparable pedestrianism, his talent for flood-cleaving, his ingenuity in robber-quelling, or his capability of sensation-creating. His light-hearted sister could have got married, and probably did get married, without his assistance. History does not furnish us with any authentic account of the reception she accorded him, but in all likelihood it was cool in the extreme; and the bridegroom must unquestionably have refused him the loan of a horse. There is absolutely no motive whatever for his expedition. All his puffing and blowing are wasted on the air. We cannot understand his conduct, unless we refer it to a passion for singularity and notoriety. Probably this is the real key to the mystery, although, if we admit it to be, it does not elevate in our eyes either his own character or that of his adventures. Viewed in combination with all the concomitant circumstances, it makes the coming up just in time for the breaking down of the bridge laughable, lends a certain air of silliness to the drubbing of the club-lawyers, and even reduces the humbug of bursting through the mob to call out, "Stop the execution!" to a level with any other melo-dramatic clap-trap.

Of the mode in which Schiller, as a mere workman, has dealt with the machinery of the story, readers will judge for themselves. For us, we pass on to our second sample, *The Glove*, which, however, is not strictly a ballad, but rather a lengthy anecdote.

[Here follows "The Glove"]

Und er wirft ihr den Handschuh in's Gesicht—and he throws to her the hand-shoe in the face, as we may gracefully render the line. Sir Guy was, like Bayard,[6] *le chevalier sans peur*, but not, like Bayard, *le chevalier sans reproche*. He was in the wrong in flinging a hand-shoe into a Countess' face, in the presence of both Human and Brute Majesty: the act was shy, shocking and shabby.[7] But what we conceive to have been most particularly reprehensible in him was the stupid chivalrous politeness that led him to risk his life for the sake of one whom he knew to be worthless, and whom he had even then predetermined to disgrace in the eyes of the whole amphitheatre. This was pushing romance a little too far, and could not, we warrant, have had the slightest tendency to humble or soften the adorable Grafinn and Frau.[8] Such mistakes, we are sorry to say, sometimes occur upon a different scale, even in our own days; but they are oftenest made by the very young and enthusiastic, whom nothing short of a series of cruellest experiences can teach that there are hearts in this world hard as the nether mill-stone, and which convert every fresh instance of generosity towards themselves into food for undissembled triumph and open mockery.

* * * * * * * * *

To the Poet.

Lasz die Sprache dir seyn, was der Körper den Liebenden.

When thy soul kindles most with thine endeavours,
  Still be thy language to the thought it covers,
  That only which the body is to lovers—
At once the great link that unites and severs.

Many of the German poets have very faithfully followed this advice; and the consequence has been that Poetry is with them an affair of moonshine and fog, the fog predominating. Surely there can be no valid reason that the language of poetry should not be as comprehensible and unambiguous as the habit of clear and correct thinking necessarily renders all language. A genius for mystifying successfully is the rarest of endowments; but even the finished mystifier hazards a step likely to be attended with failure when he attempts to mystify through any other medium than that of metaphysics and criticism. There appears to be something in the very nature and essence of true poetry—whether of the sublime or the heart-breaking order—irreconcileable with any admixture of either self-mockery or mockery of others. It would be difficult indeed to persuade us that mystification would not have been wholly out of place in the *Iliad* or *Childe Harold*—at least such mystification as had in any degree bordered upon the familiarity of quizzery.

Some of Schiller's opinions with respect to Poetry were odd. He thought, for instance, that it contributed to make a man virtuous. *Was wäre ich ohne Dich?*[9] he asks the Muse: *Ich weisz es nicht* (we could have told him)—*aber mir grauet! seh' ich, was ohne Dich Hundert und Tausende sind*[10]—that is—

To Poesy.

What had I been without thy star
  To light the pathway of my being?
I know not; but what myriads *are*
  I see—and shudder in the seeing!

Overlooking the fact that there were other myriads, despisers of poetry to a unit, each of whom was as moral and happy an individual as himself, and much more useful than he to society. In reality Poetry never had at any time more to do with rectitude of purpose or conduct than with red hair or round shoulders. The Creator has so constituted the faculties of the mind that any one of them can act independent of all the others. Were the generality of mankind poetical instead of prosaical, vice, it is probable, would exist among them in very nearly as many shapes as she displays at present. Schiller, as it happened, was a good man as well as a great poet; but he might have been either one or the other alone. Nothing can be easier, as an exercise of the imagination, than to picture him in the first place as no poet at all, and then as a still better man even than he was.

Perhaps in the opinion of some we are all this time affirming grave nonsense. Those who can think so are entitled to more than all the pity we bestow on them. It could afford us no gratification to advocate a theory of the correctness of which we were not satisfied. With respect to the possibility that our convictions may themselves depend upon erroneous judgments, we can merely state that we are not prepared to admit it.

* * * * * * * * *

Our task is completed. We have exceeded our limits. Evening, too, is deepening into night; and it is now some time since Dr. Kitchener[11] and D'Israeli the Younger[12] terrified us out of our ancient malpractice of lucubrating by candle-light. Our solitary regret in parting from our friend Schiller is that we should be under the necessity of leaving very great numbers of his broadest hexameters untouched. Future translators, however, will, we should fancy, do ample justice to all the writings— including the ballads—of this distinguished man. It is pleasant for us to look forward through the mists of the future, and imagine a period when the name of Schiller alone shall be sufficient to awaken in the bosom of him who hears it pronounced an unquenchable enthusiasm in behalf of all that is pure in principle and praiseworthy in action. As Messerschmidt impressively saith—and the unlearned have here a greater advantage over us in their ignorance than they dream—

> —an der Zukunft Sarkophage
> Donnert süsz die Hoffnungsjubelklage,
> Wenn der Todte rüstig sich ermannt,
> Wenn er in das kalte Leben springet,
> Glücklich in dem Unglück die besinget,
> Die nach kurzer Flucht ihn endlich fand.[13]

ANTHOLOGIA GERMANICA.—NO. XIII.
M. KLAUER KLATTOWSKI'S PUBLICATIONS.

THESE unrivalled little volumes have been lying before us for some time; and we now take them up in a state of the greatest puzzlemindedness. Dare we attempt a review of them? We think not. The praise they demand is so enormous, that we despair of our ability to afford it. We certainly could not find room enough in a single essay to express our opinion of them. On the other hand nothing can induce us to damn them with faint praise. Such a proceeding would inflict too severe a shock on that fine perception of justice which constitutes a portion of our intellectual nature. Every page of these books merits an interminable panegyric. In what light, therefore, would a few meagre sentences of approval appear, except as an impertinence which no person of reflecting faculties could be expected to tolerate? If we owed M. Klauer a thousand pounds, he does not suppose that we could have brass enough to tender him a groat by way of payment. No. Our sense of the magnitude of the debt would rather impose perpetual silence on us. Not one penny should we jingle against another before him. The mingled nobleness and perspicacity which have on many occasions distinguished us would enable us thoroughly to appreciate the delicacy of his feelings; and if he ever alluded to pecuniary subjects we should merely either cough him down at once, or inquire, with considerate *nonchalance*, whether he could not do himself the favour of pressing an additional thousand on our acceptation.

The position we are placed in, he will perceive, is, therefore, an embarrassing one. It is the more to be regretted too, for a reason which we shall specify. We possess, in a marvellous degree, the capability of expatiating to eternity upon a single topic. Our sentences meander onward right and left, like an unbroken stream of zigzag water through the mazes of a wilderness; and just as you, venerable Public, "see them on their winding way"[1] now, so would you see them "an endless year"[2] (as Moore says) hence, did not the barrier-walls of THE MAGAZINE restrain them. Give us but one pull from St. Leon's elixir-bottle,[3] and ages might elapse, until the grass grew over the forgotten tombs of those who shall be still unborn in the days of our great grand-children, before our monotonous drawl should cease to astound and mystify mankind. Now, with such powers at command, with both ability and will to lavish overflowing laudation upon M. Klauer, it is torture to us to write in gyves— to be compelled to clip our syllables and curtail our sentences, and defraud our friend of his due. It is true we have been offered a field of sixty pages, or thereabouts, to gambol in, if so we choose. But such niggardly liberality would never answer views expansive as ours. The idea of compressing into four sheets a rhapsody that should be *répandu*[4] through myriads of reams, is too ridiculous not to be discarded with eminent contempt. Nobody can dream of it. The thing is impossible. It cannot be. Mankind would scout it *en masse* as a humbug of intolerable magnitude. It is quite out of the question. He is, as the Persians would say, "the prince and father of jack-asses," who can for a moment contemplate its practicability or stickle for its fairness.

Nothing, then, M. Klauer, nothing remains for us except to adopt the plan of giving what are called "copious extracts" from the volumes themselves. And now for the first time, it strikes us that this is not so very bad a plan. It will afford you, M. Klauer, some slight and beggarly compensation for your labours, and so far it must be gratifying to you. True, we must in our selections, employ the Queen's English instead of the Emperor's German; but even through the medium of the vernacular the excellent taste you have displayed will be conspicuous. Besides, in thus anglicising, to whisper you the truth, we have a motive; and upon second thoughts we have another motive—and upon third thoughts, a third. We wish our readers to understand what they read. We wish to gain a prodigious deal of *éclat* by our translations, so called. Also we wish to embellish our originals, where they want embellishing. For it is now generally admitted by both Tyrian and Trojan[5] that we have awakened a wide and deep, and intense, and permanent interest in favour of the literature of Germany, solely by the bold, arrogant, audacious, judicious, and original manner in which we have dared to improve upon its poetry, and hector its poets. We have blown soapbubble after soapbubble into their legitimate dignity of rainbows; and the rudest apparent grossnesses of our originals have dazzled the eye upon coming forth from our hands as gold when it issues from the furnace seventy times purified. There was music in them (the aforesaid originals), much music of the most soul-entrancing quality; but nobody guessed whereabouts it lay,—not a ninny could elicit a note of it,—until WE arose, and, using our long goose-quill as a wand, wiled it (the aforesaid music) forth to steep the senses of millions in Elysium; performing in this respect much the same service towards it as the thaw performed towards Baron Munchausen's horn,[6] wherein, as you, M. Klauer Klattowski, a Professor, a Mecklenburg-Schwerinian, a man of extensive erudition, and, let us hope, a reverer of Munchausen, will please to recollect, the tunes of each player continued imprisoned and frozen until one of those gentler winds "that love to dally with Æolian lyres,"[7] came in pity to release the ethereal captives from their bondage of lethargy.

* * * * * * * * * *

We have no objection to the prosaic flow of these stanzas[8]—for the best poetry is that which most resembles the best prose—but there appears throughout the story a tendency to dilate unnecessarily upon trivialities and things of nothing; and against this we must enter our protest. We notice also here and there an incongruous commingling of the Moving in *conception* and the Burlesque in *expression*; as if, after some beautiful or exalted idea had occurred to the writer, he had deliberately set about clothing it in the most inappropriate language, as far as sentiment was concerned, that a poet could select. This style of writing is wholly German; even Byron, in his worst fits of cynicism, never approximates to it. Neither could it ever become popular—or, perhaps, even intelligible— among us, were it introduced; and we shall not perplex our readers by quoting specimens. They would hardly recommend themselves. We hate not sentimentality where it is genuine—where, though maudlin in itself, it is pervaded by a tone of sincerity; but the hybrid kind of composition we have alluded to must ever be at variance with that singleness of purpose and harmony of conception without which it is impossible for a man to be either a good serious poet or a good comic. Truth, indeed, compels us to admit that the great majority of German poets are, as sentimentalists, irreproachable. We have here, in M. Klauer's first volume, a song by SCHUBART, the excessive pathos of which would go far, if read aloud at a conversazione, to justify, except among the very stout, a general sympathetic syncope. *Wenn Hoffnung nicht wär', so lebt' ich nicht mehr*, If Hope were not, then I should exist no more! begins the poet:—*Wie lieblich* (he adds) *erscheint uns ihr Schimmer!* How beautifully beams her light on us!—and the same affecting strain is pursued to the close. The touching tenderness of the original it is of course difficult for a translator to give in all its perfection; but luckily for us the Lachrymose happens to be our forte; and therefore, most complaisant Reading Public, you will kindly accompany us through our version, "sighing like furnace"[9] as you proceed, and be good enough,

"If you have tears prepared, to shed them now,"[10]

over this dolorous ditty of ["Pathetic Hypothetics"].

* * * * * * * * *

In a short commentary on [Schiller's "Light and Warmth"], M. Klauer says: "A young man forms his ideas of men from what he has seen in the endearing circle of his relations and friends; and as he met on all sides with love, he gave them love in return. Experience, however, soon shows him, after his entrance into the world, that the majority of men are narrow-minded and selfish. By degrees he retires into himself, and at last becomes in his turn an Egoist." Now, we cannot subscribe to this doctrine. Seventeen-eighteenths of the men *we* meet are really right good fellows; in fact, if they have any fault it is too great a readiness to become the dupes of such fine speeches and protestations of kindness as a regard to our interests occasionally induces us to make to them. It is true, we formerly judged otherwise. When a young man, we formed our ideas of men from what we saw in the sneering circle of our friends and acquaintance; and, as we met with sneers upon all mouths, we gave sneers to the sneerers in return. Experience, however, soon after our entry into Dublin, shewed us that the majority of men, and all the women, were narrow-mouthed and unsneering. By degrees, therefore, we wriggled ourself out of ourself, and at last became in our turnings[11] a We-goist.

* * * * * * * * *

It would be rather unfair, if now, at parting with M. Klauer, we should omit to recommend the handsome volumes from which our extracts have been made to all admirers of German literature in the kingdom. Though we have not space to praise them as we could wish, we have quite enough to acknowledge that they deserve our praise. Of the three we prefer the volume containing the Songs; and from this our specimens have been chiefly taken; but no country has hitherto equalled Germany in the Ballad; and when we state that the compilation in M. Klauer's last volume embraces many of the most popular compositions in the ballad line, we have said enough to show that the book must be a treasure to all cultivated lovers of the original and marvellous. We should not pass in silence over the Lyrics, which may be regarded as a condensation of almost the whole poetic spirit of the author's country. Those persons also, for whom exterior decoration is an irresistible attraction, will be pleased with the getting-up of these volumes, which to quote a line that M. Klauer will recognise:

"Füget zum Guten den Glanz und den Schimmer,"[12]

and does infinite credit to the compiler's taste.

LITERÆ ORIENTALES.
TURKISH POETRY.—THIRD ARTICLE.

THE Ottoman Empire may be said to have reached the zenith of its literary glory under the reign of SULEIMAN II. Circumstances had never at any former period allowed the intellectual energies of all classes of the Osmanlü such ample scope for their development as they obtained in the half century during which this patronising and prosperous Prince held the reigns of government.[1] The Biographers, SEHDI, AHDI, LATIFI, AASHIK, NAZMI, KINALIZADE and KAFZADE, have compiled and illustrated the writings of no fewer than five hundred and fifty poets alone, to say nothing of other *littérateurs*, all belonging exclusively to this period. The great majority of these, it is true, hardly rose above mediocrity, but we find also many eminent and celebrated names among the number. FASLI, famous from Stambool to Samarcand, flourished at this time, and gave to the world his magnificent poems of *Gul u Bulbul* (The Rose and the Nightingale) and *Nakhlistan* (The Wood of Palms), an imitation of the *Gulistan* (Rosegarden) of the Persian poet, SAADI; and YAHYA transcended all who had preceded him in descriptive and panegyrical poetry;[2] BAKKI was universally acknowledged as the first Lyrist of modern times; ALI VASI acquired an immortal name by his *Humajun-Nameh*, a spirited translation into Turkish verse of the *Hitopodésa* of VISHNA SARMA; GHAZALI and FUZULI (of the latter of whom we purpose to speak more at large towards the close of our paper) sang Mystical Epics, the themes of which were Wine and Devotion; KHALILL produced his great work, *Firak-Nameh* (the Book of Separation): AWAZ-ZATI[3] became the founder of a school in composition which united the ease of everyday thought with an inexhaustible imaginative luxuriance; and KHIALI delighted all ranks of readers by the peculiar originality and vividness of his commonest poetical creations.

But perhaps the most distinguished of the poets of this the Augustan era of Turkey is MOHAMMED BEN OSMAN BEN ALI NAKKASH, called LAMII, or The Dazzling. We have referred to this voluminous writer elsewhere, and adduced a specimen of his manner in religious and eulogistic poetry.[4] His principal works bear the following titles:—*Nefhatol-ins* (The Breath of Humanity), *Futuhesh shadihin li tervih kullibil-mudshahidin* (An Apocalypse to quiet the hearts of the Wrestlers), *Shevahidun-nubuvvet* (Witnesses for the Prophets), *Ibret-Nameh* (The Book of Examples), *Miretól-esma* (a Mirror of Names), *Medjmaol-lataif* (A Budget of Whimwhams), and

Munazerat Nefs u Ruh (The Battle of the Spirit and the Soul.) His poems of *Vamik* and *Asra* and *Vizeh* and *Ramin* are among the most celebrated of his productions, though whether they are original or merely *rifaccimenti* of similar romances by the ancient Indian poets VALMYKI and VYASA is a point that has never been satisfactorily settled. Somewhat less known in Europe, but, if we may venture to pronounce an authoritative opinion, scarcely less deserving examination and perusal, are his *Shemi u Pervaneh* (The Waxlight and the Butterfly), *Dzsaber-Nameh* (The Book of [Sultan] Djaber), *Sherenghisi Brusa* (The Rejoicings at Brusa), *Kui u Tchougan* (The Ball and the Mall), *Heft Piker* (The Seven Beauties), and *Maktel-Husein* (The Martyrdom of Houssain.) Besides these and some other miscellaneous works, LAMII also produced a Divan of Ghazels, Kassidets, Eulogies, Elegies, Enigmas and Epigrams, highly praised by KINALIZADE, and from which KAFZADE has copiously quoted in his Life of the Author.

The Martyrdom of Houssain is a poem of great beauty. It is a sort of Elegiac Epic, after the Persian models. Its principal and most striking feature is the singular liberality of its sentiments. This was so remarkable immediately upon its appearance that an outcry was raised against the writer, and he was accused of promulgating heretical opinions. But LAMII had anticipated the attack, and was prepared to meet it. He publicly summoned the leading Imams, the Cadi, all the Khodjas and the principal nobility and gentry of Brusa to appear before him on an appointed day in the Great Mosque and hear him recite the poem; and he pledged himself to answer all objections. The step was bold, but successful. All Brusa crowded to the Mosque, predetermined to anathematise, but Nature had gifted LAMII with a voice of marvellous power and compass; and where one cannot edify, it is no contemptible advantage to be able to electrify. The result was the still higher elevation of his character in the minds of his audience as a Mussulman and a poet. Tears and sobs attested the general sympathy as he described in his most pathetic tones the last hours of his hero, his abandonment and sufferings—

> Oh!—pierced with wounds—deserted—dying,—
> Far away from ISTAMBOL!
> A thousand poisoned arrows lying
> In his sick, sore soul!
> What could he do but pine and groan?
> What could he do but groan and pine?
> *He—a lion—all alone*
> *Amid a herd of swine!*

* * * * * * * * *

According to our promise we shall conclude our article by a few extracts from FUZULI. This writer, whose title signifies The Supercilious, was a native of Bagdad, but, betaking himself to Constantinople, soon became a favorite with the Sultan, who conferred many honors on him. He died in 1562, while his renown was in full church flower. His most esteemed poem is *The Loves of Leila and Medjnoon*—names familiar to all admirers of Eastern romance—but, as a curiosity, no one of his works can compete with his *Bang u Badeh*.[5] The title of this poem, translated, means Opium and Wine, or, more properly, Hyoscyamus and Wine, for *Bang* is, in fact, the Egyptian *Benj*, (*qu.* the Νηπενθης of Homer?) which not merely operates as a simple narcotic, but produces delicious dreams, and fills the soul with rapturous anticipations. Mohammed, who wanted practical men, and not dreamers, forbade the use of narcotics generally, but *Bang* is not interdicted by name in the Koran, and probably was not known to the Arabians in Mohammed's era, for there is reason to presume that this drug is one with the *Hashishet* of the Indian, BABA RATANI, which was only introduced into Syria and Arabia some centuries after the Hejira. Partly because not prohibited by name, and partly on account of its seductive properties, *Bang* gradually rose into celebrity, until at last the throne and pulpit took the alarm; and fierce and terrible was the war which for many years both the Sultan and the Mufti waged against the heterodox opiate. It was at this period that FUZULI wrote the extraordinary and fantastic poem with some account of which we are now about to present our readers.[6]

He commences in the ordinary manner, that is, with an Invocation to the Deity, a Hymn to the Prophet and the Four Khalifs, and the Panegyric of the reigning Sultan. Then, representing himself under a feigned name, as seated at a table covered with potables of all hues in glittering flasks, "which lend their own brightness to the liquids within, as the heavenly constellations shed their beams on the sea"—he proceeds thus:—

> Queen of all those that came to grace
>   This lordly banquet, One there was
> With burning eye and wondrous face:
> She is of a royal race;
>   Everywhere she meets applause.
> Her title is WINE, the Child of the Vine....

The Drinker, at length, fancying that WINE is giving herself too many airs, interrupts her rhapsody by a fit of laughter, and then tells her that she must not talk any more in that strain. There is but little wisdom in thee, WINE, he pursues; thou art beginning to dote, methinks. Unloose the girdle of self-conceit from thy waist, and be not so hasty to light thy dwelling with the wax-taper of vain-glory.[7] Remember what the poet says; *He that crowneth himself with roses shall see his chaplet wither until only the thorns are left.* Is it for the crow to claim kindred with the eagle, or shall the daisy say to the sun-flower, Thou art my sister? Know that yesternoon I attended a festival at which was present the celebrated BANG; he was clothed in green,[8] like a Sofi; he was not drunk, as thou art, but wore a divine and philosophic air; and all the guests did homage to him, while thou wert neglected and forgotten. For it is well known, O WINE, that he is thy Sultan, thy Superior. Hereupon WINE flies into a passion. O, ingrate and driveller! she exclaims, O, viperous Drinker of Me, I am astounded at thine unexampled and detestable ingratitude. It overwhelms me on a sudden, as thunder comes down in the night time on one who stumbles over a dark mountain. I weep also for thy bad taste, which afflicts me with intense and particular melancholy: can it be that thou art sunk so low as to acknowledge thyself a *Banghi?*[9] If so, be advised by me, and recover thy senses ere it be too late; humble thyself; grasp the bottle by the neck and swear to be faithful to WINE alone.

> Swear by the Bottle's roseate hue,
> Swear by its gurgling *Glug-glug-glu,*[10]
> Swear by the Paunch of the Bottle, O Drinker,
>   Faith and Allegiance to WINE alone! . . .

WINE now turns to her companions for consolation and succour; and all, with one exception, declare BANG to be a pestiferous wretch, the continuance of whose existence no honest person can conscientiously connive at. The dissentient voice is that of BRANDY, who treats the whole affair as insignificant in the extreme and acquaints WINE that she is *tzsok szarkos* (too stupidly drunk) to understand the real relative position or importance of the parties.

> Wert thou not drunk as an owl, such a trifle
> Never could vanquish thy reason, or rifle
> Thy mind of its peace: Why, the world are thy followers! . . .

CIDER (*Nebid*) on hearing this, tartly turns round, and, like Sempronius in Addison's *Cato*, accuses Lucius BRANDY of being a traitor at heart,[11] and of secretly wishing to protect the enemy. In my opinion, observes CIDER, in an effervescence of zeal,—the most eligible, the most dignified mode of proceeding is to assassinate BANG. Let there be no more deliberation or delay, but let BANG be at once and quietly assassinated. There will then be end of him, because he will be dead. That is what I, CIDER, say.—The advice appears to gratify WINE, but BEER (*Busa*) interposing his voice, remarks that it cannot be adopted, as BANG scents poison at the distance of a farsang,[12] is not vulnerable by hatchet or bowstring, and cannot be drowned or hocussed without considerable risk to the safety of the drowner or hocusser; and he therefore suggests that stratagem and not strength should be employed on the occasion. What would you think, O BEER, demands WINE, if I were to despatch you to him as my ambassador? A superb idea! quoth BEER. Could you circumvent him? asks WINE. With the help of the Prophet, answers BEER, I should strip the gilding off his pills instantaneously; he should eat many bushels of dirt. Then, O, BEER! says WINE, I here invest you with the prerogatives of a plenipotentiary: betake yourself forthwith to the court of BANG, and so manage your embassy that your skill in diplomacy may be talked of through the world as a thing to wonder at. And whereas, I have hitherto called you only *Eshek* (the Ass), I will, in case of your success, confer upon you the title of *Bujuk Jilin*, (Grand Humbugger), and you and each of your kindred shall retain the same, until the sun and moon shall cease to shine, and wax candles be darkened in the houses of the Faithful.

BEER accordingly departs upon his mission, while the others remain behind and entertain one another by recounting scandalous anecdotes of the enemy, and singing the praises of WINE; and WINE tells a tale of a tub[13] to the effect that there was once a young man of Bagdad who from his boyhood upwards had despaired of ever finding the way to Paradise, until happening in his twenty-fourth year to take a long and merry drink of WINE from a pitcher for the first time, he exclaimed that he now saw every inch of the way to Paradise quite clearly.

After a journey of twenty-nine days BEER arrives at the Court of BANG and presents his credentials to that important personage himself, who is represented as engaged in a cloudy metaphysical discussion with ESRAR (a Persian Opiate) concerning contingent existence, and the souls of the unborn. The reception accorded by BANG to BEER is polite, but cool and guarded. BEER then tries to sift and wheedle BANG, but BANG repels all his artifices with a self-possession and vigilance which shew that he perfectly understands the designs of his wily pumper, and is determined to defeat them. My cater-cousin[14]—observes BANG, at length, desirous of closing the scene—my cater-cousin—for so thou wert once, and, I trust, wilt be again—thou but losest thy labour; it is useless all this cross-hackling of Me. I compassionate thee, for thou art the father of a jack-ass; he that will gull should seek the gullible, but thou hast come across One too enlightened to be hoodwinked. I am the profoundest of philosophers, the greatest astrologer living, a necromancer of no ordinary talent, a searcher into the future, a mirror of the past, an interminable rhapsodist, the master of the three hundred and threescore sciences, a treasury of knowledge, a gigantic phenomenon, the glory of nature, the wonder of the universe! And I, quoth ESRAR, am thy worthy co-mate, seeing that the world acknowledges my sovereignty, and is confounded with inexpressible excess of astonishment at my miraculous attributes. The height of my mind surpasses that of the pillars of TCHEL-MINAR,[15] and the divers of ORMUZ would be drowned in the depths of the ocean of my understanding. I combine within myself the virtues of a hundred convents of dervishes, and the wisdom of a thousand academies of Sofis. I possess the fluency of NIZAMI,[16] the inventiveness of BIDPAI,[17] the perspicacity of ARISTOTLE, the memory of HAFIZ,[18] and the luxuriant imagination of DJAMI.[19] IFLATUN (Plato) would have rubbed his forehead in the dust before me, and LOKMAN[20] have exclaimed in rapture, *Ferdi szenszin,* Thou takest the shine! Not from Me, however, interposes BANG—thou dost not take the shine from Me. I think I do, answers ESRAR; I think, BANG, I take the shine from thee. By green and blue, No! exclaims BANG warmly. I am BANG; thou art ESRAR; thy business is to sit at My feet and eat dirt; what dost thou talk of taking the shine from Me? I take the shine then from all others, observes ESRAR, and in the meantime I either am or will be thy Sultan. As soon as thou canst, replies BANG. But as for thee, he adds, turning to BEER, I think it is high time thou wert jogging. Go back therefore, to her who sent thee hither, and inform her that BANG is Shah of this world, that he has neither master nor brother, that the treasuries of the nine-gated Dom Daniel[21] are his, and that his knowledge and wisdom will be sung by poets, and venerated by kings, when the ignorance and infamy of thy Koran-accursed mistress shall have made her execrable in the eyes of all mankind.

BEER, perceiving the inutility of contending against such formidable odds, accordingly withdraws and resumes his journey homeward. BANG and ESRAR then jointly assail the character of WINE, and lavish upon it all the abusive epithets they can think of; and BANG blows the trumpet of his own praises over again, and gives ESRAR the history of a young man of Bassora, who was for a long time so stupid as not to know his great toe from his forefinger, but by the use of BANG became the subtlest metaphysical hairsplitter of his time, and translated besides from several languages without knowing any thing of any of them.[22]

BEER has scarcely presented himself before his mistress to detail the unsuccessful result of his embassy, when he is followed by a messenger from BANG, a huge *Habb,* (or Opium Pill of thirty grains), who comes to dilate upon the power and extraordinary attributes of his master, and to require from WINE an acknowledgment of her inferiority to him. A panegyric pronounced by BANG on himself is repeated by his envoy as follows:—

> I am BANG, a magnificent name—
> A globe of light—a pillar of flame....

This unequivocal evidence of the excellent terms upon which BANG is with himself, excites the irascible passions of WINE to a high pitch; and a plot is concerted between her and her auxiliaries to wound BANG in the tenderest point by coaxing over BIG OPIUM-PILL to their side. How to accomplish their object, however, is a puzzle, until BEER suggests the idea of intoxicating him. All immediately agree, and BIG OPIUM-PILL is accordingly made thoroughly drunk all round, and while drunk is prevailed upon to swear by the Paunch and *Glug-glug-glu* of the WINE-bottle, that he will fight the battles of WINE against BANG until the sun and moon shall cease to shine, and wax-candles no longer light the houses of the Faithful.[23]

Now comes the tug of war. Intelligence of BIG OPIUM-PILL's treachery in due time reaches BANG, and exceedingly exasperates him: he musters an army of opiates, fluid and solid, and marches against WINE. WINE on her part also rises like a giantess, and collects her forces to meet those of BANG. Hostilities involving the most destructive results to both parties appear inevitable, when, just at this juncture, SUGAR-CANDY (*Nokl*) and CINNAMON (*Muiz*), who have occupied neutral ground from the beginning of the contest, interfere between the high belligerent powers, and propose that WINE and BANG shall decide the quarrel by single combat. After some deliberation on both sides the proposal is mutually agreed to; and, the requisite preliminaries being arranged, WINE and BANG gird themselves for fight. The final decisive struggle is preceded by a wordy skirmish, in which each hero endeavours to exalt his own pretensions and to depreciate those of his antagonist.

> Says WINE: I am the Daughter
> 　　　　　　　　Of Sultan Vine.
> Says BANG: Like Eden's Water
> 　　　　　　　　Of Life I shine....

The fight now begins in earnest, and is sustained with great fierceness for eight days and eight nights.[24] Both combatants shew prodigious pluck, but as one of them must be victorious, the honor is reserved for WINE, who at last bangs BANG, and forces him to fly the field.

> Worsted and howling, BANG slunk away,
> And thenceforth never by night or day,
> Durst shew himself in his ancient array....

This bizarre poem concludes with a Hymn to God, thanking him for his mercies. After all, it is probably but an allegory of some kind or other, and Wine and Bang may be meant as personifications of some of the Divine attributes. We can come to no other conclusion when we consider the praises it lavishes on a beverage of which every Mussulman is bound by his creed to entertain an abhorrence. At the same time its latent meaning may be too obscure to be discovered, or perhaps, if discoverable, may not be worth the trouble of tracing. Our object in giving an abstract of the poem is simply to furnish the uninstructed among our readers (we hate writing for the learned) with some idea of the sort of poetry in which the Oriental mind delights to revel; for, eccentric and perhaps puerile as the sample we have exhibited may appear to them, they may be satisfied that few Mohammedans would not fancy themselves losers in bartering it for the most brilliant of the creations of Goethe or Shakespeare.

But our limits forbid us to advance any further on the present occasion. In our next paper we propose to take up and discuss the subject of *Persian* literature. New and untrodden as this field will be to us, we ought perhaps to question the wisdom of yielding to the impulse that prompts us to enter it at all. In reality we should feel oppressed by many misgivings if our distrust of our integrity could be cast into the same scale with the diffidence we entertain of our ability to do justice to our task. But the case is otherwise. In whatever degree we may fail, we shall retain the consolation of reflecting that we have been assiduous to avoid failure in even the least degree. We shall claim for our undertaking all the merit of honest intentions. If these cannot guarantee our success, they will at least enable us to remain upon good terms with ourself, and we trust will even acquire for us, to a certain extent, the suffrages of our readers.

THE THIRTY FLASKS.

Επειδαν άπας ακουσω, εκρινα, και μη προτερον προλαμβανω.
Demosthenes.[1]

"Marry, this gallant fulfils the old saw notably: give him an inch, and without more ado he hauls you off a whole ell."—*A Mad World, my Masters.*[2]

CHAPTER I.

————————————"meet me at the notary's
And I will go and purse the ducats straight."
Merch. of Ven. Act i. Scene 3.[3]

"WELL, my fine fellow, how goes it? Any news?" demanded Heinrick Flemming, as, without much preliminary ceremony, he made his way into the parlour and presence of his friend, Basil Von Rosenwald. "Whom do you think I had a glimpse of as I crossed the Platz? Guess."

"Perhaps the devil," answered the interrogated party, without raising his head from the hand that supported it, as he sat apparently in deep depression at a small cedar-wood table—his dejected tone and manner forming a singular contrast to the levity of his reply.

"Perhaps so, but in the shape of an angel of light, my boy," exclaimed Flemming. "The apparition that floated by me, all pearls, plumes, and prettiness, was none other than the Fraülein Aurelia Jacintha Wilhelmina Elsberg. Know you the fair ladye?"

A half-smothered sigh was the only response.

"And yet she looked paler than her wont," said Flemming. "Sick at heart, no doubt—bewailing the absence of her fickle swain! Ah, Baz, Baz!" He cast, as he spoke, an unobserved look around the room; for a moment his eye dwelt on the space above the mantel-piece, and was withdrawn as rapidly as it had wandered thither. "By the way," he added, "you mean of course to make an exhibition of yourself at the Villa to-morrow night?"

"I mean to make no exhibition of any kind, any where, at any time," answered the other, in the same sad or rather sullen accents as before.

"Eh! how the deuce? What crotchet have you got in your head now, Basil? To bury yourself in a hermitage?" and Heinrick, unasked, took a seat at the table opposite his friend, and looked him in the face with seeming wonder.

"Heinrick Flemming," said Basil, raising his head, "I do not want to quarrel with you. Still you are, perhaps, one of the last persons whose company I could wish for at the present moment. If you cannot remain silent, withdraw. Forgive my frankness, but I am in no mood for bandying compliments."

"So it appears," observed Flemming, quietly. "But, pray, if I may ask the question, my somewhat uncourteous host, in what lies *my* especial offence? Why should you so particularly wish *my* absence just now?"

"Since you have asked me, I will tell you," said Rosenwald. "Your presence is unwelcome, because it recalls remembrances I would give worlds to obliterate. Heinrick Flemming! I have cause to curse the day and hour we first met!"

"Good God, Rosenwald! are you mad?"

"Slight wonder if I were," said Basil, with a bitter smile. "I make you no more reproaches, Heinrick; but"—and he opened a drawer and took out a small memorandum-book—"cast your eye over the first page or two of that."

"Very ugly," observed Heinrick, but without much evident emotion, and after he had finished a hasty but accurate scrutiny of the document submitted to him. "Very ugly indeed that, I must say."

"And look around you—look up at the mantel-piece! You recollect the diamond bracelets, my mother's miniature set in brilliants, the other trinkets that hung there—each of them once dear to me as life—valuable as a world—all, Heinrick, all———." He paused, overcome with emotion, and passed his trembling hand across his brow.

"Gone?" inquired Flemming.

"Gone!" echoed Rosenwald. "As for my property, Steinhart and Groll will come down like wolves upon the Konigsmark chateau—and this house, of course, with all its rights, members, and appurtenances, as the lawyers say, goes to Elsberg. Cash I have next to none. A pleasant prospect for the approaching winter!—for come what may, I will not be guilty of the last, basest cowardice of dying." After a pause of a few moments he added—"It is strange! Surely there are impulses neither to be explained nor controlled, which sometimes urge the half-ruined wretch to anticipate the whole and the worst of what Fortune has in store for him of degrading and bitter! What will you say? Last night in my madness I rushed from the *rouge et noir*[4] room to the *roulette* table—my brain was on fire—and in twenty minutes, without well knowing how, I found that I had parted with notes for four thousand florins!"

"And you attribute your ruin to me, Basil, do you now?" and the speaker looked a sort of mild reproach and amazement at Rosenwald.

"Pardon me, I accuse you of nothing. Not your will, it may be, but that of destiny, is in fault. You are, perhaps, blameless. But, as there is a God that oversees and judges, I was as ignorant as an infant of even the existence of a Spielhaus[5] in the city, until you initiated me into the mysteries of that den of thieves in the Kaiserstrasse."

"My dear friend," said Heinrick, "be just. I could not—how could I— how could any one have imagined that a casual introduction of the kind could lead to such disastrous results? I would have laughed to scorn the man who told me that you, of all beings, were likely to prove a gambler. Your habits were so regular! so well governed! What you have told and shown me is like a thunder-clap to me. Yet, though surprised, I am not greatly grieved, believe me."

"I *do* believe you," said Basil, bitterly. "I have no friends. A ruined man is a fool to look for sympathy."

"He is a fool to expect that his neighbours will sit down and weep like church-spouts over his misfortunes," observed Flemming. "Now I, for my part, feel more inclined to laugh than cry on account of your reverses, my grave young bachelor. Take heart of grace; you have lost all; things are at the worst with you; and, of course, you must even now, according to the proverb, be on the mending hand. Tell me: who has got the jewels, and lockets, and so forth?"

"They have fallen into the cursed clutches of that old Jew, Lubeck, in the Brunnengasse," sighed Rosenwald.

"So far so middling; we know where they are, then," said Flemming.

"Ay," observed Basil; "so said the Dutch merchant when his cargo of ingots went to the bottom of the sea. The subject hardly admits of jesting, Heinrick."

"My good friend, it is you who jest, not I. I am in downright earnest. I am glad I know where your jewels are; because—I mean to recover them, or to get you to do so, which comes to pretty much the same thing."

Basil looked up. "Recover ?—get me—how—did I hear you correctly? What have you to do in the matter?"

"Suppose I choose to raise the ready?" said Flemming.

"I can tender no security," said the other, gloomily, "and my bond would not be worth the price of the stamp."

"Bonds are for bondsmen," said Heinrick, lightly; "don't talk in that manner to me—it jars upon my notions of the æsthetical in practice. You and I shall march to the man that has the sacks, and he shall shovel out without stint or ceremony. Do you jump?"

"Come, come, Heinrick, be serious, if you please."

"Serious? By Heraclitus the Howler,[6] you make me serious in spite of my teeth, which are longing to luxuriate in a grin at the present moment. Do you know the Dornensteg?"

"The Halbmond? Yes. What of it?"

"And do you know a certain uncertain old East Indian snudge,[7] vegetating there and thereabouts, any time between day and dark—a Nabob, dwarfish stature—weazened visage—invisible complexion—crooked legs—rich as Crœsus[8]—eccentric—waspish—misanthropic—generous—magnanimous—liver-grown—world-sick—and living all alone, surrounded by piles of ducats, in the vain hopes of getting them out of his hands and house?"

"Psha, Heinrick!"

"Then you do? or you don't? No matter. You shall see him to-morrow."

"See whom?"

"*C'est à dire*,[9] if you wish the introduction. By the way, it is queer, but he bears the same name as yourself."

"Who—who?"

"Hoo, hoo! why thus hoots the owl. I never thought of asking him if he was related to you. I don't mean the owl, but the man rather. What do you think yourself?"

"I think you would worry the devil," answered Basil. "Whom or what are you raving of?"

"Raving of nothing, but conversing rationally with you of this Nabob. He is your man. He will down with the dust."[10]

"An East Indian money-lender! I never heard of such a person," said Basil. "Where does he stop ? How is he called?"

"He stops at nothing, and is called, or called on, by nobody. But his name, I told you, is your own—Rosenwald. The point, you see, is that this ancient oddity has amassed an immense fortune—some millions of ducats, it is said."

"Humph ! I see—an old usurer."

"Quite in the wrong box, my penitent elbow-shaker. He *gives*, not *lends* his money."

"Gives? How—or to whom?" demanded Basil.

"As to the *how*," said Heinrick, "on certain conditions; and as to the *whom*, to all who are properly recommended."

"As a man of integrity and truth—you are not mocking me, Heinrick," said Basil, gravely.

"By my soul," said Flemming, "I am in earnest. I know him well; and, which is more to the purpose, I know that he can and will disembarrass you from all your debts and difficulties—that is, if you and he agree."

"To any thing in honor I will—I must agree," said Basil. "But do you know what the conditions are?"

"There is but one condition, in fact; that for each thousand ducats the applicant takes, he must swallow a flask of the Black Elixir."

"The Black Elixir? What is that?"

"I don't exactly know," said Flemming; "but I have tasted it, and thought it marvellously like cherry-brandy. It does no harm in the world—not the least."

"All this sounds very odd and curious," said Rosenwald. "And what may his motive be for annexing such a condition to the acceptance of his money?"

"Deuce knows!" answered Heinrick. "Some whim of his own. But I forgot. He always closets the applicant before-hand and there is a talk between them *unter vier Augen*.[11] I suppose he explains every thing then."

"Did you ever trouble him on your own account?" asked Basil.

"I? No; and I never introduced but two persons; one of these is dead, and the other gone into La Trappe."[12]

"You say he bears my name? Where is his dwelling?"

"The last house but one in the Dornensteg, as you go down from the Vogelstrasse."

Basil rose up and walked about the room in silence for some minutes.

"What you have told me," he at length said, "excites my curiosity much. My hopes I had better say nothing of, for a drowning man catches at straws. But if your friend will let me have the money I want on any conditions short of dishonorable, I will pass him my bond at twelve months."

"He won't take it. But you will come then?" said Heinrick.

"Settled, Heinrick," said Rosenwald. "To-morrow—would you say to-morrow?"

"Yes—certainly; the sooner the better. Say two o'clock to-morrow—for I should like to call on him beforehand, and arrange every thing for our visit. Besides he would prefer being forewarned—no matter why, but I know it."

"Egad," said Basil to himself, rubbing his hands, when, after some further conversation, his friend had taken his departure—"Egad, this looks providential! But who is this Nabob? and how does it happen I have never heard of him until now? A man that fills other people's purses with ducats, and their stomachs with brandy, and all for nothing! Why, he must be mad! Perhaps overtaken by remorse for some crime: they do ugly things in the East. Perhaps only eccentric. Perhaps—but no matter—it is nothing to me. We'll see to-morrow."

Basil went to bed that night in a more tranquil frame of mind than he had enjoyed for months. Hope gilded the horizon of the future with her beams; and his sleep, if not so refreshing as that of innocence and happiness, had less of a feverish character than heretofore. One resolution he was determined to adhere to, if his property were but once disencumbered, and his debts paid—never again to enter a Spielhaus. No! he would reform thoroughly—he would become the strictest of economists—a pattern for bachelor housekeepers—a light to enlighten the rising generation upon the uses of candle-ends and cheese-parings. Zittarotti and Elwes[13] should hide their diminished heads before him. Alas! for the resolutions of the gambler! A burnt child, it is said, dreads the fire. Perhaps;—yet even after the wings of the moth are singed he will persist in fluttering about the flame until he perishes in it.

CHAPTER II.

"I know that Deformed; he has been a vile thief these seven years; he goes up and down like a gentleman."—*Much Ado about Nothing*, *Act* iii. *Scene* 3.[14]

"A forsaken-looking quarter, Heinrick!" said Basil, as the friends next day proceeded along the irregular semicircular street forming the Dornensteg. "I have not been here for a long time. It seems going quite to decay."

"Why, yes," said Flemming, "it is less fashionable than it was—particularly since Ullersbruck, the lawyer, cut his throat here,—and the tourist from Berlin was murdered at the Knife and Wallet, (a curst unlucky sign, for him, with his bags, to put up at!)—and the gang of coiners was *déterré*[15] in that house opposite with the broken windows. But all these things, you know, though they *do* operate to the disparagement of a locality, make house-rent the cheaper in it—you understand?"

"Not exactly why so rich a man as your friend should select it for his abode," said Basil.

"You know nothing of the man, his ways or his whims," answered Flemming. "The Nabob Von Rosenwald has not his parallel from this to Calcutta, whence he came. But here is his house. Prepare to behold a strange being." As he spoke he knocked.

The door was opened by a servant in livery, and the friends were ushered into a parlour, Flemming having desired the man to announce their coming to his master. Basil began to survey some very characteristic paintings by Rubens and his disciple Vandyck,[16] which decorated the walls. In a few moments the sound of approaching steps was heard. The Nabob entered, but by a door at the opposite end of the room.

Basil almost started at the sight of him. No! surely he had never before looked upon such a melancholy caricature on the human form. A rich dress, a profuse abundance of rings, chains, and jewellery, and a countenance in which aristocratic pride seemed struggling with the consciousness of personal meanness, were insufficient to screen from the observer more than a few of the many very repulsive points exhibited by the rare, the almost peculiar deformity of Rupert Von Rosenwald! He was lame, crooked, and shrunken in his limbs. A few straggling hairs still adhered to his head, but his teeth had all abandoned their posts, and the jaws in consequence having collapsed, he presented at thirty-one, the appearance of a man somewhere between fifty and sixty. His eyes were small and spiritless, and his complexion had that sallow, doubtful hue which habits of intemperance are so apt to superinduce in the countenance of a man of naturally feeble constitution. His stature could not have exceeded three feet and a half;—and as he walked into the room, leaning upon an ebony stick and stooping somewhat, he seemed a thing almost too dwarfish and insignificant to be entitled to the epithet of human.

As soon as Flemming had introduced his friend, the Nabob bowed in silence, and then looking at the introducer, he pointed to the door by which the visitors had entered. Flemming seemed to comprehend the hint. Addressing Basil, he quietly said: "It is the wish of the Nabob Bahauder[17] Herr Von Rosenwald that the interview between himself and you should be private from first to last: and therefore you will excuse me for retiring. You will also pardon me for omitting to mention this to you as we came along; I know you will attribute my silence to its true cause—a fear lest some groundless suspicion should arise in your mind to the prejudice of the happy result which," he added, glancing significantly at the Nabob, "the Herr Von Rosenwald, as well as myself, I have no doubt, anticipates from this meeting." He then bowed, and took his leave. So abrupt was his departure that Basil scarcely knew he was gone, before he heard the house-door closing after him.

The Nabob now carefully fastened the door, and then turning to Basil, he requested him, in a subdued and depressed voice, to be seated; at the same time taking a chair himself.

"Your name, if I mistake not, is Basil Von Rosenwald?"

"It is, mein Herr."

"And mine is Rupert Von Rosenwald," said the Nabob.

"That," observed Basil, with a sigh, "was also the name of a brother of mine, who was drowned while I was a child."

"You mistake," said the Nabob, sadly. "He was not drowned. He is not dead. I am he."

"You!" cried Basil, half starting from the chair. "You my brother!—Impossible!"

"I am he," repeated the other, in the same sad, soft accents as before. He added no more.

"But—but—my mother," said Basil, "has always spoken of him to me as dead—as having been drowned. Besides you—you"—he added, as he glanced at the stranger's figure and face, but paused from the natural embarrassment that grew out of his apprehension of wounding the Nabob's sensibilities by an unreserved communication of his meaning.

"I know what you would say," interposed the Nabob, sadlier than before. "You would tell me that your brother was young, noble-looking, and beautiful—and that I am old, withered, deformed, a monster! Nevertheless my words are true. I am your elder brother. Hear the brief solution of the enigma. In my twelfth year (you were then but five) I was kidnapped, as your mother knew—I would say, knows, but I have heard of her death. The wretches who spirited me away sold me to the captain of a slave-ship, and about half a year afterwards, to stifle further inquiry, a letter was sent to your parents and mine—stating the truth so far, but adding that the vessel had been wrecked on the Guinea coast and none saved but the captain, the first mate, and the writer. Hence the belief that I was drowned. Happy for me had I been! The sufferings I underwent for many years were dreadful. At length—no matter how—I baffled my tyrants. I escaped. I led for some time a wandering life through the East— through Araby, Persia, Egypt, and Syria. In the end I went to India. I was then nineteen. There I spent ten years in the study of magic."

"What! Do I hear you aright?" asked Basil. "Did you say magic?"

"Suppress your surprise," said the stranger—and a melancholy smile illumined his ghastly features. "Egypt and India familiarise men with many wonders that you in these humdrum countries little wot of. Yes, I studied magic for ten years. My art profited me: I acquired rank, riches, respectability. But I paid for these advantages an awful price!"

"Heavens!" exclaimed Basil—"surely you did not—could not be so mad as to——"

"Sell my soul to the Prince of darkness?"—interposed the Nabob. "No, my dear brother," (Basil shuddered) "you do me but justice in believing me incapable of that extreme act of insanity and impiety. What I mean is, that my health and personal symmetry were destroyed. At this moment I will not trouble you with uncalled for details: I shall only say, that for months before embarking for Europe, I was unable to eat, drink, sleep, or move—I was as one who should be three-fourths dead in the midst of a living world—as a body from which the soul has all but gone out; and when at length I regained complete consciousness, I found that I had dwindled down to—the wretch and wreck you see me!"

"Marvellous!" said Basil, eyeing the narrator with an undisguised expression of incredulity. "Your tale, my friend, I fear, would not avail you much in a court of equity. But, to save trouble on your part, I may as well inform you at once that any claim you may be disposed to prefer to my property must be nugatory, for this simple reason, that I am no longer the possessor of——"

"Did I say—did I hint," asked the Nabob, reproachfully, "that I intended making any claim of the kind? Believe me, you wrong me. Besides, you forget that I am enormously rich already."

"True—true—I beg your pardon," said Basil, "I have heard as much. But what motive then——"

"Can urge me to play the impostor, would you say? My good sir,"—and he took the unoffered hand of Basil, who slightly shrunk from the contact— "my good sir, before you call me such, before you think me such, first *prove* me such. Your very question, in fact, shows the unreasonableness of your own doubts. What motive, indeed, *can* actuate *me* to claim a relationship with *you*—all the circumstances considered—your beggary and my inexhaustible wealth taken into account—what motive but the one—a yearning after the indulgence of those fraternal affections from the experience of which I have been so long and so cruelly debarred?"

At the word "beggary," in spite of himself Basil winced. He rose up. "Your story, mein Herr," he said, "you will yourself allow, is at least extraordinary; and you must pardon me if I say that a rational man cannot in one moment upon the mere *ipse dixit*[18] of another, a perfect stranger, give implicit credit to assertions which contradict all his foregone experiences. But, passing that over, I do confess myself what you have said—a beggar—and I believe you are aware of the object which has led me to intrude upon you."

"Perfectly," replied the other, also rising,—"and I wish you to understand what I have told you as an introduction to the transaction between us. Will you now accompany me into another room?"

CHAPTER III.

"I would I had thy inches."—*Ant. and Cleop. Act.* i. *Scene 3.*

He led the way into an adjoining apartment. It was of extensive dimensions and carpetted all over, but, to the surprise of the young man, contained, for furniture, merely a table in the centre, upon which, in superb candlesticks of Damascus silver, three wax lights were burning. There were no windows; while, in lieu of walls, the eye encountered presses on all sides, reaching from the floor to the ceiling, which was lofty and adorned with arabesques.

The Nabob took a small bunch of keys from his pocket and silently opened one of the presses. The sight that presented itself within was singular and startling for the eyes of Basil. Countless rows of diminutive cut-glass flasks filled with a dark liquid, surmounting one another upon shelves of parallel lengths, occupied all the space between the ceiling and the carpet. There seemed to be no end to them; they were in such great numbers that the eye ached and grew bewildered in gazing on them.

Basil was still surveying these in wonder when the Nabob unlocked an opposite press.

"See here," said he. "Look in; behold these! Here is gold enough to satiate rapacity itself. Judge, after this, if I can have any conceivable object in deluding you with a cunningly devised fable."

This press was much deeper than the other; and its shelves were stored with black money-bags, apparently well filled. As the Nabob spoke, he took out one of the bags, and, unfastening a clasp round its neck, he showed Basil that it was full of ducats.

"You may, however, suspect," said he, smiling, "that this is a decoy-bag:—if so, you are free to take out any other yourself and examine it."

"No, no," said Basil, "your word is enough;" and then looking round him, he relapsed into silence and something like abstraction, as if doubting whether he was not the dupe of a dream.

"Each of these bags," pursued the old man, "contains a thousand ducats, and there are a thousand bags;—a thousand times a thousand make a million;—and one million of ducats, brother, is no trifle. What say you?"

"Upon my word, Sir," said Basil, "you are a rich man."

"Richer than you think," said the Nabob, "for I have five other rooms in this house stored just as this is. Six millions of ducats, brother, are something to brag of. What do you think?"

"Pray, do not overwhelm me," said Basil, smiling, for in the midst of his wonder he had his doubts. "But perhaps you would gratify my curiosity on one point, and tell me what those bottles are for?"

"I will tell you *whom* they are for, if you please; they are for all who are willing to relieve me of my ducats."

"Willing to relieve you?" exclaimed Basil, opening his eyes very widely.

"I say so. I have now been four months and three weeks in town, and during all that time have been able to get rid of no more than sixty thousand—and even those have come back to me," he added, with a profound sigh.

"You speak riddles!" cried Basil, now more confounded than ever, and not well knowing what to say or think. "Is it possible that the great majority of those you meet with in this city can be so disinterested as to refuse riches when proffered to them?"

"I rather think not," said the Nabob; "but it happens that I do *not* proffer them to the great majority of those I meet."

"I beg your pardon; I understood you to mean that you did."

"I see," said the Nabob, "that your friend, Flemming, has not sufficiently instructed you. Did he say nothing of the condition upon which I give away my ducats?"

"O, yes—he said that the applicant must take from you a flask of the Black Elixir—ah! now I see—one of those flasks—for every thousand ducats you bestowed."

"So he must," said the Nabob, opening a gold snuff-box which he had produced from his pocket, and accommodating himself with a pinch of snuff.

"And surely that is no such mighty matter?" observed Basil, interrogatively.

"Ah! but he must drink the contents of the flask, too," said the elder Rosenwald, putting up his snuff-box.

"Well? and where is the harm even of that? Is the draught a disagreeable one?" inquired Basil.

"Quite the contrary: as a cordial, a restorative, a renovator, an exhilarator of the system, it beats both tea and tar-water:[19]—gin-twist, nay, jinseng itself, is but hog-wash by the comparison."

"Then, what *is* the objection?" Basil asked.

At this interrogatory the little East-Indian first looked grave, then puzzled, and then troubled. "My good brother, my excellent friend, my very dear Sir," he said, "you will, perhaps, permit me, before I enter into a detailed explanation of the difficulties in the way of answering you fully, to put a question or two of mine to you. If I have been rightly apprised, you are just now in want of money?"

"My friend, I suppose, has acquainted you with the extent of my embarrassment," replied Basil, "but if he has not, I can have no desire, with you at least, to varnish over the truth. My pecuniary resources are, I acknowledge, quite exhausted."

"Then, my dear friend," said the East-Indian, assuming as he spoke an expression of countenance so rueful that it bordered on the ludicrous— "then, my dear friend, you will not, perhaps, be disinclined to do me the favour of—of disencumbering me of some twenty or thirty of my bags?"

"Favour?—disencumbering you, my good Sir?" cried Basil. "You astonish me! Were I to accept your generous offer, I believe there could be little doubt that I, not you, would be the obliged party."

"Ah! but if you take my bags you must take my bottles," said the Nabob. "My bags and bottles go together.—No bottles, no bags; remember that!"

"But as yet," suggested Basil, "I have not been able to learn what obstacle the taking of your bottles could possibly place in my way;—and to avow the whole truth, if I accepted of your ducats I should prefer being at the pains of overcoming some difficulty or making some sacrifice to oblige you in doing so—I should prefer this, I say, to carrying off the cash without proffering you even the shadow of an equivalent. My pride would be less damaged."

"These are sentiments that do you honour!" exclaimed the elder Rosenwald, grasping Basil's hand, which, however, he did not detain. "Would that they were more generally diffused among men! But we live in an age when romance has only to show her face to be sneered at and hooted down."

"I look for none and utter none," said Basil. "But plain-dealing and justice are jewels in their way too."

There was a pause. "You are tall," said the Nabob, breaking the silence at length: "what is your precise stature?"

"Six feet," answered Basil, not a little marvelling at the oddness of the query at such a moment.

"And mine is but three feet six," observed the East-Indian; "so that you are two and a half feet taller than I. Diminutive stature, I dare say, is as contemptible in your eyes as in those of most people?"

"I have never entertained a worse or better opinion of any one on account of his inches," said Basil; "I trust I am not so absurd—so unjust;" and in the speaking he cast a look at the Nabob which seemed to say, I fear, my mannikin, that your wits are wandering!

"But," pursued the Nabob, not noticing his look, "I presume it would grieve you considerably to stand no higher in your shoes than I do?"

"If Nature had made me short, I suppose I should have reconciled myself to my lot," said the young man, carelessly.

"Ay, but if Nature had nothing to do with the matter?"

"Now you mystify me indeed," said Basil. "I am in the midst of as German a fog as you please. Plainly, I cannot comprehend you."

"Suppose that Nature had made you long?"

"No necessity for supposing what is actually the case," said Basil, getting extremely fidgetty, and glancing from side to side at the open presses.

"But, suppose that, being long, you had become short?"

"My good Sir," said Basil, turning, as if to leave the room, "excuse me if I appear rude, but this grows tiresome—I cannot understand nonsense, and I do not see what a discussion upon personal height can have to do with the subject we were previously engaged on. If you please I will take my leave, for I perceive you are trifling with me."

The Nabob at these words laid his hand on the arm of Basil. "Pity me and be patient!" he exclaimed—and with such an imploring tone and appealing look that the young man, who was naturally kind-hearted, found it impossible to resist them. "Answer me, for charity's sake," he continued, while the tears almost gathered in his eyes; "could you bear to become as short as I am?"

"To *become* as short?" said Basil—"Surely, mein Herr, you do not—cannot expect a rational answer to an insane question?"

"Who is insane?" demanded the Nabob. "The prosperous man—the applauded beauty—the worshipped monarch—the flattered millionaire! Not the wretch—the thrice-deformed—the brooder over his own thoughts, black as midnight and cheerless as the sepulchre—the being whom Heaven and Earth abandon—no—to him the blessing of madness is eternally denied! Alas! that I should be but too exquisitely alive to the unutterable loneliness and misery of my destiny! Look at me, Basil Von Rosenwald! I was once as tall as you are now. Nay, more, I had your flowing curls, your fine firm teeth, your radiant eyes, all that makes you most attractive in the estimation of woman. Even now inspect me narrowly, and you will trace a family resemblance. My nose is still aquiline, like your own. Though my cheeks have fallen in, my lips preserve their shape;—and see and say whether they are not the counterparts of yours. My forehead, separated from my other features, might be mistaken for your own. In a word, give me but your height, your hair, and a few other minor advantages, and I defy the most scrutinising to distinguish between us. These, in fact, are all that I want. But—these are *what* I want. Will you—will you give them to me?—Will you give them to me? I ask but this one gift—this one transfer—in return for my gold!"

"Ha! ha! ha!" cried Basil, laughing outright, "my good Sir, I take you at last—I *was* stupid—pardon me! I did not know you. You wish me to bestow my inches upon you in return for a few of your money bags?"

"Precisely so," said the Nabob; "and I am glad you treat the matter so lightly."

"Capital! Upon my honor, Sir, you are an inimitable wag! Ha! ha! ha!"

"Alas !"—sighed the Nabob—" I fear you——"

"Ha! ha! ha!—fear nothing! my dear Sir," said Basil. "I enter fully into the spirit of your proposition—believe me—Ha! ha! ha!"

"You rejoice me," said the Nabob. "I did not, I confess, expect this ready acquiescence on your part. You agree, then?"

"Agree—to give you my inches and take your ducats—ha! ha! ha!—yes, agree to be sure; though, to be frank, I do feel some scruple in taking such an advantage——"

"No more, my worthy friend—not a word more, I insist. I am, then, to consider the bargain as closed?"

"What can I say, dear Sir," said Basil—"what can I do—except return you my warmest acknowledgments—poor as I am in all besides? You are really very good, exceedingly noble, thus to cloak your unparalleled liberality under the guise of such eccentricity!"

"As it is a settled matter, then, you will pay attention to me now," said the Nabob, gravely. "You shall have thirty of my bags, that is, thirty thousand ducats; and with those thirty bags you shall take thirty of my flasks." He went to the press. "Here is one flask to accompany this bag. I can let you have as many as you please under six, at a time, but I would recommend you to commence by taking one. To obtain possession of the bag, you must swallow the elixir in the flask: this is an indispensable condition. Now mark and ponder: *Every time that you drain one of these black flasks you lose an inch of your stature, and I gain it*. This is not all: your appearance otherwise becomes altered for the worse; and, in short, by the time you have drained the thirtieth flask you will have sunk down to my height, and present precisely such a spectacle to the eyes of all who see you as I do now, while I, on the other hand, shall be in possession of all your present advantages of feature and figure. You understand me definitely and clearly?"

"Really, my worthy Sir," said Basil, still laughing, "your solemnity would impose on the devil himself. I do understand you—and am willing to go any length you like to countenance your joke. I trust you will not find me ungrateful."

"Observe, however," pursued the Deformed, "that if you can at any time repay me all—if you can return me the thirty thousand ducats—you get your inches back. So, in proportion, you can regain one inch for every thousand ducats you manage to restore to me. And now you are *au fait* of every article and stipulation connected with the bargain betwixt us. Will you be satisfied to take a single bag to-day? Mr. Flemming has apprised me of your address; and my servant shall leave the money at your house forthwith."

"Ten thousand thanks, my dear sir. But indeed—indeed, I feel reluctant to abuse your generosity. Could there not be a bond?"

"There is, you know," said the Nabob, quietly.

"Eh!—there is?—how?—what?" asked Basil.

"My flasks are my bonds," said the East-Indian, in the same quiet tone. "But you agree voluntarily to my proposal? You will have the ducats at the price I have stated?"

"I agree to every thing," said Basil—"and I hope that circumstances may yet enable me——"

"Never mind—never mind—don't mention repayment—as to that, if you can repay me, you will."

"Depend on that, my dear Sir."

"Yes," observed the Nabob, "you will traverse the globe to ferret me out."

"You form but a just estimate of my gratitude, Sir," said Basil.

"Of your gratitude?—Bah!—I am thinking of your probable anxiety to recover your inches."

"To recover my inches?—ha! ha!—Yes, I forgot that."

The Nabob opened a drawer in the table and took out a beer-glass, into which he decanted the elixir. He then proffered the glass to Basil, remarking, as he did so, that he would not find the beverage unpleasant.

Without hesitating a moment, the young man took the glass from his hand and drained it to the bottom in a draught. A thrill shot through his veins as he withdrew it from his lips; and instead of re-depositing it on the table he cast it from him to the end of the room. His eyes were lighted by a fierce and unwonted fire.

"Damned hot!" he said—"why does it burn the fingers? I say, you twaddling old humbug!—you'll be coming down with a smash too, one of these days. By the ghost of Merlin I—I could crush to dust all the dry bones in your shrivelled carcase!—Give me the bag, you hound!"

"Too strong," said the East-Indian calmly, as speaking to himself; and re-producing his snuff-box, he extended it to Basil, who mechanically plunged his finger and thumb into it.

"God bless me," exclaimed the young man the next moment, "where?—what ?—did I not utter some foolish thing? You will excuse me!"

"The elixir was somewhat fierier than I thought," said the Nabob—"but I shall remedy the error in the other flasks. And now all is done and settled. As to the ducats, you will find them at home before you. Nay, no more acknowledgments—our bargain is mutual and so are our obligations. When you want a second bag, come to me." And he led the way from the chamber.

"You are the truest friend I have ever had," said Basil, clasping the Nabob's hand. "I shall not forget this day."

"I imagine not," replied the Nabob drily. "Take care of yourself." He accompanied Basil to the door, and they parted.

CHAPTER IV.

"The course of true love never did run smooth."—*Midsum. Night's Dream, Act* i. *Scene* 1.

Reader! we would fain introduce thee, supposing thee a bachelor, to the lady Aurelia Von Elsberg. And yet a second reflection whispers us that we should not, for wherein could the introduction advantage thee? Bitter are hopes disappointed; and the young damsel's affections are already given away—plighted beyond the possibility of recall to Basil Rosenwald—the hero of the elixir-flasks and ducat-sacks. Content thy soul and sight, therefore, with one passing glimpse of the shining-haired apparition as she sweeps by thee into the saloon. See! she comes—she dazzles—she is gone.

Thou art not over-imaginative; and the vision thus vouchsafed thee, far from sufficing to people thy slumbers with shapes of beauty henceforward, is even now melting into misty indistinctness, like the last glories of a departing rainbow. But vain are thy supplications. More of her this night thou mayest not see. Go thy ways from Elsberg Villa, consoling thyself with the recollection that thy purse-strings remain undrawn.

Who is at the Villa to-night? They who know its owners and their guests, and ask the question, are dunces at the reading of the heart. Who, it should rather be inquired, is *not* at the Villa to-night? The Prince of Lowenfeld-Schwarzbach is not at the Villa to-night. Groups of the gay, the fashionable, the beauteous, throng those illuminated and mirrored rooms, but the Prince of Lowenfeld-Schwarzbach comes not; and many hearts are depressed and many brows clouded.

And the heart of Aurelia Von Elsberg is depressed, and her brow is clouded, but not for the absence of the Prince of Lowenfeld-Schwarzbach. Her thoughts are on another truant—on Basil—and Basil, where is he? She knows not; but her eye wanders from place to place, from figure to figure, and finds him not, and comes back again, and again wanders, and again is disappointed. Hark!—a knock!—a series of knocks!—and her heart beats responsive. He comes—Basil Theodore Von Rosenwald approaches. All is commotion, anticipation, excitement. Every eye is directed towards the door. The servant announces the new arrival, but mistakes his name and gives him a title. Aurelia prepares to greet her lover *à la mode Germanorum.*[20] Her eyes are sparkling; her bosom throbs. Another moment and the expected is in the apartment. She moves forward, grace in all her steps, and—O, stars and garters! wherefore is such sorcery permitted in ball-rooms?—beholds the vision of her fancy metamorphosed into the Prince of Lowenfeld-Schwarzbach. There he stands, bowing to the whole *beau monde* in epitome—glittering with crosses and orders, and looking as handsome as any man can look, who is not Basil Theodore Von Rosenwald.

There are bright roses in thy darkling hair, O matchless maiden! and fair pearls cluster on thy fairer bosom, and as thine airy form follows the sinuous evolutions of the dance, and thou appearest less a being of earth than heaven, none can dream that for thee Fortune has a single disappointment in store. Ah, well-a-day! Unwreathe from thy hair those blooming flowers—discard all thy bright pearls—mingle no more in the mazes of the quadrille—but retire—retire and luxuriate in the full indulgence of sorrow; for thy lover, thy beloved, he for whom thou lookest, will not smile on thee, will not sigh to thee, will not see thee to-night.

What a pity that where the affections are concerned, fathers and mothers cannot be made to see with the eyes of their sons and daughters!

So much self-immolating love is marred—so many tender hearts are broken, or, at least, get a little bruised!—and all for no reason in life, except that people at fifty pique themselves upon being thirty years older than when they were twenty! It is worse than a pity—it is monstrous!—but let us keep cool. Herr von Elsberg was an exemplary parent, an honorable man, and a good citizen, as parents, men, and citizens went and go, but he preferred seeing his daughter married to a Prince than to a beggar, and he had been telling her so for some time; and his wife, a shrewd lady in her way, though quiet, had been backing his arguments with all the abundant feminine logic she had at command. On all these occasions almost the sole resource of the poor girl had been to withdraw and weep. The absence of her lover had grieved her much; and the cause of it, when revealed by her father—who was neither slow in discovering nor shy in communicating it—had grieved her more. Unluckily, too, it had chanced that just at the time Basil began his visits to the Spielhaus, the Prince began his visits to the Villa, and fell desperately in love with the illumining star thereof—a brighter than any he had yet taken unto his bosom. Misfortunes never come singly: to miss a lover was not quite enough; the unhappy Aurelia must, to say nothing of auxiliary disadvantages, be threatened with a title and a principality. She tried, in compliance with the wishes of Papa and Mamma, to look at the Prince, but somehow the image of Basil constantly interfered with her best attempts, and she felt and acknowledged with Fenelon,[21] *qu'il est plus facile de mépriser la mort même que de réprimer les affections du cœur.*[22] And then over and over again,

> "———she said,
> I'll ne'er wed man but thee,
> The grave shall be my bridal bed
> Ere Græme my husband be."[23]

Her nineteenth birth-night arrived, and a ball was given in honor of it. Basil had been invited months before, while as yet his prospects were tolerable;—but circumstances had now assumed such a different aspect! Would he venture within the precincts of the dwelling from which he had so long remained away, a voluntary exile, self-condemned, and engrossed by one of the most degrading and powerful of all the passions? I fear he will not, whispered her doubts—and again Fear yielded to Hope. I hope, yes, I think he will—and in a moment after a saddening influence, the result of some trifle lighter than air, would overshadow her spirit, and again Hope would be banished by Fear, and she would sigh, No! no!—It is vain to expect him—He is cold—changed—cruel! He will not come!

"I wonder whether that young scapegrace, Rosenwald, intends to show himself here to-morrow," said Elsberg to his wife on the day preceding.

"Why, my dear, he has been invited, you remember—and—and I think he *will* come—and if he should, you know," she added, significantly, "we cannot quite turn him out."

Le sage entend à demi-mot.[24] "No, as you say, we cannot *turn* him out," said the husband. "...... But ......" A certain proverb with reference to the various ways the canine race have of dying occurred to him,—but we quote it not;—we eschew vulgarity.[25]

Ah! what a world of untowardnesses is this! Nobody has ever made the remark before. Why does not every thing happen just as it ought? This is the sole puzzle that continually employs our reflecting faculties, and baffles our investigations night, noon, and twilight, (for we doze away the morning.) How is it that young gentlemen are not always self-possessed and diplomatic on emergencies? Why will hall-porters prate when they should remain tongue-tied? What is the reason that a fit of remorse or apoplexy does not seize on a worldly-minded, Prince-for-a-son-in-law-seeking sire precisely at the instant when it would be most agreeable—— to one or two others? Why are lovelorn damsels moving through drawing-rooms when they should be seated in turrets, watching at lattices for the approach of their knights from afar? Why? How?

> "The little bird pipeth, 'Why, Why?'
> In the Summer woods when the sun falls low,
> And the great bird sits on the opposite bough,
> And stares in his face and shouts, 'How, how?'"[26]

We will question no more. Our spirit is a-weary of evoking shadows to be answered by echoes. It *is* tiresome. A very minute portion of contempt, too, for the philosophy that in some thousands of years has done so little towards enlightening us, may perhaps mingle, we half apprehend, with our ennui, as a drop of tartaric acid slightly relieves the insipidity of a glass of distilled water. '*Memnon*,' quoth Voltaire, '*conçut un jour le projet d'être parfaitement sage. Il n'y a guère d'hommes à qui cette folie n'ait quelquefois passé par la tête.*'[27] Very few, indeed, we admit; and we are not one of them. For the identical *folie* has just occurred to ourself; but in us it becomes the quintessence of wisdom, and as one result, we abandon moralising. Let us pursue our interesting narrative, and relate it after the fashion of the day. Amen.

The events of the afternoon had considerably elevated the spirits of Basil. The prospect of being enabled through the agency of the East-Indian to settle his debts, to regain his accustomed position in society, and above all, to re-establish himself upon his former footing at Elsberg Villa, was cheering. Basil was of a sanguine temperament, and he now changed from the extreme of despondency to that of extravagant anticipation. Very little deliberation sufficed to determine him to go to the ball. He had expected that Flemming would accompany him. But he waited until nine o'clock and neither Flemming nor any body else came; so at last, tired of waiting, away he went by himself in a hackney carriage.

Upon descending from the vehicle he glanced up at the windows of the Villa; and he fancied he saw, flitting by them, the well-remembered figure of Aurelia. His heart beat quicker for that vision; and he entered the house. He was about taking out his ticket in readiness for the inspection of the janitor at the summit of the staircase, when a door near him opened and the Herr Von Elsberg came forth, accompanied by a tall stranger in a cloak, who shook him (Elsberg) by the hand, and, bidding him farewell, passed rapidly out at the great entrance.

Von Elsberg looked at our hero, and our hero looked at him. Both gentlemen then bowed; but a not very close observer might have discerned something approaching to *hauteur* in the greeting of Elsberg, and a slight indication of embarrassment in that of Rosenwald.

"This is an unexpected pleasure, Mr. Rosenwald," said Elsberg, with repelling politeness of manner, not easily described, though frequently encountered.

"Indeed?" returned Basil. "That is somewhat strange. I come on your own invitation, given me two months since."

"Will you step into my study?" said Elsberg. "I am anxious to say a few words to you."

"Willingly," and both crossed the gallery and entered the study. There was a calm but cheerful aspect about this little room. A coal fire—so rarely met with on the Continent—burned in the grate, and a huge tom-cat was reposing upon the hearth-rug. Warm-looking paintings, set in deep gilt Florentine frames, decorated the walls. Elsberg rang for wine and glasses.

"Take a seat, Mr. Rosenwald," said he, "I hope you have not been ill lately?"

"Not particularly," said Basil.

"You are not looking by any means as well as you used," observed Von Elsberg.

"My mind has not been entirely at ease of late," Basil answered.

"I should suppose not," said Elsberg. "Habits such as you have fallen into, Mr. Rosenwald, must disturb the mind very much."

"Sir!" exclaimed our hero—and pride and mortification were both concentrated in the monosyllable.

"Well, Mr. Rosenwald?" returned the other, composedly.

"I may have been unfortunate, Sir," said Basil, "but I did not expect to be taunted with my misfortunes—at least by you. It is ungenerous—allow me to add, it is ungentlemanly."

"You are too warm, Mr. Rosenwald—you should learn to hear and to bear the truth," answered Elsberg. "I meant you no offence. Suffer me to help you to a glass of Rhenish," he added, as the servant, entering, laid a wine-flask, with glasses and silver salvers, on the table.

"Let me not detain you from your guests, Herr Von Elsberg," said Basil, abruptly rising. "I see—I can perceive——." But a certain consciousness that he was beginning to be agitated beyond what he should be, or should *appear to be*, and that any attempt to explain his feelings would but increase his agitation, checked the rest of the sentence. Basil was proud and sensitive, and, like all proud and sensitive men, he desired to be considered exceedingly impassive and self-possessed.

"Pray, sit down, sit down, Mr. Rosenwald," said Elsberg, tranquilly, and filling his own glass as he spoke. And Basil, ashamed of the emotion he had betrayed, and resolute to rival the coolness of his host during the rest of their interview, whether long or short, reseated himself.

"Mr. Rosenwald," said Elsberg, "it is right that we should come to an understanding with each other. Some weeks have now elapsed since I last saw you—and I am not ignorant of the causes that have produced your absence. It is to me, as it must be to all who know you, matter of deep regret that you, with your advantages of birth, station, and talent, should have yielded yourself up to an infatuation as degrading as it is destructive—and with eyes open to all the consequences of your own misconduct should persevere in pursuing, I may say, the direct path to perdition. This is an afflicting consideration, Mr. Rosenwald. I should be rejoiced, however, to think that your case was not yet wholly hopeless. Let me trust all has not been sacrificed?"

"If you mean my property, Sir," said Basil, "I can give no encouragement to your hopes, though I thank you for them. But this is a subject which—excuse me —I cannot recognise your right of discussing with me. I have already admitted myself to be your debtor, although only a portion of the jewels which, when in business, you disposed of to my mother, fell into my hands on her death. You have my bond for fifteen thousand crowns, payable on the first of November. If I liquidate your claim I leave you, at least, nothing to complain of."

"This is the seventeenth of October, Mr. Rosenwald," said Elsberg,—looking at his guest with an eye of triumphant pity.

"Well, Sir,—and were it the thirty-first, what then?" demanded Basil, warmly, for the glance had not passed unnoticed by him.

"You have all but admitted your inability to take up the bond," said Elsberg.

"Pardon me, I have admitted nothing of the kind," said Basil. "My circumstances it is true, are at present embarrassed, but"—and the thought of the Nabob's money-bags flashed across his mind,—"I entertain no doubt whatever of ultimately retrieving myself."

"May I ask how?" demanded Elsberg.

"I must decline answering, Sir," said Basil, "until you have satisfied me of your right to intermeddle in my affairs."

"Mr. Rosenwald," said Elsberg, in severe and reproving accents, "Mr. Rosenwald, I am Aurelia's father!"

The words told. On the instant the young man grew paler. An arrow had pierced to his soul. It seemed as though pride, and the peculiar position in which he had been placed—for his introduction into the study had obviously been a *ruse* on the part of his host to prevent him from ascending to the drawing-room—had hitherto banished every thought of love. But now, and with a force all the mightier for having been so long repressed, his heart and its affections re-asserted their prerogatives and rose paramount to all rival considerations. A thousand fond and woeful reminiscences grew into life, and crowded upon him. All the past year, clad in its lights and shadows of incident, came before him like a panoramic picture. He hid his face in his hands and groaned.

"It grieves me much, Mr. Rosenwald," said Elsberg, "if I have revived unpleasant recollections—but the first duty of a parent is to provide for his child's happiness, and to see that she herself does not mistake it. Young men and young women never look properly before them. Wealth, rank, title, the consideration of society, the more substantial advantages of life, are with them all secondary to the single passion of love, a passion which from its very nature, from its very violence, must be evanescent—and is too often succeeded by mutual disappointment and dislike. On this account I regard it as imperative on me to make every exertion for the advancement of Aurelia's *real* welfare; and you will not take it ill, Mr. Rosenwald, if I say I conceive that your present circumstances are not exactly those which could justify me in looking forward to you as her husband and my son-in-law. I am frank, you see, with you, because I am aware that you love Aurelia; and it is better, as I have said, that in so important a matter we should arrive at an explicit understanding with one another."

"And Aurelia," said the young man, as soon as he had in some degree recovered himself—"is she—does she participate in your sentiments, Sir?"

"My daughter will entertain no sentiments unworthy of her," replied Von Elsberg. "She knows, in extremity, how to sacrifice feelings that she ought not to cherish."

"Feelings she ought not to cherish!" repeated the young man. "What,

Sir, do you look then so lightly upon violated troth and falsified promises? Is the blackest of all perjuries—that in which the heart is forsworn—so innocent or venial in your estimation?"

"I do not know," said Elsberg, doubtingly, "that Aurelia has fixed her affections on *you*, Mr. Rosenwald."

"She has: lips that never lied have confessed it!" cried Basil.

"Very thoughtless, I must say," observed Elsberg, shaking his head—"the result of her youth and inexperience, Mr. Rosenwald. But she is a daughter of *mine*—and—even if what you state be true—she will—she *shall* submit to be guided by those who are competent to direct her. I have but to speak to her, to reason with her a little, and she will at once consent as she ought, to forego this foolish and inexpedient attachment!"

"Sir," cried Basil, "if those be your real sentiments, I tell you, without circumlocution, that I cannot find language sufficiently strong to express my contempt of them!"

"It is sometimes better," said Von Elsberg, imperturbably, and playing with his watch chain, as he sat back in his chair, "that we should be at a loss for words to express our meaning; our deficiency teaches us a lesson of self-diffidence and caution. *Au reste*,[28] Mr. Rosenwald, the sentiments you reprobate are such, let me inform you, as will soon be shared and professed by my daughter herself."

"It is false!" cried Basil, as Aurelia's image—the very personification of constancy and devotedness—rose upon his mind's eye—"it is false!" he repeated, standing up; "and you, her father, know it to be false as hell! Shame upon you, sir, so to slander your own blood—ay! and to glory in the slander! But your breast is cased in triple adamant. Were it not so, I would demand of you why it is I am here at this moment—why walls and doors should be permitted to separate on such a night hearts that never can know happiness asunder. I am aware that I should appeal in vain to you, otherwise I would ask you, even now, whether I could see your daughter—if but for a minute."

"Your penetration, such as it is, has not deceived you," said Elsberg. "You cannot, upon any account, see my daughter this evening. The granting of such an interview would be impolitic; I could not possibly permit it. I have every respect for you, Mr. Rosenwald, but circumstances render——"

"You have every respect for hell and damnation, sir!" exclaimed Basil, in a transport of indignation. "Where is my hat? Let me be off!"

"Here is your hat, and there are your gloves, Mr. Rosenwald," said Elsberg very quietly, as he also rose up. "Is this your handkerchief? No; I believe it is my own. You are rather hot-blooded, I think, for your own peace of mind," he added. "I have often noticed your excitability, and never without regret. I pardon you on this occasion, because you are a lover; and though I have never known what the feelings of a lover are, I can imagine them and compassionate any unfortunate individual who suffers from them. But, if *you* are a lover, Mr Rosenwald, I am a father; and, as such, I must fulfil the duties of a father. It is pure want of reflection—want of serious habits of thought—want, in short——" and the Herr Von Elsberg put on an uncommonly profound and Socratic countenance— "want, in short, Mr. Rosenwald, of a philosophical, categorical, and analytical system of investigation into the operation of correct and irrefragable principles as contradistinguished from the operation of illusory and fallacious principles, that disqualifies you from perceiving that I act for the best, and with a view to the production of the largest possible amount of good attainable under existing circumstances. If you are determined on going, Mr. Rosenwald—if you will not stop and chat with me over another glass—this Rhenish, I assure you, was four-and-twenty years old last August,—why, I can only say, I have the honour of bidding you a good evening."

All this had fallen upon the ear of Basil "like sounding brass or a tinkling cymbal."[29] There was a roaring in his head—a tempest in his heart. He put on his hat, and, without deigning even to notice the farewell salutation of his host, rushed out of the house and made his way home.

CHAPTER V.

"There's money for thee, Greek !"—*Twelfth Night*, *Act* iv. *Sc.* 1.[30]
"I prithee, let the Prince alone."—*K. Hen. IV.* 1st *part*, *Act* i. *Sc*.1.[31]

A tolerable night's sleep—for Basil "slept in spite of thunder"[32]— somewhat restored the every-day tone and temper of his mind. He got up and dressed himself and shaved—or shaved and dressed himself, we forget which—and then he actually breakfasted; and if the curious in dietetics are agog to know of what his breakfast consisted we will gratify them:— it consisted of one colossal roll and butter, two hen eggs, three slices of Westphalia ham, and four cups of Arabian coffee—a breakfast we undertake to recommend to themselves, the curious aforesaid. After he had finished his last cup, it is a fact that he drew his chair to the fire and deposited his toes on the fender; and, settled in that position, began to pick his teeth and think of Aurelia. Several minutes elapsed, and he was just deliberating whether he should or should not despatch her a succession of billet-doux, say forty-eight in twenty-four hours—were it only to plague her father, if indeed he were plagueable—when a modest knock was heard at the hall-door, and in a minute afterwards Basil's solitary servant announced, "Der Herr Grabb."

"Show him in," said Basil, rising up carelessly.

And into the room, with a slow and stealthy pace, like Wordsworth's Doe,[33] and silently, as one whose shoon are soled with velvet, came Herr Grabb. He was a short, thickset man, with a broad head, a low forehead, a small, quick, grey eye, a snub nose, and compressed, though somewhat thickish lips; and displayed altogether a *tout-ensemble*[34] both in person and habiliments, which bespoke him—not to hazard a more perilous and less general guess at his character—as one who in his time had enjoyed a much less intimate acquaintance with the romance of life than with its realities, and was considerably more at home in Alberstadt, with all its lampless alleys and *culs de sac* than he could ever feel himself in Faery-land.

"Take a chair, Mr. Grabb," said Basil. He went to a press, unlocked it, and took out the money-bag he had received the preceding day.

"Eight hundred and—a——" he said, looking at Grabb, inquiringly.

"*Vierzig*, Forty," said Grabb, in a soft voice, and with an expressive twinkle of one eye.

Basil counted out and set apart one hundred and sixty ducats, which he restored to the press. Having done so, he emptied the remaining contents of the bag out on the table.

"Try whether you have the number there," said he; and again establishing himself before the fire and fender, he re-applied himself to his silver toothpick and golden reveries.

His back was to the thickset man who knew nothing about romance; but reader! we must disappoint thee—thou art knowing, but not all-knowing, and thy chuckle is premature—the thickset man who knew nothing about romance, counted fairly, albeit his sleeves were ample and his pockets capacious. Honesty, even for rogues, is now and then the best policy. The sum was found exact to a piece—eight hundred and forty ducats.

"*Recht*, Right," said the ready-reckoner,[35] with another twinkle of the eye, lost on Basil, though not on us.

"Have you got the receipt?" asked Basil.

"*Ja*, Yes," was the answer, and the required acknowledgment was forthwith drawn from one of the recesses of a clumsy, stuffed, venerable-looking, well-handled, nondescript article, which the possessor believed to be a pocket-book,—and laid upon the table.

"Then," said Basil, "you had better put up the—O, you have done so, I see," he added, as he half turned round. "You are a handy lad, Grabb. Give me the receipt."

"*Da*, There!" said Grabb, with his peculiar visual smile.

"I say, Mr. Grabb, before you go, tell me, did you see Schmidt last night?"

"*Nein*, No," replied the little man.

"The fellow owes me four hundred and odd florins, and I can't make him out high or low. It is very hard. Have you any idea where he is gone to?"

"*Ja.*"

"You can tell me then?"

"*Ja.*"

"Well, where is he gone to?"

"*Zum Teufel gegangen*, Gone to the devil," said Grabb.

"How do you mean?"

"*Todt*, Dead."

"Dead?"

"*Ja.*"

"Dead! You astonish me. I never heard a word of it. When did he die?"

"*Gestern*, Yesterday."

"*So* late?" said Basil. "Had he been ill?"

"*Nein.*"

"Was he killed?"

"*Er hat sich die Gurgel geschnitten*, He cut his throat," said Grabb, in a very soft tone.

Basil turned his chair involuntarily round,—and fixed his eyes on Grabb in dead silence for a minute. "Cut his throat!" he at length repeated. "Unfortunate devil! What drove him to that?"

"Roulette," said Grabb.

Basil shook his head. "Where did it happen, Grabb?"

"*Im Hause*, At home," said Grabb.

Basil looked down, and appeared to be lost in absorbing study of the grotesque figure-work of the carpet. After a pause of some minutes spent thus, he lifted his head and sighed. "You may go, Grabb," said he. And out went Grabb.

As the servant opened the door for him to make his exit, up walked Heinrick Flemming.

"In the nick of time," said he. "Hey-day, Grabb!—early at business. Grabb, I must give you a good cleaning out myself one of these days. Within?" he asked of the servant.

"Yes, sir, in the parlour," said the servant, closing the door.

"You have had a dun, I see, Basil," said Heinrick, after the first salutations were over.

"Yes—Grabb; he fastened on me like a leech last night as I was turning the corner of the Kaiserstrasse; and so I told him to come this morning, and bring me a receipt in full for all."

"How much was the all?" asked Flemming.

"Eight hundred and forty ducats."

"Ha, Basil! then I take it, you sped well at the Nabob's."

"Infinitely better than I had any right to expect," said Basil. "Heinrick, you must forgive my petulance yesterday; I see and acknowledge that you are a sincere friend. I touched a thousand ducats. But what is the matter with this little Nabob? Tell me, you who know him, is he crazed, or is it merely a spirit of waggery that actuates him?"

"Faith, I can hardly divine; he is a puzzle to the few acquaintances he has. Did he say or do any thing very *outré*?"

"He assured me he was a brother of mine," returned Basil, "and told me a rigmarole cock-and-bull story about his having studied magic in the east, and his dwindling down from six feet to three feet six; and he said that for every thousand ducats I should take from him I would lose an inch."

"An inch of what?"

"An inch of my height."

"Nonsense!" cried Heinrick, laughing. "Well, you have *not* lost the inch, have you?"

"I hope not," said Basil, also laughing. "What do you think?" And he stood up.

"Egad, but that you are in your slippers," said Heinrick, measuring him with his eye, "I should think queer things." Basil laughed louder than before.

"Did he keep his countenance, Baz, though?"

"Keep his countenance? You never saw such solemnity. That was what made the thing so ridiculous. But he told me more; he said that as I lost the inches he gained them; that as I should grow short he should grow tall. Ha! ha! ha!"

"Why, he must be the devil's quiz,"[36] said Flemming. "What did he mean?"

"It is hard to say," replied Rosenwald. "I am to get thirty thousand from him. It is needless for me to acquaint *you*, Heinrick, that I accept of this only as a loan. I could not reconcile it with my conscience to take an advantage of the prodigal generosity of any man. One thing, however, is clear to me—he wishes me, I don't know why, to have the money; and I can see that I gratify him by taking it. As the case is so, why, I have the fewer scruples. Accordingly I intend troubling him to-day for a second thousand."

"Bleed him well, bleed him well, my boy, since he will have it so," said Heinrick. "Don't let your bashfulness stand in the way of your fortune. Are you coming out, now, Baz?"

"I believe I may as well taste the morning air," said Basil; "I have nothing particular to do here. Are you going any where yourself?"

"Only to the Exhibition in the Bildstrasse—I have two or three bores to meet and be stupified by there," answered Flemming.

"Talking of exhibitions," said Basil, "why were you not with me last night? I expected you up to nine."

"I didn't know we had appointed to go together," said Flemming. "But I was not at the Villa at all. A friend that I had not seen for six years dropped in on me in the afternoon, and I couldn't help spending the evening with him, for we had a good deal to talk about that nobody must be the wiser for. So I sent an apology to Elsberg. I believe he didn't care much whether I went or stayed."

"Old Elsberg is a man of marble," said Basil. And thereupon he gave his friend a succinct account of the interview of the evening before.

Heinrick listened attentively, and when Basil had finished he leaned his cheek on his hand and assumed an unusually grave and thoughtful expression of visage. "By Jove, you are diddled, Basil," said he. "I see how it is. I never paid any attention to the rumour before—but I now perceive it is founded. As sure as you have a soul inside your body, Aurelia will be the Princess von Lowenfeld-Schwarzbach before another month."

"Aurelia will be WHAT?" exclaimed Basil, starting from his chair, which he involuntarily pushed from him into the middle of the room.

"A princess," replied Flemming; "a very fine thing to be."

"Who dares to say so?" demanded the young man.

"Her father, in the first place," replied Heinrick, tapping his boot with his ebony cane, "the Prince himself, in the second—thirdly, the whole world—and, finally, your obedient humble servant."

Basil knit his brows. "The base world belies her," he said; "infamously belies her! She has pledged her troth to me and me only—and she is not— I know she is not—the girl to be coerced by tyranny or dazzled by title. But who, pray, is this Prince? What hole or corner has he come out of? How does it happen that I have never heard of him until now?"

"To answer your last question first, as I am a lover of order," said Heinrick—"Because you have been for six weeks absorbed in the unhallowed mysteries of cards, dice, tables black and red, ivory balls, and tantalising cylinders—why, man, the Emperor of Morocco—the Great Mogul—the Grand Lama himself—though I don't know if *he* marries— might have come into Alberstadt, and borne Aurelia off in triumph to his dominions, without any knowledge on your part of the abduction. What a pretty sort of lover you are! As for Lowenfeld-Schwarzbach, upon my honour, he is in every respect a very desirable *parti*[37]—rich, handsome, accomplished, and, more than all, a Prince."

"Lowenfeld-Schwarzbach!" echoed Basil, contemptuously. "In what part of space may that principality be lying *perdu*?"[38]

"Somewhere in Silesia, I think," was the answer.

"He does well not to place it in Saxony," said Basil. "The further off a vagabond pitches his tent on these occasions the less common eyes can distinguish whether it is of sattin or canvas."

"What!" exclaimed Flemming. "Does His Serene Highness the Prince Von Lowenfeld-Schwarzbach take the shape and qualities of a *chevalier d'industrie*[39] in your eyes? Come, come, Baz; this is too bad; jealousy makes you unjust. Von Lowenfeld-Schwarzbach *is* a Prince—ay !—a Prince every inch of him."

"Curse his inches!" cried Rosenwald; "I wish that old East-Indian could melt them down, as he proposes to do with mine. I tell you, Heinrick, I have my suspicions whenever I hear of your *very* foreign noblemen. If lions are got up to be stared at, tigers[40] usually get *themselves* up. I have seen something of the world, and am not easily duped. Was there not somebody sometime back who passed himself off in Berlin as the Wandering Jew?[41] You have no notion of the gullibility of people. I will tell you a fact; while I lived at Dresden last year, my tailor there, by the help of dyes, dress, moustaches, and the most damned effrontery, got himself admitted into the first circles as a Pomeranian Baron. His title was—no matter— something sounding, like Thunder-ten-Trunk;[42] and he was on the point of making his fortune or getting his scull split, I forget which now, when I exposed the rogue and forced him to shift his quarters. As soon as he found himself blown he took himself off in a twinkling, and by-the-by carried with him a splendid dress lace-coat of mine, with a green and gold collar, worth about thirty guineas. If I ever catch him I'll drub him to some purpose, even though I lay the blows on my own coat."

"Pooh! pooh!—these little incidents will happen," said Flemming. "But your inference is somewhat sweeping if you conclude that because a Dresden tailor pretended to be a Pomeranian Baron, every Silesian Prince must be a swindler. However, we'll discuss the matter more at large another time. If you are for going out now, you had better make your toilet at once, for"— and he took out his watch—" my time is at hand."[43]

"I shall not delay you," said Basil; and he tripped up the stairs. In a few minutes he again rejoined Heinrick, and both left the house.

The friends as they walked along arm in arm, resumed the subjects they had been conversing on in the house, but Basil had not arrived at any decision satisfactory to himself with respect to the course of conduct he should pursue in reference to Aurelia, by the time they reached the corner of the Blumenstrasse, where it was necessary that both should part. They therefore appointed to meet again after a short interval. Flemming hurried off to the Exhibition, while Basil, in a thoughtful and perplexed mood of mind, slowly wended his way through the winding strasses and neglected avenues that lead to the Dornensteg.

CHAPTER VI.

"————— Dreams are toys,
Yet for this once, yea superstitiously,
Thou shalt be squared by this."
Winter's Tale. Act iii. *Scene* 3.[44]

Encouraging as the issue of the interview on the previous day had been, Basil could not entirely master a few unpleasant sensations as he once more applied his fingers to the knocker of the Nabob's house-door. His proud and scrupulous nature made him feel ashamed and humbled to think that he could be tempted by any, even the most imperative circumstances, to accept of, nay to solicit, money from the hands of another without tendering or at least proposing an equivalent in some guise or other. It is accounted a proceeding so shabby to avail yourself of the simplicity and munificence of a benevolent enthusiast to the amplest extent to which he will permit you to go! One of a truly noble mode of thinking would shrink from bearing the burden of an irrepayable favour, when bestowed by such a person. He would say to himself, Here is a philanthropist who lavishes wealth upon his fellow-beings. But he does this in the conviction that he is assisting the excellent and meritorious. Let him discover that the objects of his bounty are little better than swindlers, and he draws his purse-strings together on the instant. If I grasp at that which is proffered me and seem gratified at getting it, my rapacity furnishes my benefactor with an unanswerable argument for checking the stream of his liberality towards others. Therefore I will not. So good a creature must not be led to harbour a degrading opinion of human nature through any dereliction of mine. No. I will shew him that individual aggrandisement is the remotest thing from my thoughts; that if he is generous enough to offer, I am disinterested enough to refuse. Thus I shall at once rescue my own perhaps too fastidious pride harmless, and be the means of accomplishing for those who may really stand in need of his help the best service within the sphere of my ability to render them.

Though these thoughts did not flow consecutively through Basil's mind as he walked into the parlour, he was conscious of such a feeling as might arise from the conclusion to which they conducted. He felt uneasy and qualmish, and half disposed to retrace his steps. It was consequently with no inconsiderable satisfaction that he saw the eyes of the Nabob, as he hastily rose up from a sofa, emitting sparkles of pleasure at his approach and salutation. The look of animation and gladness that greeted him was a sufficient justification of the purpose of his visit. It gave evidence that the Nabob considered himself as the obliged, not the obliging, party. In a moment every scruple that Basil had begun to cherish was dissipated, and he felt restored to his former position in his own appreciation of himself and his motives.

"Welcome, brother!" exclaimed the Nabob, as he warmly pressed his visitor's hand. "You are come to relieve me of another flask?"

"I am indeed here again to abuse your generosity," returned Basil.

"To praise it rather perhaps?" said the Nabob.

Basil smiled. "You will appreciate my delicacy in a case like this," said he; "and if you will have the patience to hear a sketch of my circumstances, perhaps I might shew you——"

"I know them already," interrupted the Nabob; "so there is no necessity. Come in; I have no time to lose, for in half an hour I must be in the Green Suburb."

So speaking, he led the way into the flask-room, followed by Basil. The apartment presented the same appearance that had characterised it the day before, except that in the interval an arm-chair had been placed opposite the table.

"Are you fond of sight-seeing?" demanded the Nabob, as he decanted the elixir.

"Not very," Basil replied.

"Well, then, would you have any objection to be mystified for a few minutes?"

"Mystified?"

"Ay, mystified. Doubtless you have a high opinion of the fidelity and extent of your own perceptive powers, your judgment, understanding, and so forth; and you laugh at every body not endowed with a sufficiency of reason to counterpoise and curb the vagaries of his imagination?"

"Why, I flatter myself"——began Basil.

"Of course," interrupted the Nabob. "Tell me news when you next speak to me. Here, drink, and take note (not notes) of what passes before you."

Basil obeyed the behest. Apparently flask the second was as strong as flask the first had been, but the effect it produced on Basil was unique and novel. For the tithe of an instant it stupified him: then a haze clouded his view, similar to that which envelopes objects about us, when after we have stooped earthwards a long while and then risen, the blood retreats from the brain like a descending cataract. He staggered. If he had not caught hold of the arm-chair probably he would have fallen.

"Walk this way, my man," said a voice. It was that of the Nabob. He was not standing where he had been, but at the end of the room, close by a window *à la chinois*.[45]

Basil looked up. He stared around. The wax-lights were extinct; but the blue beams of an Autumnal moon came ghastlily glancing into the chamber. He rubbed his eyes; he again cast them round; there was no change.

Slowly and with faltering steps he approached the Nabob. Bewilderment and awe seemed wholly to possess him. At first he could articulate nothing; and it was by an exertion that he finally exclaimed, pointing to the window—" This—was—not here *then*."

"Well; it is now," said the Nabob calmly. "But do you observe nothing stranger than the sudden appearance of the window?"

At the question Basil looked round once more, and then, as if making an effort at recollection, he said in the low, perplexed voice of a baffled self-communer, "There was light here and there is darkness, but whence the light came I do not remember, and whence the darkness is I do not know."

"Well, as you do not know whence the darkness proceeds I will tell you," said the Nabob, drily. "The darkness proceeds from the absence of the light. Keep that a secret. But, look up at the moon. Did you ever see that planet beaming more lustrously, or floating along a sky of purer blue?"

"In all my life, never!" cried Basil. "She is in truth beautiful to contemplate;" and he gazed at the moon with all the absorbing wonder of an infant.

"Yet there should be no moon up at this hour," said the Nabob. "It is mid-day. Recollect that, and recollect also that you did not recollect it before. How do you propose accounting for the double phenomenon?"

The query appeared to plunge Basil into deep meditation, but after a short pause he answered: "Spare me! spare me!"—" Oh!" he added, lifting his hand to his brow, "I have lost my senses: I try in vain to make the present harmonise with the past: my ideas are dislocated; chaos reigns in my mind. This is your doing, juggler!"

"Mine?" cried the Nabob. "Ha! ha!—excuse me if I laugh. What, pray, do you accuse *me* of?"

"Of bereaving me of reason by your spells!" exclaimed Basil. "I am no longer myself!"

"Well, at least, you are some one," remarked the East-Indian; "and that is more than I can say for myself—I am a nonentity."

"This is horrible!" cried Basil. "Man or demon, or whatever you be, restore to me the exercise of my faculties, and let me quit this accursed house for ever!"

"I am sorry to be obliged to tell you, my dear friend," said the Nabob quietly, "that I am as powerless to aid you as your shadow on the wall can be. If you wish for help you should apply to somebody or other; I am not in existence at all."

"Not in existence !" Basil exclaimed.

"Upon my honor," said the Nabob, "I speak the unequivocal truth."

"How am I to interpret your meaning?" demanded Basil.

"In the obvious sense," replied the Nabob, "and without for a moment supposing that I shelter it behind any metaphysical subterfuge. I repeat it, I have no existence whatever: I am the mere creature of your imagination, or rather of your volition, which has unconsciously operated to endow a thought with speech and appearance. Need I add after this that you are now asleep and dreaming?"

"Ah!—dreaming!" exclaimed Basil. "Yes—yes—it must be so; I see it! I feel it! Truly, there are more things in heaven and earth than are dreamt of in our philosophy[46]—or philosophised of in our dreams either. But if I dream," he added, his features assuming an intensely puzzled expression; "how is it that instead of intuitively discovering the fact from my own sensations, I should only be able to learn it from you, who are as you yourself admit, no more than the phantom of my brain?"

The Nabob laughed in derision. "Heaven mend your silly babble!" he said. "What signifies the How? Do you not perceive that in any case the knowledge must emanate from yourself? You may find it out, or I may acquaint you with it: does it not all amount to the one thing, when your own mind is the sole primary machine that works, the sole casuist that reasons not only for yourself but for me?"

"This is marvellous, and past my capacity!" cried Basil. "But why am I subjected to a delusion so inexplicable?"

"That you may think with more reverence of the Invisible and Unexplored," replied the Nabob. "You will, perhaps, now that you have seen by what a rapid and simple process a man may lose the memory of his very identity, feel less disposed to doubt that he may lose so small a matter as a part of his stature. This has been a gratuitous and supererogatory proceeding on my part; for I might leave you in your error much longer. But I take an interest in you, and I will even exert myself to undeceive you. Remember then—and let it be your first thought as you awake—that *two of your inches are already lost.*"

It seemed as though an echo adopted the word *lost*, and repeated it in thunder through the long and broad apartment; for the loudness of the sound was such as to awaken Basil. He started from the chair into which he had sunk after swallowing the elixir. He saw the Nabob's eyes fixed on his own.

"So !"—said Basil—" I *have* been mystified, mein Herr! After all, then, it was but a dream, a fancy?"

"No more; but you know that at first you mistook it for reality. So may you fall into the opposite error, and mistake reality for fancy. The dream you have just had was not without a purpose. I am desirous of shewing you that our compact of yesterday is the very reverse of the joke you imagine it. The hoaxing of greenhorns is not my forte; I repudiate it. Nature ordained me to enact a melancholy and mysterious part on the stage of life. I neither sympathise with nor understand the nature or tendency of humbuggery. I am aware that you think otherwise, and my conscience would reproach me if I longer suffered you to suppose our agreement a bottle of moonshine. No, Sir. It must be fulfilled to the letter. I now again tell you that you have lost two inches of your height. To convince you, if you please, I will measure you on the spot."

"O, no necessity, my dear Sir," said Basil, smiling; "if you insist upon it I yield—I will say *Credo—Credo quia impossibile*.[47] But if I have lost two inches, I will swear that you have gained two; you look considerably improved since yesterday."

"Precisely what I apprised you would happen," said the East-Indian. "But I see you are still sceptical. Yet, believe me, there is nothing so unworthy credence in the theory, setting the fact altogether aside."

"What!" said Basil; "nothing incredible in the theory that a man may dwindle down from six feet to three and a half?"

"Nothing that I can perceive," returned the other. "Men fall away in bulk: why not allow them to decrease in altitude?"

"Ha! ha! Seriously, now, my dear Sir, *can* you expect me to reply to you? Or can you—as from your gravity I would almost conclude—really fancy that you or any man on earth can rob me of an inch of stature? Do you indeed indulge a notion so preposterous? Surely it is not possible that in the nineteenth century a man can be found who arrogates to himself supernatural powers?"

"Before you decide that I arrogate to myself supernatural powers," said the Nabob, "you should first satisfy yourself what the precise extent is beyond which mere human powers are incapable of rivalling supernatural. Who shall determine the legitimate limits of the mind's especial territory? That there have been from time to time human beings in existence who have exercised an incomprehensible control over some of the abstruser operations of nature is not to be rationally questioned. Natural events are established results from arbitrary causes. But these results are not uniform. Evidence exists to shew that in every age diverse results have occasionally followed. Miracles have been wrought in all parts of the earth. The practice of necromancy is matter of notoriety in the east. I myself studied it for ten years. I know many others who have studied it like me. You are not to conclude, because such men are unknown and untalked of, that they have no existence. It is the characteristic of genius of a higher order to seclude itself; to shun communion with a world unworthy of it: while straws and leaves float upon the surface of the ocean the pearl disdains to ascend from its native abyss. If even *I* chose I could amaze and overwhelm you. But I have reasons of my own for not treating you to any private sample of my art. Let the dream you have had, however, serve you as material for reflection. Meantime be assured that the compact betwixt us is not of a nature to be trifled with. You have already transferred two inches of your stature to me. It is easy for you to test the truth of my assertion. All that you have to do is to measure yourself when you reach home. I confess I wish you would do so, that we might understand one another perfectly."

Basil shook his head and took up his hat. "The difficulties in the way of a mutual understanding between us," said he, "I am afraid will rather increase than diminish. But I cannot depart without again tendering you my warm acknowledgments for your generosity. The ducats I presume——"

"Will be at home before you," interrupted the other. "Well, I wish you a good morning. When we meet again you will be wiser."

"Amen!" said Basil. "And happier?"

"Alas!" sighed the Nabob.

"Good day," said Basil. And they separated.

CHAPTER VII.

I will begin at thy heel and tell what thou art by inches.
Troilus and Cressida, Act ii. *Sc.* 2.[48]

The besetting sin of Basil was a certain self-sufficiency. Until he found himself exploring with laudable but unavailing assiduity the recesses of an empty purse, it never struck him that he could lose his money. He had three or four times met and conversed with Aurelia before he dreamt that he could lose his heart. And now in the same spirit of scorn for experience when balanced against inference he laughed at the notion that he could by possibility lose his inches. His was one of those uncatholic minds which immediately reject what they cannot immediately understand, and obstinately barricade the door of conviction against any theory that menaces the destruction of their contemptible prejudices. Still, as Godwin finely remarks, it is in any event "better to be a human being than a stock or a stone;"[49] and Basil von Rosenwald was after all not one who could long persist in withholding faith from every tittle of a testimony no one tittle of which he could by any conceivable exercise of ingenuity disprove or dispute. He is our particular friend, and we have therefore every desire to exaggerate his faults in the eye of the world; but we are forced to confess that his incredulity, if not overthrown, had sustained a sensible shock from the interview between himself and the Nabob. It is singular how forcibly arguments and protestations that move us but little as they issue from the lips of others will sometimes recur to us when they and we are asunder.

That which at the time it was uttered was only the gabble of a gander, passing in at one ear and out at the other, and exciting no feeling beyond that of a languid longing to tweak the beak of the gabbler, appeals to our hearts when we are alone with a thrilling eloquence similar to that of the oracles of old. Truth would seem to demand time and solitude for her growth, as the seed must lie buried a season before the plant can blossom. Basil, on reflection, and as he walked along the Blumenstrasse, could not deny that the Nabob had spoken like a man who firmly believes what he propounds. What motive in fact could there have been for deception and bamboozling? Then he remembered the sudden sleep and the strange dream. Were these natural, or had the East-Indian any participation in the work of producing them? He thought and thought, but the longer he thought the darker the mystery grew. He felt stranded on the *Ultima Thule*[50] of Judgment's islands. Lame as his logic was, however, it was still stout enough to jump to one conclusion. "This affair," said he, "*may* be like the middle cut of a salmon, and a body may not be able to make head or tail of it. Well: what then? That which is crystal-clear is, that when anything is, it is. Pyrrho[51] himself could not have contested that. I *will* measure myself and see how the matter really stands and how I stand with it. If I am still six feet, well and good: old Hunchback is either a ninnyhammer[52] or an unfathomable wag, and I, while I pocket his ducats, laugh at his waggery or ninnyhammerism, as the case may be. But if I am but five feet ten, as he says, why then—then—all that is to be said is, that I must be content to requote against myself the passage from Hamlet that occurred to me to-day while I slept, and have myself written down a jackass[53] for the residue of my days by the impertinent scribbler who shall hereafter undertake to biographise my fortunes or misfortunes."

Just as Basil arrived at this part of his undelivered soliloquy it was his destiny to obtain a glimpse of a pair of sandalled feet,[54] petty and pretty enough to have awakened the envy of Cinderella, even with both her glass slippers on. They passed him rather twinklingly, and with a lightness that would have guaranteed the perfect safety of any one of the myriad virgin violets that about twenty years before might have been seen luxuriating in the fair suburban localities around. He turned about, but so rapidly had the damsel, whoever she was, glided by him, that she was already hidden from his eyes by the other passengers; and he never, never, saw her, then or afterwards.

He could therefore form no idea of her beauty, if indeed she were beautiful; could not tell whether she were blonde or dark, tall or short; and had no token by which memory could assist him in recognising her again, except her feet and sandals. As a natural consequence he ceased to indulge in any conjectures about herself. But he could not so readily divest himself of the associations linked with her sandals. The mind is at seasons in a very errant and erratic humour, and only requires a fillip to dispatch it careering forwards through all countries and backwards through all centuries. Basil's thoughts on this occasion extravagued abroad in a style that would have left Mr Ex-Sheriff Raphael's right to the title of "the most incomprehensible of all imaginable vagabonds"[55] exceedingly problematical. Something like the following was their orderless order: Sandals—feet—dances—Bigottini[56]— the opera—ballets—balls—Brussels—Waterloo—Childe Harolde— Byron[57]—lame feet[58] (not in poetry). Sandals again—the old Romans— Heliogabulus[59]—Nero[60]—his fiddle—dances again—silk stockings— pumps. A third time sandals—sandal-wood—isles of spice—Serendib[61]— Sindbad[62]—merchants—grocers—tradesmen—sandal-makers—boot-makers—his (Basil's) own bootmaker's exorbitant bill.

His bootmaker's bill was an unwelcome reminiscence, not so much for itself as because it reminded him of other bills; but he now bethought himself that he had intended to order a new pair of boots the day before, though other matters had intervened to prevent him. As the recollection occurred to him it chanced that he raised his eyes, and lo! on a showy blue board over a shop-door at the corner of an adjoining strass, he saw in gilded text letters the words, *Hartmann, Schuh-und-Stiefelmacher*.[63] Instantly the notion suggested itself that, involved as he was, it would be as well for him to procure the boots from a stranger, who would make them without inquiry and either take payment or a promise to pay as might suit the purchaser's convenience. This man also, it struck him at the same time, could measure his stature, and if it were found wanting he could supply the deficiency by elevating the boot-heels in the required proportion, while Basil would be spared the awkward necessity of entering into any of those explanatory details which in case he were to go home and send for his own bootmaker would be in a manner unavoidable.

Accordingly he walked into the shop. An undersized man, advanced in years, bald, rather fat, and wearing an apron, was giving some directions to his workmen within the parallelogram where they sat; but upon Basil's entrance he intermitted speaking, came forward and made a respectful obeisance.

"You are Stiefelmacher Hartmann?" said Basil.

"Ya, mein Herr, at your service."

"Well, I want a pair of boots from you," said Basil.

"Ready-made, Sir?" inquired the obsequious shopman.

"No, no; listen to me; don't be in such a hurry. I wish to bespeak a pair of boots the heels of which must be either an inch or three inches high— do you mark?"

"Will you give yourself the trouble to walk this way, Sir?"

Basil followed the speaker into an inner room, out of the hearing of the workmen.

"Please to sit down, Sir?"

Basil seated himself. "I want a pair of boots of the best quality," said he, "and mind me: they must be either one inch or three inches high in the heels—I see you don't understand me, but I will explain as soon as I am measured:—for a particular reason it is essential that I should have myself measured before-hand."

"Oh! of course, mein Herr; we always measure gentlemen first," said the shoemaker, who already began to consider his customer an extraordinary oddity.

"The devil you do?" cried Basil. "Don't let your impertinence run before your judgment, if you please. But is it with that paltry little implement in your hand that you intend to do the mensuration?"

"Certainly, mein Herr," said the bootmaker, surprised: "it is a very excellent rule this."

"Excellent as the rule may be, my good friend," said Basil, "I beg to take an exception to it. It is not the thing. You must get a measure of at least a yard."

"A yard, mein Herr?" cried the other, opening his eyes to a width somewhat less than the measure he had named.

"Ay, a yard: have you such a measure in the house?"

Surely this man is crazed, thought the singleminded maker of double soles. But no matter: I will humour his fancies: his cash is as good as the Lord Kanzler's.[64] "In the house, mein Herr?" he replied; "No; but if you wish I can borrow one from the draper next door. I say Peter! step out to neighbour Sparlingstragg and ask him for a loan of his yard-wand for a minute."

The boy went out.

"Now, Sir, if you please, we will take off this boot;" and by dint of some tugging the right boot was got off.

"Pull off the left now," said Basil.

"One will do, Sir."

"One will not do, Sir. Pull off the other, I say, and be hanged to you!" The bootmaker obeyed without any further remonstrance.

The boy now came in with the yard-wand, and up stood Basil.

"Please to sit down again, Sir," said the bootmaker.

"Why, is it sitting you propose to measure me?" asked Basil. "Perhaps you had better roll me up into a ball at once, and take the solid contents of me?"

"Your feet will be steadier sitting, Sir," said the shop-keeper, more than ever confirmed in his conviction of Basil's insanity.

"O, I beg pardon; I perceive what you mean," said Basil; "but you misconceive me; I must first be measured from top to toe."

"What, mein Herr ?—measured from top to toe for a pair of boots?"

"Ah, damn your nonsense, Sir!" cried Basil, petulantly, (We are ashamed of him) "who ever hinted at such an absurdity? You are the stupidest tradesman I ever saw! I tell you I want to have myself measured from head to foot because,—because—I—" He paused, unwilling to state his reasons, or possibly not able to communicate them at the instant with sufficient lucidness. "But no matter why," he added; "just do as I bid you, and pass no remarks. Come, try my height,—and mind,—let there be no mistake." And he stood up erect against the wall.

The puzzled bootmaker had no resource but to yield obedience. In silence, and with a hand not altogether free from tremors, he went through his task to its completion.

"Well?" interrogated Basil.

"Just five feet ten inches, mein Herr."

Basil stared his measurer in the face for a minute without speaking. "What do you say?" he fiercely demanded at length. "Impossible! Try again."

Again the same trial was gone through, and with an identical result. Basil snatched the yard-wand from the bootmaker's hand.

"Are not these inches infernally false?" he exclaimed. "Answer me. Acknowledge the truth. Is not the measure an inch too short—I mean too long?"

"Not the hundredth part of an inch, mein Herr," said the bootmaker, who was quite astounded at all this emotion and vehemence for no apparent reason.

Basil was stupified. His feelings, on thus finding himself compelled to admit the reality of that which hitherto he had treated with the ridicule due to a chimera, may, to use a form of phrase that was original when Adam was a young man, be better conceived than described. He gazed about him: he looked to the right and left; he scrutinised alternately the pattern of the carpet and the architecture of the ceiling. "Help me, Heaven!" he exclaimed, lifting his hand to his forehead, "is my brain wandering? Am I dreaming for the second time to-day? Hark'ye, honest friend! have you such a thing as a pitcher of water at hand? If you have, will you for the love of St. Crispin,[65] empty it against my face? Because," he almost shouted, as he grasped the arm of the now terrified shopkeeper, "because I want to know whether I am awake or asleep, whether I am mad or drunk, whether I stand on my head or my heels. Is then the constitution of nature really at the mercy of human caprice? Are science and philosophy but twin humbugs—the most lying of all the finger-posts that pretend to point the way to the goal of truth? Is it in short come to this, that the whole world must go to school again, and be content to acquire the first rudiments of knowledge from Egyptian jugglers and Bengal Nabobs?"

"Sir—mein Herr—Euer Gnaden[66]—" stammered forth the alarmed tradesman—"I—I—protest I don't understand this!"

"Egad," said Basil, advancing his face close to that of the bootmaker, and lowering his voice almost to a whisper—"Egad, nor I neither, my good fellow. But, come," he continued, flinging himself into the chair,—"this is idle:—do your business. Come—" and he laughed a short bitter laugh, "you at least are no conjuror. Come, what are you about, Sir? Do you mean to take root where you are standing—a species of human dwarf elder, I suppose—or what the deuce?"

"No, no;—I don't indeed, mein Herr," returned the bewildered shoemaker, with an unconscious but deprecating simplicity; as, bestirring his limbs, he repossessed himself of his rule, and proceeded to apply it to the sole use for which it was intended.

"Now, Sir," said Basil, as soon as the dimensions of his foot had been ascertained, "remember that the heels must be full three inches high: my ordinary heels have hitherto been but one inch—but as between five feet ten and six feet there is a difference of two inches, you must supply the deficiency by adding two to the one that exists[67]—otherwise, you perceive, the discrepancy between what I was and what I am will be observable, and I shall be a laughing-stock for all Alberstadt. Why do you gape at me in that way?"

"I—I do not gape indeed, Sir."

"Well, do you understand me?"

"Really, mein Herr, I—I—"

"Are you able to comprehend the common rules of arithmetic, Sir?" Basil vociferated.

"Upon my word, mein Herr——"

"Do you know how much two and one make, Sir?" roared Basil. "Curse me if ever I met your fellow for thick-headedness!"

"Yes, Sir; three, Sir."

"Well, Sir, if two and one make three, Sir," said Basil, with an angry emphasis on every second word, "then, Sir, let me have heels of three inches, Sir! Will you do that, Sir?"

"Three-inch heels, Sir, will throw you very much forward."

"Devil may care, Sir; it is a young man's business to get forward in the world. Here, help me to thrust my legs into these boots again!"

"Are those to your fancy, Sir?" asked the shop-keeper, in allusion to the boots that Basil wore.

"What is that to you?" said Basil. "Take care that your own shall be, and that's enough for you."

"Well, Sir, when do you want them?"

"I want them now," returned Basil, "but I presume I shan't have them until to-morrow or the next day. Send them to me as soon as possible—or before that. There is my address;" and so saying he laid a card on the table.

"Eight—ten—six and a half round instep"—muttered the shoemaker, as he transferred his observations to his tablets—"I'll have them set about immediately, Sir."

"Do so," said Basil, and putting on his hat, he strode out at the door, followed by the wondering stare of the shopmen, who, though they had overheard little or nothing of the colloquy in the parlour, knew that Peter had been sent for a cloth-yard wand to measure the stranger for a pair of boots, and now grinned in unison as their master, glancing towards them and tapping his left forefinger against his forehead, pronounced in a low key the word, "Touched!"

Basil had scarcely journeyed a dozen paces from the door when he espied, lounging up the pavement towards him, with a great meerschaum in hand, a foppishly dressed, effeminate looking young man, whom he remembered to have occasionally seen at the Spielhaus where he had been accustomed to indulge his gambling propensities at the economical rate of one florin and a half per night. Now, either there are some eyes which will detect the identity of an individual in spite of any alteration in his person, or else the loss of two inches had not so metamorphosed Basil as he seemed apprehensive of, for on the approach of the smoker he was immediately greeted with a salutation of recognition.

"Aw, Bawsil, my dear vellow, appy to abtain a transient view of you! Ow goes it? Ow is every inch of you ?"

"*Every* inch?" returned Basil, vouchsafing him one look and then dashing past him; "Go and ask the devil's cousin-german;[68] he is in town, and he may tell you!"

"Put that in your pipe and smoke it, young man!" said a cadger's boy, who had overheard both the query and the response, as he slowly waddled by under the load of a cradle-sized basket of hams, sausages, tripe and cowheel, collared eels, cod-sounds, pig's cheeks, and sheep's trotters, all of which excellent things he was on his way to dispense among divers of his master's anti-Pythagorean[69] customers.

"Well,—bless my sens-i-bilities!" drawled out the fop— "no-ticeably odd that! I vow by the most ponderous of Jew-Peter's thunderbolts that were it any other than Bawsil I should follow him and inflict cawndign cawstigation!"

CHAPTER VIII.

"Say that such deeds are chronicled in hell"(s.)
King Richard II., Act v., *Scene* 5.[70]

As we have already intimated, there was nothing of the idealist about Basil. His anxieties and sympathies were all "of the earth, earthly;"[71] his speculations never gave themselves the trouble to travel beyond the boundaries that girdle "this visible diurnal sphere."[72] He could boast of being young and handsome; his appearance was fashionable, his *abord* prepossessing; he was quick-thoughted and, for his years, well-informed; he could be excruciatingly agreeable when he so willed: what more did the world want of him? Nothing: certainly not that he should set up for a metaphysician; neither was he the man to do so. He suspected that he had been born and expected that he should die; but his acquaintance with all the ins and outs of existence besides was confined to a consciousness that he was in love, in debt, out at elbows—and—for the present—out of prison. While at college, it is true, he had perused with some diligence certain abstruse treatises *Ueber die Natur des Geistes*;[73] but being completely satisfied with the great proficiency which these works had enabled him to make in the knowledge of nothing at all on the subject, he had thought it better to devote himself thenceforth exclusively to studies of a more practical description. There were in fact in his nature but few of the elements that go to the composition of a philosophical character. The penetrating reader accordingly will at once divine that after the first flutter and agitation of his surprise had subsided, the sorcery to the influence of which he had been subjected did not act in any extraordinary degree as a stimulus to his curiosity. He felt somewhat astounded and still more annoyed. But his interest or enthusiasm was not awakened. His spirit did not burn with any newborn ardour of longing to plunge into the mysteries of the magical world, or throw open the portals that barrier the awful storehouse of the Unknown. The whole thing was in his eyes entirely too much of a poser to be anything better than a bore. When therefore, in the course of the evening his friend Heinrick Flemming again dropped in upon him it was rather to solicit his counsel than to bespeak his wonder that he detailed all that had happened him since their meeting in the forenoon. "Neither you nor I," pursued he in conclusion, "could ever have calculated on the possibility of this issue to our visit of yesterday. But since the thing is, why, we must only make the best of it. The question for me simply is, whether I shall load a brace of pistols, take to the highway and plunder some poltroon of a thousand ducats in addition to the thousand I have, and thus regain my inches and prospects of pulling the devil by the tail—or—proceed with the compact to its completion and see the upshot of it,—enjoying in the meanwhile the satisfaction of shaking myself loose from the grip of those hounds of bailiffs, and re-establishing myself in society in some *shape* or other, however shy and sneaking as contrasted with my former. I acknowledge I do not fancy either mode of disposing of the question. But what can be done? I have no alternative. One of the two I must choose. As both are evils, I should of course wish to choose the lesser. But which the lesser is, I may not be so competent to determine. I can hardly reconcile myself to the resolve of relinquishing the golden hopes that within these two days have been strewing my pathway with stars. Yet *de l'autre côté*,[74] I shall be guilty of a species of semi-suicide in parting with my stature. The change will be productive of a thousand inconveniences. Nobody will recognize me—not even Aurelia. Every blackguard about town can snub me with impunity. I may be kicked out of my own house by my own servants. Worst of all, that whining old scoundrel will jump into my shoes and crow over my degradation. I confess I am at my wits' end. I never in my most fanciful moments contemplated being stuck in the centre of such a perplexity. The whole series of events appear to me 'like a phantasma or a hideous dream.'[75] They combine all the horrors of the Raw-head and Bloody-bones'[76] school of romance with the ludicrous fantasies of Mother Bunch.[77] What shall I do, Heinrick? What would you advise? An imposing *personnel*[78] and a pound of black prison bread *per diem*, or three and a half feet of humanity and the purse of Fortunatus![79] Do let me hear what you have to suggest; for upon my soul I feel myself at this moment somewhat like the schoolmen's ass betwixt the two stacks of hay."[80]

"My dear friend," replied Heinrick with deep solemnity, "your predicament is truly an extraordinary one; but it appears to me that you have but one course to pursue. You have entered into an agreement and, come what may, you should abide by it. Your honor is at stake; and what are your inches when measured against your honor? No: you have crossed the Rubicon; and you cannot now draw back. You must go the whole hog. Let your motto be, 'In for a groshen, in for a guilder.'[81] I do not anticipate from your fulfilment of the terms of the bond the evils you apprehend. There will be at first a little surprise, a slight sensation, among your acquaintance; the transaction will be talked of by twaddlers over their beer-mugs; but in a short time all this will pass and circumstances will reassume their former aspect. Therefore I say, Go on and prosper.[82] You have already advanced too far to recede with dignity; nor is there any necessity for receding. You have broken the ice and so made conquest of the worst difficulty. *Ce n'est que le premier pas qui coûte.*[83] Besides, you have a resource, though such a resource, I admit, as I feel averse from counselling you to employ. It is one that the tyranny of extreme exigency might, I think, justify a man in availing himself of; but still I shrink from the responsibility of recommending it to you."

"To be candid with you," observed Basil, "I am not inclined to be over fastidious just now. What may it be that you would *not* advise? To hocus the Nabob and pillage his treasury?"

"Nothing of the sort," said Flemming. "The resource I allude to is— start not!—the gambling-table. If I dared speak my mind, I would say, Gamble again, and this time confidently! Hitherto, you have been unlucky; but Fortune's wheel is for ever turning. You will have money enough to risk: if you lose you will scarce feel the loss; if you gain, and go on gaining—and why should you not?—you triumph at once over your fate and your enemies. A few nights' success may place you in a position not only to reinstate yourself in your inches but to dazzle Aurelia's father and drive the Silesian Prince out of the field. And surely to achieve such a consummation as this last you would not greatly boggle at the trouble of shaking your elbow for half an hour at a spell over a green cloth table?"

"By the powers of brandy!" cried Basil, starting up, "the suggestion is magnificent! I will—I will do what you say. The Spielhaus is the spot! Only, as to shaking my elbow, Heinrick, I must decline—dice are the devil—no, no!—nothing but *Rouge et Noir* for me!—but at that I'll try my hand again,—and, as you observe, what is there to hinder me from winning? Well then, my lot is chalked out: —I adhere to the compact between me and Old Scratch; by hazarding a few thousands I may—at least I must—gain as much as will extricate me from all obligations and embarrassments. So far so capital. And now, Heinrick, touching my mother's jewels. Will you, like an honest youth, go and treat with the Jew Lubeck for the recovery of them? I suppose he will let me have them back for what they cost him and a bonus over—tell him I will down with twelve hundred for them. I am anxious, you observe, to secure them immediately because the fellow is such an incessant trafficker that if I don't look sharp after his whereabouts, he will dispose of them before I can stay Trapstick!"

"Set your mind at ease as to them," said Flemming; "I'll make it my business to take them all up to-morrow to the last trinket. But what do you purpose doing with yourself to-night?"

"I don't know," returned Basil; "I feel lazy and nervous and *je ne sais quoi*-ish:[84] I think I'll go to bed."

"Suppose you come down to the Spielhaus?"

"Now?"

"Ay:—just put a handful or two of ducats into your pocket, and we'll go together. We'll see how you'll get on."

"Here goes for the nonce," said Basil, donning a huge outside coat, into the capacious pockets of which he stowed away as many rouleaus[85] of ducats as he could conveniently carry about with him.

Arm in arm the associates sallied forth. It was now past five o'clock and the dusk was deepening, but the streets were not yet lighted; and Basil and Heinrick passed along unrecognised by any until they arrived in the Kaiserstrasse.

The entrance to the Spielhaus of Trigg, Bubbell and Grabb was by a long and vaulted subterranean approach, terminating in a flagged courtyard. A solitary lamp above a high, narrow door alone indicated by night the site of the building to the stranger. The principal rooms themselves could only be reached after sundry zig-zag passages, well guarded by doors and sentinels, had been traversed; for the determination of the authorities of Alberstadt to suppress all gambling monopolies not instituted by themselves had been published; and secrecy and passwords were therefore indispensable.

Basil, as soon as he had exchanged his coin for notes,—for no more than twenty gold pieces were permitted as a single stake on any table—made his way into the *Rouge et Noir* room, whither Heinrick, quitting his arm, had sauntered in before him; and both for some minutes amused or at least occupied themselves in noting the transitions of the game, and marking the varying effects that these produced upon the countenances of the players.

"Well, Heinrick, what say you?" enquired Basil. "Suppose I venture? Do you play yourself?"

"I may stake a dollar by and by," replied Flemming, carelessly. "How much have you got?"

"Three hundred."

"Ducats?"

"Yes."

"Put down fifty," said Heinrick.

"*Thut euer Spiel, meine Hernn, die Farbe ist schwarz,*" cried the krooper;[86] "Make your game, gentlemen; the color is black."

"Only look at Grabb," said Heinrick, in a whisper. "How the rascal grins! By the way, did you hear that Schmidt had slit his windpipe?"

"Poor devil !—I did," said Basil. "Fifty ducats on the red."

The cards were distributed to the alternate sides.

"I am glad you took the red," said Heinrick.

"Why?" demanded Basil.

"Seven—four; red wins," cried the krooper.

"Be that my answer," said Flemming.

"A promising commencement," remarked Basil.

"Make your game, gentlemen, the color is red."

"Take the black now," whispered Heinrick.

"A hundred ducats black," said Basil.

"Five—three; red loses."

"To be sure it does; send the rags this way, Ludwig," said Heinrick, leaning forward. "This augurs well, Basil. Stick to the plan of staking alternately on red and black: it is the only safe one, after all that has been prated about calculations and systems."

Basil continued to play, and for a while with a success that even surpassed his expectations, sanguine as they had been. At length occurred the first breaking in upon his luck: he lost five stakes in succession. He turned round to be condoled with by Heinrick; but Heinrick was no longer by his side. He looked for him up and down the room, without, however, leaving his place; but could not discover him any where.

Still, said he to himself, I am a winner, and again he played, and again he won, and his spirits mounted; but alas! he lost the next three coups, each for a hundred ducats. He now began to grow restless and fretful; and, disregarding the injunction of Heinrick, he pertinaciously persisted in staking upon black during the whole of an unlooked for run upon the red; so that in about three quarters of an hour he had not only forfeited all his previous winnings, but lost a hundred and fifty ducats of his own in addition.

He felt prodigiously annoyed; and as coup after coup still told for the red, he at length lost all patience. "Sir!" he exclaimed, addressing Trigg, who, in his capacity of banker sat upon a high stool overlooking the game—"Sir, I say this is monstrous!—no man ever witnessed such barefaced rooking! The cards must have been packed, Sir!—here has been a run upon the red eleven times one after another!"

"You had better mind what you say, Sir, when you talk of packed runs," answered Trigg with the tranquil manner of a man accustomed to those attacks: "there were at least a dozen gentlemen[87] here when the bank opened. As to a run eleven times, that's nothing—nothing at all—is it, Grabb?"

"No," returned Grabb, grinning.

"So *you* may say, Sir," exclaimed Basil, vehemently, "but a player, Sir, judges differently, let me tell you."

"Why, there was a run on the red seventeen times last night," said Trigg; "the thing is as common as deuce-ace at hazard."[88]

A strange nondescript looking animal in a bearskin coat, with terrifying whiskers and moustaches, and an immense mass besides of woolly hair surmounted by a small, conical, comical hat, which looked like a candle-extinguisher stuck on the top of an enormous head of cabbage, now came to the rescue—"I protowst," he struck in, in the drowsiest and most guttural tones that ever issued from human throat—"I have mysowlf sown a rown on the bleck twounty fower times in sucsoussion. I believe you remumber the night, Grebb?"

"I believe I do," said Grabb in his quiet way, and with his devilishly innocent smile.

"Baz,—Baz, be discreet," said the voice of Heinrick; "if you lose both your cash and temper you have no chance."

Basil turned round. "I thought you had taken yourself off," said he sullenly.

"Not I," replied Heinrick, "I have been lounging away an hour in the coffee-room."

"Well, did *you* ever see such plundering elsewhere?" Basil asked.

"Don't be a child, Basil," said Heinrick, reprovingly—"you know as well as I that *here*, with so many lynx-eyes about and a character to be maintained, the bank *must* act on the square. When a flat *is* to be landed,[89] it is always made a private affair of. But why did you forget my instructions? Had you minded them no run could have injured you: if you gained nothing, at least you could not lose."

"I had lost five coups previously by your plan," said Basil.

"You would have won five times five had you only persevered. But never mind; don't suffer a trifle like this to discompose you; try again. I am going as far as the Brunnengasse with young Lichtenmark for about an hour, to see if his sister has come back from her uncle's yet; —meanwhile keep up your spirits and play away boldly. Have a good account of your goings on and pickings up to render me by the time I return."

There he goes again, thought Basil; and I don't know how it is, but I feel as if my evil star were once more in the ascendant. He, however, resumed playing; but whether his exasperation of mind had deprived him of the power of calculating the chances of the game with sufficient precision, or whether Fortune was determined to persecute him, choose what color he might, the longer he played the more he lost. There was no further run on either black or red; so that all pretext for a charge or even a suspicion of foul play was precluded; and our hero, as he saw debt accumulating on debt, was compelled to gnaw his lip in silence or vent his wrath in half stifled oaths, or fruitless execrations of his own folly. When things are at the worst they do not always mend: just as Basil had lost the largest coup he had hitherto played for, a bell tolled thrice; the porter pronounced the words "the bank is shut for the night;" and the krooper gathered together the rakes, swept the cards down into the drawers and proceeded to fold the tables.

"You have sped ill, I see, Basil," said Heinrick Flemming, who again stood by his side.

"Miserable wretch that I am!" cried Basil—"What is to become of me?"

"How much have you lost?" Heinrick inquired.

"I owe the bank five thousand ducats!" Now Heinrick seemed for a moment petrified by this intelligence; but recovering himself as by an effort, "Come away," said he in a low tone; "they are putting out the lamps: it is twelve o'clock."

CHAPTER IX.

"I am as mad as he, if sad and merry madness be equal."

Twelfth Night, Act iii., *Sc* 4.[90]

Basil spoke not, but took the offered arm of Heinrick. In silence they left the house and entered upon the streets. The night was gusty and starless; the shops had for some time been closed; and at intervals only was the distant footfall of a solitary passenger audible. A profound dejection had taken possession of Basil; and Heinrick was evidently absorbed in some engrossing contemplation to which he did not like to give utterance. At length, as both drew near the Silberplatz, the square in which Basil dwelt, Heinrick suddenly stopped, and arresting the progress of his companion by placing a hand on his shoulder he said, in an abrupt and startling way,—

"Basil! let me bespeak your attention for a brief space."

A gleam from a house-lamp fell at this moment athwart the features of Heinrick, and disclosed a countenance the expression of which spoke of deep thoughtfulness and a share of perplexity, blended with pity. He seemed deliberating some momentous matter: his eyes were full of doubt and indecision; he stood rivetted to the spot; and his entire air and attitude were those of a man whose mind is the arena of a painful struggle, the nature of which he would fain reveal, but which he is deterred from alluding to by some constraining consideration.

The chill blast blew along the deserted streets, making the melancholy spirit more melancholy still. Its dreary tones and the hollow voice of the night-watch, gloomily proclaiming the hour from his sepulchral turret, alone broke the reigning stillness. The time, the silence, the dismal nature of the scene, the consciousness of his ruined fortunes and blighted hopes, all combined to depress Basil's mind and prostrate his energies. Tears almost flowed into his eyes as he yielded to the sense of his utter desolateness. A load lay upon his heart. He drew his breath with an effort, and felt as if the atmosphere that encompassed him were impregnated with some deadly mephitic odour.

Meanwhile he stood passive. He evinced no symptom of anxiety or impatience. With folded arms and desponding looks he awaited in silence the communication of his companion. It was obvious that the dejection which had mastered him was of too absorbing and exclusive a nature to permit the co-existence of any conflicting passion or feeling within his breast.

At length Heinrick spoke. "Basil," he said, "I sympathise with you deeplier than I can express: were there a window in this bosom you would behold how my heart is rent and bleeding for you. Hear me. You have some right to reproach me with being the creator of your misfortunes. True, I was innocent of the design to injure; but I am he who first led you into a Spielhaus; and I cannot wholly acquit myself of imprudence in doing so. Had you never met with me you would have prospered and been happy. It is a debt I owe myself and you to remedy the wrong I have wrought. I am bound to do all in my power to repair the evil I have been the unconscious instrument of inflicting on you. Suffer me, therefore, I implore you, to be henceforth your guide : place yourself in my hands. You are so situated that you cannot depend upon your unassisted judgment for the safety of your future movements. Trust then to me, and enable me at once to still the accusations of my conscience, and to render your liberation from the toils in which you have unhappily become entangled, all but a matter of certainty."

"You ought to know, Heinrick, that I have always confided in you," answered Basil. "Believe me I am now more disposed to trust you than ever. My reliance on myself begins to be dreadfully shaken. Any plan you may suggest I am ready to adopt. Say what you would have me to do."

"In the first place to come straight with me to the Dornensteg," said Heinrick, "and have an interview with the Nabob."

"It will be in vain, Heinrick;—the man has not human feelings," said Basil; "any appeal to his mercy would be thrown away. But, at all events, you do not mean to-night?—now?"

"Basil, my friend," observed Heinrick, with some hesitation—"you— you cannot remain in your own house longer. Of course you propose paying Grabb to-morrow. But five thousand ducats will require the drinking of five flasks; and recollect that those will leave you but five feet five inches."

Basil groaned.

"So transformed, you would not be known by your own servant, unless you were to place him *au fait* of the mystery; and that, I presume, you have no desire to do."

"I understand you," said Basil, with a deep sigh. "But to-night—it is so late ."

"O, as to the hour, that is nothing," said Heinrick, "I know that the Nabob seldom sleeps at all, and never retires to bed before two in the morning. *Au reste*, believe me you will find him more accommodating than you anticipate. Come—we will set out for his dwelling at once;—this short cut across the fields behind the Bildstrasse will lead us to it. To-morrow morning I will tell your servant that business requires your absence from town for a time, and any letters that may arrive at your house I will take care to have transmitted to you, wherever you may be, either in the Halbmond or elsewhere."

"I yield, my friend, I yield," said Basil, "I place myself entirely at your disposal."

The friends, accordingly, making the best of their way over the fields, soon found themselves in the straggling avenue that conducted to the Dornensteg. Little conversation was exchanged between them until they reached the house. A servant answered to the knock of Heinrick, and in reply to his inquiry informed him that his master was at supper in the small parlour.

"Then we had better wait in the large one," said Basil.

"Not at all," returned Heinrick, "the old boy and I, it is time to tell you, treat one another with very little ceremony. You shall see. Follow me." And, lifting the latch, to the surprise of Basil, he stalked into the supper-room without even heralding his intrusion by a tap at the door.

Basil would have lingered outside, but hearing the voice of the Nabob himself inviting him to step in, he conquered his scruples and entered.

"Sit down, gentlemen," said the Nabob. "I have just had my supper taken out of the frying pan. I shall be at your service in a minute. Sit down."

"You are surprised, Sir, of course," began Basil, in a sullen tone of apology, "that we should intrude upon you at such an hour; but——"

"Not at all," interposed the Nabob; "I make it a point never to be surprised at anything during meals: all unusual emotion interferes with digestion. Have the goodness to stretch yourself upon that sofa, Mr. Rosenwald. Perhaps you would choose to pick a bit? Mr. Flemming, what say you to a mouthful?"

"What have you got to tempt us withal?" demanded Heinrick.

"Gripes and grumblings—bacon and eggs," was the reply. "Have you a mind to go snacks with me in the mess? Mr. Rosenwald, will you take a slice of bacon?"—And sticking his fork in a rasher, he extended it towards Basil, apparently quite unconscious of committing any violation of table etiquette in the proffer he made.

"Thank you, Sir," said Basil, who, notwithstanding his depression, had some struggle to keep his countenance, "but I never sup."

"Will *you* have it?" asked the Nabob, offering it to Heinrick.

"My gastronomy, Sir, takes no cognizance of garbage," answered

Heinrick, "and I usually eat like a human being."

"Go to the devil, you spooney!"[91] said the Nabob, transferring the morsel to his own mouth.

Basil looked at Heinrick, as if to inquire the meaning of all this; but Heinrick's eyes were turned away.

"And so you never bolt bacon?" said the Nabob. "Now, I eat nothing else,—except eggs. You see me supping on eggs and bacon, but had you been here earlier you might have seen me dining on them; and had you been here still earlier, you might have seen me breakfasting on them. I find an exhaustless variety in those two dishes. When I am weary of bacon I recruit myself with eggs; and when eggs grow insipid I fall back on bacon. This diet, it is true, has a tendency to generate droughtiness; but I keep a barrel of glorious double stout below stairs, and here stands a can of it, full and foaming. As you refuse to eat, Mr. Rosenwald, perhaps you will drink;—if so, you are very welcome after me;" and lifting the tankard to his lips, he indulged in a protracted draught of the eulogised beverage. "There is still a good half pint left," added he, looking into the vessel as he spoke: "here, my friend!"—and he held it out towards Basil.

"I am not thirsty, Sir," said Basil, coldly.

"You are rather dry, though," retorted the Nabob. He rang the bell. The servant appeared.

"Take away the crockery and pewter, and bring in wine and glasses," said the Nabob. "Well, gentlemen, here we are. You see me in a pleasant mood to-night; and yet I have just made a discovery of a rather unpleasant nature. It emancipates me, however, from the necessity of dissembling—of supporting a character to which I have no claim. But all this is Sanscrit to you,[92] Mr. Rosenwald; so let us to business; and then I'll explain. I think, Mr. Rosenwald, you have acted judiciously in coming to my house, and I would recommend you to stop in it. To-morrow, if you pay this evening's scores, sees you fallen to five feet five, and of course a dignified seclusion under such circumstances is much preferable to an appearance in public life, among sneerers and starers."

"How then!" exclaimed Basil—"You know the events of this evening?"

"Ay, my good Sir, and of to-morrow evening also,—that is, if you again visit the Spielhaus. I cast your horoscope not two hours back; and I found that if you gamble in the Spielhaus it is written that you shall lose all, to the last stake you hazard."

"Then I am ruined," cried Basil, clasping his hands.

"How so?"

"My only hope lay in gambling—in winning enough to enable me to recover my inches!" said Basil.

"Well, you can gamble still," said the Nabob.

"Did you not say that I was destined to lose?"

"Only at the Spielhaus," said the Nabob. "You can play with others."

"Alas! with whom?" demanded Basil.

"You can play with *me*," said the Nabob.

"Play with *you*?" cried Basil in astonishment.

"I am your man—at Blind Hookey, Scaramouch, Killdevil, or Hop-the-Twig,"[93] said the Nabob.

"I do not know any of the games you have mentioned," observed Basil.

"Well then, say Pitch and Toss," said the Nabob. "You know that."

"You are sporting with my wretchedness, Sir," said Basil.

"Ask your friend whether I am," said the Nabob.

"He is NOT, Basil," said Heinrick, with an emphasis of manner that at once assured the young man.

"And if I play against you?" said Basil.

"It is prefigured by the horoscope that I am to be defeated," answered the Nabob, "and that you are to become a great and a wealthy man."

"Then, my dear Sir," cried Basil, starting up, "let us begin at once—I—I am all impatience."

"Fairly and softly, my friend," returned the other, "men are not in such a hurry to be beaten as you seem to take for granted. The hour is rather late: tomorrow, if you please, we will commence."

"Heinrick, my excellent friend!" cried Basil, "I owe this to you—Trust me, you shall not find me ungrateful—O, believe me—I shall——"

"Come, come, Baz; no heroics; you know I never could away with them," said Heinrick, as he rose. "Hereafter we will talk of these matters. Well, Nabob, I suppose I am to consider myself now as *de trop* here?"

"You may make yourself scarce as soon as you please," was the unceremonious reply.

"Many thanks, my Chesterfield.[94] Good night, Basil."

"What, Heinrick !—Are you off? Surely his Excellency will have no objection to lodge you. For my part, I——"

"It is *he* who objects, Sir, to a bed in a coal-hole," said the Nabob, in an offended tone.

"In a coal-hole!" cried Basil. "Surely——"

"Psha, Nabob," said Heinrick, "you aspire to be a wag, and you are ignorant of the first principles of waggery. Close your egg-trap, do. Good night, Basil."

"Good night, my friend, since you are determined on going. Will you be good enough to direct Grabb hither to-morrow?"

"Fear not: all shall be settled to your satisfaction," replied Heinrick.

"As to the boots," said Basil in a whisper—"you need not trouble yourself, Heinrick."

"No, they can be of no use now," returned the other. "Farewell, *auf Wiedersehn*."

"Will you take any wine, Mr. Rosenwald?" asked the Nabob, as soon as Heinrick was gone.

"If you please I would prefer retiring to rest," said Basil, "as you are good enough to accommodate me."

The Nabob rang the bell.

"Shew this gentleman to his bedchamber, Klaus," said he.

"This way, Sir, if you please," said the servant to Basil.

"And I'll toddle off to my library," said the Nabob. "Good night, Mr. Rosenwald."

"Good night, mein Herr."

CHAPTER X.

> Pr'ythee, friend
> Pour out the pack of matter to mine ear,
> The good and bad together.
> *Ant. and Cleop. Act.* ii. *Sc.* 5.

Basil's sensations on awaking the following morning were exquisitely delightful. His temperament was sanguine, as we have already noticed: he usually required therefore but a slender foundation upon which to rear a skyhigh pyramid of hopes. His heart bounded as he recalled the declaration made by the Nabob; he saw before him the enchanting prospect of wealth, honors, and happy love, stretching out endlessly into futurity. Imagination had woven for him overnight a new triumphal banner, of a texture brighter than the sunbeams, and displaying the cheering device, *Tu vainqueras*.[95] What wonder, therefore, if about mid-day he met the Nabob,—who always spent the forenoon alone, and chiefly in his library,—with an elastic step and a brow beaming with exulting anticipation? In the fulness of his heart he was about re-plunging into the topic of the previous night without preface or ceremony. His ardour, however, was somewhat chilled when the Nabob, after returning his hurried greeting with an air of magisterial coldness, said—

"Mr. Rosenwald, I come to inform you that Mr. Grabb is below stairs, and refuses to go away without being paid his demand on you."

"Confound the fellow," said Basil: "but what shall I do?—there is no getting rid of Grabb without paying him. I may hope, my dear Sir, you will have no objection to advance the money?"

"On the specific terms,—none," returned the Nabob. "Here are five flasks of the elixir, my friend," and one by one, he took the number he spoke of from his pockets;—"and here"—fetching down a large glass from a shelf,—"is a bell-glass that will hold the contents of all five!"

"It must be, I suppose," said Basil, with a sigh; "pour out; and let me have it over me. But one stipulation I would make:—there must be no shock, no mystifying in this instance; it could answer no purpose, except to bewilder and enfeeble me."

"Have no apprehensions," replied the Nabob; "I have drugged these flasks with some of my cephalic snuff. You will forfeit your inches; that's all."

"Quite enough, in all conscience," retorted Basil. "But so deep a draught as this—will it not at least intoxicate?"

"Not in the slightest degree," said the magician; "it is too well prepared: I have mixed a good quarter of a pound of snuff with it."

"In that case it must be a dose for the devil," observed Basil. "But I presume I must not be too nice—here goes!"

Just as he had emptied the glass a loud knocking was heard at the street-door.

"Who can this be?" said the Nabob. "Sit down, my friend, while I step out and try. How do you feel? A little languid, I dare say. Here, draw your chair to the fire; you will be yourself again, bating the odd inches, in the twinkling of a bed-post."

Going out, the Nabob encountered his faithful henchman, Klaus.

"The Herr Elsberg, your Excellency," announced the servitor in a stentorian voice, "to see Mr. Basil Rosenwald; I have shewn him into the ante-chamber." A wink passed between master and man; and then—

"Beg him to wait a minute there, and I shall attend him," replied the Nabob, in the same key. He then went into the parlour.

"You have an acknowledgment, Mr. Grabb?"

"Yes," said Grabb, producing it.

"Give it me; good:—now take yourself and these out of my house together;" and so saying, he brought five bags, marked each a thousand ducats out of the flask room, and deposited them on the table. "But how d'ye mean to bear off the booty? Have you a packass, or a jackass, at the door? Come, man; never stand staring at me so, as if I had got a pair of horns since you last clapped eyes on me. Answer me."

"I have a car," said Grabb.

"I wish it were about to take you to the gallows," said the Nabob. "Come, stir your stumps. Here, Klaus—come hither; and help to carry out this heavy luggage, and stow it in Mr. Grabb's waggon. I must go and see what Herr Elsberg wants."

He passed into the antechamber.

"Your servant, Mr. Elsberg," said he briefly.

"Herr von Rosenwald, I have the honour to be your most obedient servant," said Elsberg, slowly. "I have called to see a relative of your's, who, I understand, is here at present, Mr. Rosenwald."

"He is not very well," said the Nabob: "he slept here last night; but he has had a headache the whole morning. I will let him know, however, that you are here, if you think proper."

"If you think that I should not disturb him too much, I should certainly be glad to speak with him," said Elsberg.

"May I request you to excuse me then, while I go and apprise him?" said the Nabob.

In another moment he was in Basil's room. "How do you feel now, my friend ?" he asked.

"Pretty well, I thank you," said Basil.

"Mr. Elsberg is below, and wishes to speak with you," said the Nabob. "I have told him you are unwell."

"Elsberg!" echoed Basil, "is it possible? Have him shewn up, by all means, my dear Sir !—But stay, I must curtain these windows, and tumble into bed: what *would* he think if he saw me as reduced in size as I am in circumstances? There! that will do: now my dear sir, let him come up. Elsberg! bless me! what can the object of his visit be?"

The Nabob disappeared, and immediately afterwards a creaking pair of shoes was heard on the stairs.

"This room, Mr. Elsberg," said the Nabob, ushering him in.

"I beg your pardon, Mr. Rosenwald, for this intrusion," said Elsberg; "I was not aware you were confined to your bed. I hope your headache is not very severe."

"Not very, thank you, Sir," answered Basil.

"Illnesses are very rife at this season," pursued Elsberg; "I met your old friend Major Welshuck yesterday, and he complained very much of his chest."

"Of the emptiness of it, perhaps?" said Basil.

"No," replied Elsberg, who was the most literal matter-of-fact man breathing, "he did not say that he felt any sensation of emptiness or hollowness, but merely remarked in general terms that his chest was touched; upon which I took the liberty of recommending an immediate application of the stethescope[96] by a skilful physician, regularly licensed, and having sufficient practice to furnish *primâ facie* evidence of his competency to examine and prescribe—hem!"

"I see," said Basil, who felt very much inclined to yawn; and then added, for want of knowing what else to say—"The Major was once a stout man."

"He was, Sir," observed Elsberg, "but I have known some of the stoutest men, Sir, to die by inches."

"Ah!" said Basil.

"But, Mr. Rosenwald," said Elsberg, "it is time for me to acquaint you with the object of my visit. You were a little hasty, you will acknowledge, in quitting my house as you did the other night."

"I was justified, Sir, by the manner of treatment I experienced," returned Basil.

"Well, well," said Elsberg; "perhaps I was not altogether free from blame, any more than you. Let the matter rest. I wish to tell you, Mr. Rosenwald, that I do not want to press you for the fifteen thousand florins you owe me. I am aware of the state of your circumstances, and I believe you to be a young gentleman of integrity and principle; and so believing, I am willing to postpone the day of payment to any period you name within five years."

"Well, Sir," said Basil, "I shall only say that I thank you deeply, and from my heart, for your generosity. Suffer me then to request another twelvemonth's time—I will not accept of more."

"You shall have it," replied Elsberg. "Mr. Rosenwald—a—a—are you acquainted with the Prince von Lowenfeld-Schwarzbach, may I ask?"

"I am not acquainted with him, Sir," said Basil, coldly.

"A rather—a—a—curious circumstance took place at my house, in reference to him, on the evening of the ball," said Elsberg. "My wife happened to mention your name before him, and to say that you were expected at the house; and while she spoke, he grew pale as death, and shortly afterwards, pleading a sudden illness, he took his leave. I sent to his hotel yesterday, to ascertain if he was better; but to my surprise, the messenger brought me back intelligence that the Prince had—shall I say—decamped; that he had left Alberstadt at an early hour in the morning, and was not expected to return!"

"Whew!" whistled Basil, "a light breaks in upon me: I fancy I know your Prince. Is he a long-legged, short-necked, square-shouldered, round-armed, oval-faced, angular-waisted manner of man? Has he a hawk's eyes, an eagle's beak, the brains of a goose, and the strut of a turkey-cock?"

"You paint him to the life," cried Elsberg—"dark moustaches and very white teeth——

"Ay, ay," said Basil: "I know the rubbish—he is a tailor, Sir."

"A tailor" exclaimed Elsberg, in astonishment. "The Prince of Lowenfeld-Schwarzbach a tailor!"

"Ay, and a capital one, Sir, too; he made clothes for me in Berlin, the neatest I ever wore. But he chose to shut his shop and turn Pomeranian baron one morning, and when detected he fled from the city as he has fled now from this—and I should mention to you that he made a very handsome dress lace-coat of mine bear him company. What else he took from others I cannot say; but the fellow is a swindler; that is his designation, Sir."

"Well, really, I am so amazed!" cried Elsberg. "What a lucky escape Aurelia has had!"

"What! Did you intend, Mr. Elsberg," asked Basil, "to have given your daughter to that scoundrel?"

"I am ashamed to acknowledge that I did meditate such an act," replied Elsberg.

"Knowing that she loved me?" said Basil.

Elsberg rose from his chair, and after he had taken a turn about the room in silence, "Mr. Rosenwald," said he, "I cannot enter upon this topic now; and I know that you are averse from speaking upon any other with me. Permit me to wish you good-morning."

"Stay—one word, Mr. Elsberg," said Basil, "before you go. Have you any *personal* objection to me as a son-in-law?"

"None whatever, upon my honour," replied Elsberg.

"Then, I am to understand that, if my circumstances were sufficiently affluent, you would have no objection to countenance my suit?"

"On the contrary, I should be most happy to forward it."

"It is enough, Sir; I thank you: I shall detain you no longer."

"Good morning, then, Mr. Rosenwald."

"Good morning, Sir."

And so terminated this, by no means the least important interview recorded in our history.

CHAPTER XI.

"I'll devil-porter it no further."

Macbeth, Act ii., *Sc.* 3.

* * * * * * *
* * * * * * *
* * * * *

"Miscreant!" cried Basil, "is it thus you keep your promise?"

"Jackass!" retorted the Nabob; "it *is* even thus. What right have you to complain? You have had in all twenty-nine bags of ducats and twenty-nine flasks. Being five feet five inches in height, you commenced brandy-drinking and pitch-and-toss playing with me. We played in all fifty-four games, of which you it is true won but sixteen, while I gained thirty-eight, making twenty-two in my favour. Yet what right, I repeat, have you to complain? You have not been choused[97] out of a single rap.[98] The twenty-two thousand ducats which were yours by virtue of the flasks, have been fairly won from you. I have gone on the square from the beginning. I am now five feet eleven, but I have not risen to my present eminence by means of any dirty shuffling or hookemsniveying.[99] I appealed to fortune; I have been successful; I have beaten you by chalks;[100] and more power to my elbow, say I! You are but three feet seven, but you voluntarily chose, with your eyes and mouth open, to drink away one of the noblest gifts with which Providence had endowed you—your stature. And after all, notwithstanding the howl and hubbub and hullaballoo you have been raising these two hours, you are still as safe and sound as a trout in a water-barrel. Until you have lost the last, the *thirtieth* inch, your identity remains in *statu quo*. Retain that inch, and you are still you and I am still I. I do not solicit you to part with it. If you wish to do so I shall open another bottle. But I do not coerce you. At the same time I own I see no other mode by which you have any chance of retrieving yourself. You have gambled your last ducat. If you choose to have another thousand I am ready to stand Sam;[101] and I pledge upon my honor that I will play you as fairly as ever. I can assure you, for all your suspicions of my blackleggism,[102] that fifteen years have elapsed since I skied a copper[103] before."

"Infamous deceiver!" vociferated Basil; "did you not tell me that I should ultimately defeat you?"

"It is written that you shall," said the Nabob, "but *how*, I know not. There is the puzzle. Perhaps you are to blow me up with gunpowder, or tumble me headlong from some garret-window. I cannot tell. My powers of diving into futurity are limited to a certain point."

Basil made no reply. He could not attempt any. His heart was swelling, even to bursting. In despair and madness he rushed from the house. A hurricane roared through the forests of his brain, tearing up his faculties by the roots. It was a bleak night; the winds were out and howling; and two-thirds of the moon were invisible. Not a single wanderer but himself was abroad in the Dornensteg. He hurried onward until his breath nearly forsook him, and he was compelled to pause for rest. But he did not pause long. Again he dashed forward with the speed of a wild animal. Up the Brunhugel—down the Grunthal—pell-mell through the Bloody Fields—headlong into the Wildgasse—helter-skelter over the Round-mounds—hurrah! who but he? "Faint and wearily the wayworn traveller"[104] at length might be seen wending his way into the Silberplatz. Panting and exhausted, like a broken-winded draught-horse during an uphill ascent, he now nears his own house.

"I tell you, Sir," said a voice which Basil recognised as that of his own servant, "that Mr. Rosenwald is not in town, and I don't know when he will come back."

"In that case," said the party addressed, a big, burly-looking man, in a seal-skin cap and a dreadnought, "I must just call some other time. I am sorry you cannot tell me where even a letter could reach him, for my business with him is most important." And he turned away.

"Who asks for me? Who inquires for such a wretch as I am?" demanded Basil, coming up just in time to have the door slapped in his face.

"I have been inquiring for Mr. Rosenwald," said the stranger. "Can you, Sir, direct me where to find him?"

"I am he," said Basil.

"What! You!" cried the stranger.

"I am the wreck of him who *was* Basil Rosenwald," replied our metamorphosed hero.

"Let me take a survey of you, my mannikin," said the stranger. "Good heavens!" he cried, as he surveyed Basil by a street-lamp, "surely I have seen this figure and face before!—Yet no!—it is not possible—you cannot be HE. I apprehend rather some diabolical jugglery in this business. Am I right in conjecturing that you are one of those unfortunates whom the monster I allude to has swindled out of their inches?"

"I am—I am!—Then you know him?—you know the whole story? You have seen him elsewhere—and I am not his first victim?" cried Basil, gasping. "O, stranger, whosoever you are, if you have any power over the villain, exercise it, I implore you, in forcing him to restore me to that of which he has robbed me!"

"You made a compact with him, did you not?" asked the stranger, "so many inches for so many bags of gold?"

"Yes—yes—I perceive you know all," answered Basil. "The vagabond!"

"Do you know who he is?"

"No," said Basil; "I know not:—probably Satan himself?"

"No, not Satan."

"Puck?"[105]

The stranger looked as if he did not understand.

"Belphegor[106] then?" said Basil.

The stranger nodded dissent.

"Perhaps Mephistopheles?"[107]

The stranger shook his head.

"Rubezahl[108]—that is, Number Nip?"

"No, no, no; none of these."

"Who *can* he be then?" asked Basil.

"Did you ever hear of *Maugraby*?"[109]

"What !—the magician of the eight and forty-gated Domdaniel?"[110]

"Yes. This is he. The blackguard is well known in the east. I remember him, and *he remembers me*. He has diddled many as he has nearly diddled you. I presume you were introduced to him by one of his tools?"

"No: by a friend of my own, one Heinrick Flemming."

"Bah! I know the fellow,—a former victim and present accomplice. But you have not disposed of *all* the inches yet, I hope?"

"No; there is one left," said Basil.

"Lucky for you," said the stranger. "Had that one—had the last inch passed from you to him, nothing could have saved you. Your soul would then have become his property beyond redemption. Courage! you are safe; you shall now triumph over him. Come along to my lodgings, and I will tell you a piece of good news you little dream of."

Both accordingly adjourned to the stranger's domicile, which was in the next street; and here the stranger, whose name was Slickwitz, in a few words unfolded his business.

"You had an uncle," said he, "who spent a great part of his life in the east?"

"Yes," returned Basil—"my paternal uncle, Adelbert."

"The same:—this man, Sir, has lately died in Aleppo, and has left you heir to all his immense property.[111] I am his executor. The ready money alone amounts to a sum of three hundred thousand ducats, the whole of which in gold and notes I am ready to deliver into your hands immediately."

We need not dwell upon Basil's surprise and rapture. After his first transports were over, he caught hold of the arm of Slickwitz. "My friend—my preserver!" he eagerly demanded, "have you much of this sum *here* in the house?"

"I have in this house a hundred bags of a thousand ducats each," replied Slickwitz.

"Then we will call a vehicle—thrust twenty-nine of these bags into it—for this flesh-and-blood robber has twenty-nine of my inches—drive off to his dwelling,—and compel him to refund! What say you?"

"With all my heart—I like the idea," said Slickwitz.

Accordingly in about a quarter of an hour from the time of this conversation a thundering knock at the door of Maugraby's house astounded the old fellow as he sat masticating his supper of bacon and eggs. "Klaus!" he cried—"Klaus!—go and see who that is!"

No sooner was the door opened than Slickwitz and Basil rushed into the chamber together.

"Villain! ghoule! demi-devil!" cried Basil, springing at the magician's throat—"restore me my inches this moment, or die the death of a dog!"

The magician disembarrassed himself from the grasp of Basil with the ease with which a giant might put aside the embrace of an infant, and advancing on Slickwitz demanded—

"Who are you, Sir?"

"I am *Rubadubb Snooksnacker Slickwitz*," said the stranger calmly—after a pause.

At the sound of that name the magician writhed—he grew pale—in vain he attempted to conceal his emotion; for some moments he shook like a bog during an earthquake. "And you," added the stranger, "are MAUGRABY!"

"O, by thunder and brimstone!" cried a voice on the outside of the door, "all the fat is in the fire now, and the snuff will soon follow! I must cut and run, for one, before the grand flare-up!" And forthwith the legs of the eavesdropper, in whose tones Basil had at once recognised those of the magician's attendant, Klaus, were heard marshalling him the way he should go, along the passage and out of the house.

"Damnation!" cried the baffled sorcerer in a rage—"is it then come to this—is the game up? Humph!— I smoke!"[112]—I see how the cat jumps,"[113] he fiercely exclaimed, stalking up to Basil; "you are come to fork out the blunt!"[114]—And you," he added, again turning to Slickwitz—"you expect to drag me hence to the gallows—to see me making my exit from life night-capped, snaffled, handcuffed, hoodwinked, humbugged? But curse me if I gratify either of you. I will see the whole neighbourhood blown to blazes first, and the pair of you along with it!"

So saying, and with a furious look, he snatched up his snuff-box, which had been lying on the table, and shook its contents into the fire. The effect of this apparently insignificant act was tremendously terrible and German. An explosion instantly followed, louder than the roar of ten parks of artillery together, *à qui mieux mieux*.[115] The whole range of deserted buildings along one side of the Dornensteg, a short time before valued by the Commissioners of Wild Streets, were for a moment enveloped in one wide sheet of livid flame, and in the next blown into a million atoms,—the sorcerer's own house and all the wealth it contained perishing amid the common ruin. As soon as the smoke had cleared away Basil and Slickwitz were able to see themselves safe upon their legs at a distance of about twenty yards from the scene of this appalling but sublime catastrophe. Basil stood once more six feet one in his boots.

"*Fuit Ilium*,"[116] said Slickwitz, quietly, as he gazed around. "After *that*, I think *we* may go home and take our gruel."[117]

"I think so," answered Basil.

And thus was the necromancer defeated, even as he had himself predicted. He has never shewn himself in Germany since. He sailed shortly afterwards for Egypt, and is now in Alexandria,[118] where he occupies himself in mystifying, in a small way, such travellers as visit the country. His chum, Heinrick Flemming, disappeared from Saxony about the same period with himself, but of the subsequent whereabouts of this promising young man no intelligence has ever reached us.

As for Basil and Aurelia they have been now for some years married; and their union has been blessed with a large family of small children, who bid fair, upon springing up to the inches of gaffers and gafferesses,[119] to inherit all the singular beauty and plural virtues of their estimable parents. We paid the happy pair a visit last summer; upon which occasion Basil, after his third bottle of Rhenish, related to us the story we have taken the pains to chronicle in our Magazine. Towards the close of his tale his utterance became somewhat thick and misty; but he dwelt with rapture upon the amiable character of his beloved Aurelia, swearing that she as far transcended every other individual of her sex as a rose transcends a daisy, a peach a potato, or a shilling a farthing. We could see the object of this eulogy colour even beyond the circle of her rouge at the enthusiasm of his language. She is really a pretty woman; her shining red hair, slightly intermixed with yellow, admirably harmonizes with her fair and freckled complexion; and her neck is singularly long, golden, and beautiful. As she sat at the piano, encircled by her blooming family of seven girls and two boys, we could not help recalling to mind the couplet of the greatest of modern poets—

> "A lady, with her daughters or her nieces,
> Shines like a guinea and seven shilling pieces."[120]

Their dwelling, we should not omit mentioning, is a romantic chateau in the Konigsmark suburb of the town, the rear of which is beautified by rich orchards and pleasure-grounds *à la Polonais*, while the front commands a fine view of the Old Buttermarket and other interesting localities.

THE MAN IN THE CLOAK.

A VERY GERMAN STORY.

THE GREAT clock of the Banking-house of Willibald and Company struck four.

"The Bank is closed!" cried the porter, in his usual sonorous tones.

At the words there was a general opening and shutting of desks; every inmate of the Bank took off his office coat and donned his walking-habit. In five minutes the bureaus were deserted, the runners had walked out, the clerks disappeared;—the two bankers, both married men, were driving off in their curricles, one to dine with a friend, the other with a mistress. Silence reigned through the spacious building; and the daylight which found its way through the windows gradually deepened into dusk, for the season was November and the day had been cloudy. Any one who would now see to read or write must avail himself of an artificial illumination; and accordingly at twenty minutes before five a solitary lamp shed a sickly light over a heap of legers[1] and papers, notes and rouleaus, confusedly scattered to and fro through the different recesses of the Cash-office, and developed the features and part of the figure of a man seated before a desk, conning several documents, which he passed in review before him, with an anxious eye, and from time to time casting abstracted glances around him, which now rested upon vacancy and now upon the iron safes and sealed strong boxes imbedded in the walls of his temporary prison.

The Herr Johann Klaus Braunbrock, he to whom we thus introduce the reader, was cashier to the Banking-house, and had lingered somewhat beyond his time on this evening, from what motive we may possibly understand by-and-by. Let us try to depict his appearance. He was a man of the middle size, rather clumsily made, but with a finely-shaped head, and features expressive of considerable intellect—mingled, however, with a large proportion of worldly astuteness and an air of penetration and distrust that bespoke but an indifferent opinion of mankind, or, possibly, a mind ill at ease with itself. His age might be about forty. His grizzled hair had retreated from his forehead, which was broad, but not high, and indented with many wrinkles. Upon the breast of his blue coat glittered a military star, for he had served in the Imperial Army as a colonel of Austrian dragoons, and his salary of six hundred crowns a month as cashier was reinforced by a pension of five hundred dollars, paid to him quarterly by the War-office. A pen was in his hand, with which he had just completed the signature of *Willibald and Brothers* to the last of several counterpart letters of credit drawn upon the house of Puget and Bainbridge in London.

As the eye of the forger glanced rapidly but scrutinisingly over the work of his hands, to enable him to decide which of the counterfeits before him was least liable to awake suspicion, a slight noise near caused him to start, and raising his head he saw peering through the grated door of his box two dark, burning and searching eyes, which, fixed intently upon him, seemed as if they would read the most hidden secrets of his soul. The rest of the countenance was in shadow, and the figure of the gazer was completely hidden from view by a large black cloak.

Such an apparition, which would have been under even ordinary circumstances sufficiently extraordinary and startling, was now rendered peculiarly so to Braunbrock by its suddenness, the unusual time, the sepulchral dimness of the place, and, above all, the consciousness that the occupation he was engaged in was one that would scarcely bear inspection from a pair of eyes even much less inquisitorial than those of the stranger. A moment's reflection, however, served in some sort to re-assure him. The distance between himself and the intruder, whoever he might be, was, though slight, still sufficient, he flattered himself, to preclude all chance of detection. Recovering himself, therefore, he grew bold enough to return the stranger glance for glance.

"Who are you?" he demanded.

"It concerns you to know, perhaps?" was the interrogative reply, delivered in a strange and hollow voice, the accents of which thrilled through every nerve and fibre of the cashier.

"To know your business, at least," said Braunbrock. "What is it?"

"Merely to receive payment of this from you," answered the Unknown, and he handed a paper to the cashier.

"The Bank is closed," said Braunbrock.

"Your office is open," said the stranger, significantly. "To-morrow will be Sunday; you will not be here. Perhaps you may be absent on Monday, Tuesday, Wednesday—all the week, and beyond it. Do you understand? Come, then, do not delay me now. The sum, you perceive, is one hundred thousand dollars: you have so much in the drawer beside you. Be quick and let me have it."

"How did you obtain admittance?" asked the cashier, still dallying, with the bill between his fingers.

"What is that to the purpose?" said the stranger. "I am here."

The cashier now scanned the letter of exchange, and finding it, as he fancied, or chose to fancy, correct, he slowly opened the drawer and counted out bank notes and bills to the amount required. Having given them to the stranger, he again took up the letter and looked at it.

"Your signature is not to the receipt," said he. "How is this?"

"Give it to me, and a pen with it," said the other, "and I will supply the omission."

Braunbrock gave the letter and a pen to the stranger, who wrote in English, and in English characters,[2] at the foot of the receipt, *M. The Man in the Cloak.*

"What the plague sort of signature and handwriting is this?" demanded the cashier, as he tried in vain to read it; "I can make nothing of it." He looked at the stranger. "You are not German, mein Herr?"

"No."

"You are scarcely French, I should think?"

"Scarcely."

"Ah! English, I presume?"

"Your presumption is unwarrantable; I am not English," answered the stranger; "I am an Irishman. Enough: farewell: we shall meet again." In a minute more his form was lost in the gloom and shadows around. His retreat was so sudden and so silent that the cashier could not tell by which passage he had departed.

How the deuce can he get out at all? he asked himself. Or how did he come in? What eyes! he continued—and what an unreadable name! Who can he be? The circumstance is exceedingly strange altogether.——But I am wasting time. I must finish my business, and be off.

With these words he proceeded to consume at the flame of the lamp such of the forgeries as he had rejected, and carefully deposited the selected one in his pocket-book. He next took out from his desk bank notes to the amount of ten thousand ducats, and stowed them safely away in the same morocco leather repository. Then, putting on his hat, he extinguished his lamp, and taking down his umbrella from a crook, he locked the door of his office and coolly proceeded, according to his custom, to deliver up the key to Madame Wilhelmina Willibald, the wife of the principal partner in the firm.

"Ah! you fag yourself *so* much, Herr Braunbrock!" said the lady. "But I have good news for you. We have made up a party to Ilsbein on Monday, and you are to be Master of the Ceremonies, Cicerone, Factotum in short. So, be with us early—and let the cash-office mind itself for one day."

"As *you* please, Madam; I shall be most happy," answered Braunbrock. "Meantime, will you be good enough to tell your husband that the bill of exchange from the Merciers for a hundred thousand dollars was paid this evening. It came in rather late."

"I shall tell him so," said the lady. "Will you have a glass of Tokay, Herr Braunbrock?"

"I thank you; not this evening. Good night, Madam." And the cashier went out.

"That gentleman has a very marked head," said the Baron Queerkopf,[3] a determined, thick-and-thin, anti-loophole phrenologist, who had been lounging on a sofa during this short colloquy.

"Marked?—marked with what?" asked the lady.

"I mean a characteristic head," said the Baron. "He has enormous Secretiveness and but little Conscientiousness."

"You give an indifferent character of our honest cash-keeper," said the banker's wife. "But do *you* know, Baron, I think he has rather a classic head."

"Cash-keeper!—ay, he is better fitted to keep cash than pay it," returned the Baron: "I saw his Acquisitiveness at a glance. But as to classic heads, pardon me, Madam, for taking leave to differ from you: people make the most horrible and petrifying mistakes on that point. Mankind do not sufficiently consider"—and the Baron spoke with great emphasis—"that for the formation of what is popularly designated a classic head, there must be large Self-esteem, considerable Destructiveness, and deficient Veneration. The best heads—those which confer the most commanding intellects or sunshiny dispositions—are not unfrequently altogether at variance with our preconceived notions of the *beau-ideal* of physical beauty. The truth is, that to a common observer the head is any thing but an index to the nature of the man. Look, for example, at Byron's head. It is a positive and undeniable fact that what we imagine the superior appearance of that head is solely attributable to its deficiency in several of the most beneficial organs, and its redundance in some of the most morally deteriorating. It lacked Faith, Hope and Veneration, and exhibited but moderate Benevolence, while, on the other hand, though Conscientiousness was fair, an undue and preponderating proportion of cerebral development manifested itself in Self-esteem, Combativeness and Firmness."

"Well, now, Baron, do you know," said the Banker's wife, whose eyes and mind had been wandering to a thousand things while the phrenologist was lecturing; "I don't understand one word of what you have been saying."

"Suffer me to render it lucider," said the Baron. "Phrenological induction, you will please to comprehend, is grounded upon the irrefragable principle that——" and the Baron, once fairly mounted upon his hobby, galloped on at a rate that left toiling common-sense an infinity of leagues behind. At the close of a monologue of half an hour he paused to take breath, and, looking round him, he saw that his auditress had evanished. The Baron sighed. Alas! he soliloquised, it is ever thus with the sex: they have no powers of analysis, and they are incapable of continuous attention. Yet that bankeress is a beautiful and stately woman—really a fine animal. What a subject for everlasting regret that she should be so deficient in Causality and Concentrativeness!—And the Baron, sighing again, helped himself to a pinch of snuff from a box upon the lid of which were represented three separate views of the head of Goethe, phrenologically mapped out according to the very newest charts laid down by the most fashionable predecessors[4] of his darling theory.

Meanwhile Braunbrock walked into the porter's lodge. "What the devil, Karl," he asked, with an assumed sharpness, "made you leave the Bank-doors open until five o'clock this evening?"

"*I* leave the doors open till five, mein Herr!" exclaimed the menial, astonished. "No such thing at all, mein Herr; would I be mad? I locked them at four punctually, leaving ajar only the private postern for yourself, mein Herr."

Very odd, said the cashier, as talking to himself. "Are you certain you are telling the truth?" he demanded, sternly.

"Quite certain, mein Herr."

I suppose, then, muttered Braunbrock, as he walked out, I suppose that bizarre Irishman must have somehow found his way in and out through the private entrance. Well: I thought that the devil himself, exclusive of the few persons who know it, would have been puzzled to find his way in through that. But it is of no consequence. I have other and graver affairs to demand my attention. Let us see, he proceeded, as he directed his steps along the Hochstrasse. Have I managed matters with the requisite finesse? I hope so. First, here is to-night and to-morrow;—and then for Monday—egad, this party is a lucky incident, for Willibald sleeps out to-morrow night, and will not be home until noon next day; so that I have at least until Tuesday to hammer away upon the anvil;—and, by my faith, I will not let the iron cool!—I have two passports and two different disguises—such, I fancy, as would leave the cleverest police in Europe gropers in the dark. At London I shall touch half a million before any decisive steps can be taken to discover the fugitive; and then for the remainder of my days I shall play the part of the accomplished nobleman in my Italian villa at Strozzi, with the title of Count Rimbombari, or some other of the kind; I prefer his, however, as I, *and nobody else*, saw him die in the marches of Zembin, where his bones are whitening this night. But, ah!—Livonia—what shall I do with her? Do with her?—Bah! what have I, at forty, to do with foolish girls at all? I must leave her behind. Yet, confound it, I really love the girl—ay, love her, ass that I am! Shall I take her with me? Or shall I leave her where she is?"

"You shall leave her where she is," said a voice which Braunbrock had recently heard. He turned round, and saw, fixed upon his face, the terrific eyes of——the Man in the Cloak.

Braunbrock was astounded, and somewhat annoyed. "Who the devil, Sir——" he began.—But the Irishman had already glided by him and disappeared.

Damn his eyes! muttered Braunbrock, what does he mean by staring at me in that unearthly manner? 'You shall leave her where she is,' forsooth! Curse the fellow! does he dare to dictate to me? Who can he be?—The next time I see him, here, in England, in France, or in Italy, hang me if I don't tear that old cloak from his shoulders, and see whether he wears a tail or not! A tail—ha! ha! Well—if I *were* a believer in humbug I should say that there is something supernatural about the man—though I own I deprecate the idea. It would be rather too bad, faith, to have the devil and the police at one's heels together: I couldn't stand that. Hey-day! here I am, at the house of my darling. Now for a scene! I will sound the girl's feelings for me, and act accordingly.

Livonia Millenger, a pretty brunette, with the finest eyes and teeth in all the world, was reclining, while her admirer was indulging in this mental soliloquy, on a handsome ottoman, and talking to her confidante, Maud, upon that one subject nearest (if we except, perhaps, the passion for Power) to the hearts of all women—Love.

"I am afraid, Maud," she said, "you are a little of a visionary. Ah! you don't know the world like me. You are a child, Maud, an infant, a babe. Men never love in the way you speak; they have not the soul."

"Well, I am sure, I don't know," said the attendant damsel, "but I do think Rudolf unlike anybody else; if any one can love sincerely, it is he; there is no deceit, Livonia, in such blue eyes as his—in such a smile—such an angelic look. And oh! if you could see him sometimes when he fancies no one is noticing him—how he gazes on you, and sighs, and then looks away from you again—and then——"

"Ay—looks away from me again, Maud—that is just it! I would rather he would not, though! Ah! Maud, I guess his thoughts better than you, and I can tell you——"

A loud knocking at the door interrupted the conversation.

"O, Heavens!" cried Livonia, "that is Braunbrock's knock—I know it—if Rudolf should come, as he says he will, while he is here, what shall I do?"

"Have no fear," said Maud. "We'll manage matters." And down she tripped to open the door.

I must burn this note, said Livonia, snatching up a rose-colored *billet* from the table; but she lingered to take a last glance at the characters that Love had traced upon its surface; and, bounding up the stairs quicklier than was his wont, Braunbrock entered the room. Livonia flung the little missive into the fire.

"Do you destroy all your *billets-doux* in that way?" demanded he.

"No; only about nine-tenths of them," she answered; "the rest I use in papering my hair.[5] Still I think the flames the most appropriate fate for them all: words that burn, you know, are quite at home in the fire—don't you agree with me?"

"You speak, Livonia, just as if that had been a real *billet-doux*."

"A real? And do you think, then, that I am not good enough, or beautiful enough, to receive such a thing? You horrid monster!" And she stretched out her lips to Braunbrock to be kissed, but with an air of negligence and *insouciance* that would have convinced any man less blinded by love than the infatuated cashier that in so doing she considered herself merely going through a ceremony which the nature of the *liaison* between them rendered in some sort unavoidable, but which she would have willingly evaded, if circumstances had allowed her.

"I have taken a box this evening in the Crescent," said he; "we had better dine at once, to be in time; the entertainments will begin early. You will be greatly delighted."

"I?"

"Yes; you will come with me, of course; will you not?"

"O, no, no! not I," said Livonia, "I should be sick and tired to death. Take Maud with you; I'll stay at home here by my fire-side."

"Nonsense, Livonia, you must come. What should hinder you?"

"I have a head-ache."

"The theatre will cure it; you will laugh it away."

"I should be *ennuyée*[6] to excess of *you*, you beast," said Livonia, laughing, "even if my head-ache were gone."

"Bear with me this evening," said Braunbrock, also laughing, though in a different spirit, "for I shall not be here longer to kill you with either *ennui* or extacy. I am going away from you, Livonia, going to another land. I shall not return for a considerable time. But no matter; while I am absent, you know, you are mistress of this house, these gardens, every thing here in short. Will you keep your heart for me till I come back, Livonia?"

"No, nor my little finger, nor the least paring of the little nail on it," said Livonia, with a playful emphasis. "But when will you be back?"

"Aha!—is it so?" said Braunbrock. "When do I come back, indeed? Is that your cold question, Livonia?—Well, well, love, it is said, cannot be hidden—but neither, say I, can the want of love! So, you do not think of following me?"

"Why, you vain creature," said Livonia, "what right have you to exact or expect such a sacrifice on my part? Is Beauty to harness herself to the car of Ugliness? Must Youth be subservient to the caprices of Age? O, go to! I am ashamed of you: you are a monster, like every one of your sex; an ingrate, a wretch, a huge heap of animated selfishness. I have no patience with you. But I'll tell you how I'll punish you; I'll give you no dinner and turn you out of my house; that's the way I'll serve you."

"Come, come, Livonia; this is all folly. You intend to accompany me, of course?"

"To the theatre?"

"Bah! to England."

"To England !—What! and leave my troops of lovers behind me?"

"You have no lovers but me, now, surely, Livonia—and you love no one but me?"

"No one but you!" exclaimed Livonia. "Oh, positively now I shall expire"—and she burst into an uncontrollable fit of laughter. "You my lover! Why, you brute, you are half a century old, if you are a day! And, you abominable-looking barbarian, you are as ugly as an Indian idol! Then you are so frightfully made—and you have such a wheezing when the asthma takes you, that is, about fifteen times a day. O, you detestable wretch, how I hate you! Do you know, I think I shall hire somebody to assassinate you some night!"

"I wish you would drop this tone of badinage, Livonia, I am not in a mood for joking. Consider: I am bidding farewell to my Fatherland for ever."

"Oh, then, you have a balloon in readiness, I presume, waiting for floating orders," said the lively girl.

"Balloon! what do you mean?"

"Are you not going to England to-night?"

"I leave Vienna to-night for England, most certainly," said Braunbrock; "and I expect you to come with me, Livonia. I expect so much from your attachment. Really and seriously, Livonia, I am going," he added, seeing a smile of incredulity on her lips.

"Then, really and seriously, you are a greater fool than I took you to be," said she. "You may go, but I shall stay. I wish you a pleasant voyage, but I would rather abandon life itself almost than my dear, darling, delightful, native town, W***."[7]

"But Livonia, my dear girl—hear me: I do not mean to stop in England; I shall proceed to France and thence into Italy."

"Ha! ha!" laughed Livonia. "From Germany to England, from England to France, and from France to Italy! Really the Wandering Jew[8] may begin to tremble for his reputation: he has a dangerous rival in the Herr Johann Klaus Braunbrock."

"I see it is idle to talk to you," said the gentleman, pettishly, and stretching himself on a sofa. "But you will come with me to the Crescent, at least—that pleasure you will not deny me?"

"Well, my poor calf, if you are really leaving us, I will consent to oblige you so far. But see, your cravat is quite loose: let me fasten it for you." So saying she approached him, and stooping over him began to arrange the folds of his neck-kerchief. "And at what hour do you leave me?" she asked, tenderly.

"At twelve, dearest," he answered, playing with her hair.

"See, now, thus I tie a gentleman's cravat," she said, executing with her delicate hands a movement the enamoured quadragenarian had by no manner of means anticipated.

"Oh, oh! Livonia!—Death and fury, you will strangle me, woman!" and by a vigorous bound forward he disengaged his neck from her grasp. In the meantime Livonia had made a sign to Maud to approach, and while the astonished lover, half inclined to laugh, and half to scold, was recovering himself she whispered—

"Tell Rudolf, if you see him, not to venture hither until one o'clock."

The maid-servant announced dinner.

"Very good," said Braunbrock, "we will dine together, and then you will dress and accompany me."

At about seven accordingly they drove off to the Crescent, and entered a box near the stage. The entertainments consisted of three pieces. As soon as the second piece was over, Braunbrock apologised to Livonia for leaving her for a few minutes, and went out to converse with some friends whom he had observed going round to the saloon from an opposite box. He had scarcely advanced half a dozen steps, however, when he felt himself touched upon the shoulder. Turning nervously around, he saw before him for the third time the figure of the Man in the Cloak, who in a moment stepped before him and intercepted his passage onward.

"What do you mean, Sir?" asked Braunbrock.

"I mean to smoke," replied the Irishman, as he drew a long pipe, already ignited, from beneath the folds of his cloak.

"Come, come, Sir," cried Braunbrock, "I don't understand this buffoonery. Let me pass, or take the consequences!"

A number of persons had already assembled around them, to watch the issue of this singular rencontre.

"So serious a matter as forgery, I fancy, has unfitted you for relishing buffoonery," said the Irishman, aloud, and in the hearing of all.

"Forgery!" exclaimed Braunbrock, turning three colours, white, blue and yellow. "Who dares——But such language can only be resented in one way, when a gentleman has to deal with a ruffian!" So saying, he aimed a furious blow with his clenched fist at the Irishman, who received it with exemplary science and imperturbability precisely upon the bowl of his pipe, from which it did not elicit a single sparkle.

The lookers on were seized with amaze; and no wonder. "Come," said the Man in the Cloak, proffering his pipe to one by-stander, who mechanically took it, "come, Herr Braunbrock, this is child's play on both sides; you and I must know each other better. Give me your arm and we will walk and talk a little. Make way, gentlemen, if you please;" and seizing the arm of the bewildered cashier, who was now almost passive in his grasp, he dragged rather than led him to a remote and silent part of the saloon, where they might converse without hazard of *espionage* or interruption.

"Poor handful of dust!" he here exclaimed—"did *you* think to resist ME? As well might you attempt to pluck the planets from their spheres. Know that on this vile ball of earth all that man can dream of in the shape of Power is mine. I wield, or if I chose, could wield, all the engines of governments and systems. I read every heart; I see into the future; I know the past. I am here; and yet I may be elsewhere, for I am independent of time and place and distance. My eye pierces the thickest walls; my hands can dive into exhaustless treasures. At my nod proudest palaces crumble. I can overspread the waste with flowers, or blast in a moment the loveliest landscape that eye delights to revel in. Poor, degraded, imbecile being, how can you cope with me? Can you bend this iron arm? Are you able to quench the torch-light of this all-scrutinising eye? Dare you hope to humanize a heart of granite? Go to, helpless, blind, weak worm that you are! Delude not yourself. You are my slave. Though oceans should roll above your corpse, you are my bondslave. Though you should hide yourself from the eyes of men and angels in the central caverns of the earth, you are still mine, and I can trample you to impalpable powder! Neither by might nor guile can you escape me, for I am—be wide awake and listen to me—I am——"

"You are—Who?" demanded the confounded cashier.

"I am," replied the Irishman—and bending his head, he suffered his lips to approach within an inch of Braunbrock's ear—"I am——*the Man in the Cloak!*"

"Strange and mysterious being!" exclaimed Braunbrock, whose superstition was awakened, though his religion still slumbered—"and what would you with me?—you who represent yourself so powerful as to need nothing at the hands of others."

"You rightly guess," said the Man in the Cloak, "that, after all, I require your help—yes, even yours. I am all-powerful in every respect but one: I cannot conquer my own destiny. To achieve such a conquest, I require the assistance of another—a reckless and desperate man—and I have pitched on you as the aptest instrument I could find. Will you give me the aid I ask?"

"What is it?" asked Braunbrock.

"You shall know soon. Meantime let us return to our box—and I shall show you *your* destiny. Mark it well! for unless you evade it by *one mode*,—and there is no other open for you—you must undergo all its torture! You came to see a sight—ha! ha! so you shall. Come, now, and present me to the girl Livonia Millenger as one of your best friends."

Braunbrock returned to his box, accompanied by the Man in the Cloak, whom he introduced to Livonia, as a particular friend of his, but without mentioning any name, simply because he had heard none. Livonia looked at the stranger, and then testified in a whisper to Braunbrock, her astonishment at the glare of the stranger's eyes; but made no other remark. With respect to the Man in the Cloak himself, he retired to a back-seat in the box, and resumed his pipe, of which he had managed to repossess himself as he walked along with Braunbrock.

"How rude your friend is!" whispered Livonia. "Smoking such a long pipe in a box at the theatre!"

"He is a foreigner," returned Braunbrock; "and it may be the custom in his country to smoke very long pipes in the boxes of theatres."

"When we are at Rome we should do as Rome does," observed Livonia. But at that instant the curtain rose, and the closing vaudeville of the evening's entertainments began. Expectation was high, for the popular player, Twigger, was to enact four parts, as a Jew pedlar, a French dancing-master, a German student, and an English alderman, in this piece.

The cashier, however, had scarcely cast his eyes upon the boards before he uttered a half-stifled shriek of terror. Could he credit his senses? A private room, into which he had been more than once introduced, in the house of the Willibalds, was represented on the stage; and in this room Herr Willibald the elder himself was discovered in close conference with the Minister of Police upon the flight of Braunbrock and the robbery and forgery he had committed! There was a good deal of very animated discussion, which terminated in the drawing up of informations deposing to all the facts, and which were to be forthwith transmitted to the official authorities.

"After all," said Willibald, "the infernal rascal may give us the slip. Are you certain he is at the Crescent?"

"Positive," answered the Minister of Police; "and escape is quite impossible: I have planted guards at every avenue."

Braunbrock trembled from head to foot; he rose up. "I—I must leave this, Livonia," said he stammering—"Business———" He turned round and was about to make his exit from the box when the Man in the Cloak tapped him on the shoulder with his pipe. "Just stay where you are," said he, "and note what passes before you. Would you rush into the lion's mouth?"

The effect experienced by Braunbrock from the touch of the Irishman's pipe was similar to that resulting from a sudden attack of nightmare, or a blow from the tail of a torpedo. He felt paralysed; his limbs refused to sustain him; he tried to raise his arms; they sank powerless by his side. He looked imploringly at the Man in the Cloak and his regards were met by a glance of fire and a volume of smoke, which savoured considerably of a sulphury origin.

"What have I done?" he asked, faintly. "Say at once what you would have of me—and cease to torture me."

The Man in the Cloak took the pipe from his mouth and pointed towards the stage. "Look and learn or you are lost!" said he. Braunbrock, who felt as if under the influence of a spell, trembled more than before, but he obeyed the Irishman.

The scene changed to the interior of Livonia's house. Maud was conversing by the fireside in her mistress's room with a sergeant-major of cavalry in a Bavarian regiment, then in garrison at W***.

"So, Braunbrock is going," said the military man. "I am very glad of that; I shall have a clear stage, and, I hope, a great deal of favour. I love Livonia too well to suffer her to sacrifice herself to the whims of that sneaking old robber. I shall espouse her myself."

"Sneaking old robber!" muttered Braunbrock, as he heard this. "The scoundrel!—I could blow his brains out!"

The play went on; the conversation between the sergeant-major and Maud was continued. By-and-by a knocking was heard at the door.

"I vow they are come!" cried Maud. "Here, Rudolf, hide yourself in this closet: I thought to have got you out of the house before they returned—but no matter—Braunbrock will not stop many minutes. There, keep quiet as a mouse!"

Braunbrock saw the young officer thrust into the closet, and immediately afterwards beheld *himself* enter the room, accompanied by Livonia. Here, after partaking of refreshments, the double of the unfortunate cashier bade farewell to his mistress, who hung about his neck in apparent fondness and sorrow, but kept all the while silently laughing over his shoulder in the face of Maud, who grinned back her approbation, and, pointing to the closet, intimated to her mistress by signs that Rudolf was there.

"Vile girl!" cried Braunbrock, looking at her who sat by his side—"have I then at last discovered your dissimulation—your treachery!" But his exclamations were lost in the plauditory shouts and irrestrainable laughter of the audience, who were during all this time deriving the most exquisite, if not the most intellectual pleasure, from the happy manner in which Twigger, as a gouty old English alderman, was devouring an entire haunch of venison, at the rate of about half a pound a mouthful,—and swilling from time to time—O, hear it, ye fashionable British novelists and blush for the continental reputation of your aldermanic countrymen—*porter!*—and out of *a tin gallon can!*

"O, I shall expire!" cried the real Livonia, in a convulsion of laughter.

"Was there ever such a delightful man!" Then looking at Braunbrock, and round at the Irishman—she exclaimed, while the tears of mirth filled her eyes, "How *can* you forbear from laughing? Why you are both as gloomy as night-owls in the midst of all this merriment. What ails you?"

"Do you want ME to laugh, lady?" demanded the Man in the Cloak, solemnly, as he withdrew the pipe from his mouth.

"Ha! ha! ha!" cried Livonia; "that is really better than Twigger. Do you only laugh, then, by particular request?"

"I have never laughed in all my life," said the Man in the Cloak, with increased solemnity. "But if you desire it, I will exert myself to laugh now."

"Nay, nay," said Livonia, "I have no wish to balk your grave humour. But you," turning to Braunbrock—"what witchery has come over you? You sit as pallid and wordless as if you were turned into stone."

"Silence, girl!" cried Braunbrock; "you will speedily enough learn the reason of my pallor and wordlessness!"

"O, as you please," said Livonia, carelessly.

Once more the scene was changed to the eye of Braunbrock. A public Strass in W*** was dimly lighted by half-extinguished lamps. The watchmen were drowsily crying Two o'clock from their turrets. A post-chaise rolled along the street and stopped before a house which Braunbrock recognised as that of an Englishman in whose name, the better to preclude suspicion, he had really designed to hire such a conveyance. Braunbrock watched the result with intense anxiety. "How, then?" said he to himself; "have I made good my escape from the theatre? In that case there is yet a chance for me; I may escape; who is to prevent me?" The carriage drove on: the scene changed to the barrier of the city: still the post-chaise was visible and alone: Braunbrock's heart beat high with hope—alas! even then all was over. Troops of horse and foot police immediately dashed forward and surrounded the carriage. Resistance was useless. Braunbrock saw his double taken prisoner and strongly fettered on the spot. A cry of terror and despair broke from him.

"Hush!" said the Man in the Cloak. "The end is yet to come. Mark it well !"

There were now but two remaining scenes for Braunbrock. The first was the trial scene in the assize-court, which terminated in his condemnation to twenty years of hard labour in a stone fortress at G***.⁹ The second was the fortress itself, in which, after being branded on the arm and breast by the common executioner, he saw himself loaded with irons, in the midst of sixty other criminals, and driven along into a wide and drear court-yard— the place of labour and punishment—under the *surveillance* of an overseer, who carried a knotted knout in his hand for the instruction and advantage of the lazy or the refractory.

The curtain fell amid universal applause, and the audience rose to depart. Livonia took her mantle from the box-keeper, who assisted her in putting it on. As for Braunbrock, he still sat in the one position, with his eye glaring upon the fallen curtain, like a man petrified.

"Come," said the Man in the Cloak, "all is over. Do you hear, Herr Braunbrock? *All is over.*"

"Eternal Heavens! what am I to do?" cried Braunbrock, starting up. "O, let me but escape from this accursed place, and I am safe—let me breathe the fresh air in the open street!"

"Escape is impossible," said the Irishman in a low tone, "except on one condition. I would speak ten words with you: step aside." He then added, turning to Livonia. "Mein Fräulein, Herr Braunbrock and I will join you in the saloon."

"Be quick, then," said Livonia; and she tripped along the passage.

"What you have seen you remember," said the Man in the Cloak to Braunbrock. "Flight—detection—detention—trial—conviction—despair —ignominy—irons—mill-horse drudgery—black bread, and neither snuff nor coffee!—such is the prospect that awaits you. No human power can rescue you."

"Why? How?" cried the agitated betrayer of trust.

"Why?" said the Man in the Cloak, seizing the arm of Braunbrock. "Dunce! Because the adamantine hand that grasps you thus will not relinquish its grasp until you are delivered up to justice. Is that German or not?"

"Cursed be the day that I was born!" exclaimed Braunbrock, in a paroxysm of despair. "Yet—" he cried, suddenly recollecting himself— "yet, you spoke, or my memory deceives me, but just now of a condition by which I might be saved. Is there any such, or do you but mock me?"

"There is ONE," said the Man in the Cloak, after a pause.

"Name it—name it—my brain is burning—I will consent to any thing," cried Braunbrock.

"Will you really?" asked the Man in the Cloak. "Will you consent to——" and inclining his head, he whispered a few words in the ear of Braunbrock. "Could you consent to that compact?" he asked, aloud.

"Such a compact is not possible," said Braunbrock. "We live in the second quarter of the nineteenth century."

"Believe it to be possible," said the Man in the Cloak. "At any rate you had better give your consent. The century will ask you no questions."

"And will my consent ensure the possession of all you have whispered to me?"

"Of all, and more than all that."

"So be it then, I freely consent."

"Enough: you are at liberty. I will restore the sum of which you have plundered Willibald: the forgery you can yourself destroy. Then your conscience will be satisfied. There exists no longer any necessity that you should have recourse to dishonest stratagem; henceforth a word, a wish, makes you as rich as you please. Come, let us forth."

They rejoined Livonia, and proceeded towards the door. "I shall now take your place," said the Man in the Cloak to Braunbrock. "These dogs of justice must be baffled, and I shall show them a trick worth a dozen of the best they have seen yet. Help Livonia into the carriage and take care of her."

"There he is—there is your man: seize him!" cried the voice of a police-officer to three of his myrmidons,[10] who at the words instantly rushed forward and captured the Man in the Cloak.

"Gentlemen," said the latter, "I make no resistance, but I submit to you very respectfully that you are somewhat precipitate. I have committed, it is true, a robbery and a forgery—two very serious infractions of the social compact; but any man who has studied the philosophy of life with liberal views and a mind emancipated from prejudices will acknowledge that circumstances may, in some degree, be allowed to plead for me and extenuate my guilt. When I perpetrated those crimes I was under the soporific influence of bad tobacco. Gentlemen, bad tobacco is an instigator to insanity. This pipe, gentlemen,—this long and melancholy-looking pipe——"

"Gammon!"[11] cried the police-officers. "Come off with us, old cock; we stand no nonsense." And in a minute more, the Man in the Cloak, his hands and feet having been first secured by cords, was thrust into a coach and left to his meditations as it rattled over the streets towards the office of police.

At length the vehicle, having reached its destination, stopped, and the door was opened by one officer, while three others stood ready in the midst of links and flambeaux to help the prisoner out and bear him into the guard-room.

"Come, old twaddler, which are your legs?" asked the officer. "What the deuce!" he continued, as he now looked in: "what do I see? Surely this is not our prisoner." He put his hand into the carriage. "Why, grill me alive," he exclaimed, at the top of his voice, "if you haven't made prisoner of a bag of feathers!"

"A bag of devils! What are you talking of? You must be drunk, Schnapps," said the nearest, advancing closer and looking in. "I cannot well see him: hold up the light, here, Gripper, I say!" The light was held up; the policeman looked in; but he had no sooner obtained a glimpse of his prisoner than he, too, started back in dismay.

"A sack of chaff, as I am a living idiot!" he exclaimed.

"What is all this delay for," bellowed a rotund and spectacled sergeant, coming out of the office. "Why don't you take out your prisoner?"

"There is none to take out," said Gripper, sullenly.

"What, scoundrels! have you suffered him to escape!"

"No," said Schnapps, "he is inside, but he has changed himself into a bundle of hay. I thought he had a wizard look."

"I will have every mother's son of you reported to-morrow morning for this," said the sergeant. "Smash my spectacles if this thing ain't always occurring! Take out this moment whatever you have got crammed into the carriage."

The prisoner was accordingly released from durance. He proved to be a mere man of straw, with very thick legs of about ten inches in length, and a hollow pumpkin, stuffed with old rags, for a head!

"Was there ever any thing so disgraceful?" exclaimed the sergeant, as he examined this singular figure through his spectacles, and forgetting in his wrath, his previous assertion of the perpetual occurrence of similar disappointments. "Upon whom the blame of the rescue may fall I know not, but it will be no wonder, if, after a circumstance of this kind, our police should sink in the estimation of Europe, Australia, and the two Americas!"

And the story went that Braunbrock, after being captured, had been rescued, nobody knew how, and that his rescuers had supplied his place with a man of straw. This was not exactly the fact; but it is not our business to know how far the rumour differed from the reality. After a lapse of eleven years, history can offer little but vague conjectures in solution of similar enigmas.

In the meanwhile our hero and Livonia drove homeward. They had scarcely entered the house when they were again joined by the Man in the Cloak: he took Braunbrock aside and whispered in his ear a notification to the effect that the paction between them must be forthwith completed. "Lead the way, therefore," said he, "into a dark room. The talisman does not bear the light."

"May I not bring a candle?" asked Braunbrock.

"Upon no account: there is no occasion," answered the Man in the Cloak, and in fact his eyes, as they proceeded along, were as good as a gas-lamp, though rather more lurid.

"What mischief are they about, I wonder?" asked Maud of Livonia, following them with her looks. "I don't half like that fire-eyed stranger in the cloak." She then drew nearer to her mistress, and placing the forefinger of her left hand on her lips, while she glanced stealthily around, she pointed with the right to the closet in which the young cavalry-officer was immured.

"Rudolf?" interrogated Livonia, softly.

"Yes, he has been here an hour," answered Maud, in an equally subdued tone.

"Shall I speak to him?" asked Livonia. "I think I may venture. Stand at the door and see whether those brutes are coming in again."

Maud went to the door and listened. In a moment afterwards she returned. "I am afraid I have heard their footsteps," said she. "Yes, yes, here they are."

The door of the room was now pushed open violently, and Braunbrock entered alone. There was a wild and foreign expression in his features. He did not look the same man that he had been two minutes before. His swarthy complexion had given place to a ghastly paleness. His eyes had that wandering brilliancy by which a physiognomist at once detects the poet or the madman among ten thousand. Even his bearing was altered; he carried himself haughtily and sternly, and trod the floor with a step that seemed to disdain the earth.

"What, in the name of Heaven, has happened you?" inquired Livonia, looking at him in wonder, not wholly unblended with terror.

"Better ask me in the name of Hell than Heaven," said he; and his voice was deep and thrilling.

"What *have* you been doing? What has passed between that frightful man and you, and where is he?"

"Where is he?" echoed Braunbrock. "He is gone—*home*. I have taken his place. I am now *the Man in the Cloak*,—in other words, I am henceforth a being of mystery—none must see me as I really am."

"What nonsense! But really, what have you been doing to yourself? You are so changed I hardly know you. Bless me! surely you were never a dabbler in sorcery?"

"Woman! Wheedling devil! be silent! It is for *me* to speak to *you*. I know all—*all*, I tell you! You have deceived, duped, betrayed, swindled me! Therefore I cast you off. Livonia, scorn, or at best, indifference, is the only sentiment I can entertain for you henceforth. And I am justified. I trusted you; you imposed upon me. Do I speak the truth?"

"I never pretended to be able to love you," said Livonia; "and I think you might have spared me the hard words you have just uttered, if you had a spark of generosity in your bosom."

"You think so? Poor girl!" sneered Braunbrock. "How you are to be compassionated! Such innocence as yours in such a corrupt world is at once admirable and saddening! When a lover visits you, of course you know nothing of his intrusions; he might clasp you round the waist, and you would not feel the pressure of his arm; he might step into your closet before your face, and when he had closed the door you would be ready to take heaven and earth to witness that there was nobody there. Oh, you are too guileless altogether for society or for your own happiness, purest of maidens!"

While Braunbrock spoke thus, Livonia's color shifted from pale to red, from red to pale, and from pale to red again. She felt that her secret was discovered, that all was known, that the *liaison* between herself and Braunbrock was terminated. For this last consummation she did not care much—but, though fallen as regarded virtue, she was still sensitive to the opinion of society, and she dreaded the *esclandre*[12] which was likely to result from an exposure of the double part she had for some time been playing with her lover and her protector. Afraid to speak to or look upon Braunbrock, she cast her eyes downwards, and awaited in silence the conclusion to which it might please him to bring this unhappy interview.

Nor had she to wait long. Braunbrock, almost as soon as he had ceased speaking, walked to the end of the room and kicked open the closet-door. "Talking of closets," said he, "one may as well take a survey of the contents of this.—Ah!" he continued, "well, it is odd how people will stumble upon the truth by accident. Rudolf Steiglitz, I protest!—the length and breadth of as neat a gallows-bird as ever sang small before a large multitude! Come forth my good fellow, and let me see whether you stand as stout upon your pins as you did last Thursday in the Hall at the Liongate."

Livonia, trembling from head to feet and white as ashes, flung herself into a *fauteuil*, while her lover, with an air in which mortification, pride, shame, and anger were mingled, obeyed the bidding of Braunbrock.

"I am ready to give you satisfaction," said he, "when and where you please. You are an old soldier."

"And you are a young jackass," retorted Braunbrock. "You will give me satisfaction when I see the carrion-crows feeding on your carcase. Why should I take the trouble of blowing out your brains? I see a purple circle round your neck already: the gallows are groaning for you. You are the especial property of the hangman; I have no right and no desire to poach on his manor."

"I despise your vulgar vituperation, Sir, I am a man of honor."

"So they all say and swear at the Liongate, among the Devilmaycares, those new conspirators against government, who have just been *déterrés*[13] and will be thrown into prison neck and heels, all of them, before to-morrow's sun has set."

The young man grew paler as he listened, and Livonia, clasping her hands, exclaimed in anguish, "O Rudolf, Rudolf!"

"It is too true for a German ballad," pursued Braunbrock. "The Minister of Police is on the alert. The Attorney-general has already got hold of all your names, and the gaoler in a short time will get hold of all your bodies. The crown-lawyer, Kellenhoffer, is at this moment busy drawing up the indictment that is to accuse your entire gang."

"And you, monster, you have betrayed Rudolf!" cried Livonia, gathering courage and energy from her despair; and she rose, and rushing towards her lover, clasped him round the neck with passionate fondness, bursting into tears as she did so, and sobbing aloud.

"You know me too well to believe what you assert," said Braunbrock, with great and laudable *sang-froid*. "I was ignorant of the facts myself an hour ago. Since then, however, I have undergone a singular change, as you have perceived, and now I see every thing, I know every thing, I can do every thing."

"Oh, then," cried Livonia, casting herself at his feet,—"if you have the power you say, if you can do every thing, save, save *him*! Save him, and I will love you; I will adore you; I will be the slave of your wildest caprices! I will traverse the world at your bidding; —if it be possible I will plunge myself into the depths of hell for your sake. Only let not him perish, so young, so good, so noble as he is!" and her passionate tears almost blinded her.

"Maud," said Braunbrock coldly, "toddle into the next room, like a decent wench, and bring me out the pipe you will find on the table."

Maud obeyed, and Braunbrock began to smoke. The pipe was that which had belonged to the Irishman. After a few inhalations and exhalations he replied coldly:

"It is in vain, Livonia; you make yourself ridiculous merely; every man must fulfil his destiny; and that of this young gentleman is to embellish the gallows one of these days. Perhaps I could save him—perhaps not; no matter; he dies; and there is an end of discussion on the subject."

"Cruel! cruel!" cried Livonia, rising and wringing her hands. "But cold-hearted fiend! you shall not triumph! Go, Rudolf, while there is yet time. Make your escape." She attempted to open the door as she spoke, but Braunbrock stepped before her and pushed her back with a jerk into the middle of the room.

"I am master in my own house, I suppose," said he, "and doors are to be opened or closed as *I* please."

"Coward and villain!" cried Rudolf, drawing his sword. "You shall answer on the spot for your monstrous inhumanity. Draw this moment: it were but an act of justice to rid the earth of such a miscreant. Draw, I say!"

Maud shrieked, and Livonia, grasping her lover's arm, exclaimed in terror, "O, no, Rudolf, no!" He gently but determinedly disengaged his arm.

"But don't you perceive, Don Bombastes,[14] are you ass enough not to see," said Braunbrock, coolly, addressing Rudolf, "that your chance of being able to rid the earth of me is rather better while I am unarmed thus than it will be if you give me the privilege of using cold iron against you? Your own windpipe even might happen to be slit by some ugly mistake instead of mine."

"I am no assassin, sir!" exclaimed Rudolf; "and I again call on you to draw. Draw this instant, I say!"

"You would have better success in calling on me for a song; though we *are* in a *drawing*-room," said Braunbrock, "I have never learned to draw, though singing and dancing are very much in my way,— favorite amusements of mine. But this farce must end,—and now to treat you to a sample of dexterity unparalleled—observe!" He struck up as he spoke, the sword of the young officer with his pipe. The effect was instantaneous; Rudolf's arm fell relaxed and nerveless by his side, and the weapon dropped on the carpet. Braunbrock took it up again and returning it to the officer, commanded him to replace it in the sheath, a command which the astounded young man obeyed with the look and action of one who doubts whether he is awake or dreaming.

"Livonia!" cried Braunbrock, turning to the girl, who had witnessed this exercise of superhuman power with no less astonishment than her lover, "Livonia, you must leave this house." He rang the bell, and ordered a carriage to be called. "Go where you please," he pursued, "but as I do not wish to return you personally evil for evil, here is money for you—more than you have a right to expect;" and he took from his pocket a parcel of bank notes to the amount of sixty thousand crowns, and laid them down before her.

"May my right arm wither from my shoulder," replied Livonia, "when it touches a single shilling of your money! Come, Rudolf, we will leave this house together, and, in spite of the prediction you have heard, I am certain there is no fear and no peril for us. Come; I feel myself choking in this room. Come, Maud."

"Don't mention choking to him," said Braunbrock drily: "the subject is a ticklish one. Well, I am sorry you refuse to pocket the cash, for nothing can be done in this world without it. But the carriage has stopped at the door: shall I light you down the stairs?"

A look of mingled scorn, fear and hatred was the only reply which either party vouchsafed him, as they left the room and descended to the street. In another moment the sound of the carriage wheels in motion over the pavement reached his ears.

He was now alone. He resumed his pipe and continued smoking all night long.

Yes, he was thenceforth alone. And he felt that he was alone. And a presentiment mastered him even then that he should be alone through all the revolving cycles of eternity. The first use to which he was determined to put the tremendous power he had acquired by his talisman was to gratify all the tastes and animal longings of his being, hitherto in a great degree circumscribed in their indulgence by the limitedness of his means. Accordingly, changing his name, a precaution scarcely necessary, as the singular alteration in his features and person had rendered him almost unrecognizable by his former friends, he purchased a magnificent villa, furnished it in the costliest manner, stocked its cellars with the rarest wines, and spared no expense to procure every luxury that art could devise or gold purchase. He plunged into dissipation with a zest and avidity that for a time enchained all his faculties and left no room for reflection. But after a while the novelty of pleasure faded, and his dreadful situation became revealed to him in all its terrors. In the midst of his banquettings and revellings he saw inscribed as it were upon all things the same fearful handwriting that startled Belshazzar upon the wall of his palace, and told him that the days of his power were numbered;[15] he felt that every succeeding hour robbed him of a portion of his soul; and anticipations of the Future perpetually haunted him, terrible as those gigantic and indefinable images of horror which rise before the ulcerated conscience in dreams, and from which the sleeper would gladly plunge even into the unexplored abysses of Death itself. The enormous nature of his power only made him acquainted with the essential desolation of heart which flows from being alone in the universe and unsympathised with by others. The relations that had existed between his finer faculties and the external world gradually suffered an awful and indescribable change. Like his predecessor, he could in an instant transport himself into the blooming valleys of the East, or the swarthy deserts of Africa; the treasures of the earth were his, and the ocean bared her deeps, teeming with gold and lustrous jewels, before him. But the transitions and vicissitudes by which mortals are taught to appreciate pain and pleasure, and the current of life is guaranteed from stagnating, were lost to him. His tastes were palled; his passions sated. Wine ceased to excite him and woman to charm. He had exhausted all pleasures; he had fathomed every depth of voluptuousness: he had denied himself no gratification; and the eternal and uniform result, grafted by necessity on nature, followed: he became incapable of further enjoyment. He was like to a rocky beach, strewn with wrecks and redolent of barrenness, when the full and gushing spring-tide of the morning has rolled back from it to the ocean. It was then, that for the first time in his life a question he remembered having met with somewhere in his boyhood recurred to him in its full force: 'What shall it profit a man if he gain the whole world and lose his own soul?'[16] He gave to this question a more figurative interpretation than it usually receives, but on that very account, perhaps, its applicability to himself came home the stronglier to his bosom.

His soul, he felt, was lost, even while yet he lived and breathed and moved among men: between him and the Power that governs the universe in love and wisdom there was hostility; and the further his mind sought to dive into the recesses of eternity, the denser became the blackness of that darkness to which he felt himself compelled to look forward as at once his refuge and his torment. His state, in fine, was wretched beyond the power of language to shadow forth. Could such a state be endured always? Could it be endured always even upon earth? No: all the resources of human nature, aided even by infernal agency, are insufficient to battle against the mighty agony of that despair which the prospect of an eternity of woe, incessantly before the mind's eye, must of necessity generate. Before the lapse of seven years all the energies of Braunbrock—let us still call him by that name—were devoted night and day to the task of discovering a victim—a substitute—even as the Man in the Cloak had discovered *him*. Month after month he prosecuted his search wherever he thought it likely to be successful. He traversed Spain, Italy, Holland, England, and France. Crossing the Mediterranean he passed as a pilgrim through Asia from east to west. Borne on the broad waters of the Atlantic he visited America. But the day of his enfranchisement was not yet to be, and he at last returned to his native land. And there he remained, alone among men, groaning under the intolerable burden of his gifted and terrible nature, and a perpetual prey to a despair that already communicated to him a foretaste of that proper demoniacal existence upon the horrors of which he felt that he must soon and finally enter.

One night, at length, in the zenith of his wretchedness, he slumbered for a few moments, and in his slumber he had a dream: he dreamed that he stood in the aisle of the Church of St. Sulpice at Paris, and that he saw a figure in a cloak resembling that of the Irishman, leaning against a pillar, but that his face was that of a corpse. He awoke before he could approach the dead man. Next day he transported himself to Paris, and repaired to the church of St. Sulpice. A number of priests were singing the office for a departed soul around a bier. Braunbrock, seeing an ecclesiastic in the chancel alone, approached, and requested to be informed of the name of the deceased.

"His name was *Melmoth*," replied the priest. "Unless I am greatly deceived, too, that name should also be yours. There is a marked resemblance in feature between you both. Perhaps you were his brother?"

"No," said Braunbrock. "But, the name—did you say it was Melmoth?"

"Yes."

"An Irishman?"

"The same."

"Who always wore a cloak?"

"Precisely."

"And whose eyes were of a blasting brightness?"

"Right."

"And *his* name was Melmoth? I thought Melmoth had been long since in his grave—had been damned these ten years."

"So the story went," said the priest; "but it was false: Melmoth the Wanderer died within the precincts of this church only last week; and his soul, I trust, if not already in heaven, is on its way thither. He made indeed a pious and penitent end. His crimes, it is true, were great, but his repentance has cancelled them all. I am not at liberty to speak of his confession, whatever it was, either horrible or otherwise, but of his prayers I will say that I never listened to any more humble and fervent. The finger of God was visible in the conversion of such a man. He has left all his wealth, which is considerable, to the poor. He would have bestowed a portion upon this church, but after mature deliberation my reverend brethren decided upon rejecting, under the peculiar circumstances of the case, any donation for themselves or the altar on this occasion. Stranger! though not his brother, you are probably related to him; the resemblance between you and him, especially in the eyes, strikes me at this moment even more than when you spoke first. Kneel down with me here and we will offer up a short prayer for the repose of his soul."

"No," said Braunbrock. "I cannot: I have never knelt or prayed since I was sixteen years of age."

"Unfortunate man!" said the priest, surveying him with compassion. "Is it true? Yet kneel now, at least."

"I will try, since you wish," said Braunbrock. And he knelt.

The priest then offered up an audible prayer for the soul of the deceased. Braunbrock remained silent. "And that it may please thee, O Lord," added the priest, "to soften the hard heart of the living, and make of it a heart of flesh!"

Still Braunbrock was silent.

"Will you not join in the prayer?" asked the priest.

"I cannot," said Braunbrock. Yet when he cast his eyes around, and they were met by the Gothic windows, and tall pillars and solemn altars veiled in black of the sacred edifice he was in, and when the chorusing chant of the priests fell upon his ear, he could not help on the instant mentally exclaiming, "Yes, all this must have had its origin in a Something!" But Conscience and his heart, ashamed of the word, went further, and demanded, "Miserable atom! dost thou call the Author of all Existence a *Something?*"

"Invoke the assistance of God, unhappy man!" said the priest.

"Impossible," answered Braunbrock.

"Can you not call upon God for mercy?"

"I do not know what to say," replied the German.

"Repeat after me, and with as much sincerity and unction as you can command, O, God, be merciful to me, a sinner!"

And Braunbrock repeated the words, *O, God, be merciful to me a sinner!*

"It is enough," said the priest. "Rise!"

Braunbrock rose up.

"Go now in peace," said the priest; "but return hither, and be here again on this day week, a changed man—a man who need no longer shroud himself *in a cloak.*"

The sequel of our tale may be easily divined by the penetrating. Religion and Hope from that hour found their way slowly into the heart of Braunbrock. Still he was not able to disembarrass himself of the fatal gift that had been bestowed on him. But an invisible agency was at length operating in his behalf.

One evening he happened to be passing the Bourse.[17] Five days from the period of his interview with the priest in St. Sulpice had gone by, and the consciousness that the talisman still clung to him oppressed him more heavily than ever. "Oh," he exclaimed aloud, as the dusk of a chill Autumn evening descended over the city, "can I then find none—none to deliver me? Is there in this world of cupidity not one wretch to be met with, who, at such a price, will accept of inexhaustible riches and boundless power?"

"Who talks of bestowing inexhaustible riches?" said a man with a hawk's eye and a hooked nose, who at the moment came out of the Bourse. "Is it you, *mon ami?*"

"Yes," answered Braunbrock, eagerly, as he glanced at the physiognomy of the stranger, and began to hope that he had found his man at last.

"Why, you are not such a fool?" said the other.

"If I were?" demanded Braunbrock.

"*En ce cas,*" said the hook-nosed Parisian, "I would just trouble you for five hundred thousand francs. I am a ruined man, to be candid with you, unless I can obtain that sum by to-morrow."

"You shall have millions," answered Braunbrock—"on one condition."

"Ah !—a condition!" said the Hawk-eyed.

"A mere trifle."

"Its nature?"

"You must sell—"

"My pictures?"

"Pish!"

"My houses?"

"Psha!"

"My wife?"

"Bah!"

"What then?"

"Your ****," said Braunbrock, with a solemnity of tone he did not intend, but which he could not avoid.

"Is that all?" said the Parisian. "Done. It is a bargain. But how do you propose getting at my ****?"

"That is *my* affair," said Braunbrock. "Here is my card. Will you meet me in an hour hence at the hotel named here."

"I shall be punctual. *Au revoir.*"

At seven o'clock, accordingly, the Parisian, whose name was Malaventure, arrived; and the awful terms of the mutual contract were ratified on both sides. Malaventure obtained possession of the talisman which had acquired and secured for Braunbrock his tremendous prerogatives, and Braunbrock was restored to his ancient identity, which for so many years he had forfeited.

"And what will become of you now?" demanded Malaventure. "Have you any resource independent of cutting your throat and going to the devil?"

"I shall go to-morrow to the Church of St. Sulpice, to make my first and last confession to a priest," said Braunbrock. "The hand of death is upon me. I feel that I shall die, but I shall die in peace with GOD."

Church,—priest,—God! muttered the Frenchman to himself. *Pauvre imbécile!* He really believes he has a soul to be saved! And, shrugging his shoulders, he left the hotel.

Early the next morning Braunbrock repaired to St. Sulpice. It was precisely the date that the priest had signified for his return. He made his confession and was reconciled with the Church. As he had predicted, he died in a few days afterwards. His last moments were characterised by a penitence as sincere as that of Melmoth himself had been previously; and he was buried side by side with the Irishman.

Here, reader, our narrative ends. Though not, we hope, over pharisaical ourselves, we may be excused for wishing to keep ourselves aloof from such gentry as Malaventure, and any or all of those through whose hands the talisman he has purchased may hereafter pass. Besides, if we must acknowledge all the truth, we are somewhat in the dark with respect to the subsequent history and adventures of the said talisman. We have heard, indeed, that the atheist, growing frightened after he had paid his debts, disposed of it to a bankrupt notary; that the notary transferred it to a ruined speculator in the funds; that from the speculator it passed into the hands of a briefless lawyer; and that this latter made it over to a stock-broker's clerk, whom he had accidentally heard saying that for one hundred louis he would blow up the king of the barricades,[18] the pope, and the whole college of cardinals with gunpowder. But whether these reports correspond with the actual truth we cannot take it upon ourselves to decide. We can only say, for certain, that all the accounts that have reached us concur in representing the stock-broker's clerk as the latest possessor of the diabolical charm in question. This young man is described by all who knew him as of a wild and impetuous but generous character. He was unfortunate in his love, and lost large sums in play. One evening he left his lodgings, telling his landlady that he should return before midnight. He never returned more. The next day his body was taken up from the Seine, and deposited in the Morgue. Whether his death was self-inflicted or the result of accident was never ascertained. Of the talisman nothing was ever heard afterwards: in all probability it slipped from his pocket as he fell into the river, and at this moment lies embedded in the mud of the Seine.

———

As the following authentic document, in reference to the young man last-mentioned may gratify some of our readers, we have cut it out from the *Belgian Courier* newspaper and sent it to our printers as an addendum to our story.

Brussels, July 27th, 1835.—Our Parisian correspondent transmits us the following singular narrative:

Yesterday, about two o'clock, the hottest hour in the day, the whole city of Paris was thrown into a state of commotion by seeing a stranger in a German dreadnought wrap-rascal with a fur collar, admirably adapted for the climate of Siberia, passing down the rue St. Honoré. The stranger seemed totally unconscious that there was anything in his appearance to call for observation until the hootings of the boys and girls who gathered in crowds about him convinced him to the contrary. When informed of the cause of the hullaballoo, he with great good nature and politeness disencumbered himself of the offending garment and delivered it into the hands of a by-stander to keep for him while he went into the house of M. Villeroi, the stock-broker, to transact some business there. I was curious to see more of the man, and I followed him.

On stepping in he looked about him, and in accents that at once told me he was from Germany, inquired whether a young man of the name of Valdenoir had not formerly done business in that office. The reply was in the affirmative, and that he had been drowned.

"Ah!—drowned,—yes," said the stranger:—"well, he is now in the planet Jupiter."

"In the planet Jupiter?" cried the head clerk, opening his eyes.

"But whether he is happy or not is the mystery," pursued the German, who I soon found out was an astrologer[19]—"for Mercury was in the seventh house on the night he was drowned—and that is ambiguous. Borrowing a light from the old mythology, too, we should say that Jupiter was the chief of the gods—but then, saith Holy Writ, the gods of the heathens are devils—and Jupiter is thus but an arch-demon. I have a book here in my pocket—Jacob Bœhmen[20]—which—" and he fumbled in five pockets successively for the book, which at length he was so fortunate as to find.

"Is the man mad?" asked one of another.

"In the forty-eighth proposition of the book called The Threefold Life of Man,[21] we find it laid down—" began the German.

"Who is the writer of that quaint-titled volume, sir?" demanded one of the secretaries, a flippant *littérateur*, who translated German poetry and wrote German stories for the magazines, and therefore deemed himself entitled to assume the critic on the present occasion.

"Jacob Bœhmen," said the astrologer.

"Bemmen ?—Van Bemmen, the Hague banker?"

"No, no, sir; this illustrious man was a shoemaker."

"Pooh,—*un cordonnier!*—Made shoes for—what country was he of?"

"Prussia, sir, had the honor of his birth."

"Made pumps for old Freddy?"[22]

"Monsieur?"

"Made shoes for the royal family?"

"I hope not," said the German: "for not one of them was worthy to unloose the latchets of *his*."

"Permit me to look—to review for a moment—I am a—judge—"

The book accordingly was handed across the counter by the German.

"This is a very poor writer, Doctor—leaves out his hyphens—I see a semicolon in the very second sentence of the preface where there should be a full stop."

"Sir," said the German gravely, "he was one of the profoundest of philosophers."

"What did he know of *la Charte*?"[23] demanded the second clerk, twirling his moustache at the German.

"Or of Taglioni?"[24] said the third.

"Could he grin a hole through a frying-pan?" asked an understrapper, whose salary had not yet enabled him to ascend for amusement from the tavern to the theatre.

"How was he off for soap?"[25] inquired an errand-boy.

A series of similar questions recommenced with the head-clerk, and again terminated with the errand-boy. I confess I could not help laughing. As for the astrologer, he looked the very picture of stupefaction and bewilderment. He put his book up into his pocket. "*Mein Gott*," said he, as he made his way out of the office, *"was ist denn das? Sind das Menschen—oder vielleicht Troglodyten?"*[26] Shortly afterwards he turned down an adjoining street, and I lost sight of him.—Your's, *mon cher Courier Belge.*

ANTHOLOGIA GERMANICA—NO. XIV
GELLERT'S TALES AND FABLES.

T HE world is about to come to an end. Here is a book from the Leipsic press,—printed legibly—on paper in which hairs and straws do not usurp the place of every third line of types. Have the recent improvements made in *their* typography by the Calmuc Tartars and the Kirghizians of the Russian Steppes begun to awaken the jealousy of Saxony? Or is there a conspiracy to smash the glass-manufactories by enabling all classes to read without spectacles? Whatever be the cause, we rejoice in the effect, and accordingly receive this first earnest of a willingness in our German friends to send us something in the shape of books which *we* shall not be under the necessity of sending to the chandler's shop—we receive this, we say, as thankfully as if we had got it for nothing.

Our first surprise being over, let us inspect the phenomenon a little more nearly. *Gellert's Fabeln und Erzählungen.* Very good. Gellert's was the hand to spin out such articles.

> "Like a ropemaker's were his ways,
>   For still one line upon another
>   He formed; and, like his hempen brother,
> Kept going backward all his days."[1]

But the retrograde progression of our fabulist was wholly as to his corporeal man. He laboured under perpetual hypochondriacism—

> "And Melancholy marked him for her own."[2]

From nineteen to fifty-four[3]

> "that surly spirit
> Did bake his blood, and make it thick and heavy."[4]

He saw about him, within the narrow precincts of his chamber,

> "more (blue) devils than vast hell can hold;"[5]

and when he went abroad

"the sheeted Dead
Did squeak and gibber in the German streets."[6]

He was forced—thrust—carted—as Maginn would say, "pitchforked"
into a Professor's chair in Leipsic—having previously quitted the pulpit
because his congregation, who should have merely looked up *to* him, were
accustomed to look up *at* him also. Yet what matter! A modest poet may be
stared out of countenance—and be compelled to profess philosophy
malgré lui[7] —but such a man will never, even in a Professor's chair,

"Sit like his grandsire cut in alabaster,"[8]

for any length of time. Gellert was born to evoke, as Schiller hath it,

"Schöne Wesen aus dem Fabelland,"[9]

and here they be,

"Black spirits and white,
Blue spirits and grey,"[10]

imprisoned in the volume before us—and here also be the pictured faces
of our friend Osterwald,[11]

"Which, with dumb mouths, do ope their booby lips
To beg a voice and utterance in our tongue;"[12]

i.e. in the Irish tongue; and that same they shall have immediately—in the
Queen's English.

Reader! carry back your imagination a century. Yet, stay; that is going
too fast and far. Carry it back ninety-two years. You will find yourself then,
if our deduction be correct, (we mean the deduction of 92 from 1839)
somewhere about 1747. Well: at that period the only writer in Germany
who was German to the backbone, and disdained stooping to pick up the
crumbs that fell from the literary tables of other nations, was Clockstop—
we beg pardon; our pen is bad—Klopstock. All his contemporaries wore
Anglican masks or Gallican—or, to speak intelligibly, were Bodmerians or
Gottschedians;[13] and foremost among the Gottschedians stood Gellert. At
every distinguished small tea-party in Leipsic

"he beat
The kettle drum with curious heat"[14]

on behalf of Boileau[15] and Lafontaine—rather appropriate names, by the by, on the occasion.[16] Lafontaine was his especial model; and what the Frenchman was from the direct impulses of his own genius, the German determined to become by force of imitation. Gellert had some invention and a fair knowledge of arithmetic: his invention considerably assisted him in inventing; while his arithmetic helped him to count the feet in his verses. The result was a book rivalling his master's, and universally admired. "It is written in German," said the Great Frederick, "and yet it can be read!"[17] Stranger still, it was translated—but alas! into Hebrew. Before last year the book, we believe, never came to Ireland. Here, however, it now lies before us; and we hail it as an old friend,—nay, as better than a friend, *because* it lies before us, while a friend commonly lies behind our back. We must hasten to show it up. Not that *we* can pretend to Lafontainize: our originality is too mighty for us and refuses to be burked: we must therefore have *carte blanche* to out-and-out it, *i.e.* to perform our task in a mode characteristic of Ourself. And as we reckon that the first care of every man should be Number One, we will commence with that, an't please the Public.

* * * * * * * * *

Into what corner of the globe have not our paraphrases penetrated?

> "Like Psaphon's birds, speaking their master's name
> In every language syllabled by fame."[18]

Yet it is solely our stupidity which, like steam, has impelled us onward. People have often talked of "the stupidest man alive." They little dreamt that they were then talking of Us. Yes; it is time for us to proclaim it; we are that identical individual, and no mistake. Our stupidity has been growing upon us from our boyhood; and, enormous as our stock at present is, we are proud to state that we are perpetually receiving additions to it. We are stupider to-day than we were yesterday, and there is not a shadow of doubt upon our mind that we shall be stupider to-morrow than we are to-day. The man whose vanity leads him to imagine that he can by any human exertion become as stupid as we, labours under a deplorable infatuation—a delusion of rare magnitude—an hallucination afflicting even unto tears. Such a man may indeed deserve success in his endeavours; but he cannot command it: his dream is brilliant, but deceptive; and he must soon awaken from it to all the bitter agony of disappointed hope. We say it without vaunting, our stupidity is a result *sui generis*—a phenomenon to be contemplated with wonder—not to be discussed without a certain awe—to be analysed only by intellects of the first order—obscurely to be comprehended even by them—and never to be parallelled by any. Many persons are called by courtesy stupid, when in point of fact they are only smoky, or perhaps in a degree muzzy; but, for us, we are not only decidedly stupid, but we are sunken, lost, buried, immeasurable toises[19] down in the nethermost depths of the lowest gulf of the last vortex of stupidity. Not one solitary ray of intelligence relieves the dense gloom that enwraps our faculties. Friends and foes alike acknowledge that our state is one to excite the deepest sympathies of the philanthropist, as well as the unbounded amazement of the psychologist and pathognomist.[20] Hence it is that we are spared the necessity of all that exertion and solicitude which break the hearts of thousands. Our stupidity is our sheet-anchor; the bulwark of our strength; the pioneer that levels all impediments before us; the talisman whose touch converts ideas into gold. By means of our stupidity we flourish; we prosper; we laugh and grow fat; we are monthly winning greener laurels, and hourly getting on at an ever-accelerated pace, towards the Goal of Fame. Would that all mankind could imitate us!—could be as stupid and triumphant as we! But this may not be: some must be wise and others otherwise; what is one man's meat is another man's poison; that which is bred in the bone will not come out of the flesh; we cannot put old heads on young shoulders; and one man is born with a silver spoon in his mouth, and another with a wooden ladle.

* * * * * * * * * *

What, Gellert!—What! another anticipatory Peter-Pindarism?[21] Then, sir, *es ist um Sie geschehn*, it is all over with you; you have dished yourself. All the water in the Liffey, distributed into wash-hand basins—all the truncheon soaps in Sackville-street[22] would not purify you. *Hic niger est*[23]— we attach the label to your brow—you are black—

"To that complexion have you come at last."[24]

We abandon you—we turn you up—we fling you down—we cast you from us as Lear cast Goneril—we place you high upon a dusty shelf—there

"To lie in cold oblivion, and to—roost."[25]

You have repeatedly disregarded the principles established by Quintilian[26] and illustrated by La Motte[27]—and you shall pay the penalty. We remember the vow we have registered.[28] Ours is the stern determination of Bethlem Gabor when he thrust St. Leon[29] into the dungeon to woo, upon an empty stomach,

"Silence and Darkness, solemn sisters, twins!"[30]

We now close your volume with six and thirty seals of black wax, each bearing the impression of a Gorgon's head. And the volume so closed let no Irishman henceforth open,

𝕼uotɧ

THE OUT-AND-OUTER.

A SIXTY-DROP DOSE OF LAUDANUM.

Laudanum: from *laudare*, to praise, this drug being one of the most praiseworthy in the *Materia Medica.—Cullen.*[1]

You may exhibit thirty, fifty, eighty, or a hundred drops, to produce sleep; everything depends on the temperament; but where your object is to excite and enliven, I recommend you to stop short at SIXTY.—*Brown.*[2]

"A dose to dose Society!" quoth the Trumpeter—"then it must be uncommon strong, comrade!"—*Adventures of a Half-crown.*[3]

So saying, he shed sixty drops of the liquid in his black flask into a cup, muttering mysterious words all the while.—*The Rival Magicians.*[4]

————————————————————Count o'er
————————————————————threescore!
Childe Harold, c. iii. *st.* xxxiv.[5]

Drop One.

Many literary beginnings are difficult; many the reverse. Where there is much taste there is much hesitation: where energy predominates the novice enters on his career with a bold and joyous heart, eager to scale "the steep where Fame's proud temple shines afar."[6]

"Thus poets in their youth begin in gladness,
Though thereof comes in the end despondency and madness."[7]

Our first efforts, it is true, are not always our happiest. Neither are our first loves. Yet both are most dear to our recollections; for with all first things there is associated a certain mysterious magic. Who are they that can forget their first kiss—the first hand they pressed—the first fiddle they played (some few play this through life)—the first time they bade their friends farewell—

"Lo di ch' han detto a dolci amici a Dio"—[8]

or "the first dark day of nothingness"[9] after the death of a relative? Byron has celebrated the old Athenians as

"First in the race that led to Glory's goal,"[10]

and Moore deeply excites our sympathies by his song to the American damsel whom he met when a little girl, on the banks of the Schuylkill, all wool, furs, muffs and boas—

"When first I met thee, warm and young."[11]

We have all heard the antiquarian ditty concerning the period at which yews were first seen in burying-grounds—

"O do you remember the first time eye met yew?"[12]

We recall our "first grey hair"[13] which brought us wisdom,—the first of April, which made fools of us again—the first day of the year, with its bells,

—"and that sweet time
When first we heard their ding-dong chime."[14]

And shall not *I* hereafter call to mind the first specimen of the genuine "Black Drop"[15] that ever trickled from my pen with that mingling "of sweet and bitter fancies"[16] inseparable from a review of whatever is interesting in the Past?

Drop Two.

It is impossible that a man can ever make a transcendant artist, that is, that he can excel in music, sculpture, painting, &c. unless he be endowed with a capacious understanding. Just principles with reference to the Fine Arts cannot, in my opinion, coexist with illiberal or erroneous notions upon general subjects. Persuade me who can that Nincompoop Higglethwaites, Esquire, who knows neither the world nor himself—who has studied neither books nor men—can possess a genius for music! A genius for eliciting sounds of all degrees of intonation through the medium of certain machinery I readily grant him;—but how can he pretend to move the passions,—he who has himself no passions—who knows nothing about them—who regards them as superfluities—and the sum total of whose ambition is to become a correct copyist of the rules of his art? A musician, forsooth! Bah! He has about as much title to the name of musician as an ape has to that of man.

Drop Three.

This earth may be characterised as the Great Emporium of the Possible, from whence contingencies are for ever issuing like exports from a warehouse. And Necessity is to the moral world what Fashion is to the social—the parent of perpetual fluctuations. The changes through which men and nations, and their feelings, manners, and destinies are passing and must pass, are not experimental merely; they are superinduced by irresistible, though to a philosophical eye obvious, agencies. When all the varieties of all those changes shall be exhausted, "then is the end nigh;" the Emporium will be thrown down as useless; and the Possible, taught a lesson by the Past, will thenceforth take refuge in spheres from which vicissitude and destruction shall be altogether excluded.

Drop Four.

Sir L. Bulwer's last portrait—that prefixed to his *Leila*—I take to be a total failure—in fact, a regular humbug.[17] The look is precisely that of a man whom the apparition of a long-legged spider on the wall is about to send into strong hysterics. And such a look was called up for the nonce! Surely the author of Pelham must have lost all his sympathy with the ludicrous when he suffered this to be thrust under the public eye. The affectation was the more supererogatory as Bulwer is really a well-favoured gentleman, the everyday expression of his physiognomy being of quite as stare-arresting an order as he need wish to see transferred either to canvas or foolscap.

Drop Five.

If you desire to padlock a punster's lips never tell him that you loathe puns: he would then perpetrate his atrocities for the sake of annoying you. Choose another course: always affect to misunderstand him. When an excruciator has been inflicted on you, open wide your eyes and mouth for a minute, and then, closing them again abruptly, shake your head, and exclaim, "Very mysterious!" This kills him.

Drop Six.

I should far and away prefer being a great necromancer to being a great writer or even a great fighter. My natural propensities lead me rather to seek out modes of astonishing mankind than of edifying them. Herein I and my propensities are clearly wrong; but somehow I find that almost every thing that is natural in me is wrong also.

Drop Seven.

The idea entertained by all girls under twenty of literary men is, that they are *very clever*. Distinctions between one order of intellect and another they can never be brought to comprehend. With them the sonnetteer and the epic poet are on a common level as to talent; the sonnetteer, however, is usually the greater pet, as he has more small talk.

𝔇rop 𝔈ight.

Apropos of sonnets, one of the choicest in our language is that addressed to Dr. Kitchener.[18] I met with it[19] many years ago in some obscure publication, which, I suppose, has since gone the way of all paper:

> "Knight of the Kitchen—telescopic cook—
>   Beef-slicing proser—pudding-building bard—
>   Swallower of dripping—gulper down of lard—
> Equally great in beaufet[20] and in book !
> With a prophetic eye that seer did look
>   Into Fate's records who bestowed thy name,
>   By which thou floatest down the tide of fame
> As floats the jackstraw down the gurgling brook.
> He saw thee destined, by the boiler's side,
>   With veal and mutton endless war to wage:
> Had he looked further he perchance had spied
>   Thee ever scribbling, scribbling, page by page;
> Then to thy head his hand he'd have applied,
>   And said,—'This child will be a HUMBUG OF THE AGE.'"

𝔇rop 𝔑ine.

The longing which men continually feel for *rest* while engaged in the struggles and stormy turmoils of Life, is an unconscious tending of the heart towards its natural goal, the Grave.

𝔇rop 𝔗en.

My impression is that the Irish were not originally so warlike a nation at all as is popularly supposed. The Danes unquestionably beat them hollow in military ardour, as well as prowess and skill. *Imprimis,*[21] the Danes were always the invaders, the aggressors,—the Irish standing only on the defensive, *pro aris et focis.*[22] Secondly, the Irish bards usually designate the Danes as *an fionn-treabh sar-bhorb,*—"that fair-haired and most fierce tribe," manifestly leaving it to be implied that they (the bards) were not accustomed to consider the Irish as equally fierce. In the third place, the Danes first taught the Irish the use of many battle-weapons, and, among others, of the curt-axe,[23] so formidable afterwards in the hands of the galloglass.[24] If the Irish had been by nature a very martial people, instinct would have directed them to the inventing of those implements of destruction for themselves. Fourthly, the successful result of the Battle of Clontarf,[25] instead of being spoken of by Irish writers as a thing of course, is for the most part made a theme for wonder and extraordinary exultation; as if the Irish had been habituated to such drubbings by their enemies that a solitary victory on their own side was to be celebrated as scarcely less than miraculous. Besides, all are agreed that the aborigines of Ireland, the Firbolgs, meddled very little with cold iron, except when they took the scythe or spade in hand; and there is no satisfactory evidence that the Battle of Moy-Tuire[26] drove them out of the island, or did more than disperse the great bulk of them over it. The northern portions of the Irish tribes I do believe were fond enough of war, both in the way of business and pleasure; but the Heberian Milesians[27] appear to have thought that they had on occasions too much of a good thing. Upon native Irish valour no slur can ever be cast; but it certainly owes much of its renown nevertheless to the example set it by the Goths. It is remarkable in fact that the dark-haired races have ever been more prone to the cultivation of arts than arms. Three-fourths of all the eminent musicians and painters of Europe have been dark. On the other hand, disdain of the refinements of social life, impetuosity, and fierceness bordering on savageism appear to be the prominent natural characteristics of the light-haired. The happy—not the *golden*—medium is found in the auburn, who have more equanimity of disposition than either, as well as more genius for historical and metaphysical research, greater mental flexibility, and, generally speaking, superior capability of adapting themselves to any position that circumstances require them to occupy.

Drop Eleven.

Touching hair,—I never cared what the colour of a woman's was. My love laughs at locks as well as locksmiths.[28] Still I have made my observations, in an unobtrusive way, and with the eye of a simpleton. Red-haired women, I have discovered, are usually the liveliest of their sex, but also the most changeable-(never, however, *double*)-minded. There is an absolute passion for coquetry in them: you can no more steady them to one object, *i.e.* yourself, of course, than you can fix a ball of quicksilver. A very vain man, if he have more regard for his soul's weal than his heart's, will be particularly sweet on this class, for they never fail to teach him by many bitter lessons all the hollowness of the philosophy of self-love. The raven-black are not always, as people fancy, the most impassioned—unless they happen to be from Spain or Italy. Of the brown it is difficult to predicate any thing in a general way, except that their perceptions are usually very acute;—their affections also are easily won and easily wounded; they are of the nervous temperament; and I apprehend that more broken hearts are found among these than among the others. I have noticed that as to both intellect and feeling much in all cases depends on the size of the brain, and more on its activity. I believe, but am not positive, that D'Israeli (the Younger)[29] asserts that very great self-possession in women indicates want of heart. I disagree: in my opinion it merely shows a capacity for concentration of thought. But I perceive I am wandering from my text; and so, lest I lose myself altogether, I stop short without further apology.

Drop Twelve.

The most opaque of all the masques that people assume to conceal their real characters is enthusiasm. In the eyes of women enthusiasm appears so amiable that they believe no impostor *could* counterfeit it: to men it seems so ridiculous that they are satisfied nobody *would*.

Drop Thirteen.

It is a singular fact, that the great majority of French authors, whatever the nature of their subject, write as if they were haranguing.

Drop Fourteen.

Poets call women light-footed. I do not know upon what ground. Sauntering one day along, rather at my ease, I passed forty-seven of them in succession between Carlisle Bridge[30] and Granby Row.[31] As to their dancing, it never satisfied me. There always appeared to me some mysterious hugger-muggery about the movements: it was their drapery that danced,—not they. Stage *danseuses* of course I make no account of here, as they are either "to the manner born,"[32] or trained to it, and people stare at them as monstrosities.

Drop Fifteen.

If every individual were to develop his inmost dispositions to the world in writing, publishers would undoubtedly realize large fortunes by the novelties wherewith we should see the press teeming. What can be stranger, *par exemple*, than the fact that I, who, with all my sins, am not, I hope, wickeder than my neighbours, should be haunted by a continual longing to become a captain of robbers? Not that I should care much about the plunder. It is the idea of exercising influence, of controlling and coercing, that captivates my fancy. But why should I not wish rather to exercise the same influence over the mild and the amiable? Is it, that an involuntary though fallacious association connects in my mind mildness and amiability with weakness, and invests force of even the rudest kind with an air of majesty and grandeur? I cannot tell; but the fact is as I record it. Let the metaphysicians explain it in their own way.

𝔇rop 𝔖ixteen.

The modern English and Irish fashion adopted by women of wearing the hair all in a clump at the west of the head is most detestably execrable. My blood curdles when I think of it.

𝔇rop 𝔖eventeen.

There are some few women who will despise you for loving them, but none who will *hate* you without a much better reason.

𝔇rop 𝔈ighteen.

All the blank-versifying in Europe to the contrary notwithstanding, revenge of personal wrongs is a mean passion. It is the gratification of self-love in one of its most abominable forms. I am convinced that none besides grovelling minds are capable of harbouring it. Remark that hurricanes are most inclined to prostrate mud hovels: they can only rage impotently around the pyramid whose apex kisses heaven. So, the momentary sway of the fiercer passions over elevated minds leaves no perceptible trace behind: it is in base natures alone that it stimulates to havoc and destruction.

𝔇rop ℜineteen.

From the moment that any man tells me that he cannot understand the humour of Rabelais, I never care to speak to him, or to hear him speak to me, on literary topics.

𝔇rop 𝔗wenty.

There is one phenomenon sometimes attendant on dreaming, at least on *my* dreaming, which, as far as I can discover, no writer, not even Macnish,[33] has ever noticed. I allude to the marvellous power which the mind possesses during sleep of *re-creating the same images over and over with no exercise of memory on the part of the dreamer.* To me this is a mystery altogether inexplicable, nor have I ever met with any one capable of clearing it up. As the meaning of my italics may not be exactly divined, I will condescend to details. I dream, for instance, that I am compelled to traverse four and twenty chambers in succession:—let me call them A, B, C, &c. Each of these chambers is characterised by some architectural or other peculiarity of its own—a pillar perhaps in the centre of it—a strange picture on the wall—a sphynx on a marble table, or some other distinguishing feature. I journey through the entire number from A to Z; and by the time I have reached Z, I have lost all remembrance of the preceding three and twenty chambers. *I am conscious of the loss of the remembrance.* Very well. On reaching Z, I am compelled to return through the chambers back again to

A. And here we have the mystery. For now, as I open each door and enter, my memory, dormant up to the moment of my entrance, *revives*, and I recognise at once, *in the correct order of their succession*, the objects I saw as I passed along first. Having arrived at A, I again resume my journey to Z, and the same series of anomalies takes place. When I am in B, I have not the faintest recollection of C, yet, on re-entering C, I recall it again distinctly and vividly. I have no notion, however, what D may contain, till, upon opening the door, I recognise every thing. And so I progress to Z; and then travel back a second time to A, only to re-commence my involuntary pilgrimage, which is repeated perhaps thirty times over. The grand puzzle here is, *How* the imagery of the chambers is created. *Primâ facie*,[34] it would seem as though it existed altogether independent of *my* consent or that of any of my faculties. Of course it cannot so exist; but of one thing I am certain,—that what is called imagination has no share in creating it. Imagination is always conscious of exercising its own power. Moreover, unless there be a determinate effort for the purpose, the forms it produces are never twice the same. Now, in me, there is no such effort; there is no effort of any kind. My will is passive throughout. *I do not know what it is that I am about to see as I open the door.* Besides, what the will helps to fabricate the will can help to destroy; and I am painfully conscious that I cannot destroy the minutest portion of the scenery before me. The English Opium-Eater's dreams about the staircases of Piranesi will perhaps occur to the reader.[35] Between those dreams and mine, however, there is scarcely one salient point of resemblance. I doubt even whether the Opium-Eater ever had such dreams as I have been endeavouring to describe: if he had, they would have appeared too remarkable to one of his metaphysical habits of thought to be passed over in silence. I may add, that I regret he should not have been visited by them; for I believe him to be one of the few men in England qualified to supply a theory in explanation of the phenomenon which they involve.

Drop Twenty-one.

People never pardon an *avowed* want of sympathy with themselves, because it is want of respect. Xanthus was one day beginning in my presence with a rapt air Mrs. Hemans'[36] poem, "I dream of all things free," when I drily edged in, "Freestone among the rest, I presume." This *mauvaise plaisanterie*[37] cost me an acquaintance. Xanthus was hurt, not so much because I did not participate in his enthusiasm, as because I took no trouble to disguise my want of participation in it. It is the way of the world. Most of us prefer the dissimulation that flatters us to the sincerity that wounds.

Drop Twenty-two.

Not that I would insist that we are always to blame for our preference. False politeness may in no case be a virtue, but unnecessary cruelty is at all times a vice. I must hate it, in whatever shape it comes. Quarrelling with the truth and quarrelling with the motive that dictates the utterance of the truth, are two distinct things. It is lawful for me to grieve over the *malus animus*[38] that levels a shaft against my self-love. I contract an aversion towards the archer, because he is barbarous in the abstract, not because he wounds *me*. My feelings would not be a jot less bitter if he had victimized my enemy instead.

Drop Twenty-three.

The most exquisite pleasure of which we are susceptible is the state of feeling that follows a sudden cessation of intense pain. Reflection on this truth might make us melancholy, if we did not remember that our final agonies must be succeeded by repose.

Drop Twenty-four.

Want of gratitude hardly deserves to be branded as *in*gratitude. A mere negation of all sentiment should not be mistaken for the blackest of vices. Favours are often slighted from constitutional insensibility; or they may be involuntarily forgotten. Where they are, wrongs are forgotten just as soon. He who serves others and is not thanked may find that he can injure them without being hated. Heaven forefend, however, that he should make the experiment for the sake of philosophising on the result!

Drop Twenty-five.

I have noticed that those men who give bad characters of women have usually worse characters themselves.

Drop Twenty-six.

L. E. L. (poor L. E. L.!) remarks in her *Romance and Reality*[39] that memory is the least egotistical of all the faculties, forasmuch as it rather recalls to us the individual we have conversed with or the book we have read than the feelings we have experienced. I am inclined to differ. Wherever the memory of our feelings is vague it must be because the feelings themselves were equally vague. For my own part I have always a much better recollection of the emotions that were excited in my mind by hearing a certain air or perusing a particular story than I have of the music or the volume itself.

Drop Twenty-seven.

None but exalted spirits, who can calmly look down upon human events and human frailties as from an eminence, are capable of unalterable friendship; for none but they can calculate beforehand the errors they shall have to pardon as well as the excellences they can prize. Even those persons, however, though they may feel friendship, can rarely inspire it;—so much more difficult is it for mediocrity to appreciate nobleness than for nobleness to tolerate mediocrity!

Drop Twenty-eight.

Distrust nine girls in ten who instead of talking to you on a first introduction listen with apparent deference to all that your foolish tongue utters to them. Depend upon it that they are making a study of your character for their own purposes. I except the tenth girl because she is a *niaise*,[40] and has really nothing to say. It may be supposed that some of the sex remain silent on these occasions from bashfulness. I think the supposition a mistake. I have met proud girls and cold girls, and silent girls and silly girls. So have others. But when and where has any body ever met with a bashful girl? Never and nowhere.

Drop Twenty-nine.

A friend once told me that Catiline[41] was as great a man as Cæsar, but not so fortunate. I contested his assertion and maintained that the failure of Catiline's enterprises proved his mind to have been of an inferior order. I think so still. In my opinion wisdom and circumspection are indispensable essentials of greatness. A great man must not only be able to foresee what *ought* to succeed, but what *will* succeed. He must conquer all adverse circumstances. Napoleon's greatness consisted not in *being* Emperor of France, but in having made himself so. Neither was his defeat by Russia half so fatal to his reputation in the eyes of Europe as the folly he had evinced in tempting it.

Drop Thirty.

While as yet we are young—while we are unhackneyed in the sodden ways of this world—our souls dwell in our eyes, and beauty is our only loadstar. Nothing has such charms for us as the society of a being who superadds grace and animation to her native loveliness. The sense of existence is deepened and quickened within us before her. A thousand newborn pulses of tremulous delight agitate our bosoms. We are tenants of a sphere apart. Fancy is intoxicated with the present and anticipates a future all triumph and transport. We stand spell-chained within the charmed circle of an enchantress. The depth of our devotion to beauty may be estimated by the aversion we feel at this time of life for its antipodes. Sex does not so much enter into our calculations as philosophers think. An ugly woman shocks us. She may be a De Stael;[42] but what do we care at eighteen for metaphysics, from the lips of man or woman? She is ugly; and disgust and weariness constitute our paramount feelings. We are spiritless, melancholy, *lonely*. Time lags on his long path, and the burden of life presses us down towards the clay we half wish to mingle with for ever. The folding-doors of the imagination are flung to with a sound, sullen and hope-destroying, which reverberates through the innermost hollows of the heart. The desire of signalizing ourselves languishes. Fame appears as valueless as its common type, a bubble on the water. The world is robed in gloom. How mighty are even momentary influences in early youth! Well! a few years and all this sensibility passes away. Beauty and ugliness can move us no more. All that is left to us is the ability to ponder on our former feelings—to laugh at or weep for our illusions, as our temperament inclines.

> "But if we laugh at any mortal thing
> 'Tis that we may not weep; and if we weep
> 'Tis that our nature cannot always bring
> Itself to apathy."[43]

Are we the happier for the change? Certainly we are not the quieter. We create less agitation in the drawing-room, but more every-where else. Alas! we are scarcely the happier either. While we can neither adore nor abhor as of yore we are compelled to praise and scold much louder than ever. We care nothing for any thing, yet are forced to seem interested in every thing. One only hour remains to us in which we are privileged to throw off the mask and be ourselves,—and that is our death hour. Then, however, the world pays us little heed,—and we—small blame to us—return the compliment.

Drop Thirty-one.

The African Magician in *Aladdin*, traversing Isfahan, and crying out for his own private purposes, *Who will exchange old lamps for new ones?*[44] is an excellent vaticinatory hit at the *soi-disant*[45] Illuminati of modern times.

Drop Thirty-two.

Aladdin displayed infinite tact in leaving to the Sultan the honor of putting the finishing hand to the building of his palace. The Sultan was then in the position of a critic to whom a great poet submits an epic, and who adds a line to the end of it: the critic may boast that he has assisted in the composition of the work; and the Sultan might have said, I and Aladdin have constructed this palace. His vanity was tickled; and his son-in-law rose at least five stories high in his opinion. Aladdin, however, afterwards spoiled all by his impatience. The Sultan was too slow a coach for him; and he had recourse to the lamp.[46] Here was a want of *savoir faire*, for which he suffered accordingly. It is thus that the cleverest men perpetually make asses of themselves in the long run,—marring in a quarter of an hour by some piece of headstrong *gaucherie* all the advantages secured to them by previous years of prudence and industry.

Drop Thirty-three.

This same palace of Aladdin, though reared in one night, had not its parallel for beauty,—and would have remained the most durable of earthly edifices—a wonder for all after-ages—if the genii that had constructed it had not of their own accord removed it:[47]—they bore it away to an unknown land, and it returned no more. So, love at first sight, the birth of an instant, strikes nevertheless its roots far deeper in the heart than the affection which takes months in maturing,—and never could depart or die if they who excited it did not themselves contribute to abolish its existence. For they are fickle in their homage—or they were false from the beginning—or they betray a baseness of character long hidden—or time furrows their cheeks—and then the love evanishes for ever,—going down, with no hope of resurrection, into the deepest of all moral graves—the grave of indifference.

Drop Thirty-four.

Very crafty persons may be at once known by the great breadth between their eyes. I have remarked that persons with this peculiarity of feature are also better qualified than others to judge of physical beauty and the harmonies of external proportion.

Drop Thirty-five.

When you pen a common-place you should always strain a point to redeem it by a *jeu-de-mot*.[48] Yet perhaps I am unphilosophical in my advice, for most great truths are essentially common-place. So, for that matter, are all the dogmas and dictates of reason—the reason of many, *c'est à dire*,[49] not of all, for what is hight[50] reason with the Old-clothesmen is high treason with the Purple-and-Fine-lineners.

Drop Thirty-six.

Life is a game which perversely varies its character according to the age at which we play it: in youth, when much may be lost, it is a game of chance; in manhood, when little remains to be won, it is a game of skill.

𝔇𝔯𝔬𝔭 𝔗𝔥𝔦𝔯𝔱𝔶-𝔰𝔢𝔟𝔢𝔫.

Gay people commit more follies than gloomy; but gloomy people commit greater follies.

𝔇𝔯𝔬𝔭 𝔗𝔥𝔦𝔯𝔱𝔶-𝔢𝔦𝔤𝔥𝔱.

The intellect of poets feeds their vanity; that of philosophers counteracts theirs.

𝔇𝔯𝔬𝔭 𝔗𝔥𝔦𝔯𝔱𝔶-𝔫𝔦𝔫𝔢.

No neglect, no slight, no contumely from one of his own sex can mortify a man who has been much flattered and courted by women. No matter from what source it may emanate, he will always and necessarily attribute it to envy.

𝔇𝔯𝔬𝔭 𝔉𝔬𝔯𝔱𝔶.

Perseverance has enabled me to find my way to XL. Whether it will ever enable me to find *the* way to excel, *reste à savoir.*[51]

𝔇𝔯𝔬𝔭 𝔉𝔬𝔯𝔱𝔶-𝔬𝔫𝔢.

Many persons have experienced a strange sensation of uneasiness and apprehension, as it were, of undefined evil, at hearing the knolling of a deep bell in a great city at noon, amid the bustle of life and business. The source of this sensation I take to lie, not so much in the mere sound of the bell as in the knowledge that its monitions, of whatever character they may be, are wholly undictated by human feelings. We are more or less jealous of the interference of our fellow-beings in our concerns, even where their motives are purely disinterested, because, in spite of us, we associate with it the idea of ostentation and intrusiveness. But, a solemn voice from a mass of inanimate metal, especially when the hum and turmoil of the world are around us, is like the tremendous appeal of a dead man's aspect; and its power over us becomes the greater because of its own total unconsciousness of the existence of that power.

𝔇𝔯𝔬𝔭 𝔉𝔬𝔯𝔱𝔶-𝔱𝔴𝔬.

It is seldom that any one who is ingenious at finding arguments is ingenuous in stating them. A clear-headed man, for all that, may be a very candid one; and a great misfortune it is for him to be so. Being always reasonable, he is of course, from the nature of society, always engaged in controverting some absurdity. Hence *tracasseries*[52] with his friends, and all those other kinds of asseries before the world, to which these usually lead.

Drop Forty-three.

The world has less tolerance for novel theorists upon morals and metaphysics than for even *soi-disant* discoverers in the sciences. The reason is obvious. Almost every man confesses to himself his ignorance of all things relating to the mysteries of the external world; but it is difficult to persuade any man that he is not himself the best judge of what passes in his own mind.

Drop Forty-four.

If a combination of the Sublime and the Sarcastic be possible, I fancy I find it in two lines by Gleim:[53]

> Und Friedrich weint?
> Gieb ihm die Herrschaft über dich, O, Welt,
> Weil er, ob auch ein König, weinen kann![54]

> And Frederic weeps?
> Give him dominion over thee, O, Earth!
> For this, that he, albeit a king, can weep.

Drop Forty-five.

Victories, after the lapse of some years, ruin a country even more certainly than defeats. The money which governments raise from speculators for carrying on successful wars must be repaid to them with interest; and as it is the nature of wealth to go on producing wealth an enormous accumulation of the circulating medium must take place in the coffers of the few to the detriment of the many. The larger party tending to pauperism in an inverse ratio with the augmenting prosperity of the smaller party, affairs daily grow more generally worse; until at last the very continuance in existence of the nation becomes a problem to be solved only by a revolution.

Drop Forty-six.

Experience is a jewel picked up by a wrecked mariner on a desert coast—a picture-frame, purchased at a preposterous cost, when decay has done its duty on your finest Titian[55]—a prosing lecturer who sermonises a sleeping congregation—a warden who alarms the citadel when the enemy has broken through the gates—a melancholy moon after a day of darkness and tempest—a sentinel who mounts guard over a pillaged house—a surveyor who takes the dimensions of the pit we have tumbled into—a monitor that, like Friar Bacon's Brazen Head,[56] tells us that *Time is past*—a lantern brought to us after we have traversed a hundred morasses in the dark and are entering an illuminated village—a pinnace on the strand found when the tide has ebbed away—a morning lamp lighted in our saloon when our guests have departed, revealing rueful ruin—or any thing else equally pertinent and impertinent. Why then do we panegyrise it so constantly? Why do we take and make all opportunities to boast of our own? Because, wretched worms that we are! we are so proud of our despicable knowledge that we cannot afford to shroud from view even that portion of it which we have purchased at the price of our happiness. Parade and ostentation—ostentation and parade for ever!—"they are the air we breathe—without them we expire."[57]

Drop Forty-seven.

"How populous—how vital is the grave!" cried Young.[58] He was in the right in the sense he contemplated. He was in the right, too, in a separate sense. The grave is vital to the renown of those great men who had none during life. "Silent as the grave," say some:—bah! the grave is your only betrayer of secrets. It is the *camera obscura* which the student of human nature must enter to behold sights unrevealable by "garish day,"[59] and "amid the hum, the crowd, and shock of men."[60] Stagnant waters picture the sky better than stormy:

> "Nicht im trüben Schlamm der Bache
> Der von wilden Regenguszen schwillt,
> Auf des stillen Baches eb'ner Flache
> Spiegelt sich das Sonnenbild."[61]

"The day of a man's death is better than the day of his birth," saith Solomon.[62] To the man of genius at least it proves so. If his friends do not embalm him like the Egyptians, or give him money like the Greeks, to pay Charon his fare, they do more—they write recommendatory letters to Posterity in his behalf. Yes: fame, like Mrs. Shelley's Frankenstein,[63] is a genuine production of the sepulchre. "The night-mare Life-in-Death is she."[64] She springs up from the dust of him who seeks her no more, as the phoenix rises from its own ashes. "The grave-dews winnowing through the rotting clay"[65] are distilled into an *elixir vitæ* which, unlike St. Leon's,[66] turns out no burden to its possessor. The season of requital is come, and the crowd cry out, *Le roi est mort, vive le roi!*[67] What is the reason? How is the anomaly explained? Why all this hullaballoo, begotten on a sudden? Because the man *is* dead: because he is *out of the way*. He is "fallen from his high estate."[68] He has ceased personally to excite the wonder and wrath and envy of others. His works are before the world, to be sure, and that is mortifying, but he, the worker, is behind the world, and that is fortifying. No fear of pleasing him now by flattery. He can no more "hear the voice of the charmer, charm he never so wisely."[69] Walls have ears, quoth the proverb, but those of the tomb are an exception. "Can honor's voice provoke the silent dust"[70] to smile a reply to a compliment? Low in the arms of the Mighty Mother he lies, no more the unconscious stirrer-up of heart-burnings among those whom he overlooked, but hated not, and who hated him because they could not overlook him. Therefore let the shell and lute now resound with his praises! Ah! after all, human nature has been libelled. "We are not stocks and stones."[71] We are glad of all opportunities to effect a compromise between our jealousy and our justice. And is not this much? Let him who thinks it little remodel society upon a plan that shall enable men to possess passions "as though they possessed them not,"[72] for otherwise he is scarce likely to be satisfied on this side of the Millennium.

Drop Forty-eight.

Horace Smith's shop-board with "Going, Staymaker,"[73] is very good, and better still if true; but I certainly once saw over a gateway the notification, "John Reilly, Carpenter *and Timberyard*."[74]

Drop Forty-nine.

The Irish Annalists sustain the literary character of their country famously. I like samples of style such as those *que voici*. "Mac-Giolla-Ruadh plunged into the river and swam to the shore, but was drowned before he landed." "The Kinel-Owen defeated the Kinel-Connell with terrible slaughter, *for* Niall Garbh O'Donnell lost one leg in the battle." "The Lord Lieutenant and Maurice Fitzgerald then returned to Ireland, both in good health, except that Maurice Fitzgerald caught a fever on the way, from which he did not recover." "Hugh Roe now sent word to the Italians to come and assist him, but this they were not then able to do, for they had all been killed sometime before by," &c. Pope, it occurs to me, has an Irish line in his *Essay on Man*:

> Virtuous and vicious every man must be;
> *Few* in the extreme, but *all* in the *degree*.[75]

And Schiller another in his *Robbers*:

> "Death's kingdom—*waked* from its *eternal* sleep!"[76]

And Milton another in his *Paradise Lost*:

> "And in the *lowest* deep a *lower* deep."[77]

Drop Fifty.

Poets are the least sympathising of breathing beings. They have few or none of the softer feelings. One cause of their deficiency in these is that they have already vented them in verse. Pour the wine out of a flask and you leave the flask void. A second and better reason for their insensibility is this, that two master-sentiments cannot coexist in one bosom. The imagination refuses to share its sovereignty with the heart. "One fire tires out another's burning,"[78] says Shakespeare, who, I fancy, took a much deeper interest in the fate of his own dramas than in all the affairs of the world besides. The use of poetry to poets is that it preserves them from great crimes and gross vices. If it quenches every spark of sympathy in their breasts, on the other hand it absorbs them too much to allow them to seek a reputation by throat-cutting or city-burning. Negatively poetry is thus of use to mankind. With regard to its positive use to them, as this is an age of discoveries we may perhaps find it out by-and-by.

Drop Fifty-one.

A translator from Spanish, French, High Dutch, &c. should always improve on his original if he can. Most continental writers are dull plodders, and require spurring and furbishing. I see no harm in now and then giving them a lift and a shove. If I receive two or three dozen of sherry for a dinner-party, and by some chemical process can convert the sherry into champagne, my friends are all the merrier, and nobody is a loser. As to translations from the Oriental tongues, no one should attempt them, unless for the purpose of adducing them as documentary evidences in support of some antiquarian theory, about which the world does not care three halfpence. By the way, I submissively insist that Mr. Lane's new version of the *Arabian Nights*,[79] now coming out in numbers, is the most quackish jackassicality of latter days. Mr. Lane is a good writer and a shrewd observer, but he cannot—no man can—Europeanize Orientalism. One might as well think of introducing Harlequin's costume into the Court of Chancery.

Drop Fifty-two.

Shelley was remarkable for very bright eyes; so was La Harpe;[80] and so was Burns.[81] Maturin's eyes were mild and meditative, but not particularly lustrous: when he raised them suddenly, however, the effect was startling. Byron's did not strike the observer as much as might have been expected, probably because of his ill health. As De Quincey correctly remarks, the state of the eyes greatly depends on that of the stomach.[82] Carleton has a fine intelligent eye, filled with deep, speculative thought, "looking before and after."[83] My idea, nevertheless, is, that in general too much stress is laid on the expression of the eyes. In many faces their supposed character is derived from the other features. What eye can be more beautiful and expressive than that of an infant, who has no passions, and whose mind is as yet a blank?

Drop Fifty-three.

I disapprove of encouraging the working classes to read too much. One inevitable result of their knowledge must be, that their wants will become multiplied in a greater degree than their resources. For a successful and summary method, however, of enlightening the multitude by means of books, I refer readers to the history of the Caliph Omar and the Alexandrian Library.[84]

Drop Fifty-four.

"Murder," says Shakespeare, "though it hath no tongue, will speak with most miraculous organ."[85] Here is evidence that the existence of the organ of Destructiveness was not unknown to our ancestors. Or perhaps "will speak" points to the nineteenth century, and the passage is a prophecy. I neither know nor care.

Drop Fifty-five.

Apropos of poetical prophecies, Shelley has recorded a remarkable prediction by Byron anent the mode of his (Shelley's) own death:

> ———————— " 'O, ho!
> You talk as in times past,' said Maddalo.
> ''Tis strange men change not: you were ever still
> Among Christ's flock a perilous infidel,—
> A wolf for the meek lambs: *if you can't swim,*
> *Beware of Providence!*' I looked at him,
> But the gay smile had faded from his eye."
> *Shelley's Julian and Maddalo.*[86]

Drop Fifty-six.

One word more upon Craniology. Whence, I should like to learn, springs the propensity to general ridicule?—to scout most things and people as humbugs? Spurzheim's theory[87] makes it a product of deficient Veneration and great Destructiveness and Congruity, *i.e.* Wit or Humour. I largely doubt. Rabelais lacked Congruity; so did Swift. Curran's[88] masque exhibits but a moderate share of it. In Godwin and Wordsworth it appears full; yet to both wit is an abhorrence. Voltaire had large Veneration. Sterne's head, it is true, answers to the required *laid ideal*,[89] but making Sterne's head do

duty for the head of every man who is the reverse of stern is something too
bad. For myself I place faith in but four of the thirty-two organs:
Self-esteem, Secretiveness, Firmness, and Hope; but this last I would call
Castle-building; and I conceive that it and Ideality are the same faculty.

Drop Fifty-seven.

One of the finest passages in modern fiction is the meeting between
Watson and Welbeck in Brockden Brown's *Arthur Mervyn*.[90] The stern
concentrated rage of the avenger—the more awful from its calmness—and
the wordless resignation and despair of the wretched seducer are portrayed
with a terrible faithfulness to nature. The introductory words of Watson—
"It is well. The hour my vengeance has long thirsted for is arrived.
Welbeck! that my first words could strike thee dead! They will so, if thou
hast any claim to the name of man,"—prepare us for the harrowing
disclosures that follow—the death of Watson's sister "from anguish and a
broken heart," and the suicide of their lunatic father[91] in consequence. And
when Watson, having narrated the latter circumstance, draws a pistol from
his breast, and, approaching Welbeck, places the muzzle against his
forehead, saying with forced calmness—"This is the instrument with
which the deed was performed," who, even of those that cannot *feel* the
scene, but must acknowledge the graphic nature of the conception? The
duel, also, across the table, with its unlooked for result in the death of
Watson, and the whole of the subsequent narrative of the interment of the
corpse in the cellar—how peculiarly, but how powerfully they are given!
Our interest in the entire affair is heightened by the singular character of
Welbeck, who, by the way, is not at all like the Falkland of *Caleb Williams*,[92]
though Dunlop,[93] Brown's biographer, fancies he perceives a marked
resemblance between them. Let us hope that *Arthur Mervyn* will find a
place among the Standard Novels. It deserves the honor fully as much as
Edgar Huntly.[94]

Drop Fifty-eight.

Writing a poem for the sake of developing a metaphysical theory, is like
kindling a fire for the sake of the smoke.

Drop Fifty-nine.

Love, even fortunate love, never leaves the heart as it found it. An angel
once dwelled in the palace of Zohir, and his presence was the sun and soul of
that edifice. But, after years, there came a devil, stronger than the angel; and
the devil drove the angel from the palace and took up his own abode therein.
And a woeful day was that for the palace, for the devil brake up the costly
furniture and put all things at sixes and sevens, and the mark of his hoof was

every where visible on the carpets. But when some time had passed, he too, went away; and now the palace was left a lonely wreck, for the angel never more would return to a dwelling that had been desecrated by a devil. So it continued to wax older and crazier, till at last one night a high wind came and swept it to the earth, where it lay ever after in ruins. Many say, however, that the angel might have remained in it to this day had he combated the intruder with might and main in the beginning, but that he chose rather to hold parley with him, and even invited him to come under the roof.

Drop Sixty.

Inscribed in the Chronicle of the Forty-four Mandarins is the record of the confessions of A-HA-HO-HUM, Man of Many Sciences, Son of the Dogstar, and Cousin to the Turkey-cock; and thus it runneth: I, A-HA-HO-HUM, HAVE TRAVERSED THE EARTH, AND THE HEARTS OF MEN HAVE BEEN LAID BARE TO ME; AND LO! MY TESTIMONY CONCERNING ALL THINGS IS THIS:—No Wall is Dense, and no Well is Deep, where a Will is Daring.

A POLYGLOTT ANTHOLOGY.

DEVELOPED IN FORM OF A DIALOGUE.

COLLOQUII PERSONÆ.

THE HERR HOPPANDGOÖN VON BAUGTRAUTER, A CELEBRATED TRAVELLER.
THE HERR POPPANDGOÖFF VON TUTSCHEMUPP, A DISTINGUISHED CRITIC.

SCENE.—*A parlour in* BAUGTRAUTER's *domicile.* BAUGTRAUTER *and his friend* TUTSCHEMUPP *are discovered seated at a table near the fire, with a bottle of Tokay between them. A pause has occurred in the conversation.* BAUGTRAUTER *seems about to light a cigar, which, nevertheless, he merely continues to hold up between his fingers, while his elbow rests on the mahogany. A universe of reminiscences may be detected in his eye. He sighs very peculiarly.*

TUTSCHEMUPP.
Who are to be your publishers?

BAUGTRAUTER.
Humm and Co. of Bamberg.

TUTSCHEMUPP.
Humm—Humm?—yes, I recollect. BLINKMANN's *Book of Bubbles* was one of their affairs. Some tolerable epigrams in that too.

BAUGTRAUTER.
I understand that Pultrowski, the Polish exile, found one of them rather *in*tolerable.

TUTSCHEMUPP.
Yes—and he threatened to sacrifice BLINKMANN—but BLINKMANN luckily escaped to Seringapatam, where an appointment awaited him; and in some months afterwards a letter came "from Indus to the *Pole*,"[1] frankly confessing the delinquency, and soliciting forgiveness.

BAUGTRAUTER.
Why, it must have been quite a musquito in metre.

TUTSCHEMUPP.

Not at all. Merely this:—

𝕰pigram.

"Strzemlejno sztdrosztj Pujltrzouskj ojpol dzcnek a gyeza."

Quoth Prince Pultrowski, while darning his clothing,
"'Tish odd! I can't patch von singale hole!"
"*Very* odd," said a hearer, "for folks think nothing
As true as the Needle to the Pole."

BAUGTRAUTER.

Fill your glass. Your epigram reminds me of a reply that a Fakir once made me at Delhi. His coat, like Pultrowski's, was a mere thing of shreds and patches.[2] 'My friend,' said I, 'your garment is extremely full of holes.' 'So you imagine,' he replied, 'but POPE, who examined the matter more narrowly, acquaints me that

'All are but parts of one stupendous hole.'[3]

TUTSCHEMUPP.

I should like to hear a German beggar quoting the *Gulistan* of SAADI.[4] Well: let us have the sequel of your *escapade*.

BAUGTRAUTER.

You mean in Japan? Why, as I was telling you, when I saw affairs grow blacker and blacker there every day, I at last thought it bootless to tarry in it longer. I saw I must pitch my tent elsewhere. Fresh jars were continually occurring between me and the nobles, whose manners were none of the most polished at the best of times. So, finding I could not recover my former footing at court, I apprised the Emperor of my wish to depart; and he kindly granted me liberty, on condition that I should go to Transoxania,[5] and be the bearer of some dispatches from him to the king of that country.

TUTSCHEMUPP.

Transoxania? In what *mappe-monde* is that visible?

BAUGTRAUTER.

Fill your glass. ABULFEDA[6] will tell you all about Transoxania. Did you never meet some verses that were presented to a beautiful European slave in Tunis, by one of the old Transoxanian monarchs, who accompanied the

Caliph Mookh-tahder on his expedition against Morocco? The first stanza runs thus:—

"Chailehouc locmah, failehouc chind-roumahl."

Fair child of Northern climes and skies,
       I don't know what should chain you,
With those brown locks and light blue eyes,
       To swarthy Mauritania!
O come with me, my pretty prize,
       And, if you wish to reign, you
Shall be the queen of a Paradise
       In bowery Transoxania!

TUTSCHEMUPP.

I wish you would give me the Tartarian entire.

BAUGTRAUTER.

So I will. But to resume: off I went to Transoxania, and executed my commission. I would then have sailed for Europe, but the king had a very young wife——

TUTSCHEMUPP.

Who fell in love with you.

BAUGTRAUTER.

Bah! The king had a young wife—a girl half-past twelve, or thirteen; and this baby matron had an album. One day I requested as a favor that she would permit me to copy from it a certain ancient Arabic song, the composition of AL MAKEENAH, a warrior who had survived the glory of the Barmecidian nobles fifty-eight years. She gave me leave at once, the dear little thing; but her husband, who was the devil for jealousy——

TUTSCHEMUPP.

Let us hear the song, Hoppandgöon. You can afterwards fabricate the particulars of the *esclandre* at your leisure.

BAUGTRAUTER.

You are incorrigible, Poppandgoöff. Open your ADELUNG.[7] The music is wild and plaintive. I need not commend the words, for even according to AUGUSTUS SCHLEGEL,[8] Arabic admits of no comparison with any language besides.

𝕿𝖍𝖊 𝕿𝖎𝖒𝖊 𝖔𝖋 𝖙𝖍𝖊 𝕭𝖆𝖗𝖒𝖊𝖈𝖎𝖉𝖊𝖘.[9]

"Hudukahum ba daikhish, dilehim pirish."

My eyes are dimmed, my hair is grey,
    I am bowed by the weight of years:
I would I were stretched in my bed of clay,
    With my long-lost youth's compeers!

  . . . .

TUTSCHEMUPP.

There is a marvellous resemblance between the first line of your song and the beginning of that stanza in PERGLESI, in which the Milanese Mayor says—

    'Il mio naso e rosso, la mia perucca e canuto'—[10]

I'll extemporise it for you in German.

Stanʒa from the Italian.

Ere my nose was red, or my wig was grey,
    Or I sat in the civic chair,
I often left Rome on a soft Spring day
    To taste the country air—
All sattin and plush were my bran-new clothes—
    All white my lace cravat—
All square my buskins about the toes—
    And oh! all round my hat!

BAUGTRAUTER.

My dear friend, that last expression of yours is RICCIARDETTO's, not PERGLESI's. Surely you can't pretend to forget the triumphant reply of Sigismondo to Gianetto in the *Fantasmi*—when Gianetto in vain endeavours to strip his antagonist's helmet of the contested laurel-sprig:

Indarno vuoi, te dico, prender' quello,
Perch'e tutt' all' intorno il mio cappello![11]

TUTSCHEMUPP.

Come, come; no improvising!

BAUGTRAUTER.

To return, then, to Transoxania. I found also in the album what I thought a very philosophical sentiment by a native poet; and I transferred it to my tablets. The king, on discovering that his wife had allowed me to abstract the song and the sentiment, had the unfortunate girl sewn up in a sack and thrown into the Djoorah. As for me he literally *caged* me for six months. At the end of that time he liberated me, and told me that I was at liberty to decamp from Transoxania if I could enlighten him with respect to something that had latterly puzzled him very much. About two years before, he said, an Englishman had been a visitor at his court, and had written this inscription over the door leading into the court of King's Bench: WI*SDOM AND POW*ER. 'Now,' said the king, 'Wisdom and Power are intelligible enough, but the most eminent of my astrologers can make nothing of the stars. Something is evidently wanting.' 'Good,' said I, quietly. 'What do you mean by Good?' asked the monarch. 'G, O, O, D, is wanting to make the sense perfect,' returned I; 'but as twice nought is nothing, we will omit the centre capitals, and only take the extremes. Put G in the place of one star, and D in the place of the other, and you have WIGSDOM and POWDER. The head-gear of your Majesty's lawyers, I believe, is that of our own.' I said all this with astonishing gravity. Well: the king was so delighted! When he had finished laughing at my explication, he ordered me ten purses of gold. He was a liberal fellow in all respects, and especially lavish of the bowstring, which was in requisition at his court about thirty times a day.

TUTSCHEMUPP.

Then he must have had a prodigious number of strings to his bow. What was the extract you spoke of?

BAUGTRAUTER.

A trifle, but perfect in its way:

Transoxanian Philosophy.

"Aalem bakkilse ssaafhi ibbret deilmiddir!"

Make the round world thy Book of Examples!
 Man and his mind are a study for sages:
He who would mount to the firmament tramples
 Under his feet the experience of ages.
Love what thou hast with a willing devotion!
 Drink of the stream, if thou meet not the fountain!
Though the best pearls lie low in the ocean,
 Gold is at hand in the mines of the mountain!
      TUTSCHEMUPP.

Poor Cocking,[12] the Englishman, lately illustrated the truths of the third and fourth lines to his cost. You came to Europe with your ten purses?

BAUGTRAUTER.

Not immediately. I first took a trip to China. There I lent considerable assistance to PAUTHIER[13] in his translation of the *Tao-te-king* of LAO-TSEU. It is a noble work that—and for the age most wonderful!

TUTSCHEMUPP.

Have the Celestials any poetry?

BAUGTRAUTER.

All sorts, from epic to epigram. Here is an elegy on the death of a fisher-man, by WHANG-HUM, the laureate, who passes for the first wit in Pe-king.

𝔈legy

ON THE DEATH OF TCHAO-KING, FISHER AND ANGLER.
"Kien-yen-fo-ho-tsing-mao-lou-kloung-fi-tchao-king."

Tchao-king (Joe King) the fisherman, has paid
  That weightiest of debts, called Nature's debt;
The only debt he paid, I'm much afraid,
  For all was fish that came into *his* net.

· ·

What think you of that? As a sample of the epigram take this from the same poet.

𝔈pigram.

"Mou-chen-ka-fong-te-lien-ya-ying-tso."

A costly pearl tea-urn was made by Ya-ying
  A present of to Lao-lang-hi, his brother;
Who sent the donor one of silver, saying,
  'Ya-ying!—one good T-urn deserves another!'

TUTSCHEMUPP.

Very Chinese indeed.

* * * * * * * * *

TUTSCHEMUPP.

... You never kissed the Blarney-stone,[14] I believe.

BAUGTRAUTER.

No, but I made an acquaintance with a very clever Corkonian in the United States; and poor fellow! before the Yellow Fever carried him off at Natchez he left me all his papers. He was a poet. He introduced himself to me as an O'GALLAGHER; and I, in turn, let him know that I was a BAUGTRAUTER; so that there was at once a common bond of sympathy between us. His "sponsorial appellative," as he called his Christian name, was Felix; and he usually signed his letters and other productions F.O'G, 'because,' said he, confidentially, 'I am here under a sort of cloud.' I intend to publish the entire of his literary remains, as soon as I can get them done into German. There is in particular a metaphysical poem of his which I admire: the measure is that of the following stanza, which is the opening of the third canto.

Nŗ conṭŗáŗóáċṫ ȝul ꝺoŋ ŋ-ȝáŗŗe.

Though Laughter seems, it never is, the antithesis to Tears:
  The gayest births of Circumstance or Fancy
But minister in masquerade to Sovereign Grief, who rears
  Her temple by that moral necromancy
Which fuses down to one dark mass all passions of Life's years;
  And, as from even adverse facts VALLANCEY[15]
Proved us mere Irish to be Orientals,
Nature makes Grinning Schools turn men out Sentimentals.

Although most of his compositions are Irish, he was well acquainted with modern English literature, as I find from a poem which he left behind him in a fragmentary state, and which he calls

The Rule of Three In-Verse.

Men seem to have supposed in olden time Rhyme
     Crime:
At least, we never find that they rehearse terse
     Verse
Embellished with that all-transcending ending
     Lending
Fresh grace and vivifying vigour, bigger
     Figure,

> And soul to Song,—making the dimmest dream-theme
> > Beam
> In colors of sublimer weaving,—giving
> > Living
> Fire to the page, making a faint, though fine, line
> > Shine,
> Rendering the sloven metre neater, meeter,
> > Sweeter,
> And shedding, equally for soul and sight, bright
> > Light
> Over the darkest cabalistic mystic
> > Distich.
> They scribbled much, indeed, but I must add, had
> > Bad
> Taste, and are, therefore, like (I'm thinking) winking,
> > Sinking.

F.O'G's opinion is that rhyme should be the vehicle of ordinary conversation—but while as a philosopher I pardon his eccentricities, as a man of taste I burke them.

* * * * * * * * *

TUTSCHEMUPP.

Αλις ουτος,[16] O my friend! Forgive me the interruption, but I am two-thirds asleep. Have you anything very heart-breaking by way of variety? The Irish, I am told, is a lachrymose language.

BAUGTRAUTER.

Affected to the last degree as you are at times, Poppandgooff, I should despair of affecting you farther, even by the exhibition of O'REILLY's[17] entire vocabulary. But I will try to meet your wishes. Fill your glass.

* * * * * * * * *

TUTSCHEMUPP.

The nationality of Ireland appears to be rapidly vanishing.

BAUGTRAUTER.

It has vanished. Ir múċṫa an ṫıne a ṫ-ṫealaċ ġaoıḋeal.[18] The lament is two centuries old.

O! the fire is quenched on the hearth of the Gadelian!
The diadem of Banba is stripped of its cornelian!
Her prop is gone—her mighty one—her hero in a million—
      And she weeps, as a widow, for Aodha Ruadh Ua-Domhnaill![19]

TUTSCHEMUPP.

Who was he?

BAUGTRAUTER.

"The noblest Roman of them all."[20] Fill your glass,—fill—fill—fill!

TUTSCHEMUPP.

Have you seen DRECHSLER's last volumes?[21]

BAUGTRAUTER.

Yes: they grow thicker and thicker.

TUTSCHEMUPP.

While he himself grows thinner and thinner.

BAUGTRAUTER.

We should never judge of authors from their works. Is DRECHSLER
progressing?

TUTSCHEMUPP.

Yes, in unintelligibility. Every day spoils him more and more. He has
been too popular. $Τοις$ $πλεισοις$ $ειμαρμαι$ $μηδεποτ'$ $ευ$ $πραττοντες$
$φρονειν$.[22] so observes DEMOSTHENES, and DRECHSLER illustrates the
truth of the observation. It is a pity, for his faults are the result of sheer
wilfulness. However, I think he lacks judgment somewhat, too....

BAUGTRAUTER.

The taste, or no-taste, of the age encourages *persiflage* too much; but
anything is preferable to that pestiferous sentimentality that prevailed a
generation back. Look at SCHILLER——

TUTSCHEMUPP.

O Hoppandgoön!

BAUGTRAUTER.

O Poppandgoöff! I say, look at his *Hero and Leander*—

TUTSCHEMUPP.

Which opens with a fine stanza:

> Mark ye well those crumbling castle-walls,
> Where the sun-light ever gladlier falls,
>   Where the moonbeam ever sadlier dwells,
> Where the Hellespont, with angering shock,
> Foams and rolls and rushes through the rock
>   Portals of the dœdal Dardanelles?
> Hark! how stuns again that sullen thunder!
>   But the power and fierceness that of old
> Tore two mighty continents asunder,
>   Fail to daunt where Love is young and bold!

BAUGTRAUTER.

One swallow makes no summer. By the way, I made a neat application of that saying last year in reference to the son of the Starost of Molinsky. His tutor, "one Michael Cassio, an arithmetician,"[23] had set him the task of summing up a number of vulgar fractions into one aristocratic integer. The young man swallowed a glass of 'hot without'[24] to quicken his intellect, but still looked puzzled. 'Very strange that he can't do it,' said the tutor to me. 'O!' observed I, 'one *swallow* makes no *summer.*' However, as I spoke in the Magyar tongue, I suppose the cream of the joke must have been spilt. To return to SCHILLER:—I was talking——

TUTSCHEMUPP.

Blasphemy. What do you say of LA MOTTE FOUQUE?[25]

BAUGTRAUTER.

That the dull weed that rots itself at ease on Lethe's wharf[26] is a model of liveliness by a comparison with him.

TUTSCHEMUPP.

My impression is that his poetry requires a peculiar talent in the reader.

BAUGTRAUTER.

Ay! such a talent as GOETHE exhibited when he read for his friends *out* of the *Musenalmanach* that which nobody could find *in* it....

Now, rather than travesty my author I would let him alone altogether. Better no version, say I, than a perversion. Hence I entertain an unconquerable disgust against all translations, except those into German, which are improvements on the originals. Indeed German bids fair to become in another century the great literary language of Europe.

TUTSCHEMUPP.

And America?

BAUGTRAUTER.

Never mind. *Apropos* of America: did you ever read Captain ALEXANDER's *Transatlantic Sketches*?

TUTSCHEMUPP.

I have no time to read books: you forget that I am a reviewer.

BAUGTRAUTER.

The Captain gives an interesting account of an English recluse—Francis Abbott—who took up his abode for two years on Iris Island, near the Falls of Niagara, and was at last drowned in the river. I happened to meet with this being in one of my solitary rambles, in the Summer of 1830; and he was kind enough to let me rest in his hut for a week. He was the mildest creature I ever met. He had written a good deal of rather fantastic poetry, in which his own disposition and feelings were the themes he most delighted to dwell on. I made transcripts of several of the shorter pieces.[27]

TUTSCHEMUPP. (*Yawning.*)

Well: I grant you permission to repeat the shortest of the short.

BAUGTRAUTER.

Don't fall asleep, then. Take another glass.

[Here follow "My Mausoleum" and "On the Occasion of the Truce"]

TUTSCHEMUPP.

Too didactic for metre. I confess I think love the only proper theme of poetry, as poetry is said to be the only proper language of love.

BAUGTRAUTER.

You will have the better half of the world your allies in that sentiment. You will also have the Oriental poet, MUSTAFA REEZAH, for he lays an emphatic injunction on his own honey-dropping mouth, to sing of nothing else for ever! *Szoileh hali izek uk u mashuki shireen dihen!*

TUTSCHEMUPP.

Shall I read you a little poem by CASCAGNI? You know he is a favorite of mine.[28]

BAUGTRAUTER.

You should have asked me whether I would listen. Read any nonsense you please, my dear fellow.

TUTSCHEMUPP.

Yes, but I'll stand none; remember that.

BAUGTRAUTER.

And I'll understand none; remember that.

TUTSCHEMUPP.

If you can *with*stand what I am about to read I shall give you every credit for a want of understanding.

[Here follows "To Laura"]

BAUGTRAUTER. (*taking out his watch.*)

Half past ten. I shall be late at the Club.

TUTSCHEMUPP.

And I shall be early at the Spade. I work my own garden, you know.

BAUGTRAUTER.

Mindful of the counsel of ISOCRATES, Πειραομαι το μεν σωμα ειναι φιλοπονος, η δε ψυχη φιλοσοφος.[29]

TUTSCHEMUPP.

Τα οντα αγαθα και καλα ουδεν ανευ πονος κ' επιμελεια θεοι διδοασιν ανθρωπος.[30]

BAUGTRAUTER.

Rich widows and lottery-prizes excepted. You may as well come out with me now, though. I have a few good things to tell you.

TUTSCHEMUPP.

And a multiplicity of *niaiseries*.[31]

BAUGTRAUTER.

Well: "a friend should bear a friend's infirmities."[32]

TUTSCHEMUPP.
My reading of that is, A friend should *bare* a friend's infirmities.

BAUGTRAUTER.
Nonsense, Poppandgoöff;—Come!

TUTSCHEMUPP.
Me voila tout prêt.[33]

(*Exeunt ambo.*)

ANTHOLOGIA GERMANICA.—NO. XV.
WETZEL'S POEMS.

WHEN one enthusiast takes up the cudgels for another, men witness a more than usually apt instance of the zeal that lacks discretion. Herr Zachariah Funck, we venture to predict, will not redeem the reputation of his late friend, Frederick Conrad Wetzel, from the oblivion into which it is fast falling, by taking upon himself the editorship of his poems. People may sometimes bear to be lectured into the belief that madness is inspiration, but certainly never where the lecturer is himself a madman. Paine[1] was patronised rather to the detriment of his own celebrity by Cobbett.[2] Hunt's glowing eulogies of Shelley[3] have not tended to dissipate the cloud that rests upon the latter's character. We do, therefore, apprehend that the sober-minded Germans will continue to discountenance the poetical and political extravagances of Wetzel, notwithstanding Editor Funck's tempestuous vindication of both, and the scalding hot tide of invective in which his indignation finds vent against all who happen to be prosaic and apathetic enough to feel no sympathy with either.

But with this We have nothing to do. The sole regret that the publisher's choice has caused us is occasioned by the absence from the volume before us of any biographical details respecting the poet. The verbose rhapsody that does the duty of preface to it talks of "culmination-points," "halls of immortality," "paracentric æsthetics," "objectivity," and so forth, and denounces the age in a dialect that illustrates the vast advantage of having a dictionary at one's elbow; but it does not tell us where, when, why, or how it came to pass that Wetzel was so unfortunate as to die—as we understand was the case—a neglected poet and a broken-hearted man. On these points we wanted to gain as much information as we possibly could; and on these points Editor F. has given us as little information as he possibly could, *viz.* none whatever. He talks instead—being obliged to talk of something—of the signs of the times, and the melancholy prevalence of an anti-mystic materialism in modern poetry. We desire facts, and he treats us to disquisitions, as "germane to the matter"[4] in hand as an air by Neukomm[5] might be to a problem in algebra. His mode of establishing his *protégé's* claim to the title of poet strikes us also as rather inconclusive. "Dasz Wetzel," he demands, "ein rechter Dichter war, wer vermag das zu bestreiten?" "Who will dare to dispute that Wetzel was a genuine poet?"

No argument is attempted; no evidence is tendered; the interrogatory is put, Who will dare, &c.; and so the matter is decided. One might, however, tolerate any little deficiency his logic exhibits for the sake of its brevity: the shortest follies are the best. But, alas, for his interminable metaphysics! their only recommendation is the strong probability that, as they are wholly and hopelessly incomprehensible, they must, after the first glance given to them, perforce compel the reader to pass them over altogether: the cloud that envelopes them is in fact the densest we have come into contact with since our first acquaintanceship with Kant, and as completely veils the writer's meaning from ordinary apprehension as the volume of smoke which filled the room while, pipe in mouth, he went through with his task, shrouded the characters he scrawled from his own eyes.

His favourite theme of panegyric is the poet's soul, which, nevertheless, he describes as loaded with rubbish—somewhat like his own meerschaum—and the poet's spirit, in reference to which we have a vivid picture of a Bedlamite[6] escaping from his keepers. Hear him blow the trumpet. "Die mannichfaltigsten Fesseln lähmender Erdgewalten, Schutt and [*sic*] Staub der erbärmlichsten Prosa, legten wie Berge sich auf seine Seele, und doch vermochten sie nicht seine Dichterkraft niederzubeugen, geschweige seinen Genius zu begraben. Sein junger, freier und kräftiger Geist durchbrach jeder äuszern Zwang, machte sich Platz mit seinen gewaltigen Adlerschwingen, entfloh der niedern Erde, reinigte mit raschem Flügelschlage die verpestete Luft und flog, dem ewigen Phönix gleich, dem Lande seiner Geburt, der Sonne, zu!" "The most multitudinous and multifarious manacles of the crippling and shackling earth-authorities, the rubbish and dust of the paltriest prose, cast themselves like mountains upon his soul, and yet prevailed not to bow down his poet's might, far less to sepulchre his genius. His young, chainless, and powerful spirit broke through every external barrier, made room for itself with its stupendous eagle-pinions, soared above this base earth, purified with the rapid rushing of its wings the pestilential atmosphere, and flew, like the eternal Phoenix, to its native clime—the sun!"

If this be true, "that other great traveller," Munchausen,[7] is left far behind, for he visited only the moon—the account of the voyage to the dog-star being now generally admitted by the learned to be spurious. Poor Wetzel! the coolness of his reception upon earth was indeed such as might naturally enough have induced in him a wish to exchange his habitation for warmer quarters. While, however, we lament his destiny, we do not go the length of blaming the world for it. No: Wetzel was a man of mere middling genius—and one fate alone awaits such men. Themselves are unsought, their books unbought; so was it always; so will it continue; it must be thus; there is no remedy for it. People somehow will not purchase an inferior article when they can have a superior one as cheap. If Herr Funck and a few like him mistake crockery for porcelain and potatoes for peaches, they have no right to fall foul of others for being better-sighted. Nay, even supposing the public in the wrong, these are still the best judges of what pleases themselves. This is a truth so obvious as to force itself upon the commonest minds; and they who abuse the public because of their taste or want of taste prove themselves either very splenetic or very irrational. We pity a man of talent, like Wetzel, for his sufferings—in conscience we can afford to do no more. If we thought his deserts to be such as to have made the treatment he received unjustifiable we should perhaps be almost as indignant as Orator Funck himself. He is dead; the grave has closed over him; and, whatever his defects may have been, we can have no wish to quarrel either with his memory or his executors—even though he gained little fame, and made less money, and has got an editor to edit him who assumes that the secret of his want of success lay in the paramount sublimity of his genius—that is to say, that he was so magnificent and so fascinating a writer—and so grandiloquent and so "up-soaring," and so "down-diving" a thinker that— nobody cared to read him.

We believe it were as well, to preclude any misconception with reference to the point, if we at once gave the reader a few samples of the poems. None of them are certainly of a worse order than any we have hitherto published; and some of them may perhaps be of a better. Our own anti-poetical modes of thought and tendencies of mind, indeed, license the likelihood that we see in them blemishes which to those better qualified for understanding them may be invisible. We give one dozen of specimens; not extracting at random, but selecting the best that offer.

* * * * * * * * *

Some German poets are singularly fond of trying to pass themselves off as persons who ought to be shut up in desarts and transported to desolate islands. Scattered through their books we encounter occasional mysterious allusions to certain dark incidents in their lives—much meeting the eye and more being meant for the mind. Now this is disgusting affectation. It is a claptrap unworthy of intellectual men. Byron tried it and got credit for sincerity from some half dozen persons, of whom Goethe, poor old man, was one. Yet Byron's was a wild life, and he *might* have done something to "plunge his years in fatal penitence".[8] Where he failed to pass for worse than he could be, who is likely to succeed? With that silvery voice, those courtly manners, does Tieck stand any chance of being regarded as a villain at heart? Can a man so brimful of the milk and water of human kindness[9] as Kerner have poisoned his mother-in-law and set the Spree on fire? Who will believe that the delicate lemonhued handshoe[10] of Klinger[11] is assumed only to hide such an accusing stain as might "the multitudinous sea incarnadine?"[12] These follies, however, are peculiar to a few. Our friend Wetzel does not pretend to be a very *mauvais sujet*:[13] he has nothing to confess; he "sleeps in spite of thunder."[14] He is, in fact, "more sinned against than sinning"[15]—wretched only, not guilty—he weeps blood, but has drawn none—writes daggers,[16] but never brandishes them. His characteristic fault is that of talking *à la* Jacob Bœhmen[17]—

> "His thoughts are theorems—his words a problem—
> As if he deemed that mystery would ennoble 'em."[18]

* * * * * * * * * *

The rudeness of our versions generally is a fair presumption for their faithfulness. We know that we have been charged with paraphrasing and even travestying our originals; and the charge may be true or false; we neither admit it nor deny; but good-natured judges will perhaps be inclined to consider that we are as literal as the difference between the structure of English and the structure of German allows us to be. In reality there is no reason that we should perpetrate paraphrases. Translations are considerably easier. To give the words of an author as he has given them himself is obviously less of a task than to be at the trouble of inventing for him words that he never intended to give. The *dolce far niente*[19] of literal rendering must in any case be preferable to the supererogatory fatigue of circumlocutory wantonness. Moreover, a paraphrase, palmed upon the public as a translation, is an imposture, and the palmer is an impostor; and the character of an impostor is one that no man assumes for nothing.

The privilege of individual opinion, however, we have always respected; and on that account we decline to offer any formal exculpation of our Anthologies. Were we to pledge our word of honor that we have not deceived the public they would be in a manner coerced into the adoption of a particular belief with regard to the question at issue. We deem it more eligible to leave them the unshackled exercise of their proper judgement. It is the course that liberal feeling dictates; and we disdain precedents.

* * * * * * * * * *

THE METEOR OF KASAN.——A TRAGEDY.

THE reading public has doubtless long before this decided that we have altogether forgotten our friend Wetzel. To be frank, we will acknowledge that since he and we parted company he has not often intruded on our speculations, and this because of reasons that we shall state. It so happened that about three months back we had the misfortune to sustain a severe attack of intellectual hypochondriasis, the effect of which was to revolutionise for a season all our literary tastes; insomuch that the admiration we had thitherto cherished of the fine land of our dreams, her cloudy philosophy and wizard poetry, was exchanged for a stupid antipathy, worthy the contempt of an Esquimaux. Neither physicians nor metaphysicians were able to comprehend, far less remove, our malady. Whence it originated we ourself can hazard no conjecture; for who shall fathom the abysses of the human mind? Enough, that while it lasted it either paralysed or perverted all our faculties,—converting us, even while we fancied ourself an eagle, by turns into an owl, a raven, and a gander. We attribute our recovery from it, which was gradual, to the combined agencies of gymnastics and toast-water[1]—a sober beverage in the main, though frequently drunk twice a-day for weeks in succession. The majority of our acquaintance have already transmitted us their compliments, congratulations, and cards by the hundred—perhaps we should rather say by the hundred weight—and that in a manner the most flattering to us. Among those worthy individuals we would beg to particularly particularise our world-renowned friend, William Carleton of Richmond Castle,[2] who has fraternally counselled us to make the most of the great change that has overtaken us. We thank this distinguished man from the bottom of our inkstand, and shall endeavour to act upon the injunction, the more especially as any small change that may overtake us stands, we lament to observe, a very slender chance of being made the most of in such hands as ours.

So far, so fair, in explanation of the past; and now to business. As we are about to close accounts with poor Wetzel, and are anxious that the balance should appear in his favour, we must abandon his minor poems to their fate, for we have already selected all of these that we thought readable. A review of the tragedy before us,[3] appears better adapted to answer our purposes. With regard to the authorship of this tragedy, it is true, we confess we are somewhat in the dark. No evidence establishing Wetzel's right to that authorship has yet been made public. Many persons even go so far as to attribute it to Baron Auffenberg, and among these is the Baron himself, for he has emblazoned his name on the title-page. Fortunately, however, the inquiry is not of paramount importance. If Wetzel be not the author of the book, somebody else is. It could not have started spontaneously into existence out of a stack of old rags on the road to a paper-mill, reasonable as that theory of universal possibilities may be which led Godwin to imagine that human beings might one day spring from the muzzles of muskets.[4] Wetzel produced it—or—if you will, reader—Chrononhotonthologos[5] produced it, or, in default of either of these two, a third person. Who that third person may be it is not at present material to ascertain. At some future period the requisite light will perhaps be thrown upon the points that baffle investigation in this intricate question. In the meanwhile the laurel will shade Wetzel's brow with quite as green a gracefulness as it could confer upon that of the Baron, who has his *Prophet von Florenz* to keep him in celebrity, independent of a version of *The Warden of Galway*,[6] which he has recently put off upon the Carlsruhers[7] as an original sin of his own.

The scene of the tragedy is Russia, and the story is founded upon the Tartar revolt of 1774, when the impostor Pugatsheff, under the title of Peter III. placed himself at the head of a large army, with the intention of marching against the Empress Catherine and depriving her of the crown. The following are the characters of the drama:—

THE CZAR.
SOPHIA NIKOSOROFF, *his Consort.*
DEMETRIUS NIKOSOROFF, *her Father.*
GURKA, *Sister of Demetrius.*
PETRONELLA, *Waiting-woman to Sophia.*
A KAPIDAN–ISPRAFFNIK.[8]
IVANNA, *his Daughter.*
GOROOD, *a Major* ⎱ *of Artillery in the service of the Czar.*
FEODOR WERESHIN, *a Captain* ⎰
THE HERMIT OF THE MOUNTAIN, *Patriarch of the Roskolniks.*
ALEXIS PETROWITZ FOMA, *a Roskolnick Priest.*
MICHELSON, *the Russian General.*
MICHAILA JAGUNOFF, *Hetman of the Volga Cossacks.*
IVAN PERSILSHEV, *a Don Cossack.*
JUVALANKA, *Chief of the Baskirians.*
RUSSIAN SOLDIERS, NOGAY AND KASANKA TARTARS. DON AND VOLGA COSSACKS. KIRGHEES. BASHKIRIANS. TCHEREMISSES. TCHUVASHES. KALMUCKS. WOTIAKS, &c.

Time of Action, 1775.
Place—KASAN[9] AND THE SHORES OF THE VOLGA.

The opening of the piece represents Feodor Wereshin and Gorood in conversation on the subject of the war.

* * * * * * * * *

The dialogue continues some time longer, but is at length interrupted by the entrance of a Tartar girl, who brings a letter to Feodor from Ivanna, his betrothed. By this it appears that the Czar has imprisoned Ivanna's father for refusing the oath of allegiance to him; and she implores her lover to rescue the prisoner, if possible. While Feodor is reading the cannon is heard, announcing the approach of the Czar to Kasán; upon which the friends separate, after some arrangements unnecessary to be detailed.

Scene the next introduces us to the Czarina Sophia, in her gorgeous pavilion before Kasán. Her aunt Gurka occupies a seat beside her. From the dialogue that follows we learn that the Czarina married her husband without the knowledge of her father, a noble of high birth but ruined fortune, who was absent in the East during the wooing and wedding. She harbours a vague and apparently unreasonable apprehension of her father's wrath on his now hourly-expected return, principally on account of Gurka, who was mainly instrumental in the success of the Czar's suit. While they converse the cannon and trumpets are heard, as before; whereupon *exeunt* both ladies to make preparations for greeting the victor.

The closing scene of the Act represents a square in Kasán, with a vacant throne in the centre. The nobles and burghers are present to do homage to the Czar. A splendid cavalcade of Kirgheese and Kalmucks occupies the back-ground. Gloom, nevertheless, sits on every countenance. Silence prevails. At length Foma, the Roskolnik priest, comes forward.

* * * * * * * * *

The Czar now enters with all the "pride, pomp and circumstance of glorious war,"[10] bells ringing, cannon firing, bands of music playing, and so forth; and accompanied by cavalcades of Tcheremisses, Tchuvashes, Wotiaks, Bashkirians, and all the other Tartars he has caught by his promises.[11] He is enthroned, Sophia by his side, and from the throne graciously narrates the story of his life and adventures to the multitude. It proves rather tedious, but the substance is that he was never murdered at all, and could not have been, because, if we may take his word for it,—

> To plunge into the unrefunding crypts
> Of ghastliest hell for all eternity
> Were easy by comparison with the task
> Of butchering on his bed the unconscious sleeper
> Whose awful brows a diadem encircles!

There was, however, at this period a man in Moscow whom nobody knew, but amazingly like the Czar in figure and features, and this man was made the scapegoat on the occasion. The assassins kept their places, and Catherine ascended the throne all the same; the Czar being forced to fly for his life. He travelled, like Ulysses, through many countries—

> "Mores hominum multorum vidit."[12]

Twelve years thus passed on; and, like Beppo,[13] he grew anxious to return home. He observes that he would have abandoned his vagabond mode of life much sooner, but that the time was not ripe for his projects.—At this moment a bell tolls dismally.

> *Czar* (*agitated*)—Ha! What is that?
> (*A voice among the crowd*)—   O woe!
> *Czar* (*yet more agitated*)—   What bell is that?
>   Why knells it thus?
>   (*All are silent.*)
>   No answer! What means this?
> *A Noble* (*trembling*)—Sire!—that bell—is—the death-bell of Saint
>   Nicholas!
>   Which never tolls but—when—but—when—
> *Czar*—   Say on!
> *Noble*—But when State-criminals are—doomed to die!

The Czar, unaccountably upset by this intelligence, commands that strict search be made for the ringers. Word, however, is brought him that there are no ringers; whereupon he very naturally concludes that he is the sport of sorcery, and expresses his settled conviction to that effect. At this juncture the Don Cossack Ivan Persilshev gallops into the square, proclaiming the unexpected approach of Michelson, the Empress's Field-Marshal, with a vast hostile force. The announcement, of course, spoils all appetite for further festivities; the Czar and his cavalry, after a speech, which the former makes and the latter cheer, are off to the camp; and so closes the first Act.

In Act II. we are again in the battered Tartar village. A battle has been fought and Kasán is in ashes. The Czarina and her aunt are conversing on the affair, when the room-door opens, and Demetrius Nikosoroff, the Czarina's father, suddenly startles them by his appearance.

* * * * * * * * *

A confidential colloquy ensues between father and daughter. Demetrius acquaints Sophia that he has returned from the East a rich man, and desires to know whether the Czar possesses her heart as well as her hand. Her reply is affirmative:

> I love him with the full love of my nature—
> I love him passionately as my husband—
> I love him reverently as my sovereign.

On which Demetrius groans—

> I feared as much: the cure will prove the bitterer.

This excites her alarm, and she solicits an explanation, which he diplomatically evades. After some further talk he tells her that he must see her alone at his own dwelling, and accordingly gives her an opiate to mix in her duenna of an aunt's gruel, that she may not suspect the visit. Follow mutual leave-takings, very tender and tearful on both sides.

Scene changes to the interior of a spacious cave in the rocks, artificially illuminated. To the right is seen a Roskolnik in the habit of an Armenian monk, with a book open before him. From the left advance Foma and the Czar, attended by two Roskolnik priests. The Czar is clad in the long flowing habiliments of the Tartar princes.

* * * * * * * * *

The scene again changes to a still more spacious cavern, in form of a chapel, with shrines and sacred paintings. Here are assembled a convocation of the Roskolnik priests, each with a stone altar before him, on which stand a lamp and a crucifix; while their Patriarch, the Hermit of the Mountain, is seated on a throne in front. He is clad in white robes, is blind, and would seem from his features to have passed his hundredth year. The paraphernalia of the chapel are described with prolix minuteness in the drama. The Czar is conducted with much solemnity before the Patriarch. The object of his visit is to ascertain from the Patriarch, to whom popular report ascribes the gift of prophecy, whether his present campaign shall eventuate in success or in defeat.

* * * * * * * * *

The interview progresses, but is destined to close in a manner not at all agreeable to the Czar.

[*The Patriarch denounces the Czar as an impostor*]

To this denunciation the Czar replies by a furious burst of invective against his denouncer. Turning to Foma, he asks him whether he should be condemned upon the *ipse dixit*[14] of a sorcerer; and for proof that the Patriarch deals in sorcery, he refers to his physiognomy—

> His sightless eye-balls, as thou mayest perceive,
> Glare with a dull, dead, hazy, spectral light,
> Like gaping graves on which the blue moon shines.

He then invokes the spirits of his ancestors to avenge the insult offered him, but without effect; and, his harangue being concluded, the Patriarch and the priests go through the solemn ceremony of anathematizing him by bell, book, and candle. On the extinction of the last light the Czar, who is of a nervous temperament, lapses into a swoon, and Foma clasps his hands and groans, and then the members of the convocation make their way out in the dark as well as they can; and the Second Act finishes.

The tide of contingencies is now upon the turn with the Czar. A sudden gloom has fallen upon the pathway of his existence. He is no more the man he was. Before his fatal visit to the Patriarch no man could have been more prosperous in all his undertakings. Fortune had woven a triumphal banner for her minion, of hues brighter than sunbeams. Now the scene is shifted. Henceforward his life must be a series of unsuccessful battles against circumstances. In all the architecture of his future dreams, the scaffold, the scaffold stands appallingly foremost. Man and Destiny have conspired against him. He must perish. Yet surely he might have anticipated the consequences that lay in ambush to overwhelm so criminal a curiosity as that which would penetrate the secrets of Unborn Time. His foresightless folly is to us mortals a beacon and a warning. Alas, for our peace, when we cease to think the common diurnal circle of our duties sufficiently exciting and diversified! One false step, and lo! the Uncalculating Doomed is precipitated into an abyss of evils from which all the throes of Penitence— all the excellence of Worth—all the resources of Genius, are powerless to deliver him. One error of judgment, and Man, even while to the many he seems unchanged, may be exiled from the domains of light—from the home of his tranquillity, to a land of darkness and horror, "where no order, but eternal confusion reigneth."[15] There the solitary privilege that remains to him is liberty to hopelessly ponder the calamities his imprudence has generated, and to water the dreary sands of the Past with the everflowing fountain of his tears.

Demetrius reveals to his daughter the imposition that has been practised on her. Her husband is by birth a Tartar. His real name is Borovoskitsch.[16] He has no title whatever to the Crown of Russia; and she has been duped into a marriage with an outlawed rebel. Dreadful is her anguish on ascertaining the truth. We must pass over the vivid and circumstantial description she furnishes of her own sensations. Her father exerts himself to soothe her by beautiful phraseology. By and by she grows calmer; and, Ivanna being about to meet her lover Feodor, by moonlight in a grove at the end of a vale, it is settled by Demetrius, for reasons, that Sophia shall accompany her. On their arrival at the spot, Sophia conceals herself; and Ivanna, whose father, the Kapidan-Ispraffnik, knowing all how and about the Czar's life and adventures, has been imprisoned for denouncing him as an impostor, details to her lover the entire history, to which he listens with surprise and horror. She then produces a ring which the Czar, when a Don Cossack, had sent her father in liquidation of a debt, and is about to give it to Feodor. On the instant Sophia rushes forward declaring that she alone has the right to it, and that by its instrumentality she will obtain justice for all parties. After the requisite astonishment is gone through by Feodor, and the requisite explanation by Ivanna, Sophia obtains the ring; whereupon she hurries home to have a scene with her husband. . . .

[The Czar maintains that he and Sophia are bound together as husband and wife]

Sophia's reply is in substance the same as before, viz. that when she married she imagined that she bestowed herself upon Peter the Third, and that therefore she cannot be considered the wife of any other man. The argument poses the Czar, whose intellect is not Aristotelian enough to detect its fallacy. We regret his deficiency, for Sophia thus obtains an unfair advantage. A man of the requisite skill and experience in dialectics would have shewn her the nullity of her assumption at once. "True," he would have observed, placing the upper moiety of his dexter forefinger in contact with the palm of his sinister hand, "true, you imagined that you bestowed your hand on Peter. But you did not bestow your hand on Peter; therefore your bestowal of your hand on Peter is purely imaginary; therefore you are married to Peter only in imagination; therefore you are not married to Peter at all. But you admit that you are married. Now, I have shewn you that you are not married to Peter. If, therefore, you admit that you are married, and if I have shewn you that you are not married to Peter, it follows that you are married to me, for there is no question between us of a possible third husband. But you still insist that as you married in the *bonâ fide* belief that you married Peter, Peter, and none other, must be your husband *de jure*. To this I reply, that Peter either is your husband or he is not. If Peter, and none other, be your husband, then he and I are the same individual, which is an impossibility: if Peter be not your husband, away with casuistical subtleties! Will you finally outrage all reason, and assert that you are the wife *de facto* of Peter? Even to that assertion I have a ready answer. You are a wife *de facto*—good. Now, Peter has ceased to exist; therefore Peter is not your husband; therefore you are not Peter's wife. But if you be not Peter's wife, you are my wife, for you acknowledge yourself a wife *de facto*; and, as I have already remarked, there is no question between us of a third husband. Such, Madam, is my view of the case; and I confess I do not see how you can controvert an iota of the reasoning it comprises. To me it appears as indisputable as the proposition that if two straight lines cut each other—as you propose that we should do[17]—the opposite angles will be mutually equal—like your folly and mine." Possibly the Czar's inherent loftiness of sentiment disdained stooping to the pettiness inseparable, after all, from a mode of remonstrance like this. Moreover, he was a fond husband; his affections were bruised: what wonder that under such circumstances the natural pathos and passion of his character should achieve a conquest over the suggestions of worldly reason? The Czarina [declares] her determination to be the death of him. . . .

* * * * * * * * *

He makes, however, a pathetic appeal to her generosity. Can it be that she will belie all her past professions of devotion in his hour of tribulation? He has been excommunicated by the Roskolniks. His troops are beginning to falter in their fidelity. Misgivings of the success of his enterprise disturb his nightly dreams. He is harassed by troubles from within and without. Will she, who plighted her faith to him through good and ill, desert him at such an awkward juncture? Surely she must feel eternally self-upbraided by the consciousness that her love was unable to withstand so trifling a circumstance as the change of a name! To all this she succinctly answers that she will not be the receiver of plundered property, the receiver being as bad as the thief—

> Auf meine innre Kraft will ich mich stützen,
> Doch kein gestohlnes Erdengut besitzen.[18]

> I'll go ahead where I can make progression,
> But won't keep stolen goods in my possession.

"Was aber liegt am Namen?" But what's in a name? demands the Czar, with Juliet.[19]

> The rank is but the guinea stamp.
> The man's the gowd for a' that.[20]

Sophia thinks differently—

> Der Staub bleibt Staub, fliegt er auch himmelhoch.

> Dust is but dust, though it be blown sky-high.

The scene in fine terminates, as might have been predicted, with an open rupture between the parties. The Czar orders the Czarina under lock and key—alas! to what purpose? Already the pale Parcæ have received their behest—

> Weave the warp, and weave the woof,
> The winding sheet of Borovoskitsch![21]

The Meteor of Kasán, in lieu of expanding into a sun, must explode like a sky-rocket! "How art thou fallen from heaven, O Lucifer!"[22] We track his whereabouts anxiously into the Fourth Act, and there the painful spectacle of his public exposure strikes sorrow to our soul. Yet, though

> Deserted in his utmost need
> By those his former Bounty fee'd[23]

and proclaimed an impostor besides, he still for a brief space maintains his assumed character. Yes—

> ——exposed, he lies!
> Without a friend.[24]

But proofs accumulate—he must succumb; the Kapidan-Ispraffnik, boon companion of his youth, has escaped from prison, and appears before him to confront and confound him. Shame upon thee, Ivan Persilshev, Cossack of the Don, that thou couldst stoop to bribe a gaoler!

[*The Czar is publicly exposed*]

"Thus bad begins, but worse remains behind:"[25] the revolt from his banner now becomes general; Jagunoff, the Hetman of the Volga Cossacks, setting the example. The appeal of the Czar to this portion of his troops, as soon as they have announced their determination to leave him, is finely characteristic of the man, to whose generosity of feeling and peculiar high-mindedness the dramatist, we regret to observe, has not upon all occasions done equal justice.

[*The Czar asks his troops to kill him*]

For all response to this magnanimous harangue the Hetman merely answers "Das ist nicht unser Amt!"[26] That is not the ticket!—but the Czar alas! is spared only for further discomfitures and disasters. Battle follows battle until, what with desertion and defeat, he is left without a single cohort, and compelled to seek refuge from his enemies in a cavern among the Ural Mountains. Here his fate, long held at bay, at length overtakes him. A veiled figure appears to him pointing with the finger in a northernly direction. Although sufficiently far north[27] already, as we should fancy, he accepts the omen, and, pursuing the path indicated to him, finds himself accordingly—in the midst of the Imperial Army.

> *Czar*—Betrayed! The Enemy round me! Come then, soul!
>   Nerve thyself for the final struggle!—Now!—
>   Ah!—Ah!—my arm!—it sinks!—my sword—it drops!
>   All—all is over!

(*He is seized, disarmed, and bound with cords.*)

Whither do you lead me?

> *Field-Marshal*—To that which thou hast earned—the rebel's death!

(*At this moment Borovoskitsch, looking up, beholds the Veiled Figure standing on a rock to his right in the foreground. The last rays of the setting sun fall upon her dress.*)

> *Czar*—Who art thou, shrouded and mysterious being,
>   That hast betrayed me to my doom?

(*The Figure slowly unveils. It is the Czarina!*)

Sophia—   Behold Me!

(*Boroskovitsch sinks to the earth with an outcry of horror;
and the curtain falls.*)

The length to which our review has extended precludes us from offering any formal comment on this powerful tragedy. As a whole we must be allowed to consider it inferior to *Macbeth*: perhaps it might better bear a comparison with *Richard III.*, especially in its author's judicious adaptation of language to character. Its cardinal fault is in the management of the catastrophe. Auffenetzel,—Wetzenberg, we mean, would have been pardoned a slight violation of historical truth here. As it is, we have no sympathies with Sophia Nikosoroff. The loyalty of the subject can never claim precedence of the fidelity of the spouse. If we do not go the length of stigmatizing the Czarina's conduct as monstrous, we must maintain it to have been at least shabby in the extreme—impolitic in her as a public personage, dishonourable to her as a woman, and ungenerous in her as a wife.

NOTES

THE TWO FLATS; OR, OUR QUACKSTITUTION [(J.C.M.), *Comet*, 3 June 1832]. This, the first known of Mangan's political squibs, appeared in the year of the first Reform Bill, which is obviously its theme. Mangan burlesques the two Houses of Parliament as Flats (tenement apartments), and the Constitution as Quackery. His word-play is in most cases so self-evident as to require no gloss: *Kingland/England, the Thing/the King, Erralls/Earls, Ducks/Dukes.* The notes are therefore confined to clarifying less obvious proper names and historical allusions.

1 *Ce gouvernement ... oisifs*: "That government would be worthy of the Hottentots in which a certain number of men would be allowed to say, 'Those who work should pay; we owe nothing because we do nothing'": Voltaire, "La Voix du sage et du peuple" (1750).

2 *mosey*: soft-minded person; idiot.

3 *Longdulldreary*: Charles William Stewart, third Marquis of Londonderry (1778–1854), uncompromising Tory and conspicuous opponent of parliamentary reform.

4 *a tenth part*: reference to the Tithe War (1830–1838), in which the Catholic Irish refused to support the Established Church with the forced payment of a tenth of their income. The *Comet* was founded as an anti-Tithe paper.

5 *Blockwood's Magazine*: *Blackwood's Magazine*, a Tory monthly founded in 1817.

6 *John Gull*: *John Bull*, a weekly review founded in 1820.

7 *'Alf-read*: the *Alfred*, a Tory paper published from 1831 to 1833, then incorporated into *Old England*.

8 *Stand-hard*: the *Standard*, a Tory paper launched in 1827 to oppose Catholic Emancipation. It had, in fact, a huge circulation.

9 *Billingsgate*: foul language, as attributed to the Billingsgate fish market, London.

10 *burrowed their passage into the House*: got themselves elected through "rotten boroughs"; cf. "Lord Henry was a great electioneerer, / Burrowing for boroughs like a rat or rabbit" (Byron, *Don Juan* XVI. lxx).

11 *Burke-ing traps and Pitt-falls*: rotten boroughs were condoned and exploited by such statesmen as Edmund Burke (1729–1797) and William Pitt (1759–1806).

12 *peculators*: embezzlers of public money.

13 *Ten Teapots*: anagram for "Potentates".

14 *Ten Predicables*: Aristotle, in fact, recognised only four: *genus, definition, property, accident*.

15 *Ann Tiquity*: mocking reference to "the inscrutable antiquity of the English Constitution"—an accretion of legal wisdom down the ages, not embodied in any single document.

16 *Wailingtone*: Arthur Wellesley, Duke of Wellington (1769–1852), English general, defeated Napoleon at Waterloo. Prime Minister from 1828 to 1830.

17 *Society for the Confusion of Useful Knowledge*: Mangan mocks the Society for the Diffusion of Useful Knowledge, founded 1825/26, by the Whig politician Henry Peter, Lord Brougham and Vaux; its first publication was Brougham's *Pleasures and Advantages of Science*. Mangan's distrust of Brougham's enterprise is largely due to its Utilitarian bias.

18 *hight*: named (*arch.*).

19 *Drones and Halters*: Thrones and Altars, the civil and ecclesiastical establishments.

20 *House of Hangover*: House of Hanover—British royal family from 1714 to 1917.

21 *Cumbertheland*: H.R.H. Ernest Augustus, Duke of Cumberland (1771–1851), a leader of the ultra-Tories in the Lords in their opposition to parliamentary reform.

22 *Burgersdicious*: Francis Burgersdyk (1590–1629), Dutch logician and moral philosopher.

23 *Machiavel*: Niccolo Machiavelli (1469–1527), Florentine political philosopher.

24 *Vattel*: Emeric de Vattel (1714–1767), Swiss jurist and philosopher.

25 *Puffendorff*: Samuel Puffendorf (1632–1694), German jurist, philosopher, economist, historian and statesman.

26 *Bombastes Paracelsus*: Theophrastus Bombastus von Hohenheim, called Paracelsus (1493–1541), Swiss physician and alchemist.

27 *mulctedude*: portmanteau word combining "multitude" and "mulcted"—*i.e.* unjustly taxed.

28 *Macbeth* I. vii. 5.

29 *Quart. Rev.*: the *Quarterly Review*, a Tory magazine, founded in 1809.

30 *Warder*: a "Dublin Castle" newspaper, founded in 1823.

ITALIAN LITERATURE [(A Constant Reader), *Dublin Penny Journal*, 13 October 1832]. This "letter" is the follow-up to John O'Donovan's unsigned article "Irish Literature", published in the *DPJ* of 15 September 1832, which contained Mangan's translation of an aria by Metastasio, "Timid Love". The poem was supposedly sent by an "Italian gentleman residing in Liverpool", who challenged the editors of the *DPJ* "to produce in all Irish poetry a match" to it. After a few disparaging remarks on Italian poetry, some of which Mangan quotes in the present "letter", O'Donovan asserted that "our friend's challenge ... will only stimulate our previously-formed intention of entering the MINE of ancient Irish literature" and followed his article with a translation of an Irish poem attributed to King Aldfred.

1 *The Editor of the* Liverpool Mercury ... *very warmly*: the *Liverpool Mercury* for 21 September 1832 reprinted Mangan's "Timid Love" together with its Italian original, prefacing it with the following editorial comment:

> Happening a few days ago to glance at a number of a Dublin miscellany, we were much struck with the following *morceau*, which we transcribe, under the impression that it will interest our readers. The translation is tender, and highly poetical, and would be an excellent theme for some of our popular melodists.

2 *prose*: O'Donovan's translation of Aldfred's poem is presented as "strictly literal" and does not rhyme.

VERY ORIGINAL CORRESPONDENCE [(Clarence), *Comet*, 13 January 1833]

1 *Philander*: pseudonym of *Comet* editor John Sheehan.

2 *Blackwood*: William Blackwood (1776–1834), Edinburgh publisher, founder of the Tory monthly, *Blackwood's Magazine*.

3 *Castlereagh's crocodile ... shedding barrels of tears*: Mangan seems to have misremembered a passage in Thomas Moore's political satire *The Fudge Family in Paris* (1818). The second letter in this work is supposed to be addressed by Mr. Fudge to Lord Castlereagh, whose style it imitates. Hence the following footnote: "This excellent imitation of the noble Lord's style shows how deeply Mr. Fudge must have studied his great original. Irish oratory, indeed, abounds with such startling peculiarities. Thus the elegant Counsellor B——, in describing some hypocritical pretender to charity, said, 'He put his hand in his breeches-pocket, like a crocodile, and,' &c. &c."

4 *à qui mieux mieux*: "emulously, trying to go one better".

5 *Epictetus*: of Greece (c.55–c.135), Stoic philosopher.

6 *by bell, book, and gaslight*: humorous "updating" of the ritual phrase "by bell, book, and candle", used for excommunication in the Roman Catholic Church.

7 *The Gorgon's head*: in Greek mythology, any one of the three terrible sisters, Stheno, Euryale and Medusa, the sight of whose face turned men to stone.

8 *the triple-faced hell dog*: Cerberus, watch-dog of Hades.

9 *Belthasar's palace-wall*: before the sack of his city, Babylon, in 538 BC, Belshazzar saw his doom in writing which appeared on the wall of his palace. See Daniel 5: 5–28.

10 *Medusa*: the only mortal in the Gorgon trinity.

11 *Cock-lane ghost*: a supposed ghost that haunted Cock-Lane, Smithfield (London), in 1762.

12 *the Abaddon-born visions of Quincy the opium-chewer*: hellish visions recorded in Thomas de Quincey's *Confessions of an English Opium Eater* (1822); Abaddon, in rabbinical literature, is part of Gehenna.

13 *the devil that perpetually stood opposite to Spinello*: "St. Benedict expelling the Devil" (1387) by Spinello Aretino (1346–c.1410) shows the saint face to face with a very colourful devil, whom he is forcing out of the fictive space through a combination of physical and spiritual force.

14 *Dom-Daniel*: abode of evil spirits in Chavis and Cazotte's *Continuation of the Arabian Nights* (1788–1793).

15 *the fire-globe that burned below the feet of Pascal*: Mangan combines two elements. On the one hand, in the night of November 23, 1654, Blaise Pascal underwent a mystical experience, which he summarized through the word FIRE. On the other hand, there is a story, which appears to have been circulated by Voltaire, that in his last years of life Pascal sometimes saw an abyss gaping on the left of his desk and had a chair placed over it to reassure himself.

16 *Othello* III. iii. 373.

17 *Lord Castlereagh*: Robert Stewart, second Marquis of Londonderry, better known as Viscount Castlereagh (1769–1822), British statesman, committed suicide.

18 *Au pis aller*: "at the worst".

19 *Charles Wetherell*: Sir Charles Wetherell (1770–1846), Tory politician and lawyer, violently opposed both Reform and Catholic Emancipation. He was so unpopular that when, as Recorder, he proceeded to open the assizes at Bristol in October 1831 a riot broke out which lasted three days. Mobbed, hooted and stoned, Sir Charles had to make his escape from Bristol by night.

20 *Hinc illæ lachrymæ*: "hence those tears", Terence, *Andria* I. i. 99.

21 *trafficker in boroughs*: the Conservatives sought to preserve the institution of "rotten" or "pocket boroughs" where votes could be controlled or purchased by the wealthy.

22 *Habeas Corpus*: "thou shalt have the body"; a basic right in the British Constitution that a prisoner be produced bodily in court for his trial.

23 *the battle of Bunker's Hill*: first major battle (17 June 1775) in the

American War of Independence.

24 *Almack's*: fashionable gambling club in London's Pall Mall.

25 *B.A.M.*: bam, hoax (*slang*).

AN EXTRAORDINARY ADVENTURE IN THE SHADES [(Clarence), *Comet*, 20 & 27 January 1833]

1 *De mortuis nil nisi bonum*: "Of the dead [speak] well or not at all".

2 *Bentham*: Jeremy Bentham (1748–1832), English philosopher, the founder of Utilitarianism.

3 *Tout est perdu, mes amis*: "All is lost, my friends".

4 *Shades Tavern*: the Royal Shades, in the Royal Arcade on College Green.

5 *unutterables*: trousers, "unmentionables".

6 *stückweise*: "bit by bit."

7 *Quarterly Reviewer*: contributor to the Tory *Quarterly Review* (1809–1967).

8 *Professor Wilson*: John Wilson (1785–1854), Scottish writer. Wilson was one of the principal contributors to *Blackwood's Magazine*, using the pseudonym "Christopher North". From 1820 he held the chair of moral philosophy in Edinburgh.

9 *Ahasuerus the wanderer*: the Wandering Jew of medieval legend.

10 Cf. Psalm 4: 6.

11 *Tugendbund*: "League of Virtue", secret association (1790–1813) whose aim was to promote civic virtues and work for the liberation of Prussia.

12 *Orestes and Pylades*: respectively son and nephew of Agamemnon; their friendship was proverbial.

13 *Cuvier*: Georges Léopold Chrétien Frédéric Dagobert Cuvier (1769–1832), French naturalist and palaeontologist.

14 *Dr. Bowring*: John Bowring (1792–1872), well-known translator and champion of the founder of Utilitarianism, Jeremy Bentham, whose works he edited; in later years Mangan was to use Bowring's translations of Russian, Serbian and Cheskian poetry.

15 *the Rubicon*: a small river between ancient Italy and the province of Cisalpine Gaul, which Julius Caesar crossed with his army in 49 BC, thus breaking the rule that a Roman general should disband his troops before re-entering Italy. Hence, *to cross the Rubicon* means "to take an irrevocable step".

16 *the wand of Prospero*: Prospero, hero of Shakespeare's *Tempest*, manages much of the play's business by means of his magic staff.

17 *the lamp of Aladdin*: Aladdin, hero of a tale in the *Arabian Nights*, has a lamp which when rubbed summons a genie of prodigious obligingness.

18 *the violin of Paganini*: Niccolo Paganini (1782–1840), Italian virtuoso

violinist of such uncanny skill that he was rumoured to be in league with the devil.

19 *March of Intellect's*: the "march of intellect"—or "march of mind"—was a phrase commonly used (especially with ironical intent) in the second quarter of the 19th century, following the foundation of the Society for the Diffusion of Useful Knowledge.

20 *primâ facie*: "at first sight".

21 *con amore*: "with love".

22 *Calderon*: Pedro Calderón de la Barca (1600–1681), Spanish dramatist.

23 *Corneille*: Pierre Corneille (1606–1684), French dramatist.

24 *Malherbe*: François de Malherbe (1555–1628), French poet and translator.

25 *Opitz*: Martin Opitz von Boberfeld (1597–1639), German man of letters.

26 *Canitz*: Friedrich Rudolf Ludwig, Freiherr von Canitz (1654–1699), German poet and diplomat.

27 *Uz*: Johann Peter Uz (1720–1796), German poet.

28 *Wieland*: Christoph Martin Wieland (1733–1813), German poet, novelist and translator.

29 *meines Herzens Richter — (ach! wenn ich ein Herz habe)*: a literal translation would read "Richter of my heart (alas! if I have a heart)" .

30 *the Reverend Ned Irving*: Edward Irving (1792–1834), fundamentalist Scottish minister, whose followers espoused the pentecostal practice of "speaking in tongues".

31 *The great Utilitarian*: Bowring, see note 14 above.

32 *the Westminster*: the *Westminster Review*, a radical magazine founded by Bentham in 1824, edited by Bowring and James Mill.

33 *Oliver Yorke*: pseudonym of Francis Mahony in his *Reliques of Father Prout*. Mangan is quibbling on the names of the prudent Oliver and the more reckless Roland, contrasting characters in the French epic *Chanson de Roland*.

34 *Lardner*: Dionysius Lardner (1793–1859), Irish scientific writer and encyclopedist. He was frequently the butt of Mahony's sarcasm.

35 *enbonpoint*: Mangan's spelling—instead of *embonpoint*—corresponds with the origin of the word: *en bon point*, "in good condition".

36 *Alnaschar*: see "The Tale of the Barber's Fifth Brother" in the *Arabian Nights*.

37 *the tower of Lebanon*: Song of Solomon 7: 4: "thy nose is as the tower of Lebanon which looketh towards Damascus".

38 *Maugraby*: great magician, master of the Dom Daniel hall of evil spirits, who figures in Chavis and Cazotte's *Continuation of the Arabian Nights* (1788–1793); he plays a villainous role in Mangan's story "The

Thirty Flasks".

39 *de haut en bas*: "from top to bottom".

40 *Sir Morgan O'Doherty*: one of the many pen-names used by the Irish writer William Maginn (1793–1842).

41 *manches à gigot*: "leg-of-mutton sleeves".

42 *Lock-und-Gaukel-Werk*: "conjuring trick, deception".

43 *Berkeleyans*: followers of the Idealist philosopher George Berkeley (1685–1753).

44 *Tempest* V. i. 56.

45 *the Thunderer*: the London *Times*.

46 *Slawkenbergius*: a name invented by Sterne; supposedly the author of a long treatise on noses, whose "Tale" appears in *Tristram Shandy* Vol. IV. Nosology means "science of diseases" and does not derive from the word *nose*. Strangely enough, Edgar Allan Poe, who resembles Mangan in many ways, made the same pun in his story "Lionizing", which first appeared in the *Southern Literary Messenger* in May 1835.

47 *Paradise Lost* II. 142–143: Belial's actual words are "our final hope / Is flat despair".

48 *Anacharsis Clootz*: Jean Baptiste du Val de Grâce, Baron von Clootz (1755–1794), revolutionary Prussian nobleman, self-styled "Orator of the Human Race", in which character he asserted before the French Assembly, 19 June 1790, that the world adhered to the Declaration of Human Rights; guillotined in time by Robespierre.

49 *pour toute compagnie*: "for my sole companion".

50 *Dom-Daniel*: see note 38 above.

51 Byron, *Childe Harold* III. xcviii.

52 *Dr Stokes*: Whitley Stokes (1763–1845), patriot and scholar, professor of medicine at Trinity College, Dublin.

53 *Brasspen*: pseudonym of Joseph L'Estrange, one of the *Comet* writers.

54 *Tout est mystère dans ce monde-ci...je ne sais trop qu'en croire*: "All is a mystery in this world, I don't know what to make of it".

FLASHES OF LIGHTNING [(Unsigned), *Comet*, 27 January 1833]

1 Maria Edgeworth, in *Belinda* (1801) Vol. I, ch. x, quotes 'an old Scotch song':

'Tis good to be merry and wise,
'Tis good to be honest and true,
'Tis good to be off with the old love,
Before you be on with the new.

2 *the Age*: London newspaper (1825–1842), which was entertainingly quoted in a regular section of the *Comet* called "Gems of the British Press".

3 *Philander*: pseudonym of *Comet* editor John Sheehan.

4 *Irish Radicals and the Whigs*: Irish Radicals supported the British Whig Administration of Earl Grey (1830–1834) in introducing the Reform Act of 1832.

5 *Peel*: Sir Robert Peel (1788–1850), Conservative statesman; he opposed O'Connell's agitation for the repeal of the Act of Union.

6 *Apropos des bottes*: "with regard to nothing at all"; correctly *Apropos de bottes*.

7 *Mother Mute's Mag*: jocular reference to Trinity College, (sometimes called the "silent sister" of Oxford and Cambridge) and to the *Dublin University Magazine*, which had just been founded in 1833 by Isaac Butt and other members of the College. Mangan was to become one of its main contributors.

8 *pour manger*: a pun on the English word meaning "trough" and the French phrase for "to eat".

9 *Bessy Bell and Mary Gray*: characters in a story which appeared in the first number of the *DUM*, January 1833; intended as the first in a series, it had, in the event, no successors.

10 *Brasspen*: pseudonym of Joseph L'Estrange, one of the *Comet* writers.

11 *Hume-Anne*: Joseph Hume (1777–1855), Radical M.P. for Middlesex, 1830–1837; Anne, we presume, is meant to be Brasspen's thirty-first cousin.

A TREATISE ON A PAIR OF TONGS [(Clarence), *Comet*, 17 February, 10 March & 17 March 1833]

1 R.B. Sheridan, *The Duenna* II. ii.: "Ah! sure a pair was never seen / So justly form'd to meet by nature!".

2 *Julius Caesar* I. ii. 134–135. For "it", read "he".

3 *Celestial Empire*: China.

4 *Van Dieman's land*: now Tasmania.

5 *New Burlington Street*: the London street where the well-known publisher H.D. Colburn had his office.

6 *Bulwer*: Edward George Bulwer-Lytton, first Baron Lytton (1803–1873), popular English writer.

7 *D'Israeli*: Benjamin Disraeli, Earl of Beaconsfield (1804–1881), British Conservative politician and novelist.

8 *Colburn's lunacy*: see note 5 above.

9 *the Age*: London newspaper; see "Flashes of Lightning" note 1.

10 *surphiz*: surface—macaronic pun; "phiz" (jocular abbreviation of "physiognomy"): face.

11 *Prometheus*: the Titan who stole fire from heaven.

12 *Kilkenny*: possible allusion to coal-mines at Castlecomer, Co. Kilkenny.

13 *punch-jug*: "Punch was made formerly in a jug. The practice, even today, has some disciples in the suburbs." *(Mangan's note)*.

14 *Cartesius*: René Descartes (1596–1650), French philosopher, mathematician and scientist.

15 *Burked*: smothered or suppressed—after the Irish murderer and body-snatcher, William Burke, of "Burke and Hare" notoriety, executed in Edinburgh in 1829.

16 *Schelling*: Friedrich Wilhelm Joseph von Schelling (1775–1854), chief philosopher of the German Romantic movement.

17 *Gassendi*: Pierre Gassendi (1592–1655), French philosopher.

18 *Reid*: Thomas Reid (1710–1796), Scottish philosopher, author of *Essays on the Intellectual Powers of Man* (1785).

19 *Mallebranche*: Nicolas Malebranche (1638–1715), French philosopher and theologian.

20 *Wolfe*: probably Christian Wolff (1657–1754), German philosopher and mathematician.

21 *Leibnitz*: Gottfried Wilhelm, Baron von Leibnitz (1646–1716), German philosopher and mathematician.

22 *Berkeleyans*: followers of the Idealist philosopher George Berkeley (1685–1753).

23 *in esse vel posse*: "in actuality or possibility".

24 *Reid's Powers*: see note 18 above.

25 *Mill's Phenomena*: James Mill (1773–1836), author of *Analysis of the Phenomena of the Human Mind* (1829).

26 *Brown's Philosophy*: Thomas Brown (1778–1820), Scottish philosopher. His *Lectures on the Philosophy of the Human Mind* was published posthumously.

27 *muddler*: a small churning stick for mixing toddies.

28 *Philander*: pseudonym of *Comet* editor, John Sheehan.

29 *Bully's Acre*: free burial ground for Dublin's poor in Kilmainham up to 1832.

30 *Brobdignagian*: correctly, Brobdingnagian, "enormous", after Swift's giant men and women in Book III of *Gulliver's Travels*.

31 *De l'autre coté*: (correctly, *côté*) "on the other hand".

32 *Trenck in Magdeburgh*: Friedrich, Freiherr von der Trenck (1726–1794), writer of a celebrated autobiography, was incarcerated in 1754 in Magdeburg for ten years.

33 *Tasso in Ferrara*: Torquato Tasso (1544–1595), Italian epic poet, author of *Gerusalemme Liberata*, was incarcerated at a lunatic asylum in Ferrara in 1579.

34 *Galileo in Florence*: Galileo Galilei (1564–1642), Italian astronomer and physicist; imprisoned by the Inquisition in Rome, Galileo was released

to the Duke of Tuscany in 1633 on condition that he remain on Tuscan territory; he continued to live and work in Florence.

35 *Philander in Kilmainham*: John Sheehan ("Philander") and his co-editor Thomas Browne, whose pseudonym was "Jonathan Buckthorn", were sentenced to twelve months' imprisonment and a fine of £100 following the appearance in the *Comet* of the article, "A Buckthorn for the Black Slugs", an attack against the clergy of the Established Church. Sheehan was imprisoned in Kilmainham Gaol in February 1833.

36 *under Dunn*: George Dunn was chief warder of Kilmainham prison. The square brackets are Mangan's.

37 *Eglantine*: Mangan's sonnet, "Symptoms of Disease of the Heart", published 17 March 1833, is also addressed to "Eglantine".

38 *Zeno*: Zeno of Elea (c.490–c.430 BC), Greek philosopher, inventor of dialectics.

39 *Robert Owen*: Welsh social reformer (1771–1858), pioneer of the co-operative movement. He recommended that "villages of unity and co-operation" be established for the unemployed. Each village would consist of about 1,200 persons, living on 1,000–1,500 acres; all would live in one large structure, built in the form of a square.

40 *Tom Steele*: Thomas Steele (1788–1848), Irish politician and writer; fought as a volunteer in Spain in 1823; returned to Ireland to work for Catholic Emancipation.

41 *Brougham's Useless Knowledge books*: the Society for the Diffusion of Useful Knowledge, founded in 1825/26 by Henry Peter, 1st Baron Brougham *et al.*, produced a large range of cheap "useful knowledge" books; see "The Two Flats", note 17.

42 *Bowring*: Sir John Bowring (1792–1872), English linguist, political economist and translator; see "An Extraordinary Adventure in the Shades", note 14.

43 Thomas Warton, "The Pleasures of Melancholy", l. 209: "The due clock swinging slow with sweepy sway."

44 *Dr. Southey*: Robert Southey (1774–1843) had been appointed Poet Laureate in 1813. Mangan had already attacked Southey in "Sonnets by an Aristocrat" (*Comet*, 24 June 1832): "Southey who strings / Hexameters for butts of sack".

45 *Helvetius*: Claude Adrien Helvetius (1715–1771), French materialist philosopher, whose *De l'Esprit* appeared in 1758.

46 William Godwin, Preface to *St. Leon* (1799): " . . . it is better that man should be a living being, than a stock or a stone."

47 *black stock*: clergyman's necktie.

48 *Crichton*: James Crichton (1560–1582), Scottish scholar and linguist; known as the "Admirable Crichton" after Urquhart's glowing

characterisation of him in *The Discovery of a Most Exquisite Jewel* (1652).

49 *c'est là une affaire finie*: "that business is settled".

50 *gaffer*: in Hiberno-English usage the word could mean "youngster"—see Synge's *Playboy of the Western World*, Act III: "dreading that young gaffer who'd capsize the stars".

51 *Saint Dunstan*: archbishop of Canterbury (925–988), was believed to have seized the devil by the nose with a pair of red-hot tongs.

52 *the Comet Club*: previously called the *Political Tract Society*, had for its main object the abolition of the Tithe system. Its main publications were *The Parson's Horn-Book* (1831), to which Mangan contributed, and the *Comet* newspaper, launched on 1 May 1831.

53 *Black*: "Any allusion to the Editor of the *Morning Chronicle*? PHIL.". It cannot be ascertained whether this note is by "Philander" (John Sheehan, *Comet* editor) or by Mangan.

54 *Grey-headed*: Lord Grey was then the head of the Government.

55 *Blue-devilled*: hallucinating with *delirium tremens*; may refer also to the fact that the Tories were currently adopting blue as their party's colour.

56 *Globe, Sun*: contemporary English newspapers.

57 *pia mater*: a delicate membrane of the brain.

58 *Prometheus Unbound* IV. 334.

59 *Francis Blackburne*: Irish lawyer (1782–1867), became Attorney-General for Ireland in 1830.

60 *William Conyngham Plunket*: 1st Baron Plunket (1764–1854), became Lord Chancellor in 1830.

61 *posting the coal*: *to post the cole* (or *coal*) is slang for *to pay down the money*.

62 *a better on the Turf*: "*Turf*—3. A slab or block of peat dug for use as fuel. 4. The turf (often with capital T): The grassy track of course over which horse-racing takes place; hence, the institution, action, or practice of horse-racing; the racing world." (O.E.D.)

63 *Coke on Littleton*: lawyer's shorthand for Sir Edward Coke's edition (1628) of Lyttelton's *Tenures* (c.1481). "Coke upon Lyttleton" was also slang for a mixture of Spanish wine and brandy.

64 *Blackstone's Commentaries*: *Commentaries on the Laws of England* (1765–1769) by Sir William Blackstone.

65 *Dey of Algiers*: France invaded Algiers in 1830, ousting the Dey.

66 *the ex-Rex Charles X*: Charles X (1757–1836), king of France, abdicated after the July Revolution of 1830.

67 *otto of rose*: another term for "attar of rose", *i.e.* essence of rose-scent.

68 *ex uno disce omnes*: "you may infer all from one instance".

69 *Moses Cohen*: proprietor of a cigar divan at 70 Dame Street—mentioned, *a.o.*, in Mangan's "A Railway of Rhyme" (1835).

70 *Dame-street*: shopping street in the centre of Dublin.

71 *the fifth book of the Jewish Ethics*: Mangan is in fact expanding upon a famous passage in the *Mishnah*, "Ethics of the Fathers" V. 9; in the original catalogue, the first item is normally given as "the mouth of the earth".

72 *Levi*: the *Mishnah*, basis of the Talmud, is a second-century consolidation of Hebrew oral law established by a team of Jewish scholars which does not include a Levi.

73 *the shameer*: a supernatural small green stone, which was first used at the time of the construction of the Tabernacle to engrave the names of the tribes on the precious jewels of the High Priest's breastplate.

74 *ens rationis*: "being of the mind", *i.e.* something that can exist only as an object of thought, but does not exist "in itself".

75 *Othello* III. iii. 360: "Farewell! Othello's occupation's gone".

76 *toploftical*: elevated, overbearing.

77 The quotation is not from Shakespeare but from Milton's *Comus*, III. 208–209: "And airy tongues, that syllable men's names / On Sands, and Shores, and desert Wildernesses".

78 *King Tongataboo*: Tongatabu—the Sacred Tonga—is the largest of the Tonga Islands.

79 *pour couper court*: "to be brief".

80 *Das Jahrhundert...werden*: "This age is not ripe for my theories. I live a denizen of the centuries that are to come". *(Mangan's note)*. Schiller, *Don Carlos* III. x. 3076–8.

81 *Every one...black stockings*: Henry, Marquess of Anglesey, was Lord Lieutenant of Ireland, from 1 March 1828 to 6 March 1829, and from 23 December 1830 to 26 September 1833. When, on his second entrance, the procession passed along College Green, Marcus Costello, a young barrister and a member of Daniel O'Connell's recently founded Association of Irish Volunteers for the Repeal of the Union, stood at a window holding a black stocking with a pair of tongs, presumably to laugh at the Marquis, who had lost a leg at the Battle of Waterloo.

82 *keep up the* game *"at all* hazards"*: an involved combination of puns, since "hazard" was a popular gambling game, and the adjective "game", when used of an arm or a leg, means "lame".

83 *blacklegs*: cheating gamesters.

84 *White feet*: the Whitefeet were one of the secret societies formed in Ireland in the 1830s and associated with agrarian disorder.

85 *l-e-g.*: the word "leg" when it is spelt produces the word "elegy".

THE IRISH LANGUAGE [(A Constant Reader, Clarence-Street, Liverpool), *Dublin Penny Journal*, 20 April 1833]
1   "Of the letters ᵭ, ᵽ, ᵹ." *(Mangan's note)*. Mangan's "letter" is followed by a reply by J.Ó'D[onovan], commencing:
    Our Italian correspondent has mistaken the passage which he extracted from the "Transactions of the Gaelic Society".... [The] letters are not ᵭ, ᵽ, ᵹ, as our learned correspondent imagines, (for their powers are well regulated,) but the liquids *l*, *n*, *ʀ*, the sounds of which are not so fixed.
2   *Count Marcel*: Mangan may be referring to Jean-Joseph Marcel, French linguist, author of an *Alphabet irlandais, précédé d'une notice historique, littéraire et typographique* (1804); the French quotes are not from this work.
3   *the grammars of O'Byrne and Neilson*: no grammar by an O'Byrne has been found; Mangan may have meant O'Brien (see following note). William Neilson wrote *An Introduction to the Irish Language* (1808).
4   *Rev. Paul O'Brien's grammar: A Practical Grammar of the Irish Language* (1809).
5   *who "ama la sua patria"*: who "loves his fatherland".
6   *L'Alfabet Européen appliqué aux langues Asiatiques*: a linguistic study (1819) by Constantin François Chasseboeuf, Comte de Volney (1757–1820).
7   "See Preface to Vol. I. Gaelic Society." *(Mangan's note)*.

MY TRANSFORMATION. A WONDERFUL TALE [(Clarence), *Dublin Satirist*, 19 October 1833]
1   *1 Henry IV*. III. i. 58.
2   Byron, *The Giaour* 1101–1102: "[My love] was like the lava flood / That boils in Aetna's breast of flame". The phrase occurs also in Mangan's poem, "Moreen: a Love-Lament", *DUM*, October 1847.
3   *the change... the spirit of my dream*: cf. Byron's poem, "The Dream", in which six stanzas out of nine begin with the line, "A change came o'er the spirit of my dream".
4   Psalm 105: 18: "The iron entered into his soul", a mistranslation in the Vulgate of the Hebrew (literally "his person entered into the iron", *i.e.* fetters, chains), which has passed into figurative use to express the impression made by captivity or affliction upon the very "soul" or inner being of the sufferer.
5   *The denunciatory handwriting... destiny*: Belshazzar, king of Babylon, saw a hand writing on the wall of his palace a message which Daniel interpreted thus: "God hath numbered thy kingdom and finished it.... Thou art weighed in the balances and art found wanting.... Thy

kingdom is divided, and given to the Medes and Persians" (Daniel 5).

6 *aspect*: face.

7 *Monkstown*: a seaside suburb of Dublin.

8 *Carlisle Bridge*: now re-named O'Connell Bridge.

9 *lycanthropy*: magic which turns man into wolf.

10 *Burton's Anatomie of Melancholie*: Robert Burton, *The Anatomy of Melancholy, what it is, with all the kinds, causes, symptoms, prognostics, and several cures of it: In three partitions, with their several sections, members, and sub-sections, philosophically, medicinally, historically opened and cut up: by Democritus Junior, with a satyrical preface conducing to the following discourse* (1621).

11 Godwin, Preface to *St. Leon*; correctly, "a stock or a stone" (see "Treatise on a Pair of Tongs", note 46).

12 See "Tale of the Fisherman", *Arabian Nights*.

13 *blue devils*: depression of spirits.

14 *Henry-street*: still a busy shopping area on the north side of the Liffey in Dublin.

15 *Prometheus Unbound* IV. 334.

16 *Clootz*: Jean Baptiste du Val de Grâce, Baron von Clootz; see "An Extraordinary Adventure in the Shades", note 48.

17 *Democritus*: Democritus (c.460–c.370 BC), Greek philosopher; sometimes styled "the laughing philosopher".

18 *Lord Chesterfield's Letters*: Philip Dormer Stanhope, 4th Earl of Chesterfield (1694–1773), English politician and writer; letter to his son, 9 March 1748: "Many people... have got a very disagreeable and silly trick of laughing whenever they speak".

19 *Hamlet* III. iv. 53: "Look here upon this picture, and on this".

20 *cloud-compelling*: Homeric epithet, sometimes used humorously in English to refer to smoking.

21 *Cohen's cloud-compelling Divan in Dame-street*: see "A Treatise on a Pair of Tongs", note 69.

A DIALOGUE IN THE SHADES; BUT NOT A "DIALOGUE OF THE DEAD" [(Clarence), *Weekly Dublin Satirist*, 21 June 1834]. The Shades was a Dublin tavern, on College Green. *Dialogues of the Dead* is a satirical work by the Greek writer, Lucian (c.120–180).

The Dialogue is followed by endnotes, headed "Comments and Queries, By Solomon Dryasdust, L.L.D. and A.S.S."

1 Maria Edgeworth, in *Belinda* (1801) Vol. I, ch. x, quotes "an old Scotch song":

'Tis good to be merry and wise,

'Tis good to be honest and true,
'Tis good to be off with the old love,
Before you be on with the new.

2 *hic, haec, hock*: parodic declension of Latin demonstrative, "hock" being a German white wine.

3 "Truly, this seemeth to be a most bare and evident plagiarism from William Shakspeare, Gent.
'Cowards die many times before their death,
The valiant never taste of death but once.'" *(Dryasdust's note)*.
Mangan parodies *Julius Caesar* II. ii. 32–33.

4 *Romeo and Juliet* II. ii. 43–44: "What's in a name? That which we call a rose / By any other name would smell as sweet".

5 Pope, "Thoughts on Various Subjects" (1711).

6 *Castle-market to Coppinger's-row*: the present Dublin City Market and adjacent Coppinger Row.

7 *a hog*: a shilling (*slang*).

8 *Rock-road*: seaside road on the way to Blackrock, a southern suburb of Dublin.

9 *Julius Caesar* IV. iii. 72–73: "By heaven, I had rather coin my heart, / And drop my blood for drachmas".

10 *bibber*: booser.

11 *Julius Caesar* III. ii. 74: "Friends, Romans, countrymen".

12 *Firbolgs*: in the *Book of Invasions*, which recounts the legendary history of Ireland, the *Fir Bolg* or "Bag-men" were an unlovely race conquered in battle by the Milesians, admired ancestors of the historic Irish. *O'Hoollaghan* therefore is fictional, a satiric type for the bibulous Irish poet.

13 *Potteen*: "poitín"; in Irish literally the "little pot", from which the illegal whiskey was served.

14 "*Trom-ól se munloch ó mhaidin go n-oídche*": source not found; corrected, the line would read: "*Trom-ólann sé múnloch ó mhaidin go h-oidhche*", that is, "He is forever drinking piss (*i.e.* bad liquor) from morning till night". Mangan's polite translation quibbles on two meanings of the word *muddle*: "to bathe or wallow in mud or muddy water" (*obs.*), and to stir punch with a 'muddler'".

15 "Of a verity the passage doth occur in the Iliad:

Οινοβαρες κυνος ομματ' εχων, κραδιην δ' ελαφοιο,
Ουτε ποτ' ες πολεμόν άμα λαώ θωρηχθηναι,
Ουτε λοχονδ' ιεναι συν αριστηεσσιν ΤΙΠΠΡΑΡΙΩΝ,
Τετληχας θυμώ." *(Dryasdust's note)*.

The original (*Iliad* I. 225–228) has Αχαιων instead of ΤΙΠΠΡΑΡΙΩΝ and translates:

> You old soak, with the eyes of a dog and the heart of a doe, you never had the courage to join your people in arming for battle, or risk an ambush with Achaia's [Tipperary's] picked men.

16 *exflunctify*: appears to be a Mangan coinage for "destroy" or "extinguish". "To flunk" is "to give up, back out, fail utterly" (O.E.D.).

17 *Pomponious Atticus*: Titus Pomponius Atticus (109–32 BC), Roman *eques* ("knight"), friend of Cicero.

18 "*Quere—Et tu Brute?* For it hath not yet been supported by any notable authority that Caius Julius (titularly called Cæsar,) was wont to hold parlance in the English tongue; neither doth it, *primâ facie*, appear duly consonant with reason that he should have been used so to do, seeing that such tongue had in his epoch no accredited existence, and was, properly speaking, then merely an *ens in posse*." *(Dryasdust's note)*. Mangan parodies *Julius Caesar* III. i. 77.

19 *cross*: to write across what is already written.

20 Byron, *Beppo* lxxx.

21 *The Deserted Village*, l. 208: "'Twas certain he could write, and cipher too".

22 Byron, *Childe Harold* III. xxxiii. For *bottle* read *mirror*.

23 Thomas Moore, "Farewell! but whenever you welcome the hour" (*Irish Melodies*): "You may break, you may shatter the vase if you will, / But the scent of the roses will hang round it still".

24 *Ballygruddery road*: fictitious place-name, probably compounded of such names as Ballyporeen and Kilruddery ("bally" is the anglicised version of the Irish *baile*, "town", "village").

25 Pope, *Essay on Man* I. 267.

26 *Lord Burleigh*: in Act III of Sheridan's comedy, *The Critic*, there is a play-within-the-play, *The Spanish Armada*, in which Lord Burleigh makes a brief appearance; too busy with the affairs of state, he declines to speak, but the shake of his head is prodigiously interpreted by the character Puff.

27 *Hamlet* III. i. 81–82: "rather bear those ills we have, / Than fly to others that we know not of?"

28 *gaffer*: youngster.

29 *Hamlet* III. i. 83: "Thus conscience does make cowards of us all".

30 *Apropos de rein du tout*: properly "*Apropos de rien du tout*", apropos of nothing ("rein" is "kidney" or "small of the back / waist").

31 *Crabtree*: fictitious poet.

32 The lines are Mangan's own: "Verses to a Friend", *Comet*, 27 January 1833.

33 "The Deep, Deep Sea", a cavatina from the musical comedy *Honest Frauds* (1830); music by Charles Edward Horn (1786–1849), words by Mrs George Sharpe. The first stanza reads:

> Oh, come with me, my love,
> And our fairy home shall be,
> Where the water spirits rove,
> In the deep, deep sea.

34 pries ... blank: a *blank* is a lottery ticket which does not get a *prize*.

35 "*Quere—I've hereafter named?* The venerable canons of our English orthography do notoriously repudiate and anathemise those fantastical combinations of words and disjointings of syllables, whereof we here witness a specimen. Neither in Vattel nor yet in Blackstone hath any man been hitherto able to discover the *materies* of a pun." *(Dryasdust's note)*.

36 "*Quere—O'Connell might?* A duplicate and counterpart (transcribed *verbatim, literatim et punctuatim*) of the foregoing apposite, and, in truth, seasonable criticism might be introduced here with not only great profit, but also exceeding advantage, and likewise, I opine, considerable benefit, utility, and usefulness." *(Dryasdust's note)*. Mangan's pun, "*oak*-on-*elm*-ight"/ "O'Connell might", refers to the lawyer and politician, Daniel O'Connell (1774–1847).

37 *soal*: obsolete spelling of "sole".

38 "*Lament of Tasso*": a poem by Byron (1817).

39 "*Elegy in a Country Churchyard*": a poem by Thomas Gray (1750).

40 *Schiller's "Wail of Ceres"*: Mangan had translated the last four stanzas of "Klage der Ceres" for the *Dublin Penny Journal*, 20 July 1833, and was to translate the whole poem for the *DUM*, January 1835.

41 "*Death and Burial of Cock Robin*": popular seventeenth-century English song, mock-heroic elegy in which the birds and beasts lament the robin's death and arrange for his burial.

42 *Robert Owen*: Welsh social reformer (1771–1858); see "A Treatise on a Pair of Tongs", note 39.

43 *Mendicity Asylum*: later renamed the Mendicity Institution, for the city's poor, situated on Island St. by the Liffey.

44 Thomas Moore, "Lesbia hath a beaming eye" (*Irish Melodies*), l. 21: "To sink or swell as Heaven pleases".

45 Thomas Moore, "Remember thee!" (*Irish Melodies*).

46 *On voit bien ... allons*: "It is clear my friend that you are what we call hoxmontary. Let us go.—You have some nerve indeed calling me hoxmontary, considering you are now as blind as an owl. If I felt like it I could exflunctify you teetotaceously. But let us go." Like *exflunctify*

(see note 16 above), the words *hoxmontary* and *teetotacieusement* may have been coined by Mangan. Note, however, that *hoxmontary* (meaning "drunk") appears also in an article not written by Mangan, "Annals of Ireland, 2008–2034", *Weekly Dublin Satirist*, 30 August 1834, and that *teetotacieusement* has been derived from *teetotally*, "in complete abstinence from intoxicants".

LOVE, MYSTERY, AND MURDER. A TALE. [(Clarence), *Weekly Dublin Satirist*, 30 August & 6 September 1834]

1 *Taming of the Shrew* IV. i. 52–58: "Let's ha't, good Grumio. . . . "
2 *Ugolino di Bulbruzzi*: cf. Ugolino della Gherardesca, Count of Pisa, eternalised by Dante in the *Inferno*, canto xxxiii.
3 "Beneath a mountain's brow, the most remote
  And *inaccessible by shepherds trod.*
                                    HOME's *Douglas.*" *(Mangan's note)*.
  Douglas is a tragedy by John Home (1722–1808).
4 *Cocker*: Edward Cocker (1631–1675), whose text-book *Arithmetic* sold prodigiously. The answers provided in its final section occasioned the proverb "All right according to Cocker".
5 *Mrs Radcliffe's romances*: Anne Radcliffe (1764–1823), English novelist in the Gothic tradition, many of whose novels were set in Italy.
6 *The name of the monk was Hugo Gundalpho*: a comic conflation of the titles of two famous Gothic novels, M.G. Lewis's *The Monk* (1796) and Radcliffe's *The Mysteries of Udolpho* (1794).
7 *cup*: presumably misprint for *lamp.*
8 *pluck*: Mangan exploits two senses of the word: the "heart, lungs and liver of a beast" and "resolution".
9 *Apicius*: famous gormandiser at the court of Augustus who, when his means ran out, took his life rather than submit to plain rations.
10 *the Lord Lieutenant of the Castle*: a thrust at Ireland's Lord Lieutenant, who ruled from Dublin Castle.
11 *Ariosto*: Ludovico Ariosto (1474–1533), Italian poet and playwright, author of the epic *Orlando Furioso* (1516–1532).
12 *Hole in the Wall*: then a colloquial name for the Black Horse Tavern near the Ashtown Gate of Dublin's Phoenix Park.
13 *Stone Jug*: slang for "prison".
14 *muriatic phlogiston*: "muriatic" means "obtainable from the sea"; "phlogiston" is a principle formerly supposed to exist in all bodies and to be disengaged in the process of combustion. The theory of phlogiston was generally abandoned after the discovery of oxygen by Antoine Lavoisier (1743–1794), but Joseph Priestley, in *The Doctrine of Phlogiston Established, and that of the Composition of Water refuted*,

published in 1800, still maintained that phlogiston was a constituent part of water.

15 *two-pair floor*: second floor.

16 *castor*: a hat, originally of beaver's fur.

17 Cf. "Frailty thy name is woman", *Hamlet* I. ii. 146.

18 *A mad world, my masters!*: title of a comedy by Thomas Middleton (1604).

19 *bonnet rouge*: red cap worn by the French revolutionaries.

ANTHOLOGIA GERMANICA NO. I. THE LYRICAL AND SMALLER POEMS OF SCHILLER [(Unsigned), *DUM*, January 1835]

1 *Father Bouhours*: Dominique Bouhours S.J. (1628–1702), grammarian, historian and autobiographer.

2 *Un Allemand peut-il avoir de l'esprit?*: "Is it possible for a German to be witty?"

3 *Point du tout*: "Not at all".

4 Mangan appears to have remembered here a passage in Carlyle's essay, "State of German Literature": "Above a century ago, the Père Bouhours propounded to himself the pregnant question: *Si un Allemand peut avoir de l'esprit?*"

5 *Pelion piled upon Ossa*: the Titans were said to have piled Mount Ossa upon Mount Pelion in an attempt to storm the Olympian heaven.

6 *Le maître l'a dit; cela suffit*: "The master has said it; that's enough".

7 *Il ne faut pas s'en étonner; je demande des hommes et l'on me donne des Allemands!*: "One should not be surprised; I asked for men and you gave me Germans!"

8 Job 38: 2.

9 *Leidenschaften des jungen Werthers*: Goethe's novel, *The Sorrows of Young Werther* (1774).

10 *Hamlet* I. iv. 51–53: "What may this mean, / That thou, dead corse, again in complete steel / Revisits thus the glimpses of the moon".

11 *1788*: it is not clear why, on several occasions, Mangan thus dates the French Revolution of 1789.

12 *Martin Opitz*: Opitz von Boberfeld (1597–1639), German man of letters.

13 *Gellert and Hagedorn*: Christian Fuerchtegott Gellert (1715–1769) and Friedrich von Hagedorn (1708–1754), German poets and fabulists.

14 *Rabener*: Gottlieb Wilhelm Rabener (1714–1771), popular German satirist.

15 *Haller*: Albrecht von Haller (1708–1777), German poet and scientist.

16 *Weiss*: Christian Felix Weisze (1726–1804), German poet and playwright.

17 *Klopstock*: "The poetry of Klopstock is like the tolling of a deep-

mouthed bell, powerful perhaps, but one-toned even to tediousness. No man repeats himself half so often. We occasionally meet in his Odes, it must be confessed, thoughts we seek elsewhere in vain, thoughts abounding in pathos to very overflowing, and serving as indications of what the man was capable of, had he granted more exuberant license to his imaginations. The following, which occurs in his Ode to Bodmer (and under other forms by the by, in two or three of his Odes besides) will strike upon an answering chord in the bosoms of many: —

> Ah! they meet not each other, those burning hearts,
>   For love and each other created—*these*
> *The nightwide Heaven of sundering climates parts,*
>   *Or the barrier-wall of centuries.*

But notwithstanding this and a few similarly charactered conceptions of undoubted beauty, scantily scattered through his blank verses, it is every day becoming more apparent that Klopstock was over-appreciated from the beginning. His partizans have exalted him as the originator of the German hexameter. But the Greek had the priority. It is just as though when an artificer had constructed a splendid pair of chariot-wheels, the admiration of all who saw them, a fellow were to come forward and exclaim, But I know a man who has made a pair of waggon-wheels on the same plan, a great deal heavier and clumsier than these! The heaviness and clumsiness of the German wheels are not the fault of Klopstock, but as little do they entitle him to our applause. Yet Klopstock has received the epithet of Miltonic. Sounder criticism would probably style him Mill-stoneic." *(Mangan's note).*

18 Byron, *Childe Harold* III. xxix: "Their praise is hymned by loftier harps than mine".

19 *Julius Caesar* II. i. 14.

20 *Götz von Berlichingen* (1773), Goethe's first play; *Die Räuber* (1781), Schiller's first play.

21 *Parabeln und Räthsel*: "Parables and Enigmas".

22 *comme il faut*: "decorously".

23 *Voyez un peu*: "have a look".

24 *Rousseau*: Jean-Jacques Rousseau (1712–1778), French writer and philosopher.

25 *Emilius*: Jean-Jacques Rousseau's novel *Emile* (1762), outlining a new theory of education, revolutionised fashionable Europe.

26 *Grand Panoramic View of the French Revolution*: oblique reference to the then evolving fashion of "panoramas" presenting sites or historical scenes on a cylindrical screen with the spectators standing on the inside. The panorama was invented by the Irish painter Robert Barker in 1785.

Among the most travelled panoramas was The Battle of Waterloo.

27 *Francis Arouet*: François-Marie Arouet *alias* Voltaire wrote a scurrilous poem on Joan of Arc, *La Pucelle*, for which he was rebuked by Schiller in the poem which Mangan now goes on to translate as "The Maid of Orleans".

28 *Champollion*: Jean François Champollion (1790–1832), French Egyptologist, pioneer in the modern study of hieroglyphics.

29 *Jackpuddingism*: buffoonery.

30 "He had at one time collected materials for a comedy, but soon felt that his genius was too foreign from this species of composition." *(Mangan's note)*.

31 *Manichæus*: also known as Mani or Manes (c.216–276), heresiarch who gave his name to Manichæism.

32 *Hoffman's*: Ernst Theodor Amadeus Hoffman (1776–1822), German novelist and short story writer, whose tales include "The Devil's Elixir".

33 *the Denier*: the devil.

ANTHOLOGIA GERMANICA.—NO. II. SCHILLER'S LAY OF THE BELL AND MESSAGE TO THE IRON FOUNDRY [(Unsigned), *DUM*, February 1835]

 1 Pope, *Iliad*, II. 572n: "that Omnipresence he [Homer] gives to the Muses, their Post in the highest Heaven, their comprehensive Survey thro' the whole Extent of the Creation, are Circumstances greatly imagined".

 2 *St. Leon*: novel by William Godwin (1799) to which Mangan makes frequent reference.

 3 *Macbeth* I. vii. 60: "But screw your courage to the sticking-place".

 4 *Monmouth and Macedon*: "I think it is in Macedon where Alexander is porn. I tell you, captain, if you look in the maps of the 'orld, I warrant you sall find, in the comparisons between Macedon and Monmouth, that the situations, look you, is both alike...." *Henry V*. IV. vii. 23–27.

 5 *Wieland*: Christoph Martin Wieland (1733–1813), German poet, novelist and translator.

 6 *Hero and Leander*: "Hero und Leander" (1802); Mangan was to translate only the first stanza of this ballad (see *DUM*, April 1839).

 7 *The Cranes of Ibycus*: "Die Kraniche der Ibykus" (1797); Mangan published no translation of this ballad.

 8 *The Hostage*: "Die Bürgschaft" (1798), literally "The Pledge"; see *DUM*, July 1838.

 9 *Damon and Pythias*: legendary models of friendship in 4th century Syracuse under the tyrant Dionysius.

10 *The Diver*: "Der Taucher" (1797); see *DUM*, May 1835.

11 *The Combat with the Dragon*: "Der Kampf mit der Drachen" (1798);

Mangan published no translation of this poem.

12 *Der Geisterseher*: lit. "The Ghostseer" (1787–1789), a fragmentary novel.

13 *Böttiger*: Karl August Bötttiger (1760–1835), Weimar academic and man of letters.

14 *Rodriguez*: Alonso Rodriguez S.J. wrote *Exercicio de Perfecion id virtudes religiosas*, Seville, 1609. In his Preface to *The Hind and the Panther*, Dryden accuses an English Protestant divine, "T.B.", of passing off as original his *Treatise of Humilitie* (1631), whereas it "was translated from the Spanish of Rodriguez".

ANTHOLOGIA GERMANICA.—NO III. MISCELLANEOUS POEMS AND
METRICAL TALES [(Unsigned), *DUM*, April 1835]

1 *Quand des hommes... n'est pas claire*: "When clear-sighted men dispute about some matter for a long time, there is every likelihood that the matter is not clear", Voltaire, *Le Siècle de Louis XIV* (1733), ch. 35, where the wording is slightly different: "Quand des hommes éclairés disputent longtemps, il y a grande apparence que la question n'est pas claire".

2 *Castelvetro*: Ludovico Castelvetro (1505–1571), Italian jurist and literary scholar.

3 *Tasso*: Torquato Tasso (1544–1595), Italian epic poet.

4 *Epopee*: epic (*arch.*).

5 *Gottsched and Co.*: Johann Christoph Gottsched (1700–1766), German philosopher and critic; he attempted to purify German literature according to the canons of French Classicism; "and Co." refers, among others, to his wife, the playwright Louise Adelgunde Victoria Kulmus, known as "Gottschedin".

6 *Camöens*: Luis de Camões (1524–1580) Portuguese epic poet, author of *Os Lusíadas* (1572).

7 *Scudérys*: George de Scudéry (1601–1667), French playwright, poet and critic.

8 *Perraults*: Charles Perrault (1628–1703), French poet, fabulist and critic.

9 *Mambruns*: Pierre Mambrun S.J. (1600–1661), French classicist, author of *De Poemato Epico* (1652).

10 *Chapelains*: Jean Chapelain (1595–1674), French poet and litterateur; notorious butt of Boileau's parodies.

11 *Grab*: "grave".

12 *Kalchberg*: Johann von Kalchberg (1765–1827), German poet.

13 *Kotzebue*: August von Kotzebue (1761–1819), prolific German playwright, murdered for his political activities.

14 *a translation from Hölty*: Mangan refers to "Song", *DUM*, December 1834.

15 Schiller remarked that Richter would have been admired "if he had made as good use of his riches as other men have made of their poverty".

ANTHOLOGIA GERMANICA — NO. IV. [(Unsigned), *DUM*, October 1835]

1 "Gedichte von F. Matthison and [*sic*] T. G. Salis. In einem Bande. Zürich, 1831." *(Mangan's note)*. Friedrich von Matthisson (1761–1831), German poet; Johann Gaudenz Freiherr von Salis-Seewis (1762–1834), Swiss poet.

2 Correctly, εἶς νόμος τὸ δοξάν ποιητῇ: "(There is) only one law for the poet—wha t he regards as good". Source unidentified.

3 *The Tempest* III. iii. 101: "deeper than e'er plummet sounded".

4 *Schelling*: Friedrich Wilhelm Joseph Schelling (1775–1854), chief philosopher of the German Romantic movement.

5 *Novalis*: Friedrich Leopold, Freiherr von Hardenberg Novalis (1772–1801), German poet and critic.

6 *Tiedge*: Christoph August Tiedge (1752–1841), German Romantic poet. Mangan translated his poem "The Field of Kunnersdorf" twice.

7 *Castaly*: famous well at the foot of Parnassus, sacred to Apollo, and considered the fountain of the Muses.

8 Wordsworth, "The Rainbow", ll. 1–2: "My heart leaps up when I behold / A rainbow in the sky".

9 Mangan's brother John had died in May of that year.

10 "*Nought under Heaven's wide hollowness*": this quotation has not been traced.

11 1 Thessalonians 4: 13: "But I would not have you to be ignorant, brethren, concerning them which are asleep [*i.e.* dead], that ye sorrow not, even as others which have no hope".

12 A review of the *DUM* number for April 1835 had appeared in the *Weekly Dublin Satirist*, 4 April 1835. It contained the following observation: "Anthologia Germanica No. 3 possesses some interest but is deficient in the information which a paper on such a subject should afford. We would advise the clever author to indulge his readers with critiques on the distinctive genius of German Poetry, rather than on abstract questions of a cloudy philosophy with which the generality of mankind has no sympathy".

13 *Tom Thumb*: person of small stature. The hero of the nursery tale is the protagonist in Richard Johnson's *Tom Thumb* (1621), and gained further glory in Fielding's burlesque *Tom Thumb the Great* (acted 1730).

14 Byron, *Sardanapalus* I. ii. 249–250: "Sardanapalus, / The King, and

son of Anacyndaraxes, / In one day built Anchialus and Tarsus."

15 Pope, *Essay on Man* IV. 204.

ANTHOLOGIA GERMANICA.—NO. V. FAUST, AND THE MINOR POEMS OF GOETHE [(Unsigned), *DUM*, March 1836]

1 *Werther*: Goethe's *Sorrows of Young Werther* (1774).

2 *Wilhelm Meister*: Goethe's bildungsroman of 1795–1796, translated by Thomas Carlyle (1824–1827).

3 *Dichtung und Wahrheit*: Goethe's autobiography, the full title of which is *Aus meinem Leben: Dichtung und Wahrheit* (1811–1833).

4 *Manfred*: Byron's poetic drama of 1817.

5 Cf. *Hamlet* IV. v. 123–124: "There's such divinity doth hedge a king / That treason can but peep to what it would. . . . "

6 First line of a sonnet by Wordsworth; for "them" read "us".

7 "*Foreign Quarterly Review*, No. II. Art. V." *(Mangan's note)*. The article to which Mangan refers does not mention Goethe.

8 *Hamlet* III. iv. 53: "Look here upon this picture, and on this".

9 Proverbs 14: 10.

10 *Zeno*: Zeno of Elea (c.490–c.430), Greek philosopher, inventor of dialectics.

11 *Paradise Lost* VII. 22.

12 *Dr. Anster*: John Anster (1793–1867), frequent contributor to the *DUM* and friend of Mangan's. His translation of Faust (Part One) appeared in 1835.

13 *Mr. Blackie*: John Stuart Blackie (1809–1895), contributor to *Blackwood's* and the *Foreign Quarterly Review*. His translation of *Faust* (Part One) appeared in 1834.

14 *Lord Francis Egerton*: statesman and poet (1800–1857). His translation of *Faust* (Part One) appeared in 1823.

15 *Mr. Syme*: David Syme translated *Faust* (Part One) in 1834.

16 *Honorable Mr. Talbot*: Robert Talbot translated *Faust* (Part One) in 1835.

17 "*presque toujours de tenir une pensée en arrière*": Pascal, *Pensées* No. 181, Lafuma edition. Correctly, "Il faut avoir une pensée de derrière, et juger de tout par là": "One should have a hidden standpoint from which one should judge all things".

18 *the best of all possible worlds*: "le meilleur des mondes possibles", a phrase repeatedly used by Dr. Pangloss in Voltaire's *Candide*.

19 *Les hommes . . . elle est courante*: "Men reflect little; they read carelessly, they judge hastily, they receive opinions as they receive coins, because of their currency." Voltaire, *Des mensonges imprimés* (1749) ch. 3, No. xx.

20 Francis Bacon, *Apothegms* (1624): "Quidquid recipitur, recipitur secundum modum recipientis".

21 *Macbeth* IV. i. 111.

22 "Goethe's Works—Vol. III. Stutgard and Tübingen. 1828". *(Mangan's note).*The lines are quoted, with a few inaccuracies, from "Zur Logenfeier des dritten Septembers 1825" ("On the Occasion of the Masonic Feast of September 3, 1825"), and translate:

> Let go of what is all-too transient!
>> It will be of no help to you.
> What was well done in the past endures,
>> Lent permanence by fine actions.
>
> And so what is now alive gains,
>> Turn by turn, new life;
> For steadfastness alone
>> Gives permanence to humankind.
>
> This answers the big question
>> As to our second fatherland.
> For what has permanence in our earthly days
>> Assures us there is permanence eternally.

ANTHOLOGIA GERMANICA.—NO. VI. THE GERMAN FABULISTS [(Unsigned), *DUM*, May 1836].

1 Thomas Gray, "Elegy Written in a Country Churchyard", l. 88.

2 *Aladdin's lamp*: Aladdin, hero of a tale in the *Arabian Nights*, had a lamp which, when rubbed, summoned a genie of prodigious obligingness.

3 *Gyges' Ring*: Gyges, King of Lydia (7th century BC), had a magic ring conferring invisibility.

4 *Fortunatus*: hero of German folk-tale who had an inexhaustible purse and a cap which could transport him, at his wish, all over the earth.

5 *Paganini's violin*: Niccolo Paganini (1782–1840), Italian violinist, was named "Mephisto" for his virtuosity and demonic appearance.

6 *Orpheus*: semi-divine hero of Greek legend whose lyre drew iron tears from Pluto, god of the underworld.

7 *Moran*: legendary Irish judge, whose collar tended to choke him if he made a wrong verdict.

8 *Harlequin*: in the *Commedia dell'Arte*, a sprightly stock character who often carried a wooden sword and was sometimes conventionally invisible to other characters in the *ensemble*.

9 *Prospero's wand*: Prospero, hero of Shakespeare's *Tempest*, manages much of the play's business by means of his magic staff.

10 *St. Leon's elixir vitae*: "the *elixir vitae*, which was to restore youth, and make him who possessed it immortal", Preface to *St. Leon* (1799) by William Godwin.

11 *Midas*: legendary Phrygian king whose wish, that everything he touched would turn to gold, was granted with unhappy consequences for himself.

12 *Icarus*: legendary Greek youth whose father, Dædalus, made him wings to enable his flight out of the labyrinth on Crete.

13 *Camaralzaman*: hero of a tale in the *Arabian Nights*, owner of a magic precious stone.

14 *Prince Firouz Schah*: Persian prince, hero—with magic horse—of a tale in the *Arabian Nights*.

15 Coleridge, *The Death of Wallenstein* V. i. 68.

16 *Gay*: John Gay (1685–1732), English poet, playwright and fabulist.

17 *Béranger*: Pierre-Jean de Béranger (1780–1857), French poet and satirist.

18 *Aesop*: Phrygian fabulist (c.620–550 BC).

19 *Casti*: Giambattista Casti (1724–1803), Italian poet whose extended fable, *Court and Parliament of Beasts*, was translated into English in 1819. Mangan was to translate part of his sonnet-sequence *I Tre Giulii* in 1842.

20 *La Mothe*: Antoine Houdar de Lamotte (1672–1731) whose *Fables* appeared in 1719.

21 *Phaedrus*: Caius Julius Phaedrus (c.15 BC–AD 50), Latin fabulist, imitator of Aesop.

22 *Hagedorn*: Friedrich von Hagedorn (1708–1754); gained fame as a fabulist with his *Versuch in poetischen Fabeln und Erzählungen* in 1738.

23 *Yriarte*: Tomás de Iriarte (1750–1791), Spanish writer, who published his *Fabulas Literarias* in 1782.

24 *Weiss*: Christian Felix Weisze (1726–1804), German poet and playwright.

25 *Karamsin*: Nikolay Mikhaylovich Karamzin (1765–1826), Russian writer, famous for his novels and his *History of Russia*. Mangan, however, appears to have had in mind his translations from the French of Marmontel and Mme de Genlis.

26 *Sennacherib*: Assyrian general whose army, in Byron's poem, "The Destruction of Sennacherib", was destroyed by "a glance of the Lord".

27 *Alles Schöne. . . .*: "All that is beautiful, / All that is high they took away with them; / All the colours, all the tones of life / And to us remained but the soul-less word". These lines are from the last stanza of "Die Götter Griechenlands" ("The Gods of Greece"), a poem which Mangan did not translate.

28 *Fuit Ilium*: "Troy is no more", *Aeneid* II. 325.

29 W. Cowper, *The Task* III. 838–839: "Much that I love, and more that I admire, / And all that I abhor".

30 *c'est précisement par des détails que la poësie nous charme*: "it is specifically for its details that poetry charms us." Voltaire, *Essai sur la poésie épique* (1727), ch. 2. Correctly: "Et c'est précisément par ces détails que la poésie charme les hommes".

31 *Swift's Laputan architect*: in the kingdom of Laputa, described in Book Three of *Gulliver's Travels*, members of the Academy of Legado keep busy with such hare-brained experiments .

32 *Hamlet* II. ii. 433: "caviare to the general".

33 *le bon sens qui court les rues*: "commonsense that is everywhere to be found".

34 *Quintilian*: Marcus Fabius Quintilianus (c.30–100), *De Institutione Oratoria*, V. xi. 19: "Illae quoque fabellae...ducere animos solent praecipue rusticorum et imperitorum...."

35 *William Cobbett*: William Cobbett (1762–1835), influential English radical thinker and political historian. The present reference is probably to Cobbett's *The Life and Adventures of Peter Porcupine, with a full account of all his authoring transactions, by Peter Porcupine himself* (Philadelphia: 1796), the second edition of which (London: 1809) was entitled *The Life of William Cobbett by Himself. Intended as an encouraging example to all young men of humble fortune; being a proof of what can be effected by steady application and honest efforts.*

36 Byron, *Don Juan* XII. xxvi.

37 The fable summarized by Mangan, "Anus ad amphoram" ("What the old woman said to the wine-jar") is by Phaedrus (c. 15 BC–c. AD 50), not Aesop.

38 Milton, *Paradise Lost* II. 266.

39 *Leibnitz*: Gottfried Wilhelm Leibnitz (1646–1716), German philosopher.

40 *Pro tem*: "for the time being".

41 *outré*: "out-of-the-way, eccentric".

42 *Brougham*: Henry Peter, 1st Baron Brougham and Vaux (1778–1868), lord chancellor of England; see "The Two Flats", note 17.

43 William Godwin, "Of the Rebelliousness of Man", *Thoughts on Man* (1831): "I want to be alive, to be something more than I commonly am, to change the scene, to cut the cable that binds my bark to the shore, to launch into the wide sea of possibilities, and to nourish my thoughts with observing a train of unforeseen consequences as they arise." (96–97)

44 "*To act, to suffer, may be nobly great / But Nature's hardest lesson is—to*

wait": this quotation has not been traced.

45 *St Augustine's dream-child*: legend has it that, when still a young man, Augustine contemplated a treatise on the Holy Trinity. Walking along a beach one day, he saw a boy trying to spoon the waters of the sea into a small hole in the sand. Upon being told that this was an impossible task, the child replied that he would accomplish it sooner than Augustine, with the sole help of *his* intellect, would manage to understand the mystery of the Trinity. The saint gave up his project there and then, and did not write his *De Trinitate* until many years later.

46 *That situation...Eblis*: unlike the other monarchs imprisoned in the Palace of Eblis (Satan) because of their sins, King Soliman Ben Daoud is not totally destitute of hope, for he has been promised that his woes shall come to an end when the cataract which is partly visible through one of the grated portals, and whose roar is the only sound to be heard in the place, "shall—for ever cease to flow". *Vathek*, an oriental tale by William Beckford (1760–1844), appeared in 1786.

47 *levius fit patientia / Quidquid corrigere est nefas*: "whatever cannot be healed / Can be made more bearable by patience". Horace, *Odes* I. xxiv. 19–20.

48 *revenons à nos moutons*: "let us return to the subject"—literally, let us get back to our sheep. The phrase is borrowed from Rabelais.

49 *Guichard*: Jean-François Guichard (1731–1811), French man of letters, author of *Fables, contes, et autres poésies* (1803).

50 *Dorat*: Claude-Joseph Dorat (1734–1780), French writer, whose *Fables Nouvelles* appeared in 1773.

51 *come out of the crucible seven times purified*: cf. Psalm 12: 6: "The words of the Lord are pure words: as silver tried in a furnace of earth, purified seven times".

52 *Pilpay*: supposed author of a famed collection of Indian fables, the *Hitopadesa*.

ANTHOLOGIA GERMANICA.—NO. VII. KERNER'S LYRICAL POEMS [(Unsigned), *DUM*, August 1836].

1 Job 38: 2.

2 *Man of Uz*: Job.

3 Edmund Burke, *Reflections on the French Revolution* (1790), Penguin Classics, p.182.

4 *the Coat of Darkness in the Nursery-story*: Jack the Giant-Killer has a cloak which makes him invisible.

5 "One step above the sublime, makes the ridiculous," Thomas Paine, *The Age of Reason* (1795), II, 22.

6 *Glorious Apollo*: song written in 1787 by the British composer Samuel

Webbe (1740–1816) on the foundation of the Glee Club; it was sung at every meeting of the Club. In classical mythology, Apollo was the sun-god and the patron of poetry and music.

7 Byron, *Don Juan* I. xii: "Her serious sayings darken'd to sublimity".

8 *gallimaufry*: medley; hodge-podge.

9 *ale-draper*: publican.

10 *the Barmecide in the Arabian tale*: in the "Barber's Story of his Sixth Brother" (*Arabian Nights*), a prince of the Barmecides plays a joke on the beggar Schacabac by entertaining him to non-existent viands on splendid dishes.

11 James Boswell, *The Life of Samuel Johnson* (1791), ch. IV; correctly, "Lay your knife and your fork, across your plate".

12 *A bas la bagatelle, mais au diable la sottise*: "Down with frivolity, but to the devil with stupidity".

13 *Paradise Lost* III. 44.

14 John 4: 44.

15 *lieber Deutschland's*: "dear Germany's".

16 *Tiedge*: Christoph August Tiedge (1752–1841), German Romantic poet. Mangan translated his poem "The Field of Kunnersdorf" twice.

17 *Novalis*: Friedrich Leopold, Freiherr von Hardenberg Novalis (1772–1801), German poet and critic.

18 *Solon*: Athenian statesman legendary for his wisdom (c.638–558 BC).

19 *Della Cruscan*: literary clique founded by English poets in 18th century Florence, proverbial for its affectation.

20 *Ex pede Herculem*: "by extrapolation". Hercules's height can be inferred from the length of his foot.

21 *The Merry Wives of Windsor* V. v. 196–197: "I went to her in white and cried 'mum', and she cried 'budget'".

22 *Le Bourgeois gentilhomme* (1670) III. iii.

23 Cf. 2 Samuel 1: 20: "Tell it not in Gath, publish it not in the streets of Askelon".

24 *the tenth heaven*: "The supposed outermost sphere (at first reckoned the ninth, later the tenth), added in the Middle Ages to the Ptolemaic system of astronomy, and supposed to revolve round the earth from east to west in twenty-four hours, carrying with it the (eight or nine) contained spheres". (O.E.D.).

25 *pococurante*: "carefree". Pococurante is the name of a character in Voltaire's *Candide*.

26 *the Magnetic Mountain in the Persian Tale*: in the "Story of the Third Calendar" (from the *Arabian Nights*), Prince Agib's ship drifts out of course to this 'Black Mountain', and falls to pieces.

27 *experimentalist in Gulliver*: member of the Legado Academy described

in Book III of *Gulliver's Travels*.

28 *Matthissonian*: after Friedrich von Matthisson (1761–1831), German lyric poet; see "Anthologia Germanica No. IV", *DUM*, October 1835.

29 *Bernays*: Adolphus Bernays (d.1864), Professor of German language and literature at King's College, London. His *German Poetical Anthology* (1829) went into several editions.

30 *Thränen, Vögel, Blumen, Bäche, Sterne…Grab*: "tears, birds, flowers, brooks, stars…grave".

31 *Rip-Van-Winklish*: reference to the hero of Washington Irving's fable, *Rip Van Winkle* (1819), who slept for twenty years.

32 *Somnus*: god of sleep.

33 *Morpheus*: god of dreams.

34 *Spahi*: Turkish horseman.

35 *chibouque*: long curled pipe.

36 Pope, *Essay on Man* IV. 380: "From grave to gay, from lively to severe".

37 *Dr. Macnish*: Robert Macnish (1802–1837), Scottish writer and physician, author of *The Anatomy of Drunkenness* (1827) and *The Philosophy of Sleep* (1830).

38 *Kepler*: Johann Kepler (1571–1630), German mathematician and astronomer.

39 *Frischlin*: Philipp Nikodemus Frischlin (1547–1590), German poet and philologist, found his death while attempting to escape from the fortress of Hohenurach, where he had been imprisoned for having written a pamphlet against the Council of Wurtemberg.

40 "They prisoned him within gaunt rocks—him, for whom the wide regions of the earth were too narrow. But he, full of strength, broke through the rocky stone, *and let himself down by a rope which was none of the stoutest*; and they found him, in the pale moonlight, himself bruised *and his clothes in tatters*. Alas, Mother Earth! that thou didst not mercifully extend thy gentle arms and afford him shelter and protection!" *(Mangan's note)*.

41 Milton, *Paradise Lost* II. 933–934: "Fluttring his pennons vain plumb down he drops / Ten thousand fadom deep".

42 *Rabelais' giant*: see *Gargantua and Pantagruel* Book IV, Chapter XVII; the Giant's name is Widenostrils in Peter Antony Motteux's English translation (1694).

43 *coup d'oeil*: "prospect".

44 "Schiller's *Verschleierte Bild zu Sais*". *(Mangan's note)*. A literal translation of these lines reads: "Take one tone from a harmony, / Take one colour out of the rainbow, / And all that you've left is Nothing, as long / As the beautiful All lacks the tones and colours".

ANTHOLOGIA   GERMANICA.—NO.   VIII.   SCHILLER'S   DRAMA   OF
WALLENSTEIN'S CAMP [(Unsigned), *DUM*, December 1836]

1 *a former paper*: "Anthologia Germanica No. II", in which Mangan had
   appended the following footnote to his translation of Schiller's "Lay of
   the Bell":

> The great propensity of German verse to form *double rhymes* has
> frequently been noticed. Several writers have contrasted the
> multitudinous display of those rhymes in German with the apparent
> paucity of similar rhymes in English, and very much, of course, to the
> disparagement of the latter. The German language certainly
> comprehends an extensive number of words applicable to double-
> rhyming purposes. But it is an error to imagine that it is more copious
> in this respect than the English. The fallacy by which it is made to
> appear more copious is easily detected. At least nine-tenths of all the
> German double rhymes may be said to be *of one class*. The infinitive of
> every German verb (with two or three exceptions) is a polysyllable, and
> terminates in *en*. This termination is also found in other forms of the
> verb and constitutes the plural of many nouns. All the words thus
> terminated are available as double rhymes, and as, of course, nouns and
> verbs are in constant use, it is from the frequent employment of such
> words, and from this only, that the apparent superabundance of the
> rhymes results. Thus, in Schiller's Address "*An die Freunde*" (taking a
> sample at random) the first sixteen double rhymes run consecutively as
> follows: Zeit*en*, streit*en*, schweig*en*, zeug*en*, verschwund*en*, Stund*en*,
> Zon*en*, wohn*en*, entzog*en*, gewog*en*, gewöhn*en*, bekrön*en*, rausch*en*,
> tausch*en*, geh*en*, seh*en*. Now to enable us to rival the unrelieved
> monotony of this array, all that in the majority of instances it is
> necessary for us to do, is to transform the German infinitive into the
> English active participle, *i.e.* to substitute, for example, think*ing*,
> sink*ing*, drink*ing*, for denk*en*, sink*en*, trink*en*; and our show of
> resources becomes quite as respectable as that of our neighbours.
> Whether we choose to do so or not, however, the capability of doing so
> remains with us. As to the rest of our double rhymes, their variety, it
> may be remarked, finds no parallel in any poetry in the world besides,
> for even the Italian—another language inordinately vaunted for the
> prodigal use it makes of double terminations, does nothing, when all is
> said, but ring the changes upon four weariful vowels, *a*, *e*, *i*, and *o*.

2 *the waggoner in the fable*: La Fontaine, *Fables* VI, 18.
3 Pope, *Essay on Criticism* III. 66.
4 Psalm 8: 5.
5 *Praxiteles*: of Athens (4th century BC), sculptor, famous for shaping the
   first nude statue of Aphrodite.

6 Pope, *Essay on Man* I. 244–246: "Where, one step broken, the great scale's destroyed: / From Nature's chain whatever link you strike, / Tenth or ten thousandth, breaks the chain alike".

7 Goldsmith, *The Vicar of Wakefield*, Chapter 18: " 'So then, I suppose,' cried I, 'that our modern dramatists are rather imitators of Shakespeare than of nature.'—'To say the truth,' returned my companion, 'I don't know that they imitate any thing at all....' "

8 *Pope's Homer*: Alexander Pope's translations of the *Iliad* (1715–1720) and the *Odyssey* (1725–1726) are written in rhyming couplets.

9 *Chapman's*: George Chapman translated the *Iliad* (1598, 1611) in rhyming fourteeners; his translation of the *Odyssey* (1614–1615) is written in rhyming pentameter.

10 Dryden, *Absalom and Achitophel*, l. 548: "Was every thing by starts, and nothing long."

11 *tournure*: "shape".

12 Thomas Campbell, *The Pleasures of Hope* (1799) II. 6.

ANTHOLOGIA GERMANICA. — NO. X. TIECK AND THE OTHER SONG-SINGERS OF GERMANY [(Unsigned), *DUM*, March 1837]. The title carries the following note by Mangan:
Poems and Songs, by Lewis [*sic*] Tieck; 2 vols. Leipsic, 1835.
Popular Songs of the Germans, with Explanatory Notes, by Wilhelm Klauer-Klattowski. London, Simpkin and Marshall, 1836.

1 *Newgate Calendar*: a biographical record of the most infamous inmates of Newgate Gaol, London, begun in 1773 and consolidated in four volumes by Knapp and Baldwin, 1824–1828.

2 *Robert Owen*: Welsh social reformer (1771–1858); see "A Treatise on a Pair of Tongs", note 39.

3 *Omnia vincit veritatis amor*: "The love of truth conquers all"; wry adaptation of Virgil's dictum *Omnia vincit amor*, "Love conquers all", *Bucolics* X. 69.

4 *Ferdinand Mendez Pinto*: Ferdinand Mendez Pinto (c.1510–1583), Portuguese traveller who became a byword for tall tales with the publication of his *Peregrinaçam* ("Peregrination", 1614).

5 *Cimmerian*: the legendary "Cimmerii" were believed by the Ancients to live in a world of dense darkness.

6 *the human face divine*: *Paradise Lost* III. 44.

7 *the children of men*: human beings (*bibl.*).

8 *Whip-Poor-Will*: cf. Washington Irving, *A History of New-York, from the beginning of the world to the end of the Dutch dynasty* (1809) VI. iii: "the melancholy plaint of the Whip-poor-will, who, perched on some lone tree, wearied the ear of night with his incessant moanings". Irving is

describing the banks of the Hudson, not the "forests of South America".

9 *La Serva Padrona*: opera by the Italian composer Giovanni Battista Pergolesi (1710–1736).

10 *O un certo che nel core... m'imbroglio*: "I have a certain something in my heart; / And am unable to say / Whether it is hate or love; / I'm between yes and no, / Between wanting and not wanting, / And I am more and more confused". *La Serva Padrona* (libretto by G.A. Federico), *intermezzo secondo*:

> *Ho un certo che nel core,*
> *Che dir per me non so*
> *S'è amore, o s'è pietà.*
>
> . . . .
>
> *Io sto fra il sì e il no,*
> *Fra il voglio e fra il non voglio,*
> *E sempre più m'imbroglio.*

11 *Hamlet* III. i. 75–76: "When he himself might his quietus make / With a bare bodkin".

12 *1 Henry IV* I. iii. 49.

13 *Tristram Shandy's uncle*: Toby, uncle of the eponymous hero of Laurence Sterne's *Tristram Shandy* (1759–1767).

14 *Gulliver... Lilliputians*: Lilliput, one of the imaginary countries visited by Gulliver in Swift's *Gulliver's Travels* (1726), is peopled by pygmies six inches high.

15 *My wound is great because it is so small*: the attribution of this line to Dryden stems from the following story in Joseph Spence's *Anecdotes, Observations, and Characters, of Books and Men, collected from the Conversation of Mr. Pope, and other eminent persons of his time* (published posthumously in 1820):

> "In one of Dryden's plays there was this line, which the actress endeavoured to speak in as moving and affecting a tone as she could:
>
> > My wound is great, because it is so small!
>
> ...The Duke of Buckingham, who was in one of the boxes, rose immediately from his seat and added in a loud, ridiculing voice:
>
> > Then 'twould be greater, were it none at all!"

The story is in fact spurious. The earliest known version of the two lines occurs in one of the tracts of the Marvell–Parker controversy of 1673, where they read:

> (The Wound was great because it was but *small*)
> Th'adst been a *Bishop* needed *none* at all.

See Spence's *Anecdotes*, ed. James M. Osborn (Oxford: Clarendon Press, 1966) I, 275.

16 *sous silence*: "silently".

17 *Fergusson*: Sir Samuel Ferguson (1810–1886), Irish poet and scholar, frequent contributor to the *DUM*.

18 Pope, *Essay on Man* I. 200. For *one* read *a*.

19 *the frogs in the fable*: the fable is "The Boys and the Frogs", in which a company of boys playing ducks and drakes on the margin of a lake are thus addressed by a frog: "Consider, I beseech you, that though this may be sport to you, 'tis death to us". See Robert Dodsley's *Select Fables of Esop and other Fabulists*, a popular selection first published in 1761.

20 *rack-rent*: term used in nineteenth century Ireland for unjust rents imposed on tenant farmers.

21 *Sindbad in the Valley of Diamonds*: see Sindbad's second voyage in the *Arabian Nights*.

22 *Hudibras*: a poetic satire by Samuel Butler, published in three parts between 1663 and 1680.

23 Samuel Butler, "Repartees between Cat and Puss", ll. 57–58; for "And sets them off" read "That sets it off".

24 *Zeno*: Zeno of Elea (c.490–c.430 BC), Greek philosopher, inventor of dialectics.

25 *Brother Jack*: character, standing for Calvinism, in Swift's satiric allegory, *A Tale of a Tub* (1704).

26 *Zobeide's porter....*: see the "Story of the Three Calenders, Sons of Kings, and of Five Ladies of Bagdad".

27 Wordsworth, "London, 1802"; the reference is to Milton: "Thy soul was like a Star, and dwelt apart".

28 *the Bhurrampooter*: the River Brahmaputra, which has its source in Tibet and flows into the Gulf of Bengal.

29 *barter an estate for a Dutch tulip*: reference to the reckless mania for the purchase of tulip bulbs that arose in Holland and spread all over Europe in the first half of the 17th century.

30 *Goldsmith's Chinese*: character-narrator in Oliver Goldsmith's epistolary *Citizen of the World* (1762), Letter XIII.

31 *sanctum sanctorum*: "holy of holies".

32 *Bedlamite*: lunatic, after London's infamous Bethlehem Asylum for the insane.

33 Wordsworth, *Peter Bell*, Prologue, ll. 133–135: "The common growth of Mother Earth / Suffices me—her tears, her mirth, / Her humblest mirth and tears".

34 On the feast of Michaelmas, 29 September, goose is traditionally served.

35 *Phoenix-Park*: Dublin's largest public park.

36 *Bluebeard*: "Der Blaubart", a tale by Tieck, in his *Phantasus* (1812–1816).

37 *The Titian of* The Pictures, *the Prometheus of* The Old Man of the Mountain: respectively, "Die Gemälde" (1821) and "Der Alte vom Berge"(1828), two tales by Tieck, who as a writer is extravagantly compared to the painter Titian and the Titan Prometheus.

38 *The Love-charm*: "Liebeszauber", a tale by Tieck, in his *Phantasus* (1812–1816).

39 *Jackpudding*: normally "Jack Pudding", a buffoon.

40 *Howling Dervish*: member of a Sufi cult which practises ecstatic chanting.

41 Thomas Gray, "The Bard", l. 51: "Give ample room and verge enough."

42 *The Tempest* IV. i. 153–154: "the great globe itself, / Yea, all which it inherit...."

43 *tertium quid*: "third entity".

44 *Mirabeau*: Honoré Gabriel Riqueti, Comte de Mirabeau (1749–1791), French statesman, whose life-style was notoriously extravagant. He is reported to have said shortly before his death: "My friend, I am going to die today; when one has reached that stage, the only thing to do is to envelope oneself in perfumes, to crown oneself with flowers, and to intoxicate oneself with music, in order to enter eternal sleep in a pleasant way."

45 Consider, however, Mangan's sonnet, "Life", *DUM*, September 1839, in which he exclaims "O Life! thou art a mystery!"

46 *amas*: "heap, pile, mass".

47 Byron, *Manfred* I. ii. 10.

48 *utile*: "useful"; *dulce*: "pleasant".

49 "He gravely asked me one day, 'What it was that convinced me in an argument?' I said, I thought I was convinced by the strongest reasoning. 'For my part,' said he, 'it is the last speaker that convinces me.'" (Leigh Hunt, *Lord Byron and Some of his Contemporaries*, I. 71–72).

50 *Dr. South*: Robert South, D.D. (1634–1716), renowned for his polemic with Dr William Sherlock, which gained such proportions that William III interposed to stop it.

51 *Twelfth Night* I. i. 5–7, "O, it came o'er my ear like the sweet sound / That breathes upon a bank of violets, / Stealing and giving odour!"; *sound*, the Folio reading, which most modern editors retain, was changed to *south* by Pope in his edition of Shakespeare's works (1725).

52 *Horne Tooke*: John Horne Tooke (1736–1812), English politician and philologist; far from being "puzzled" by the word *more*, he writes in *The Diversions of Purley* (1786): "These adverbs [*much, more, most*] have

exceedingly gravelled all our etymologists, and they touch them as tenderly as possible", and then proceeds to give what he feels sure is the right etymology.

53 *Mort* in French means "death".

54 Byron, *Childe Harold* IV. clxxxv; Byron has *My* instead of *Our*.

55 *Much Ado About Nothing* III. iii. 15–16: "to write and read comes by nature".

56 Pope, *An Epistle to Dr Arbuthnot*, l. 128 : "I lisp'd in numbers, for the numbers came".

57 Byron, *The Giaour*, l. 393: "A weary chase and wasted hour".

58 *many Priors and few Popes*: many poets of the stature of Matthew Prior (1664–1721), few of the stature of Alexander Pope (1688–1744); there is a clerical pun on the two surnames.

59 *Reading-made-Difficult*: "Reading Made Easy" was the title of various reading-books for children.

LITERÆ ORIENTALES. PERSIAN AND TURKISH POETRY. — FIRST ARTICLE
[(Unsigned), *DUM*, September 1837]

1 *"Ce n'est pas la route ordinaire de l'esprit humain de voyager vers le nord"*: "It is not the ordinary bent of the human spirit to journey north".

2 *Count Segur*: Philippe-Paul, comte de Ségur (1780–1873), French general in Napoleon's army; the last chapter of his *Histoire de Napoléon et de la grande armée en 1812* (1825) contains the remark: "Sans doute le genre humain ne marche point ainsi; sa pente est vers le sud, il tourne le dos au nord".

3 *ens rationis*: something that has no existence of its own, but can only exist as an object of thought.

4 *Pelion... Ossa*: mountains piled one on the other by the Titans in their attempt to storm the Olympian heaven.

5 *Cheops' Pyramid*: the "Great Pyramid" at Giza.

6 *Beaupré*: Pierre Jean Moricheau-Beaupré (1778–?), French surgeon in Napoleon's army, published in 1817 a treatise entitled *Des effets et des propriétés du froid, avec un aperçu historique et médical sur la campagne de Russie*. An English translation appeared in 1826.

7 *So in* Candide... *Europe*: Mangan's reference is to the first paragraph in Chapter 22 of Voltaire's satirical novel *Candide* (1759).

8 *Poussin*: Nicolas Poussin (1594–1665), French painter. The reference is to his famous *Les Bergers d'Arcadie*.

9 *The Greater and Lesser Lights of Dante's Paradiso*: as Dante moves through the nine heavens below the Empyrean the souls of the blessed appear to him as lights whose greater or lesser brightness corresponds to the degree of virtue they have reached.

10 Opening line of "The Irishman" by James Orr (1770–1816), Ulster poet and United Irishman.

11 *Houzouana*: Hottentots.

12 *La Vaillant*: Francois Levaillant (1753–1824), French naturalist and ornithologist, author of *Voyages dans l'intérieur de l'Afrique*.

13 *Dan and Beersheeba*: "from Dan to Beersheeba" is a phrase used in the Bible to describe the entirety of Israel.

14 Byron, *Childe Harold* IV. cxxii.

15 *the Wonderful Lamp*: see the story of Aladdin in the *Arabian Nights*.

16 *Mareses...from human view*: in the ancient Egyptian city of Sais there was a veiled statue representing truth.

17 *"the mother of science, and the house of gods"*: this quotation has not been traced.

18 Cf. Genesis 3: 24.

19 "'Les ruines de 'I'chéhel-minar,' writes Le Blonde, (Chelminar, the Forty Pillars, is the native name of Persepolis,) 'presentent aujourd'hui les débris de plus de deux cents colonnes et de treize cents figures d'hommes ou d'animaux. Deux siècles auront-ils suffi pour exécuter des travaux aussi multipliés? On ne trouve dans le monde connu que les pyramides d'Egypte qui puissent être comparées à la majesté de ces ruines. En se rappellant cependant que les Egyptiens n'ont eu pour construire les pyramides qu'à employer une multitude d'ouvriers peu instruits, et que ces vastes amas de pierres n'offrent aucun relief, aucune figure, hésitera-t-on à les placer au-dessous des monumens de Tchéhel-minar?'" *(Mangan's note)*.

"Today the ruins of Chelminar display the remains of over two hundred pillars and one thousand three hundred figures of men or animals. Can two centuries have sufficed to produce so numerous pieces of work? In the known world only the Pyramids of Egypt can be compared to those majestic ruins. When we remember, however, that all the Egyptians had to do in order to build the pyramids was to employ crowds of unskilled workers and that those huge heaps of stones show no reliefs or figures, we cannot but place them below the Chelminar monuments".

By Le Blonde, Mangan probably means Gaspard Michel Leblond (1738–1809), French archæologist.

20 *Tabor*: Mount Tabor was believed to have been the site of Christ's transfiguration as described in the New Testament.

21 *"the Mythi of the breast"*: this quotation has not been traced.

22 Sir Walter Scott, *Lay of the Last Minstrel* VI. i.

23 This quotation has not been traced; cf. the conclusion of Carlyle's *Life of Friedrich Schiller* (1825): "On the whole, we may pronounce him

happy.... It is true, he died early; but the student will exclaim with Charles XII, in another case, Was it not enough of life when he had conquered kingdoms?"

24 *Voltaire... of his favors*: probably a reference to the entry "History" in *Questions sur l'Encyclopédie* (1752–1770), where Voltaire ridicules the idea that "the God of all the peoples and of all the inhabitants of the other worlds cared about the revolutions in Asia only in relation to the small Jewish people"—that, for instance, "if Alexander defeated Darius, it was in order that Jewish cast-clothes men might settle in Alexandria".

25 *Wieland*: Christoph Martin Wieland (1733–1813), German poet, novelist and translator.

26 *Cicero's daughter*: Tullia (78–45 BC), much beloved of her father. In April 1485 a tomb was discovered along the Appian Way which was identified as being that of Tullia. Among other things it contained a lamp which was supposedly still burning after over 1500 years.

27 *Appian Way*: longest and most famous Roman road, putative site of Tullia's tomb.

28 Romans 13: 12.

29 In Benjamin Disraeli's novel, *Contarini Fleming* (1832), Part the Sixth, Chapter VII, certain characters gathered in a house in Jerusalem are invited to "inscribe on a panel of the wall some sentence as a memorial of [their] sojourn". The passage ends:
   "Sheriff Effendi wrote: 'God is great; man should be charitable'.
   Contarini Fleming wrote: 'Time'."

30 Mark 5: 9: "My name is Legion: for we are many".

31 Cf. *Othello* II. iii. 166–167: "Silence that dreadful bell, it frights the isle/From her propriety".

32 *pantoufles*: "slippers".

33 Revelation 5: 11.

34 Byron, *Don Juan* XI. lxxxv.

35 hue *and* cry: usually means "outcry", but Mangan uses *hue* in the sense of "colour".

36 *White and Omar, or Green and Ali*: the two major branches of Islam—the Sunites, followers of Omar, the second Caliph, and the Shiites, followers of Ali, the fourth Caliph.

37 *Macbeth* II. i. 58: "The very stones prate of my where-about".

38 *Macbeth* IV. i. 111.

39 *Hamlet* I. v. 79: "With all my imperfections on my head".

40 *D'Herbelot*: Barthélemy d'Herbelot, *Bibliothèque orientale* (The Hague: Neaulme & Van Daalen, 1777–1779), II, 369–370. The *Bibliothèque orientale* first appeared in 1697. The volume and page numbers given

in these notes are those of the edition Mangan used.

41 *de Sacy*: Antoine Isaac Silvestre de Sacy (1758–1838), French Orientalist, author of an *Arabic Grammar*.

42 *Schlegel*: either Friedrich von Schlegel (1772–1829), German writer and critic (a student of Sanskrit, he published *Über die Sprache und Weisheit der Indier*, 1808), or Friedrich's brother, Augustus Wilhelm (1767–1845), critic and Orientalist. He published the scholarly journal *Indische Bibliotek* (1820–1830) and founded Sanskrit studies in Germany.

43 *Casiri*: Miguel Casiri (1710–1791), Syrian-born Orientalist.

44 *Von Hammer*: Josef von Hammer-Purgstall (1774–1856), Austrian Orientalist. Later in the article Mangan states that he "attentively perused and studied" the works of "that accomplished scholar." He does not acknowledge that he got most of his originals from Hammer-Purgstall's *Geschichte der osmanischen Dichtkunst* (Pest: Conrad Adolph Hartleben, 1836–1838).

45 *Bibliothèque Orientale*: see note 40 above.

46 *Aide-toi, le ciel t'aidera*: "Help yourself, and Heaven will help you", La Fontaine, *Fables* VI, 18.

47 *Augustus Schlegel*: see note 42 above.

48 *Sir William Jones*: British Orientalist (1746–1794), author of *Grammar of the Persian Language* (1771).

49 *Langlès*: Louis Mathieu Langlès (1763–1824), French Orientalist; translator of *Les Instituts politiques de Timur Lang* (1787), and editor of a *Manchu Lexicon* (1789–1790).

50 *Abel-Remusat*: Abel Rémusat (1788–1832), French sinologist, author of *Essai sur la langue et la littérature chinoises* (1822).

51 "Sir William Jones, we may as well observe here, has fallen into a strange error, as to the time of the introduction of the Persian language into Hindostan. He states that 'the descendants of Tamerlane carried into India the language and poetry of the Persians.' This was not the case; long antecedent to the birth of Tamerlane, that language and poetry had been introduced into India by the Patan princes of Delhi and the Deccan; and the works of the Indian poet, Mir Khosru, who flourished a century before Tamerlane, and yet wrote in Persian, are still extant". *(Mangan's note)*. See *The Poetical Works of Sir William Jones* (London: 1810) II, 227.

52 "The Koran, the production of the Arabian prophet, embodies the loftiest poetry of Arabia". *(Mangan's note)*. See Hammer-Purgstall, I, 3.

53 "The Seven Poems which were suspended in the temple of Mecca. They belong to an age anterior to Mohammed". *(Mangan's note)*.

54 *Mohammed in truth hated poetry...*: Mangan is disingenuous here and in the lines that follow. He uses pp. 3–6 of Hammer-Purgstall's Vol. I, but distorts his argument. The Orientalist carefully weighs the pros

and cons in Mohammed's attitude to poets, insisting in particular that he attacked mainly the unbelieving satirical poets and those who followed false prophets. Hammer-Purgstall also quotes those sayings of Mohammed that are favourable to poets, such as "Coffers lie under the throne of God and their keys are the poets' tongues". Mangan omits all this, and then declares that Hammer-Purgstall is mistaken.

55 Wordsworth, *The Excursion* I. 79.

56 These two quotations from the Koran are in Hammer-Purgstall, I, 5. Mangan gives them in George Sale's translation: Sale, *The Koran* (London: n.p., 1801), II, 306 and 457–458.

57 *"Mismar min mesamiri Ibbis".(Mangan's note)*.

58 *"Lienne jomtela djuf ahadiküm kihen chairen lehu min in jomtela djüren". (Mangan's note)*.

59 *"Ahassu et-turab si wudjuhil-meddahin". (Mangan's note)*. Mangan took this and the other Arabic quotations in notes 57 and 58 from Hammer-Purgstall, I, 3.

60 Byron, *The Prophecy of Dante* III. 92.

61 Wordsworth, *Peter Bell*, Prologue, l. 133.

62 *Toute leur littérature consiste à réciter des contes et des histoires dans le genre des Mille et une Nuits*: "All their literature consists in reciting tales and stories similar to those in the *Thousand and One Nights*". C. F. Volney, *Voyage en Egypte et en Syrie* (Paris: Bossange, 5th edition, 1822) I, 373.

63 *Shemseddin Mohammed Hafiz*: Persian poet (c.1325–1390).

64 "Persian Poetry is the sun, Turkish the sun-flower; the last naturally turns towards the first, and is indebted to it for its hues and growth". *(Mangan's note)*. The German quotation is from Hammer-Purgstall, I, 51.

65 *Drechsler*: a pseudonym meaning (wood-) turner, (hence translator), which Mangan uses when passing off as translations some of his own compositions in the "Anthologia Germanica" series.

66 This quotation is lifted, with small modifications, from Hammer-Purgstall, I, 1.

67 *Philosopher Square*: "Mr Square, the philosopher" in Fielding's *The History of Tom Jones* measures "all actions by the unalterable rule of right, and the eternal fitness of things".

68 *"One Introductory Part.... does not astonish us"*: freely translated from Hammer-Purgstall, I, 2 except that where the German scholar expresses astonishment Mangan states the reverse and adds mischievous comments of his own.

69 Matthew Prior, "Henry and Emma", l. 430.

70 Byron, *Don Juan* IV. x.

71 *Sir William Ouseley*: English Orientalist (1767–1842), author of *Persian Miscellanies* (1795).

72 The item to which Mangan refers is indeed in No. 293 of the *Spectator* where it is entitled "A Little Persian Fable".

73 Lope de Vega (1562–1635), *Arcadia*, Book I. Mangan's transcription has two errors: for *invidioso* read *envidioso*; for *sali* read *salia*. The lines can be translated as follows: "The sea, as if jealous, / Invades the land for those tears / And, happy to have gathered them, / Keeps them in shells and turns them into pearls".

74 *a scarcity of Pearl Necklaces, and thence French Revolutions*: an allusion to a notorious scandal in French history (1784–1786), involving the purchase of a *diamond* necklace for Queen Marie-Antoinette (for 1,600,000 livres) and its subsequent disappearance.

75 *the pupil of the Dervish Noureddin*: this person has not been identified.

76 *Alexis Ruganoff*: this person has not been identified.

77 *Scaliger*: Joseph Justus Scaliger (1540–1609), famous Franco-Italian scholar.

78 Pope, "Epistle to Dr Arbuthnot", l. 62.

79 *Fichtean*: after Johann Gottlieb Fichte (1762–1814), German subjectivist philosopher, who postulated the pre-eminence of the ego.

80 William Cowper, "Verses supposed to be written by Alexander Selkirk", ll. 9–10: "I am out of humanity's reach / I must finish my journey alone".

81 *Abbé Sieyès*: Emmanuel Joseph Sieyès (1748–1836), French statesman, author of the pamphlet *Qu'est-ce que le Tiers Etat?*, *i.e.* "What is the Third Estate?" (1789). The answer to the question in the title, "Nothing!", is followed by another question, "What ought it to be?" to which the answer supplied is "Everything!"

ANTHOLOGIA GERMANICA.—NO. XI. MISCELLANEOUS POEMS [(Unsigned), *DUM*, December 1837]. The title carries the following note by Mangan:

> Sammlung Vermischter Gedichte, &c. A Selection of Miscellaneous Pieces in Verse and Prose, extracted from the most approved German Authors. 1 vol. pp. 984. Frankfort, 1837.

1 Wordsworth, "Intimations of Immortality", l. 207: "Thoughts that do often lie too deep for tears".

2 *Goethe*: Goethe's *Werke—Vollständige Ausgabe letzter Hand* (1827–1830) comprised forty volumes; his *Nachgelassene Werke* (1832–1834), a posthumous continuation of this edition, consisted of fifteen volumes.

3 *Faust and Werther*: the drama *Faust* and the novel *Werther* are Goethe's most famous works.

4 *Wieland*: Christoph Martin Wieland (1733–1813), German poet, novelist and translator.

5 *Phantasus*: Tieck's *Phantasus* (1812–1817), a collection of German folk tales.

6 *Brockden Brown's Carwin*: Charles Brockden Brown (1771–1810), American Gothic novelist. Carwin is the evil ventriloquist in his novel *Wieland* (1798).

7 *Hoffmann's Medardus*: Ernest Theodor Wilhelm Hoffmann (1776–1822), German writer and musician. His gruesome novel, *Die Elixire des Teufels*, detailing the evil-doings of Brother Medardus, *Doppelgänger* of Victorin, was translated by Carlyle under the title *The Devil's Elixir* (1824).

8 *Doppelgänger*: "a person's double".

9 *Scheuchvogel*: in fact, "Die Vogelscheuche"(The Scarecrow), a tale by Tieck (1835).

10 Shelley, *Scenes from the Faust of Goethe*, II. 78.

11 *chiaro oscuro*: in English more commonly *chiaroscuro*; contrast of light and shade in painting.

12 "We allude to the *Reiseschatten*, or Shadows of Travel; a monstrous compound of grotesque description and bloated dialogue. As all the characters introduced into the book talk precisely in the style in which the following sentence is couched, the reader will require no additional specimen of its merits.

'I tell you,' said Moses, 'I tell you, my excellent, rather talented and in all probability still young friend, I tell you that the sentinel hears nothing and sees nothing; for, step out and cry aloud once, twice, thrice, four, five, and six times, *exempli gratia*, "Fire! fire! ho! Robbery! Murder! Stop thief! Stop the robber! the incendiary! the cut-purse and cut-throat! the coiner! the Jew!"—to which you may subjoin as an appendix, "the gipsy! the tinker! the curry-comb and mousetrapmaker!"—and shout this in the following languages, *viz*: 1. High-German,—2. Low-German,—3. Suabian,—4. Swiss,—5. French,—6. Dutch,—7. Bohemian, and 8. Italian, in the first instance with your mouth after the common mode, then through the medium of a sizeable pipe or horn, and then successively through two speaking tubes or trumpets, one very long and straight, the other curved like a serpent, at the distance of ten, six, four, and two paces from the sentinel—and finally walk up to him and putting your lips to his ear, roar until your lungs crack, concluding by giving him a sore and serious punch in the ribs—do all this, and yet the fellow will neither hear nor see, nor say anything,—because, my friend, he is only—a painted sentinel!'

The author's apology for the work is found in the first line of his poetical preface:

'Das sind die Schatten *aus der jungen Tagen,*'
["These are the shadows from our young days"]

An apology certainly more available in Germany than among us."
(Mangan's note).

13 *Maturin's Montorio... Filippo*: the character Filippo occurs in *The Fatal Revenge; or, The Family of Montorio* (1807), Charles Robert Maturin's first Gothic novel.

14 *Ravaillac*: François Ravaillac (1578–1610), assassin of Henry IV of France; sentenced to death by quartering.

15 *Sindbad the Sailor*: see Sinbad's fourth voyage in the *Arabian Nights*.

16 *"We call aloud... a chasm"*: this quotation has not been traced.

17 Wordsworth, "The Fountain", ll. 1–2: "We talked with open heart, and tongue / Affectionate and true".

18 *noli me tangere*: "Touch me not" (John 20: 17).

19 Thomas Campbell, *Pleasures of Hope* (1799) I, 7: "'Tis distance lends enchantment to the view".

20 *Sisyphus*: in Greek mythology Sisyphus was condemned to perform this never-ending task in the underworld.

21 *Goliah*: (usually "Goliath") Philistine giant whom David slew with a sling and a stone. See 1 Samuel 17.

22 Matthew Green, *The Spleen* (1737) l. 92: "Fling but a stone, the giant dies."

23 *veni, vidi, vici*: "I came, I saw, I vanquished", words which Julius Caesar is said to have used to announce to a friend his victory at Zela (47 BC).

24 "It is a part of German book-making to print for leaves together three or four lines on a page, and leave the rest of the page blank". *(Mangan's note)*.

25 *Van Wodenblock*: see Mangan's poem "Mynheer Van Woodenblock", *DUM*, August 1838.

26 *Hamlet* III. ii. 375: "They fool me to the top of my bent."

27 1 Corinthians, 13:12.

28 Charles Lamb, "The Old Familiar Faces".

29 *Gil Blas*: picaresque novel (1715–1735) by the French writer Alain-René Lesage. In the Preface, a student finds the soul of Pedro Garcias in a leather bag hidden beneath a stone.

30 *Twelfth Night* II. iv. 114: "green and yellow melancholy".

31 Cf. *Othello* I. iii. 250–251: "My heart's subdued / Even to the very quality of my lord".

32 In "My Bugle, and How I Blow It" (*Vindicator*, 27 March 1841) Mangan has "fold over fold, inveterately convolved"; on both occasions

he appears to have misremembered Wordsworth's lines "... a growth /
Of intertwisted fibres serpentine / Up-coiling, and inveterately
convolved" ("Yew-trees", ll. 16–18).

33 George Canning, "The Friend of Humanity and the Knife-grinder"
(1797), l. 21. The original reads *I have*, not *he has*.

34   "Blumen sind uns nah befreundet,
           Pflanzen unserm Blut verwandt,
       Und sie werden angefeindet
           Und wir thun so unbekannt.
       Unser Kopf lenkt sich zum Denken,
           Und die Blume nach dem Licht,
       Und wann Nacht und Thau einbricht,
           Sieht man sie die Blätter senken,
       Wie der Mensch zum Schlaf einnickt
           Schlummert sie in sich gebückt.

       Flowers are to us near befriended, (allied)
           Plants to our blood related.
       And they become at-hated, (they are objects of dislike)
           And we do so unknown. (we are so distant with them)
       Our head turns itself to the thinking,
           And the flower after the light,
       And when night and dew breaks in,
           Sees one her the leaves sink, (we see her leaves drooping)
       As the man to the sleep nods in, (as man nods asleep)
           Slumbers she in herself wrapped."
                                   (Mangan's note).

35 *und damit Lied am Ende*: "and there the song ends".

36 *Gregory Hipkins*: this character has not been identified.

37 *Miss Edgeworth's Murad*: see "Murad the Unlucky", in Maria
Edgeworth's *Popular Tales* (1805).

38 *Trenck*: Friedrich, Freiherr von der Trenck (1726–1794), writer of a
celebrated autobiography, was incarcerated in Magdeburg for ten
years.

39 *Novalis*: Friedrich Leopold, Freiherr von Hardenberg Novalis
(1772–1801), German poet and critic.

LITERÆ ORIENTALES. TURKISH POETRY.—SECOND ARTICLE [(Unsigned),
DUM, March 1838]

1 See "Literæ Orientales I", note 44.

2 See "Literæ Orientales I", note 48.

3 *sapernientes*: "ignoramuses".

4 "Geschichte der Osmanischen Dichtkunst". *(Mangan's note)*.

5 *p. 150*: in Volume II.

6 "Divan, a collection of poems". *(Mangan's note)*.

7 *p. 145*: also in Volume II.

8 *Nat. Lee*: Nathaniel Lee (1653–1692), English dramatist, wrote a number of extravagant tragedies. However, the line quoted by Mangan is from an extravaganza which may have been written by the Irish scholar John O'Donovan. See Ellen Shannon-Mangan, *James Clarence Mangan: A Biography*, 118–119.

9 *at random*: the poem below is actually the first in volume II.

10 *ghazel*: a type of Oriental lyric, usually of erotic import.

11 *There are… into English*: Mangan would have his readers believe that he went to the original MSS. In fact, at least twenty of the translations in this article can be traced to Hammer-Purgstall's German versions, the rest being either of doubtful origin or clearly spurious.

12 *The Prophet spoke…. of this world*: Mangan takes many liberties with Hammer-Purgstall's rendering. For instance, after stating that "there will be ten divisions of the wicked" (which is correct), he only lists nine, omitting, for some reason, the dumb. As for the last sentence, it has no equivalent in the German source.

13 "'Comme l'Alcoran est d'un grand usage, on le met ordinairement dans un étui de drap pour le conserver.' D'HERBELOT, *tome IV*". *(Mangan's note)*. This anecdote is indeed told, with less embroidering, nameless characters, and no mention of Kafzade in d'Herbelot's *Bibliothèque orientale*, IV, 463.

14 *From this authority we learn*: Mangan takes many liberties with his "authority". Hammer-Purgstall's translation states, for instance, that no work should be done on Saturday, the day of rest, and that on Thursdays all prayers are granted ("perilous undertakings"are not mentioned).

15 *King Pharaoh*: "pharaoh king of Egypt" is how these Egyptian rulers are styled in Hebrew and Assyrian records from their eighteenth dynasty (16th century BC). Pharaoh was never a personal name.

16 *Nimrod, the Mighty Hunter*: Genesis 10: 8–10.

17 *Lot*: Genesis 19.

18 *Core, Dathan and Abiron*: Dathan and his brother Abiram combined with Korah, the Levite, in rebellion against Moses. Numbers 16: 1–34.

19 *Og*: semi-legendary giant who crops up here and there in the earlier books of the Old Testament (Numbers and Deuteronomy).

20 *Iskander Nameh*: Mangan's account of this work is based on Hammer-Purgstall's prose summary of the same, which it abridges and distorts in various ways.

21 *Alexander the Great*: (356–323 BC), famous conqueror of the East.

22 *a long list of his own names*: the only list mentioned in the source at this point is that of the names of God.

23 *Metempsychosis*: theory of transmigration of souls. It is not mentioned in the source.

24 *Philip of Macedon*: ruled Macedonia (359–336 BC), assassinated in 336 BC as he moved against Persia.

25 *Darius of Persia*: Darius III, ruled Persia 336–330 BC; was defeated by Alexander the Great.

26 *Wise Men of Greece*: the "seven Sages": Bias, Chilon, Cleobulus, Periander, Pittacus, Solon, Thales.

27 *Hippocrates*: the "father of medicine" (460–c.375 BC), Greek philosopher.

28 *Khisra, the Guardian of the Fountain of Life*: cf. Mangan's lines, "Bright streamlets rill through Paradise, and KHEES'R guards their waters / For Heaven's immortal sons and daughters" ("Kasseedeh", *DUM*, April 1840). Khisra, or Kheeser, is identical with "Khidder the ever young", about whom Mangan wrote two poems, "Khidder" and "The World's Changes".

29 *the cock, who is Religion*: in the source the cock is the Pure Man (*der Reine*).

30 *farsang*: Persian unit of measure approximately four miles.

31 *The soul is an abstraction ... any one spot*: this actually contradicts the source, in which the soul is divided into three parts, the second of which is divided into two parts, the first of which is divided into *inner* and *outer*, the outer part being divided into the five senses. At which point even Hammer-Purgstall finds himself unable to go on and concludes with *u.s.w.* ("etc.").

32 *the twelve gates are ...*: Mangan's "&c." stands for the nostrils, navel, mouth and excretory orifices.

33 *from thence he proceeds ... visits the place*: the German source translates: "[He goes] to the island of Wakwak, where the fruits on the trees are birds which cry *Wakwak*." Mangan is having great fun here, for while *quackquack* is the cry of a duck, a *quack* is an impostor—"one who professes a knowledge or skill concerning subjects of which he is ignorant" (O.E.D.). The birds, "by an instinctive intelligence" (which *DUM* readers do not have), denounce Mangan the quack Orientalist, a stowaway on Hammer-Purgstall's boat.

34 "*Shadkiem*, or, more correctly, *Shad-u-kiam*, (Pleasure and Love) is an appellative now bestowed by the Orientals upon many cities, real and imaginary; but it was originally the proper name of the capital of *Djinnestan* (Genii-land,) and it is as such that Beckford and Moore allude to it in their tales: —

'They imagined they saw in the gorgeous clouds of the west the domes of Shaddukian and Ambreabad, (the City of Amber,) where the

Peries have fixed their abode.'— *Vathek. Sixth. Ed. p.125.*

> 'O! am I not happy? I am, I am!
> To thee, sweet EDEN, how dark and sad
> Are the diamond turrets of SHADUKIAM,
> And the fragrant bowers of AMBERABAD!'
>
> *Paradise and the Peri."*
> *(Mangan's note).*

35 *Canto IX treats exclusively... mankind:* this is inaccurate for the canto begins with an account of Alexander's love-affair with Kaidafa, Queen of the Amazons.

36 *The author pronounces... as black as it is:* Mangan gets slightly carried away here; the source merely says "Diatribe against women; the author laughs at his old head".

37 *The last Canto... not obvious:* the German source translates: "Fable of the fox who, when the sun played on his fur, thought he was a peacock".

38 "The variance between this account of the last days and the death of Alexander and that furnished by Diodorus Siculus, Quintus Curtius, Plutarch, and other writers, will be sufficiently explained, when it is considered that AHMEDI merely copied the narrative of the Persian historian, NIZAMI, whose compilations are in general little better than splendid fable". *(Mangan's note).*

39 *Philo:* of Alexandria (c.20 BC–AD 50), Jewish philosopher; or Philo of Larissa, Greek philosopher of the first half of the first century BC.

40 *Bias:* of Priene (6th century BC), one of the Seven Sages.

41 *Pythagoras:* of Samos, Greek philosopher and mathematician (6th century BC).

42 *Aristippus:* of Cyrene (5th century BC), disciple of Socrates.

43 *Solon:* of Athens (early 6th century BC), poet and statesman; one of the Seven Sages.

44 *Zeno:* of Elea (c.490–430 BC), Greek philosopher, inventor of dialectics; or Zeno of Citium (c.335–262 BC), founder of the Stoics.

45 *Heraclitus:* of Ephesus, (c.540–c.480 BC), Greek philosopher.

46 Hammer-Purgstall lists eight obscure philosophers, *viz.* Matrimus, Rufus, Bertas and Bidagoras, Balo, Emrio, Mirawe and Maino. Mangan adopts the first four and for the latter he substitutes Bias, Aristippus, Heraclitus and Aristotle.

47 *we dislike Eastern poetry:* the task of having given an account of the *Iskander Nameh* may explain this flat statement; however, Mangan had already made a plea for "perspicuity" in "Anthologia Germanica IV" (October 1835).

48 *"march of mind":* phrase commonly used (especially with ironical intent) in the second quarter of the 19th century, following the

foundation of the Society for the Diffusion of Useful Knowledge.

49 Ecclesiastes 1: 9: "The thing that hath been, it is that which shall be".

50 *Hoogly*: (Hugli) channel by which the Ganges enters the Bay of Bengal.

ANTHOLOGIA GERMANICA.—NO. XII. THE LESS TRANSLATABLE POEMS OF
SCHILLER [(Unsigned), *DUM*, July 1838]

1 *Mother Bunch*: legendary 16th century London alewife famous for telling tall tales.

2 *Balaam-box*: the receptacle or file in a newspaper office for material kept to fill empty spaces on the printed page.

3 *The conduct of Pythias*: Pythias, condemned to death by the tyrant he had attempted to kill, begged for a three days' reprieve in order to attend his sister's wedding, offering his friend Damon as hostage for this period.

4 *amende honorable*: "public apology and reparation".

5 *Macbeth* IV. i. 10: "Double, double, toil and trouble."

6 *Bayard*: Pierre Terrail, seigneur de Bayard (1475–1524), styled "*le chevalier sans peur et sans reproche*" ("the knight without fear and without blame").

7 *the act was... shabby*: in the poem Sir Guy risks his life to retrieve from a lion-pit the glove which the cruel Countess drops there, as a test of his chivalry; he then throws it in her face.

8 *Grafinn and Frau*: "Countess and Lady".

9 *Was wäre ich ohne Dich?*: "What would I be without you?"

10 *Ich weisz es nicht... Hundert und Tausende sind*: "I do not know... but I am terrified as I see what hundreds and thousands are without you".

11 *Dr. Kitchener*: William Kitchiner (?1779–1827), author of a great variety of books, including *The Economy of the Eyes: Precepts for the Improvement and Preservation of the Sight* (London: 1824).

12 *D'Israeli the Younger*: Benjamin Disraeli (1804–1881), novelist and statesman. Mangan appears to be fusing together two episodes in Disraeli's novel *Contarini Fleming* (1832). In Part II, ch. 8–9, the young hero spends every night during three weeks writing a tragedy which turns out to be "a laboured exaggeration of the most unnatural features of the German school", while, years later, in Part IV, ch. 5–8, he indulges so much in meditation—though not especially at night—that his health breaks down completely.

13 These lines, which have not been traced, translate literally:
    At the sarcophagus of the future
    Sweetly thunders the rejoicing complaint of Hope,
    When the dead man rises sprightly,
    When he jumps into cold life,

And happy in unhappiness praises her
Who after short flight found him in the end.

ANTHOLOGIA GERMANICA—NO. XIII. M. KLAUER KLATTOWSKI'S PUBLICATIONS [(Unsigned), *DUM*, August 1838]. The title carries the following note by Mangan:

> Popular Songs of the Germans, with explanatory notes, &c. By Wilhelm Klauer Klattowski, Professor of the German and Northern Languages and Literature. London, Simpkin and Marshall, 1836.
>
> Select Lyrical Poems of the Germans, with explanatory notes. By Wilhelm Klauer Klattowski. London, Simpkin and Marshall, 1837.
>
> Ballads and Romances, Poetical Tales, Legends and Idylls of the Germans, with explanatory notes. By Wilhelm Klauer Klattowski. London, Simpkin and Marshall, 1837.

1 Reginald Heber (1783–1826), "Lines written to a March composed in imitation of a military band", l. 1: "I see them on their winding way".

2 Thomas Moore, "I'd Mourn the Hopes" (*Irish Melodies*), l. 14.

3 *St. Leon's elixir bottle*: the *elixir vitae* (elixir of life) possessed by the hero of William Godwin's novel *St. Leon* (1799).

4 *répandu*: "spread".

5 *both Tyrian and Trojan*: an echo of Dido's words in Virgil's *Aeneid*, I. 574: "Tros Tyriusque mihi nullo discrimine agetur" ("Between Trojan and Tyrian I will make no discrimination").

6 *Baron Munchausen's horn*: Baron Munchausen, a type of the tall-story teller, the hero of R.E. Raspe's *The Surprising Travels and Adventures of Baron Munchausen* (1785). At one point during the Baron's winter travels in Russia his postilion blows his horn but cannot make it sound. After they arrive at an inn the horn is hung near the fire, whereupon the tunes that were frozen up in it issue forth.

7 "*that love to dally with Aeolian lyres*": this quotation has not been traced.

8 Mangan is referring to his own poem, presented as a translation from Drechsler, "Mynheer Van Woodenblock".

9 *As You Like It* II. vii. 148.

10 Julius Caesar III. ii. 171: "If you have tears, prepare to shed them now."

11 *turnings*: translations.

12 "*Füget zum Guten den Glanz und den Schimmer*": "Adds to the Good the shine and the gleam". Translated by Mangan as "And blends with the Useful, the Brilliant and Pleasing" in his rendering of Schiller's "Lay of the Bell", *DUM*, February 1835.

LITERÆ ORIENTALES. TURKISH POETRY.—THIRD ARTICLE [(Unsigned), *DUM*, September 1838]

1 "From 1521 to 1572". *(Mangan's note)*.

2 "He also wrote two mystical poems, *The Treasury of Secret Knowledge* and *The King and the Beggar*, still in high repute. Yahya professed Christianity, but it does not appear that his religion was any barrier to his success as a poet. Now and then, however, he was rallied on the subject. One day having sent the following distich to the poet Khiali—

> With a yellow visage and a nose the color of a tulip,
> Is it not astonishing that Khiali should look so like an owl?

Khiali replied—

> Benim erbabi nasmun douleti, *el shapkali kafir!*
> Khari nadan deil isen douletun nitshun depelersun sen.

> I am the Glory of the Princes of Song, thou *hat-wearing infidel!*
> If thou be not an ass thou wilt try to win Glory to thyself.

i.e. to make a friend of the writer. On one occasion a conspiracy was formed against Yahya by some enemies at court, but Suleiman, with his characteristic generosity, refused to listen to any accusation against so distinguished a poet. Yahya's life was long and prosperous. His death occurred in 1582". *(Mangan's note)*.

3 "Author of *The Candle and the Moth, The Book of Ferrukh, Ahmed and Mahmoud, Shireen and Mouloud*, and many other poems. He died in 1546, of a complication of diseases, brought on chiefly by intemperance. He was a native of Persia, and at first practised astrology for a livelihood, but finding the stars adverse to his success in that profession, he went to Turkey and turned poet. The following sketch of his subsequent fortunes we render from RIAZI, to whom it was communicated by ZATI himself:—

'When I came to Constantinople, Sultan Bajazet II. being then the reigning monarch, I found there a great number of rich Ulemas, to whom I presented Kassidets for the feast of Bairam and the Winter and Spring Festivals; I also, in a fortunate hour, gave Sultan Bajazet several Panegyrics, for which he rewarded me with a pension of three thousand aspers yearly and a yearly largess of half a sheep and a number of red shawls, only stipulating that I should every year write one Kassidet for the Feast of the Roses and two Kassidets for both

Feasts of the Bairam. I protested against the sheep and the shawls in the following quatrain:

> I am a stilly ocean, lying bare under the Moon of Poetry;
> Give to thy warriors the red shawls and the blood of the sheep.
> But to ZATI give silks of blue (the color of the ocean),
> Which are agitated like the waves when the winds begin to woo them.

As soon as the Grand Vizier Ali Pasha saw these lines he commanded the Defterdar to let me have wardrobes of blue Angora silks in future. These were my bright days; my particular friends were the Viziers Ali Pasha and Herzekzade, and the threetailed Bashaw Tadjizade Djaafer and his brother Saadi; and I often supped at table with them. My particularly particular friend was the poet Kadri Effendi; with him I spent a good deal of my time; we usually lived together, sometimes in the College of St. Sophia,—at others in the suburb of Tashtolkala; and at one time, we had a delightful little Paradise of a house opposite the Fountain of Aya-jokshurli. When Piri, afterwards Grand Vizier of Selim I., was Defterdar, I gave him a Kassidet, the burden of which was this:

> All the buds burst into roses and new stars were born in the heavens
> On the night of the day that saw Piri made a Defterdar.

At this time the Sultan made me an offer of a stewardship at Brusa, worth thirty aspers a day, but I declined it, not liking to be separated from my Constantinople friends. The Sultan took umbrage at my refusal; and what was worse, towards the end of his reign Ali Pasha died, and Herzekzade and Tadjizade fell into disgrace; so that I remained some time without any patron or protector.—On the accession of Sultan Selim I. I presented him with a Kassidet; and he gave me in requital two villages, which brought me in yearly eleven thousand five hundred aspers. My former patron Tadjizade Djaafer, the three-tailed Bashaw, was bowstrung, and Sultan Selim, during his short reign, was mostly in the field of battle; however I had still my villages. When Sultan Suleiman ascended the throne I also gave him Kassidets, and he loaded me with presents and honors. It happened that the poet Habsi was then in prison for saying some saucy thing to the Grand Vizier Ibrahim Pasha; and Keshfi, Habsi's brother, coming into office shortly afterwards, he, I, Bassiri, Khandi and other poets presented ourselves before Ibrahim in the Divan and requested him to liberate Habsi. But the Grand Vizier took this intrusion of ours in ill part; and though the Sultan still favored me and gave me presents, Ibrahim did not like me too well. Not long afterwards Destiny declared against me altogether; Khiali began to slander me, and he found many to listen to him; my own habits of life, too, had always been the reverse of regular; and what with one piece of ill luck and another I went down the hill of fortune even faster than I had mounted it; so that at last I found myself obliged to turn astrologer once more, and cast horoscopes for all who would pay for their peepings into futurity. I am now old; I suffer greatly from gout; my powers of mind begin to fail me; and I am labouring continually under a dreadful nervous debility, not to be described". *(Mangan's note)*. The sketch allegedly rendered from Riazi is attributed to Aaschik in Hammer-Purgstall (II, 240–242). Mangan's rendering is faithful enough even though he renames the Fountain mentioned halfway through: where the German text reads *Aja-jokuschi*, Mangan has *Aya-jokshurly* (*i.e. Ah! you joke surely!*).

4 *"Dub. Univ. Mag. No. LXIII"*. *(Mangan's note)*. See "Literæ Orientales. Second Article", March 1838.

5 "A magnificently illustrated copy of this poem, made for Hassan Pasha, Governor of Bagdad, in 1599, is deposited in the Royal Library of Dresden. A description of it will be found in Fleischer's *Cataloge der Orientalischen Handschriften* under No. 362". *(Mangan's note)*.

6 *with some account... our readers*: Mangan's "account" is based on Hammer Purgstall's (II, 295–302) which it now shortens, now embroiders with fanciful details, some of which are pointed out in the notes below.

7 *Unloose... vain-glory*: these "Oriental" metaphors are not in the source.

8 "The Sofis were generally distinguished by blue dresses, but some of the orders wore green". *(Mangan's note)*.

9 "Opium-eater". *(Mangan's note)*.

10 "The sound made by the wine as it issues from the neck of the bottle". *(Mangan's note)*.

11 *like Sempronius... a traitor at heart*: "This smooth discourse and wild behaviour oft / Conceal a traitor—something whispers me / All is not right—Cato, beware of Lucius". Joseph Addison, *Cato* (1713) II. i. 77–79.

12 *farsang*: Persian unit of measure, about four miles.

13 *a tale of a tub*: an incredible story.

14 *cater-cousin*: good friend.

15 *Tchel-Minar*: Persepolis. See "Literæ Orientales I", note 19.

16 *Nizami*: Persian poet of the twelfth century.

17 *Bidpay*: (or Pilpay) supposed author of a famed collection of Indian fables, the *Hitopadesa*.

18 *Hafiz*: (or Hafez) Persian poet of the fourteenth century.

19 *Djami*: Persian poet of the fifteenth century.

20 *Lokman*: legendary Oriental moralist, said to have flourished a thousand years before the Christian era. His wisdom, like Solomon's, is supposed to have been of divine origin.

21 *Dom Daniel*: abode of evil spirits in Chavis and Cazotte's *Continuation of the Arabian Nights* (1788–1793).

22 *a young man of Bassora... any of them*: Mangan is laughing up his sleeve here; the corresponding passage in the German source translates: "a holy man of Bassora, who took to opium, and by the use of it attained heavenly illumination and inspiration".

23 *until the sun... the Faithful*: this formula, already used four paragraphs previously, is not in the source.

24 "It is a coincidence deserving notice, that this is also the precise period which we find the Irish Ⰾⰰⰻⰳ ⱀⰰ Ⰳⰰⰻⱃⰶⰵ alotting to the continuance of the celebrated combat between Goll of the Fian and the King of Lochlin: Ⱅⰻⰳ Ⰳⱁⰾⰾ ⰰⰽⰰⱃ ⰰⱀ Ⱇⰵⰰⱀ ⰿⱁⱀ ⰰⰾⱀ ⰰⱀ ⱅⱅⱃⰰⰻⰳ, acas bhádur ocht lá acas ocht n-oídhche ag comhrac, ⰳⱆⱀ ⰿⱁⱀⱁⱃⰰⱅ ⱀⰻ Ⰾⱁⰽⰾⰰⱀ ⱀⰵ Ⰳⱁⰾⰾ, ⰰⰽⰰⱃ ⰰ ⰿⰻⱀⱀⱅⰵⱀ ⱆⰻⰾⰵ ⰾⰵⱀ ⰰⱀ Ⱇⱇⰵⰻⱀ". *(Mangan's note)*. In fact the German source does not specify the duration of the fight between Opium and Wine. As for the Irish quotation, though not taken from the *Laid na Gaisge* ("Lay of Prowess") itself, but from some gloss on that poem or from a prose tale of the combat, it is correct and translates: "Goll and the big man came to the strand and the king of Lochlainn was defeated by Goll and all his people [were defeated] by the Fian".

THE THIRTY FLASKS [(An Out-and-Outer), *DUM*, October 1838 & December 1838]. Mangan's story is partly a burlesque adaptation of Balzac's *La Peau de chagrin* (1831), in which, after losing his last shilling at the gambling table, the hero Raphaël de Valentin is given a shagreen talisman. The skin makes each of his wishes come true but shrinks a little each time, and his own health deteriorates correspondingly. Some of the minor correspondences between the two texts are pointed out in the notes below.

1 *Επειδαν... προλαμβανω*: very faulty transcription in the first person singular of "ἐπειδὰν ἅπαντ' ἀκούσητε, κρίνατε, μὴ πρότερον προλαμβάνετε" ("when you have heard everything, make up your mind, do not judge in advance"), Demosthenes, *Philippic 1*, 3, 14.

2 *A Mad World, my Masters*: play by Thomas Middleton (1608).

3 *Merchant of Venice* I. iii. 167–169: "Then meet me forthwith at the notary's, / Give him direction for this merry bond— / And I will go and purse the ducats straight".

4 *rouge et noir*: "red and black"; a gambling card-game.

5 *Spielhaus*: "gambling club".

6   *Heraclitus the Howler*: Heraclitus (c.540–c.480 BC), Greek philosopher; was called the "Dark Philosopher" or the "Weeping Philosopher", in contrast to Democritus, the "Laughing Philosopher".

7   *snudge*: miser.

8   *Croesus*: last king of Lydia (ruled c.560–546 BC), proverbial for his wealth.

9   *C'est à dire*: "that is to say".

10   *dust*: money (*slang*).

11   *unter vier Augen*: "in private" (lit. "under four eyes").

12   *La Trappe*: Notre-Dame de la Trappe, French abbey where a severe reform of the Cistercian rule was imposed in 1664.

13   *Zittarotti and Elwes*: John Elwes of Meggott (1714–1789), famous English miser. Zittarotti has not been identified.

14   *Much Ado About Nothing* III. iii. 122–124: "I know that Deformed; a' has been a vile thief this seven year; a' goes up and down like a gentleman".

15   *déterré*: "unearthed".

16   *Rubens... Vandyck*: Peter Paul Rubens (1577–1640), and Sir Anthony Van Dyck (1599–1641), Flemish painters.

17   *Bahauder*: usually "Bahadur", title of respect used in India and added to other titles with the name.

18   *ipse dixit*: (lit. "he himself said so") a mere assertion, totally unsupported.

19   *tar-water*: a favourite specific of Mangan's, a concoction of tar steeped in water.

20   *à la mode Germanorum*: "in the manner (*Fr.*) of the Germans (*Lat.*)".

21   *Fenelon*: François Salignac de la Mothe Fénelon (1651–1715), French bishop and writer.

22   *qu'il est plus facile de mépriser la mort même que de réprimer les affections du coeur*: "that it is easier to scorn death itself than to suppress the affections of the heart". The quotation has not been traced.

23   "Minstrelsy of the Scottish Border". *(Mangan's note)*. The lines are actually from "Sir James the Ross", a ballad by Michael Bruce (1740–1767), not included in Sir Walter Scott's *Minstrelsy of the Scottish Border*.

24   *Le sage entend à demi-mot*: "a wise man can take a hint".

25   *A certain proverb... vulgarity*: "There are more ways of killing a dog than by hanging".

26   "Alfred Tennyson." *(Mangan's note)*. "The How and the Why" is from *Poems, Chiefly Lyrical* (1830).

27   *Memnon... par la tête*: "Memnon once designed the project of being perfectly wise. Few men have not taken this crazy notion into their

heads." This is the opening sentence of Voltaire's tale "Memnon, ou la sagesse humaine" (1750).

28 *Au reste*: "besides".

29 1 Corinthians 13: 1.

30 *Twelfth Night* IV. i. 18–19: "I prithee, foolish Greek, depart from me. / There's money for thee."

31 *1 Henry IV* I. ii. 147: "I prithee leave the Prince and me alone".

32 *Macbeth* IV. i. 86.

33 *like Wordsworth's Doe*: the Doe's soft pace is mentioned several times in Wordsworth's "The White Doe of Rylstone"; Mangan may have had especially in mind "And then advanced with stealth-like pace" VII, 1650.

34 *tout-ensemble*: "general effect".

35 *ready-reckoner*: Mangan is making a joke: a "ready reckoner" is a book of computations of the sort used frequently in business. Mangan uses the phrase to mean "the man who counts the ready (*i.e.* the money)".

36 *quiz*: odd or eccentric person.

37 *parti*: "match".

38 *perdu*: "lost, out-of-the-way".

39 *chevalier d'industrie*: "crook, swindler".

40 *tigers*: parasites, or rakes (*slang*).

41 *Wandering Jew*: in Germany this legendary figure was associated with a man named Buttadæus, who "appeared" in the 13th, 15th, 16th and 18th centuries, then disappeared.

42 *Thunder-ten-Trunk*: "Monsieur le baron de Thunder-ten-tronckh" is a character in Voltaire's *Candide*.

43 Matthew 26: 18: "And he [Jesus] said, Go into the city to such a man, and say unto him, The Master saith, My time is at hand".

44 For "thou shalt" read "I will".

45 *à la chinois*: "Chinese style".

46 *Hamlet* I. v. 174–175: "There are more things in heaven and earth, Horatio, / Than are dreamt of in your philosophy".

47 *Credo quia impossibile*: "I believe because it is impossible". Saying ascribed to St. Augustine, but founded on a passage in Tertullian's *De Carne Christi*, IV: "Credibile est, quia ineptum est... certum est quia impossibile".

48 Correctly, Act II. Sc. i.

49 William Godwin, Preface to *St. Leon* (1799): "It is better that man should be a living being, than a stock or a stone".

50 *Ultima Thule*: "end of the world, last extremity". From the name given by the Ancients, and recorded by Polybius (c.150 BC), to an island far north of Britain at their world's farthest reach.

51 *Pyrrho*: of Elis (c.360–c.272 BC), Greek philosopher renowned for his continual suspense and doubt, and his avoidance of conclusions.

52 *ninnyhammer*: frivolous fool.

53 *Much Ado About Nothing* IV. ii. 84: "O that I had been writ down an ass!"

54 *a pair of sandalled feet*: in *La Peau de chagrin*, Raphaël de Valentin catches a glimpse of a woman's leg "dont les fins contours étaient dessinés par un bas blanc et bien tiré".

55 *Mr Ex-Sheriff Raphael's right to the title of "the most incomprehensible of all imaginable vagabonds"*: Alexander Raphael was Sheriff of the City of London from July 1834 to June 1835. In that same month he was elected M.P. for Carlow, but the election was annulled on petition and a commission set up to look into the matter. Raphael retired from the contest and wrote a "Letter to the Electors of Carlow" (*Times*, 31 October 1835), stating that he had given £3000 to Daniel O'Connell, the Irish politician, in order to secure the seat. O'Connell riposted with his own "Letter to the Electors of Carlow" (*Pilot*, 9 November 1835), which began: "Fellow-countrymen—I beg your pardon—I humbly beg your pardon, for having recommended to your suffrages that most incomprehensible of all imaginable vagabonds, Alexander Raphael."

56 *Bigottini*: Emilie Bigottini (1784–1858), French prima ballerina at the Paris Opera Ballet.

57 *balls… Byron*: a reference to a ball in Brussels on the eve of the battle of Waterloo in Byron's *Childe Harold* III. xxi–xxiii.

58 *lame feet*: Byron had a club foot.

59 *Heliogabulus*: Heliogabalus, Roman emperor from 218 to 222, famous for his eccentric behaviour.

60 *Nero*: Roman emperor from 54 to 68. He fancied himself an artist and a musician and is said to have played the lyre (Mangan's "fiddle") while Rome was on fire.

61 *Serendib*: (usually, *Serendip*) ancient name for Sri Lanka.

62 *Sindbad*: Sindbad the Sailor, the hero of a tale in the *Arabian Nights*, whose sixth voyage takes him to the island of Serendib.

63 *Schuh-und-Stiefelmacher*: "shoe-and-bootmaker". The scene that follows is Mangan's burlesque adaptation of the measuring of the shagreen talisman by Raphaël de Valentin.

64 *the Lord Kanzler's*: the Lord Chancellor's.

65 *St. Crispin*: traditional patron saint of shoemakers.

66 *Euer Gnaden*: "your Grace".

67 *by adding… exists*: the *DUM* text reads, "by adding other two to that one; an additional two to the one that exists"—obviously a mistake.

68   *cousin-german*: first cousin.

69   *anti-Pythagorean*: Pythagoras, Greek philosopher and mathematician of the sixth century BC, advocated vegetarianism.

70   Correctly "... the devil... / Says that this deed is chronicled in hell". Mangan is punning on hell / ell (obsolete measure of length).

71   1 Corinthians 15: 47: "The first man is of the earth, earthy".

72   Milton, *Paradise Lost* VII. 22: "the visible diurnal sphere".

73   *Ueber die Natur des Geistes*: "On the Nature of the Spirit".

74   *de l'autre côté*: "on the other hand".

75   *Julius Caesar* II. i. 65.

76   *Raw-head and Bloody-bones*: a bogy-man, once used to frighten children.

77   *Mother Bunch*: legendary 16th century London alewife famous for telling tall tales.

78   *personnel*: "personal or physical appearance".

79   *Fortunatus*: hero of German folk-tale who had an inexhaustible purse.

80   *the schoolmen's ass betwixt the two stacks of hay*: the French scholastic philosopher Buridan (d. c.1360) argued that if you placed an ass exactly between two identical haystacks it would starve to death through indecision. Buridan is referred to in *La Peau de chagrin* as well.

81   *In for a groshen, in for a guilder*: Mangan's "German" adaptation of the phrase, "in for a penny, in for a pound".

82   1 Kings 22: 15: "Go, and prosper".

83   *Ce n'est que le premier pas qui coûte*: "Only the first step is difficult to take"; a remark attributed to Mme du Deffand (1697–1780) on hearing the legend of St. Denis, who is said after martyrdom to have carried his head in his hands for two miles and to have laid it on the spot where stands the cathedral bearing his name, outside Paris.

84   *je ne sais quoi-ish*: "full of indefinable feeling".

85   *rouleaus*: cylindrical packets of gold coins.

86   "Croupier". *(Mangan's note)*.

87   *packed runs... a dozen gentlemen*: to "pack cards" means to arrange or shuffle them so as to cheat; to "pack a jury"—which consists of twelve members—is to select it in such a way as to secure a partial decision.

88   *hazard*: a game at dice. The total of the throw must be above four and not exceed nine. A deuce-ace makes a total of three.

89   *When a flat is to be landed*: "when a fool is to be caught".

90   Correctly, "I am as mad as he, if sad and merry madness equal be".

91   *spooney*: simpleton (*slang*)

92   *But all this is Sanscrit to you*: the use of *Sanscrit*, instead of *Greek*, is an ironical echo of the remark made to Raphaël de Valentin by the old

man who gives him the shagreen skin: "Ah, vous lisez couramment le sanscrit" ("Ah, you read Sanskrit fluently").

93 *Blind Hookey... Hop-the-Twig*: all gambling games which derive their names from some deceptive practice or criminal behaviour: "Blind Hookey" is a card game sometimes called "Wilful Murder"; a "Scaramouch" or "Saltimbanco" is a mountebank or quack; a "Killdevil" is an artificial bait designed to spin in the water and lure fish; to "Hop-the-Twig" is a slang term meaning to abscond or to die.

94 *Chesterfield*: Lord Chesterfield, whose *Letters* (1774), advising his stepson how to get on, stress the value of politeness and good manners.

95 *Tu vainqueras*: (correctly *vaincras*) "you shall conquer".

96 *stethescope*: mistaken spelling of "stethoscope".

97 *choused*: swindled (*colloq.*).

98 *rap*: "A counterfeit coin, worth about half a farthing, which passed current for a halfpenny in Ireland in the 18th c., owing to the scarcity of genuine money" (O.E.D.).

99 *hookemsniveying*: "hook and snivey" was the name of a wire and handle contrivance for undoing a door's wooden bolt from the outside; it later became a slang expression meaning to cheat, especially by pretending to be sick.

100 *by chalks*: by far; from the use of chalks to score points in games.

101 *stand Sam*: pay the reckoning.

102 *blackleggism*: from "blackleg", a swindler.

103 *skied a copper*: tossed up a penny (a mild form of gambling).

104 First lines of a duet in *The Mountaineers* (performed 1793) by George Colman the Younger (1762–1836); music by Samuel Arnold (1740–1802):

>   Faint and wearily,
>   The way worn Traveller
>   Plods uncheerily,
>   Afraid to stop....

105 *Puck*: a mischievous sprite of English folklore.

106 *Belphegor*: a licentious, malicious deity originating among the Moabites.

107 *Mephistopheles*: name of the devil in the mediaeval legend of Faust, and in Goethe's *Faust*.

108 *Rubezahl*: German spirit; also called "Number Nip", the gnome king of the Giant Mountains.

109 *Maugraby*: great magician, who figures in Chavis and Cazotte's *Continuation of the Arabian Nights* (1788–1789), and whom Mangan had already used in "An Extraordinary Adventure in the Shades". His

introduction here may be due to the fact that a doctor in Balzac's *La Peau de chagrin* is named Maugredie.

110 *Domdaniel*: "The great College of Magic at Tunis, once so celebrated over Barbary, but destroyed by the Arabs when they achieved the conquest of Mauritania". *(Mangan's note)*.

111 In *La Peau de chagrin*, Raphaël de Valentin inherits the fortune of an uncle who has just died in Calcutta.

112 *I smoke*: I get the intent (in the cant of pickpocketry, "to smoke" is to discover, espy).

113 *see how the cat jumps*: see what direction events are taking.

114 *fork out the blunt*: hand over the money (*slang*).

115 *à qui mieux mieux*: "emulously, trying to go one better".

116 *Fuit Ilium*: "Troy is no more". *Aeneid* II. 325.

117 *take our gruel*: Mangan seems to use the phrase antiphrastically.

118 "*Vide* the Quarterly Review, No. CXVII., which is our authority for the statement". *(Mangan's note)*. In this issue of the *Quarterly Review* (July 1837), a review of Edward William Lane's *Account of the Manners and Customs of the Modern Egyptians* contains the following: "Being determined to have ocular proof of what he had heard, he [Mr Lane] applied to the interpreter of the British consulate, who brought to him the *Sheeykh Abd El-Chadir El-Mughrebee*... whose designation will remind every reader of the excellent tale of 'Maugraby the Magician'".

119 *gaffers and gafferesses*: young men and young women.

120 *Don Juan* III. lx. For *Shines* read *Shine*.

THE MAN IN THE CLOAK. A VERY GERMAN STORY [(B.A.M.), *DUM*, November 1838]. The story is a version of Balzac's *Melmoth réconcilié* (1834), itself a kind of sequel to *Melmoth the Wanderer* (1820), by the Irish novelist C.R. Maturin. Mangan has shortened the story, changed the characters' names, moved the scene from Paris to Vienna, and added a few burlesque touches, but he follows Balzac's narrative closely enough. The most significant change may be his referring to Melmoth as "The Man in the Cloak", a phrase which he was soon to use as a pseudonym for himself.

1 *legers*: obsolete spelling of "ledgers".

2 "The German manuscript characters differ considerably from the English". *(Mangan's note)*.

3 *Queerkopf*: *Kopf* means *head* in German.

4 *predecessors*: presumably a misprint for "professors".

5 *papering my hair*: using the small pieces of paper to wrap curls.

6 *ennuyée*: "bored; wearied".

7 *W****: Wien, *i.e.* Vienna. Since the English name of the Austrian capital

appears in full in the preceding paragraph, we may assume that Mangan is laughing at the use of asterisks in contemporary writing to "disguise" place-names.

8 *the Wandering Jew*: legendary figure who was condemned to wander over the face of the earth till Judgment Day for spurning Christ on his way to Calvary.

9 *G****: Graz.

10 *myrmidons*: policemen (*derog.*).

11 *Gammon!*: Nonsense!

12 *esclandre*: "scandal".

13 *déterrés*: "unearthed".

14 *Don Bombastes*: Bombastes Furioso, one who talks big and uses turgid language. After the eponymous character in William Barnes Rhodes' burlesque opera (1813).

15 Daniel 5.

16 Mark 8: 36.

17 *the Bourse*: the Paris Stock Echange.

18 *the king of the barricades*: Louis Philippe I (1773–1850); after the July 1830 revolution in Paris, he became King by "the will of the people".

19 *astrologer*: in Balzac the German is a demonologist.

20 *Jacob Bœhmen*: German mystic writer (1575–1624).

21 *The Threefold Life of Man*: *Vom dreifacher Leben des Menschen* (1619–1620).

22 *old Freddy*: Frederick the Great (1712–1786), king of Prussia. Mangan missed the joke here; the French text reads:

    —Ha! il était cordonnier…

    —En Prusse!

    —Travaillait-il pour le roi?

"Travailler pour le roi de Prusse" ("to work for the king of Prussia") means "to work for nothing".

23 *la Charte*: the constitution granted by Louis XVIII in 1815. Charles X's attempt to abolish it led to the Revolution of July 1830.

24 *Taglioni*: Marie Taglioni (1804–1884) renowned Italian ballet dancer.

25 *How was he off for soap?*: common mid-19th century street-saying of indeterminate meaning. It could be intended to mean "What is he good for?" in the way of cash.

26 *was ist denn das? Sind das Menschen—oder vielleicht Troglodyten?*: "what is that, then? Are those humans—or maybe troglodytes?"

ANTHOLOGIA GERMANICA — NO XIV. GELLERT'S TALES AND FABLES [(The Out-and-Outer), *DUM*, January 1839]. The title carries the following note by Mangan:

C.F. Gellert's sämmtliche Fabeln und Erzählungen, in drei Büchern. Vignetten von G. Osterwald. Leipzig; in der Hahnschen Verlagsbuchhandlung; 1838.

1 Horatio Smith, "The Poet and the Alchemist", ll. 20–23. For "formed" read "spun", and for "backward" read "backwards".
2 Thomas Gray, "Elegy in a Country Churchyard", 1. 120.
3 "As a slight biographical notice of Gellert may be acceptable, we subjoin the following from *Hirsching's Memoiren.*

'Christian Feargod Gellert was born in 1715, near Freyberg in Saxony. In 1734 he studied theology at Leipsic, and at the end of four years returned home and commenced preaching; but his constitutional bashfulness and cautiousness prevented him from attaining success as an orator. Accordingly, in 1739 he accepted the situation of preceptor to a young gentleman living near Dresden, and soon afterwards to a nephew of his own, whom he accompanied to Leipsic in 1741. About this period his literary tastes began to be developed; and in 1742 he produced his first work, *Belustigungen des Verstandes und Witzes*, The Recreations of Reason and Wit, which procured him a considerable share of notice. His bad state of health and the labour which his sermons cost him now induced him to relinquish his ecclesiastical views and devote himself exclusively to the instruction of youth. In 1744 he took the degree of Master of Arts, and in 1745 appeared the first volume of his Fables, a few plays and *Das Leben der Swedischen Gräfinn*, The History of a Swedish Countess, the first readable work in the shape of a prose tale that Germany had produced. He now formed an intimacy with all the literary characters of the day, and among others with Klopstock, who has made honorable mention of him in one of his earliest odes. (The passage here alluded to is this—

Ach! in schweigender Nacht erblickt' ich die offenen Gräber,
      Und der unsterblichen Schaar.
Wenn mir nicht mehr das Auge des zärtlichen GISEKE lächelt,
      Wenn, von dem Lande fern,
Unser redlicher CRAMER verwes't; wenn GARTNER, wenn RABNER
      Nicht sokratisch mehr spricht,
Wenn in des edelmüthigen GELLERT harmonischem Leben
      Jede Saite verstummt.

Oh! in the depths of the night I saw the graves laid bare!
      Around me thronged the Immortal Band!

O, woe! when GISECKE's eye no longer its lustre shall wear!
        When upright CRAMER, lost to our land,
Shall moulder in dust! when the words that GARTNER and RABNER have
    spoken
        Shall only be echoed through years in distance!
When every sweetly-sounding chord shall be ruefully broken
        In the noble GELLERT's harmonious existence!)

[Except for a couple of minor changes, this translation reproduces lines
33–40 of "To Ebert", which Mangan had published in the *DUM* in
April 1835. As for the German lines, the poet seems to have quoted
them from memory, for they contain several inaccuracies and
grammatical mistakes.]

Henceforward the reputation of Gellert continued progressively
increasing, but, alas! at the expense of his health and tranquillity.
He was attacked with incurable hypochondriasis; a disease which
had first invaded his constitution in early youth; and in 1751 he was
with difficulty prevailed on to accept the Professorship of Moral
Philosophy in the College of Leipsic, though a liberal salary was
attached to it. Notwithstanding his constant ill-health he still
continued his exertions to entertain and edify the reading public,
until death at length in the year 1769 put a period to his labours and
sufferings. His loss was deeply and universally lamented, for he had
rendered himself in some measure the instructor of the nation.
Every person capable of handling a pen immediately turned writer
in his praise. His likeness was cast in gypsum and moulded in wax;
it was engraved on copper and represented in all forms of painting.
A century will perhaps elapse, says Kutner, before we have another
poet capable of exciting the love and admiration of his
contemporaries in so eminent a degree as Gellert; and of exercising
so powerful an influence on the taste and way of thinking of all
ranks. Though not a genius of the first order, he was an agreeable
and versatile writer; the poet of religion and virtue, and an able
reformer of public morals. His private character also was one of the
highest worth. He was humane, benevolent and tolerant of the
infirmities of others. Timidity rendered him exceedingly modest.
No literary man was ever readier to allow the superior merit of
other writers. He set the greatest value on talents which he himself
did not possess: he preferred learning to genius. As long as the
Germans shall understand their present language will the works of
Gellert be read, and his character will be honored while virtue is
known and respected"'. *(Mangan's note)*.

4 *King John* III. ii. 42–43: "Or if that surly spirit, melancholy, / Had bak'd thy blood and made it heavy-thick".

5 *Midsummer Night's Dream* V. i. 9; Mangan inserts the word "blue" before "devils" to suggest depression of spirits.

6 *Hamlet* I. i. 118–119; for "German" read "Roman".

7 *malgré lui*: "despite himself".

8 *The Merchant of Venice* I. i. 84.

9 "Fair creations from the Land of Fable". *(Mangan's note)*. From Schiller's "Die Götter Griechenlands", l. 4.

10 Thomas Middleton, *The Witch* V. ii ; for "blue" read "red".

11 *Osterwald*: the illustrator of Gellert's volumes.

12 *Julius Caesar* III. i. 260–261: "Which like dumb mouths do ope their ruby lips, / To beg the voice and utterance of my tongue".

13 *Bodmerians and Gottschedians*: Johann Jakob Bodmer (1698–1783) and Johann Christoph Gottsched (1700–1766), literary theorists, advocated imitation—the former, of Shakespeare and Milton, and the latter, of the French writers of the seventeenth century.

14 William Collins, "The Passions. An Ode for Music", ll. 46–47: "And ever and anon he beat / The doubling drum with furious heat". While Mangan's "curious", instead of "furious", may have been a mistake, the substitution of "kettle" for "doubling" was certainly deliberate, given the tea-party context.

15 *Boileau*: Nicolas Boileau-Despréaux (1636–1711), French poet, satirist and critic.

16 Mangan is punning on the names *Boileau* (drink the water) and *Lafontaine* (the fountain).

17 *Great Frederick*: Frederick the Great of Prussia (1712–1786); one of his many aspersions on the German language.

18 Thomas Moore, *Rhymes on the Road* VII. 13–14. Psaphon, in order to attract the attention of the world, taught multitudes of birds to pronounce his name, and then let them fly away in all directions.

19 *toise(s)*: obsolete French unit of measurement, roughly = 1.949 metres.

20 *pathognomist*: one who studies the emotions and the signs or expressions of them.

21 Mangan has just presented a fable of his as a translation from Gellert and now charges the German poet with plagiarism; "Peter Pindar" was the pseudonym of John Wolcot (1738–1819), a writer of satirical verse.

22 *Sackville-street*: now O'Connell Street.

23 *Hic niger est*: "His soul is black", Horace, *Satires* I. iv. 85.

24 David Garrick, "Epitaph on James Quinn": "To this complexion thou must come at last".

25 *Measure for Measure* III. i. 118: "To lie in cold obstruction and to rot."

26 *Quintilian*: Marcus Fabius Quintilianus (c.30–c.100), Latin rhetorician.
27 *La Motte*: Antoine Houdar de Lamotte (1672–1731), French writer and critic, author of *Réflexions sur la critique* and *Fables*.
28 A few pages earlier, Mangan had already accused Gellert of being a plagiarist and declared: "If you again inveigle us, we vow to stop short, and never more, through all the centuries of eternity, to overset another page of your poetry".
29 *St. Leon*: eponymous hero of a novel by William Godwin (1799); Mangan is referring to Vol. IV, ch. 7 of that work.
30 Edward Young, *Night Thoughts* I. 28.

A SIXTY DROP DOSE OF LAUDANUM [(The Out-and-Outer), *DUM*, March 1839]. Laudanum is a mixture of alcohol and opium.
 1 *Cullen*: William Cullen (1710–1790), Scottish physician. His *Treatise of the Materia Medica* (1789) gives a list of medicines with an explanation of their Latin names; laudanum is not included.
 2 *Brown*: John Brown (1735–1788), Scottish physician. Paragraphs 1183 and 1184 of his *Elements of Medicine* (1788) recommend dosages of laudanum for various cases. Mangan's "quotation" bears no relation to these.
 3 *Adventures of a Half-Crown*: this source has not been traced.
 4 *The Rival Magicians*: this source has not been traced.
 5 *Childe Harold* III. xxxiv:
> . . . Did man compute
> Existence by enjoyment, and count o'er
> Such hours 'gainst years of life,—say, would he name threescore?
 6 James Beattie, *The Minstrel* (1771–1774) I. i.
 7 Wordsworth, "Resolution and Independence", ll. 48–49: "We poets in our youth begin in gladness; / But thereof comes in the end despondency and madness."
 8 *Lo di ch' han detto a dolci amici a Dio*: "The day when they bade sweet friends, farewell". Dante, *Purgatorio* VIII. 3.
 9 Byron, *The Giaour* l. 70.
10 *Childe Harold* II. ii.
11 Mangan is joking: Moore's bitter poem, "When First I met Thee", spoken by a faded beauty to the man who had slighted her, appeared in *Irish Melodies* and has no connection with the River Schuylkill which figures in his *Poems Relating to America*.
12 *the first time eye met yew*: i.e. "the first time I met you", another oblique reference to Moore's poem.
13 W.S. Landor, "Lines": "Who would believe it e'er could be / That one, erewhile so dear to me, / Who, when she found the first grey hair, / Kist it. . . . "

14 Thomas Moore, "Those Evening Bells": "——and that sweet time / When last we heard their soothing chime".

15 *Black Drop*: a liquid medicine chiefly composed of opium, which Mangan here identifies with laudanum.

16 *As You Like It* IV. iii. 101: "Chewing the food of sweet and bitter fancy".

17 *Sir L. Bulwer*: Edward Bulwer-Lytton, first Baron Lytton (1803–1873), popular English writer, author of, *a.o.*, *Pelham* (1828), a novel of fashion and politics, and *Leila* (1838), a historical romance set in Spain.

18 *Dr. Kitchener*: William Kitchiner (?1779–1827), author of a great variety of books, including *A Companion to the Telescope*, *The Cook's Oracle*, and *Peptic Precepts to prevent and relieve Indigestion*.

19 *I met with it*: in fact the sonnet appears to be Mangan's.

20 *beaufet*: buffet.

21 *Imprimis*: "in the first place".

22 *pro aris et focis*: "for altars and hearths", Cicero, *De Natura Deorum* 3, 40, 94.

23 *curt-axe*: cutlass.

24 *galloglass*: "One of a particular class of soldiers formerly maintained by Irish chiefs" (*obs.*). (O.E.D.)

25 *Battle of Clontarf*: the decisive battle in which the Irish defeated the Danes in 1014.

26 *Battle of Moy-Tuire*: in the first mythical Battle of Moytirra, described in the *Book of Invasions*, the shambling Fir Bolg were defeated by the ingenious Tuatha Dé Dannan.

27 *Heberian Milesians*: the descendants of Heber, son of Milesius, king of Spain, who invaded Ireland with his two brothers Ir and Heremon, and defeated the Tuatha Dé Dannan.

28 *love laughs at locks as well as locksmiths*: *Love Laughs at Locksmiths* is the title of a comedy by George Colman the Younger (1803).

29 *D'Israeli (the Younger)*: Benjamin Disraeli, Earl of Beaconsfield (1804–1881), English novelist and statesman.

30 *Carlisle Bridge*: now O'Connell Bridge.

31 *Granby Row*: a small street off the north side of Parnell Square, about half a mile from O'Connell (Carlisle) Bridge.

32 *Hamlet* I. iv. 15.

33 *Macnish*: Robert Macnish (1802–1837), Scottish writer and physician, author of *The Philosophy of Sleep* (1830).

34 *Primâ facie*: "at first glance".

35 Thomas de Quincey, *Confessions of an English Opium-Eater* (1821).

36 *Mrs. Hemans*: Felicia Dorothea Hemans (1793–1835), popular English poet.

37 *mauvaise plaisanterie*: "bad joke".

38 *malus animus*: "bad intent"; cf. *Don Juan* I. xxx: "... what the lawyers call a '*malus animus*'".

39 *L.E.L.... Romance and Reality*: Lætitia Elizabeth Landon (1802–1838), English poet—"poor L.E.L.!" because she died in mysterious circumstances, supposedly from accidental poisoning by prussic acid. *Romance and Reality* was published in 1831.

40 *niaise*: "foolish girl"; "a silly".

41 *Catiline*: dissolute noble who led an unsuccessful conspiracy against the Roman Senate in 63 BC.

42 *De Stael*: Anne-Louise-Germaine de Staël (1766–1817), French novelist and intellectual.

43 Byron, *Don Juan* IV. iv; for *we* read *I*.

44 *African magician in Aladdin*: Moorish sorcerer in the *Arabian Nights*, who unintentionally delivers up the Wonderful Lamp to Aladdin. He retrieves the lamp from Aladdin's foolish servant by offering new lamps for old.

45 *soi-disant*: "so-called".

46 *Aladdin... had recourse to the lamp*: the hall of Aladdin's palace, built in one night by the genie, had twenty-three windows enriched with precious stones. The twenty-fourth was left for the Sultan to finish. But the Sultan's jewellers and goldsmiths could not get the work done in a month. So Aladdin asked the genie to make the twenty-fourth window like the rest.

47 *of their own accord removed it*: this is inaccurate; the African magician (see note 44 above), having recovered the Wonderful Lamp, orders the genie (there is only one) to transport him and the palace to Africa.

48 *jeu-de-mot*: "play on words".

49 *c'est à dire*: "that is to say".

50 *hight*: called (*arch.*).

51 *reste à savoir*: "remains to be seen".

52 *tracasseries*: "annoyances".

53 *Gleim*: Johann Wilhelm Ludwig Gleim (1719–1803), German poet.

54 Gleim, "An die Kriegesmuse":
————Ein König weint?
Gib ihm die Herrschaft über dich, O Welt,
Dieweil er weinen kann!

55 *Titian*: Tiziano Vecellio (c. 1487–1576), Italian painter.

56 *Friar Bacon's Brazen Head*: the speaking, omniscient head of brass fabled to have been made by Roger Bacon. It spoke while Bacon was asleep, saying "Time is"; half an hour later it said, "Time was." In another half-hour it said, "Time's past", fell down and broke to pieces. The legend is told in Robert Greene's *Honourable History of Friar*

Bacon and Friar Bungay (first performed in 1592).

57 George Soane, *Pride shall have a fall* (1824), II. ii: "No! freedom is like the air we breathe, without it we die!"

58 Edward Young, *Night Thoughts* I. 115.

59 Cf. John Henry Newman, "'Lead, kindly Light'" (1834), l. 11: "I loved the garish day...".

60 Byron, *Childe Harold* II. xxvi: "But 'midst the crowd, the hum, the shock of men".

61   "Never in the bosom of the stream
        Dulled and troubled by the flooding rains,
        Rather on the stilly lake the beam
        Of the mirrored sun remains.
                                   SCHILLER." *(Mangan's note)*.
For Mangan's previous translation of Schiller's lines, see "To my Friends", *DUM*, October 1834.

62 Ecclesiastes 7: 1. This Old Testament book is traditionally but erroneously attributed to Solomon.

63 *Mrs. Shelley's Frankenstein*: in Mary Shelley's novel *Frankenstein* (1818) the monster, made from parts of dead bodies, has no name; "Frankenstein" is the name of its maker.

64 Coleridge, "Rime of the Ancient Mariner", l. 193: "The Night-mare LIFE-IN-DEATH was she".

65 John Walker Ord, *The Wandering Bard* (1833) III. 196: "Do grave-dews winnow through the rotting clay?"

66 *an* elixir vitæ *which, unlike St. Leon's*: "the *elixir vitae*, which was to restore youth, and make him who possessed it immortal", Preface to *St. Leon* by William Godwin (1799).

67 *Le roi est mort, vive le roi!*: "The king is dead, long live the king!"

68 Dryden, "Alexander's Feast", l. 78.

69 Psalm 58: 5: "Which will not hearken to the voice of charmers, charming never so wisely".

70 Gray, "Elegy Written in a Country Churchyard", l. 43.

71 William Godwin, preface to *St. Leon* (1799): "...it is better that man should be a living being, than a stock or a stone".

72 Cf. 1 Corinthians 7: 30.

73 *Going, Staymaker*: Horace (or Horatio) Smith lists several comical shop-boards in his "First Letter to the Royal Literary Society", in *Gaieties and Gravities* (1826); the one Mangan refers to actually reads: "Gowing, Stay-maker".

74 *John Reilly, Carpenter and Timberyard*: Pettigrew and Oulton's Dublin Directory for 1840 gives the occupant of 2 and 3 Peter Street (Mangan's parents and, at times, the poet himself, lived at No. 9) as

"Thomas Powell, cabinet maker, and timber yard".

75 Pope, *Essay on Man* II. 231–232.

76 Schiller, *Die Raüber* V. i: "Losgerüttelt das Totenreich aus dem ewigen Schlaf".

77 Milton, *Paradise Lost* IV. 76.

78 *Romeo and Juliet* I. ii. 45: "... one fire burns out another's burning".

79 *Mr Lane's new version of the Arabian Nights*: Edward William Lane (1801–1876), Arabic scholar, published in 1836 his *Account of the Manners and Customs of the Modern Egyptians*, and in 1838–1841 a translation of the *Arabian Nights*.

80 *La Harpe*: Jean-Francois de La Harpe (1739–1803), French dramatist and critic.

81 *Burns*: Robert Burns (1759–1796), Scotland's national poet.

82 *As De Quincey correctly remarks... the stomach*: Thomas de Quincey, "William Wordsworth", *Tait's Magazine*, VI (January 1839), 8: "the depth and subtlety of eyes varies accordingly with the state of the stomach".

83 *Hamlet* IV. iv. 37.

84 *Caliph Omar*: Omar-ibn al-Khattab (c.581–644), second of the Mahommedan caliphs. In reply to a request about saving the books in the Great Library of Alexandria, Omar is said to have ordered their burning, on the basis that those books which contained the same doctrine as the Koran were redundant, whereas those which diverged from the Koran were blasphemous.

85 *Hamlet* II. ii. 589–590: "For murder, though it have no tongue, will speak / With most miraculous organ".

86 Shelley, *Julian and Maddalo* (1824) ll. 113–119:

> "O ho!
> You talk as in years past," said Maddalo.
> "'Tis strange men change not. You were ever still
> Among Christ's flock a perilous infidel,
> A wolf for the meek lambs—if you can't swim
> Beware of Providence." I looked on him,
> But the gay smile had faded in his eye.

87 *Spurzheim*: Johann Kaspar Spurzheim (1776–1832), German phrenologist.

88 *Curran*: John Philpot Curran (1750–1817), Irish lawyer, orator and wit.

89 *laid ideal*: "ugliness in its ideal perfection". The usual phrase is the antithesis of this, the *beau idéal*.

90 *Arthur Mervyn*: Gothic novel (1799–1800) by the American writer Charles Brockden Brown (1771–1810).

91 *the suicide of their lunatic father*: Mangan's memory fails him here. The father does go mad, but it is Watson's brother-in-law who shoots

himself. There are a few slight inaccuracies in the quotations, besides.

92 *Caleb Williams*: *Things as They Are, or, The Adventures of Caleb Williams*, novel by William Godwin (1794), in which Falkland is exposed as a murderer by Caleb Williams.

93 *Dunlop*: William Dunlap (1766–1839), American painter, dramatist and biographer; wrote a *Life of Charles Brockden Brown* (1815).

94 *Edgar Huntly*: novel by Charles Brockden Brown (1799). In 1831 it appeared in the Standard Novels Series published by Colburn and Bentley in London.

A POLYGLOTT ANTHOLOGY. DEVELOPED IN FORM OF A DIALOGUE [(The Out-and-Outer), *DUM*, April 1839]

1 Pope, "Eloisa to Abelard", l. 58.

2 *Hamlet* III. iv. 103: "A king of shreds and patches".

3 Pope, *Essay on Man* I. 267. For "hole" read "whole".

4 *Saadi*: Persian poet (c.1213–1291).

5 *Transoxania*: Transoxiana, a province of the Achæmenian Empire.

6 *Abulfeda*: famous Arab geographer and historian (1273–1331). Mangan may be punning on the *bul(l)* in *Abulfeda* and the *ox* in *Transoxania*.

7 *Adelung*: Jakob Adlung, or Adelung (1699–1762), German musicographer; or Johann Christoph Adelung (1732–1806), German philologist, author of *Mithridates*, a polyglot grammar and dictionary.

8 *Augustus Schlegel*: German Orientalist (1767–1845).

9 "The final downfall of the *Barameka*, or Barmecides, the most illustrious of the Arabian nobility, is supposed to have occurred in the reign of Haroun al Raschid, about the beginning of the ninth century". *(Mangan's note)*.

10 *Il mio naso e rosso, la mia perucca e canuto*: "My nose is red, my wig is grey." (*canuto* should be *canuta*). No Milanese mayor has been found in the works of the Italian composer Giambattista Pergolesi (1710–1736).

11 *Indarno vuoi… cappello!*: "Vainly, I tell you, do you try to take this, / Because it is all round my hat!" In fact, *Ricciardetto* is not the name of a writer, but the title of a heroi-comic poem, a parody of Ariosto's *Orlando Furioso*, by Nicolò Forteguerri (1674–1735), in which no characters named Sigismondo or Gianetto are to be found.

12 *Poor Cocking*: Robert Cocking crashed and died on 24 July 1837, on the try-out of the parachute which he had designed.

13 *Pauthier*: Jean-Pierre-Guillaume Pauthier (1801–1873), French sinologist. His translation of the *Tao-Te-King* appeared in 1838.

14 *the Blarney-stone*: a stone set in a wall of Blarney Castle, near Cork; kissing it was supposed to make you fluent. Tutschemupp's remark is prompted by Baugtrauter's having just recited two epigrams

supposedly translated from the Irish.

15 *Vallancey*: Colonel Charles Vallancey (1724–1812), Irish antiquarian whose researches tended to prove, as Mangan puts it in the fourth "Literæ Orientales" article (*DUM*, April 1840), that "every Irishman is an Arab".

16 Ἄλις ουτος: correctly, Ἄλις οὖτως: "Enough!".

17 *O'Reilly*: Edward O'Reilly was the author of an *Irish-English Dictionary* (1817).

18 *Is múchta an tine ad-thealach gaoidheal*: "The fire is extinguished on the hearth of the Gaels" (more correctly, "...d-tealach Gaoidheal").

19 "Hugh Roe O'Donnell". *(Mangan's note)*. His correct Irish name is *Aodh Ruadh Ua Domhnaill*.

20 *Julius Caesar* V. v. 68.

21 *Drechsler's last volumes*: "Drechsler" (i.e. "turner", hence "translator") was one of Mangan's German personæ.

22 Τοις πλεισοις ειμαρμαι μηδεποτ' ευ πραττοντες φρονειν: even allowing for printer's mistakes, Mangan's Greek does not pass muster. Demosthenes wrote: οὐ μὴν ἀλλ' ἴσως τούτοις μὲν ἔμαρται μηδέποτ' εὖ πράττουσιν εὖ φρονῆσαι (*Exordia* 24. 4)—"Maybe, however, they are doomed never to be wise as long as they are successful".

23 *Othello* I. i. 18–19: "Forsooth, a great arithmetician, / One Michael Cassio, a Florentine".

24 *hot without*: hot spirits and water without sugar.

25 *La Motte Fouqué*: Friedrich Heinrich Karl de La Motte Fouqué (1777–1843), German poet and prose-writer.

26 *Hamlet* I. v. 32–33: "And duller shouldst thou be than the fat weed / That roots [some editions have *rots*] itself in ease on Lethe wharf".

27 *The Captain...shorter pieces*: in his *Transatlantic Sketches* (London: 1833), Captain James Edward Alexander does indeed tell the story of Francis Abbott; his account ends as follows: "He composed much, and generally in Latin, but destroyed his writings as fast almost as he produced them. When his cottage was examined [after his death] hopes were entertained that some manuscript or memorial might be found of his composition; but he had left nothing of the kind" (II, 154).

28 No Cascagni has been found among Italian poets.

29 Πειραομαι το μεν σωμα ειναι φιλοπονος, η δε ψυχη φιλοσοφος: again, Mangan ignores the rules of Greek grammar. Isocrates wrote: Πειρῶ τῷ μὲν σώματι εἶναι φιλόπονος, τῇ δὲ ψυχῇ φιλόσοφος—"Strive to teach your body to love exertion, and your soul to love wisdom" (*To Demonicos* 40).

30 Τα οντα αγαθα και καλα ουδεν ανευ πονος κ' επιμελεια θεοι

διδοασιν ανθρωπος: the (mis)quotation is from Xenophon, who wrote: τῶν γὰρ ὄντων ἀγαθῶν καὶ καλῶν οὐδὲν ἄνευ πόνου καὶ ἐπιμελείας θεοί διδόασιν ἀνθρώποις—"For men are given by the gods nothing that is good and fine without toil and effort" (*Memorabilia* II. i. 28).

31 *niaiseries*: "foolish things".

32 *Julius Caesar* IV. iii. 85.

33 *Me voila tout prêt*: "I am ready".

ANTHOLOGIA GERMANICA.—NO. XV. WETZEL'S POEMS. FIRST NOTICE [(Unsigned), *DUM*, July 1839]. The title carries the following note by Mangan:

> F.C. Wetzel's gesammelte Gedichte und Nachlasz. Herausgegeben von Z. Funck. Leipsig: Brockhaus. 1839.
>
> F.C. Wetzel's Poems and Remains, complete. Edited by Z. Funck. Leipsic: Brockhaus, 1839.

 1 *Paine*: Thomas Paine (1737–1809), English-American writer and political pamphleteer.

 2 *Cobbett*: William Cobbett (1762–1835), English radical writer and politician.

 3 *Hunt's glowing eulogies of Shelley*: English poet and critic, James Henry Leigh Hunt (1784–1859), published and promoted Shelley's work in his journal, the *Examiner*.

 4 *Hamlet* V. ii. 155: "more german to the matter".

 5 *Neukomm*: Sigismund Neukomm (1778–1858), German composer.

 6 *Bedlamite*: inmate of a lunatic asylum.

 7 *Munchausen*: a type of the tall-story teller, the hero of R.E. Raspe's *The Surprising Travels and Adventures of Baron Munchausen* (London: 1785).

 8 Byron, *Childe Harold* III. lxx: "There, in a moment we may plunge our years / In fatal penitence".

 9 *Macbeth* I. v. 17: "full o' th' milk of human kindness".

10 *handshoe*: comic literal translation of the German word for *glove*.

11 *Klinger*: Friedrich Maximilian von Klinger (1752–1831), German writer. His play *Der Wirrwarr, oder Sturm und Drang* (1776) gave its name to the Sturm und Drang ("Storm and Stress") movement in German literature.

12 *Macbeth* II. ii. 61. For *sea* read *seas*.

13 *mauvais sujet*: "bad character; hard case".

14 *Macbeth* IV. i. 86.

15 *King Lear* III. ii. 60.

16 "Noted weapons, *en passant*, with 'all the tribe'". *(Mangan's note)*; *write*

daggers: cf. *Hamlet* III. ii. 387: "I'll speak daggers to her, but use none"; *all the tribe*: "Hoc genus omne", Horace, *Satires* I. ii. 2.

17 *Jacob Boehmen*: German mystic writer (1575–1624).

18 Byron, *Don Juan* I. xiii: "Her thoughts were theorems, her words a problem, / As if she deem'd that mystery would ennoble 'em".

19 *dolce far niente*: "sweet idleness".

ANTHOLOGIA GERMANICA.—NO. XV. WETZEL'S REMAINS.—SECOND ARTICLE. THE METEOR OF KASAN.—A TRAGEDY [(Unsigned), *DUM*, December 1839]

1 *Toast-water*: water in which toasted bread has been steeped, used as a drink for invalids.

2 *William Carleton of Richmond Castle*: this *was* Carleton's lofty-sounding address according to Pettigrew and Oulton's directories for 1839 and 1840. Richmond Castle was in Richmond, a northern suburb of Dublin.

3 "Das Nordlicht von Kasán; Trauerspiel in fünf Aufzugen. Von Joseph Frhrn v. Auffenberg. Carlsruhe; Müller, 1839". *(Mangan's note)*. The play was first published in 1828. It was indeed written by Joseph von Auffenberg (1798–1857).

4 *Godwin...muzzles of muskets*: Mangan probably refers to the following passage in "Of the Sources of Genius" in *The Enquirer, a Series of Essays* (1797):

> ...if a man were to tell me that, if I pull the trigger of my gun, a swift and beautiful horse will immediately appear starting from the mouth of the tube; I can only answer that I do not expect it, and that it is contrary to the tenor of my former experience. But I can assign no reason, why this is an event intrinsically more absurd, or less likely, than the event I have been accustomed to witness.
>
> This is well known to those who are acquainted with the latest speculations and discoveries of philosophers. It may be familiarly illustrated to the unlearned reader by remarking that the process of generation, in consequence of which men and horses are born, has obviously no more perceivable correspondence with that event, than it would have, for me to pull the trigger of a gun.

5 *Chrononhotonthologos*: bombastic king, eponymous hero of a farce by Henry Carey (1734).

6 *The Warden of Galway*: tragedy by the Rev. Edward Groves, first performed in Dublin in 1831. It was not published until 1876, so that Auffenberg is unlikely to have plagiarised it. Mangan is probably mocking the German playwright's fondness for titles of a similar format, such as *Der Löwe von Kurdistan, Die Schwestern von Amiens*,

Der Renegat von Granada, and *Die Furie von Toledo*.

7 *Carlsruhers*: inhabitants of the town of Karlsruhe in Germany.

8 "Constable of Police". *(Mangan's note)*. The corresponding character in the German play is a pope.

9 "A town in Eastern Russia, containing about 70,000 inhabitants. It was formerly the capital of a Tartar kingdom, but was conquered by Ivan the Terrible in 1552". *(Mangan's note)*.

10 *Othello* III. iii. 356.

11 *all the other Tartars...promises*: Mangan is playing on the colloquial phrase *to catch a Tartar*, "to get hold of one who cannot be controlled".

12 *Mores hominum multorum vidit*: "He saw the customs of many men": Horace, *Ars Poetica* 141.

13 *Beppo*: eponymous hero of a poem by Byron.

14 *ipse dixit*: "he himself said so" (a mere assertion, totally unsupported).

15 Cf. Job 10: 22 (Rheims and Douai version): "A land of miserie and darkenesse, where is the shadow of death, and no order, but everlasting horrour inhabiteth".

16 *Borovoskitsch*: the impostor's real name, mentioned by Mangan in his introduction, is Pugatscheff.

17 *cut each other...we should do*: Mangan is punning on the colloquial meaning of *to cut* ("to break off acquaintance with").

18 *Auf meine...besitzen*: literally: "On my inner strength I shall rely, / And not possess a stolen earthly good".

19 *Romeo and Juliet* II. i. 85.

20 Robert Burns, "For a' that and a' that". The original has "guinea's".

21 Thomas Gray, "The Bard", ll. 49–50; for "Borovoskitsch" read "Edward's race".

22 Isaiah 14: 12.

23 Dryden, "Alexander's Feast", ll. 80–81.

24 Dryden, *ibid.*, ll. 82–83: "On the bare earth exposed he lies, / With no friend to close his eyes."

25 *Hamlet* III. iv. 181. For "but" read "and".

26 *Das ist nicht unser Amt!*: literally, "That's not our job!"

27 *sufficiently far north*: Mangan's adaptation of the slang phrase *too far north* ("too knowing").

APPENDIX TO THE NOTES

The following is a list of persons who are so well-known and/or whom Mangan quotes or mentions so often that their presence in the main body of notes would have been supererogatory or would have taken up too much space.

John Anster (1793–1867), poet, scholar and translator of Goethe's *Faust*. He was a frequent contributor to the *DUM* and a friend of Mangan's. He was among the few who helped Mangan financially towards the end of his life.

Aristotle (384–322 BC), Greek philosopher. Studied in Athens under Plato. Teacher of Alexander the Great. His system of classification and terminology has left a lasting influence on Western thinking.

St. Augustine of Hippo (354–430), early Christian writer; Father of the Church. Author of the apologetic treatise *The City of God*, and of the spiritual autobiography *The Confessions*.

Francis Bacon (1561–1626), English statesman, philosopher and scientist. His main works are *The Advancement of Learning* and the *Novum Organum*, a landmark in natural science.

Honoré de Balzac (1799–1850), French novelist. Mangan seems to have been interested mainly in his *Etudes philosophiques*, adapting *Melmoth réconcilié* into "The Man in the Cloak", and using *La Peau de chagrin* as the basis for "The Thirty Flasks".

Gottfried August Bürger (1747–1794), German poet, famous for his experiments with the ballad form. His best-known poem "Lenore" was translated twice by Mangan.

George Gordon, Lord Byron (1788–1824), English poet and dramatist; had a deep and varied influence on Mangan, not least for the flamboyance of his rhyming. Echoes of *Beppo*, *Don Juan*, *Childe Harold* and *Manfred* recur in Mangan's poetry and prose.

William Carleton (1794–1869), Irish novelist. A frequent contributor to the *DUM.*, and a friend of Mangan, who occasionally refers to him in a tone of gentle banter.

Samuel Taylor Coleridge (1796–1849), English Romantic poet, literary theorist and translator. Mangan was intimately acquainted with Coleridge's work, including the translations of Schiller's *Wallenstein* plays. Echoes from Coleridge's "Kubla Kahn" and "Dejection: An Ode" resound in Mangan's "A Vision of Connaught in the Thirteenth Century" and "Life is the Desert and the Solitude". In his prose, Mangan refers several times to Coleridge's famous poem, "The Rime of the Ancient Mariner".

Dante Alighieri (1265–1321), Italian poet and political philosopher. His masterpiece is the visionary *Divine Comedy*.

Charles Gavan Duffy (1816–1903), Irish journalist and politician. Editor of the *Vindicator* (Belfast) and the *Nation*. Friend and patron of Mangan's.

Friedrich Heinrich Karl, Baron de la Motte Fouqué (1777–1843), German poet and prose-writer; author of many romances of medieval chivalry. Mangan translated a handful of his poems, but in his prose he makes disparaging comments about Fouqué's style.

Ferdinand Freiligrath (1810–1876), German poet. Moved from imaginative and exotic to political poetry, a change which Mangan criticized in the *DUM* at the very time when he himself was beginning to write for the *Nation*.

Christian Fürchtegott Gellert (1715–1769), popular poet and fabulist of the German Enlightenment. Mangan translated quite a few of his fables, as well as fathering on him two of Lafontaine's.

William Godwin (1756–1836), radical philosopher and novelist. His philosophical writings include *An Enquiry Concerning Political Justice* (1793), *The Enquirer* (1797), and *Thoughts on Man* (1831), but Mangan quotes more frequently from his novels *Caleb Williams* (1794) and, above all, *St. Leon* (1799).

Johann Wolfgang von Goethe (1749–1832), Germany's foremost poet, novelist and playwright. Mangan translated scenes from his play *Faust* (Part One), as well as a number of his shorter poems.

Oliver Goldsmith (1728–1774), Irish poet, playwright and novelist. Mangan quotes mainly from his collection of epistolary essays *The Citizen of the World* (1762), his novel *The Vicar of Wakefield* (1766), and his poem *The Deserted Village* (1770).

Josef von Hammer-Purgstall (1774–1856), Austrian Orientalist. His *Geschichte der osmanischen Dichtkunst* provided Mangan with most of his material for the *Literæ Orientales*.

Heinrich Heine (1797–1856), German poet and critic, saw himself as "the last Romantic". While Mangan reproached him for his Voltairean irony, it was Heine's sarcastic poems, rather than his lyrical work, that he translated with greatest gusto.

Johann Gottfried von Herder (1774–1803), prolific and influential German philosopher, critic and poet. Mangan translated some of his original poems, and some of his renderings of popular verse. In his prose Mangan expresses his regard for Herder's intellectual powers.

Ludwig Heinrich Christoph Hölty (1748–1776), German lyric poet. His poems are characterised by a subdued melancholy and love of nature at which Mangan occasionally pokes fun.

Homer (8th c. BC), Greek epic poet, to whom have been attributed the *Iliad* and the *Odyssey*.

Horace (Quintus Horatius Flaccus, 65–8 BC), Roman poet. Author of epistles, satires, odes, epodes, and an *Art of Poetry*.

Samuel Johnson (1709–1784), influential English author and critic. His famous *Dictionary of the English Language* was published in 1755.

Immanuel Kant (1724–1804), German philosopher. Author of the seminal *Critique of Pure Reason* (1781), *Critique of Practical Reason* (1788), and *Critique of Judgment* (1790).

John Keats (1795–1821), English Romantic poet. It is worth noting that Mangan refers to him only once, and never quotes him.

Justinus Andreas Christian Kerner (1786–1862), German poet and prose-writer. Mangan translated a good few of his poems, yet mostly makes fun of his poetry; he treats Kerner's prose works on spiritualism more seriously.

Friedrich Gottlieb Klopstock (1724–1803), German poet, who endeavoured to surpass Milton in his epic *Der Messias* (*The Messiah*). Mangan repeatedly makes fun of his poetry.

Charles Lamb (1775–1834), English poet, essayist and critic. Mangan appreciated what he calls his "dry drollery".

Gottlieb Ephraim Lessing (1729–1781), German poet, essayist and playwright. Most important representative of German Enlightenment. Mangan translated some of his epigrams, and, without acknowledgement, from his Fables and from his play, *Nathan der Weise*.

William Maginn (1793–1842), Irish poet and journalist. A constant contributor to *Blackwood's Magazine* and founder of *Fraser's Magazine* (1830). His witty, and at times ebullient style may have influenced Mangan's.

Charles Robert Maturin (1782–1824), Irish novelist and playwright, whose sensational novel *Melmoth the Wanderer* (1820) created a stir throughout Europe. Although at the end of his life Mangan criticized the novel, its eponymous hero lies at the basis of his own persona, "The Man in the Cloak".

John Milton (1608–1674), English poet. Author of the famous Christian epic *Paradise Lost* and of the masque *Comus*. Mangan quotes from these two works frequently.

Thomas Moore (1779–1852), Irish poet, biographer and satirist. Author of *Irish Melodies* and *Lalla Rookh*. His verse is frequently quoted and parodied by Mangan.

John O'Donovan (1806–1861), Irish scholar, worked for the Topographical Section of the Ordnance Survey and for the Irish Archaeological Society; edited and translated many Irish texts, including the *Annals of the Four Masters* (1848–1851). He was a friend of Mangan's from the early '30s.

Blaise Pascal (1623–1662), French philosopher and mathematician. Mangan quotes from his defence of the Christian religion, *Les Pensées*.

Plato (c.429–347 BC), Greek philosopher. Pupil of Socrates. Teacher of Aristotle. His moral philosophy has exerted a huge influence on Western thought.

Alexander Pope (1688–1744), foremost English poet of his time; his *Essay on Criticism* (1711) established the principles of taste for the Augustan age; together with *Epistle to Dr Arbuthnot* (1735) and *Essay on Man* (1733–1734) it is a frequent source of reference for Mangan.

François Rabelais (c.1490–1553), French comic writer whose uninhibited satiric vision of society as expressed in *Pantagruel* (1532) and *Gargantua* (1534) influenced such English writers as Swift, Butler, Sterne, and Mangan in his more ludic excursions.

Johann Paul Friedrich Richter (1763–1825), German humorist writer, usually referred to as Jean Paul, renowned for his unbridled imagination. Mangan's poem "The New Year's Night of an Unhappy Man" (1830), one of his earliest forays in translation, is rendered from Richter's prose apologue "Die Neujahrsnacht eines Unglücklichen".

Friedrich Rückert (1788–1866), German poet and Orientalist. Mangan translated nearly thirty poems of Rückert's, including the well-known "And Then No More" and "Gone in the Wind", which are based on Rückert's "Oriental" verse.

Johann Christoph Friedrich von Schiller (1759–1805), poet, dramatist and historian. His great plays *Die Räuber* (1781), *Don Carlos* (1787), *Wilhelm Tell* (1804) won him heroic stature among the German Romantics. Mangan translated over seventy of his poems, as well as his drama *Wallensteins Lager*.

Christian Friedrich Daniel Schubart (1739–1791), German *Sturm und Drang* poet. Mangan expresses sympathy with the persecution Schubart endured on account of his attacks upon the establishment, but is less appreciative of his poetic style.

Sir Walter Scott (1771–1832), Scottish poet and novelist. Mangan quotes mostly from his long poem *The Lay of the Last Minstrel*.

William Shakespeare (1564–1616), English dramatist and poet. The greatest English playwright. Mangan quotes him copiously.

Percy Bysshe Shelley (1792–1822), English Romantic poet. Mangan shows considerable affinity with Shelley's work, from which he often quotes.

Karl Joseph Simrock (1802–1876), German poet. Mangan calls him "one of the most popular of the second-rate order of German poets", and dedicates an entire article to his verse.

Socrates (c.469–399 BC), Greek philosopher. He never wrote anything himself; we know of his ideas thanks to Plato's Dialogues.

Laurence Sterne (1713–1768), Irish novelist. Mangan felt affinity with his whimsical humour, and frequently quotes from his most famous book *Tristram Shandy*.

Jonathan Swift (1667–1745), Irish writer and Anglican cleric. Mangan admired his satirical vein, and refers repeatedly to his most famous work *Gulliver's Travels*.

Ludwig Tieck (1773–1853), German poet, collector of folk-tales and critic. Mangan praises his criticism and tales, but disparages his poems with considerable gusto, translating six of them.

Ludwig Uhland (1787–1862), German poet and political activist. Mangan translated eighteen of his poems, mostly ballads.

Virgil (Publius Vergilius Maro, 70–19 BC), Roman poet. Author of the *Bucolics*, the *Georgics*, and the famous epic, the *Aeneid*.

Voltaire: pen-name of François-Marie Arouet (1694–1778). One of the greatest and most prolific writers of the French eighteenth century. Though he wrote many plays and poems, his best work is found in his prose tales and philosophical or polemical essays, and it is from these that Mangan quotes repeatedly.

Friedrich Gottlob Wetzel (1779–1819), German poet. Mangan thought poorly of his verse, which he used mainly as a pretext for voicing his own views on authorship and translation.

William Wordsworth (1770–1850), English Romantic poet. Mangan quotes from a wide variety of his poems.

Edward Young (1683–1765), English poet; author of *The Complaint, or Night Thoughts on Life, Death and Immortality*, from which Mangan quotes frequently.